Culturally and Linguistically Diverse
Exceptional Students

I dedicate this book to my family, who has provided support and inspiration throughout: Greg, Sam, and Mario Everett, and Ronald and Catherine Grassi.

For my parents, my husband, and my children: Heinz and Sandra Bulmahn, John Barker, and Grace, Elizabeth, and Katherine Barker.

With love and appreciation,
Liz and Heidi

Culturally and Linguistically Diverse Exceptional Students

Strategies for Teaching and Assessment

Elizabeth A. Grassi
Regis University

Heidi Bulmahn Barker
Regis University

Los Angeles | London | New Delhi
Singapore | Washington DC

For information:

SAGE Publications, Inc.
2455 Teller Road
Thousand Oaks, California 91320
E-mail: order@sagepub.com

SAGE Publications Ltd.
1 Oliver's Yard
55 City Road
London EC1Y 1SP
United Kingdom

SAGE Publications India Pvt. Ltd.
B 1/I 1 Mohan Cooperative Industrial Area
Mathura Road, New Delhi 110 044
India

SAGE Publications Asia-Pacific Pte. Ltd.
33 Pekin Street #02-01
Far East Square
Singapore 048763

Printed in the United States of America

Library of Congress Cataloging-in-Publication Data

Grassi, Elizabeth A.
Culturally and linguistically diverse exceptional students: Strategies for teaching and assessment/ Elizabeth A. Grassi, Heidi Bulmahn Barker.
   p. cm.
Includes bibliographical references and index.
ISBN 978-1-4129-5213-2 (pbk.)
   1. English language—Study and teaching—Foreign speakers. 2. Learning disabled—Education. 3. Individualized instruction. 4. Learning disabilities. 5. Special education. I. Barker, Heidi Bulmahn. II. Title.

PE1128.A2G679 2010
371.9′043—dc22   2009019872

Printed on acid-free paper.

09   10   11   12   13   10   9   8   7   6   5   4   3   2   1

Acquiring Editor:	Diane McDaniel
Associate Editor:	Deya Saoud
Editorial Assistant:	Ashley Conlon
Production Editor:	Sarah K. Quesenberry
Copy Editors:	Taryn Bigelow and Alison Hope
Typesetter:	C&M Digitals (P) Ltd.
Proofreader:	Sue Schon
Indexer:	Rick Hurd
Cover Designer:	Bryan Fishman

Brief Contents

Foreword   xv
  Byron Plumley

Preface   xxi

Chapter 1. Introduction   1

SECTION I. UNDERSTANDING STUDENT BACKGROUNDS   29

Chapter 2. Collaborating With Families   31

Chapter 3. Understanding Language Acquisition   49

Chapter 4. Understanding Fluency   75

SECTION II. STRATEGIES FOR ASSESSMENT
         AND PLANNING FOR INSTRUCTION   107

Chapter 5. Strategies for the Assessment Process   109

Chapter 6. Collaboration Skills   139

Chapter 7. Planning Instruction   163

Chapter 8. Culturally Relevant Pedagogy   187
  Sandra L. Mitchell

SECTION III. STRATEGIES FOR CONTENT
         AND LANGUAGE ACQUISITION   199

Chapter 9. Teaching Strategies: An Integrated
     Content-Language Approach   201

Chapter 10. Strategies for Promoting Participation   231

Chapter 11. Strategies for Explicit Grammar Instruction   255

SECTION IV. STRATEGIES FOR LITERACY INSTRUCTION   **271**

Chapter 12. Strategies for Teaching Reading   273

Chapter 13. Strategies for Teaching the Writing Process   297

Chapter 14. Challenges When Teaching Writing   317

Chapter 15. Strategies for Written Error Correction   335

SECTION V. NEW DIRECTIONS IN THE EDUCATION
       OF CLDE STUDENTS

Chapter 16. Policy Considerations for Working with CLDE Students

Glossary   349

References   359

Index   373

About the Authors   399

This section can be found
in PDF at www.sagepub
.com/grassi

Detailed Contents

Foreword   xv

Preface   xxi

Chapter 1. Introduction   1

Establishing the Rationale: Demographics
    of Students in Our Classrooms   3
        Demographics of English Language Learners   3
        Demographics of CLDE Students   5
        Looking at Labels: Overrepresentation
            and Underrepresentation   6
Setting the Context: Laws That Impact Program
    Options for CLDE Students   8
        Bilingual Education Laws   8
        Program Placement of ELL Students   13
        Bilingual or Bicultural Program Options   14
        Programs Designed to Develop English-Only
            Skills and Assimilation   15
        Special Education Laws   16
        Placement Options for Students With Special Needs   20
        The Least Restrictive Environment for CLDE Students   22
        Recent Trends in Placement   24
New Directions in Teacher Training   25
Summary   27
Key Terms 27
Activities for Further Understanding   27

Section I. Understanding Student Backgrounds 29

Chapter 2. Collaborating With Families 31
  Creating Relationships With CLD Families 34
    Informal Meetings 34
    Formal Meetings 35
  Considerations of Culture When Working With CLD Families 39
    Perceptions of Disability 40
    Perceptions of Goal Setting 41
    Understandings of the Process 41
  Empowering Families 42
    MAPs: Gaining the Family Story 42
  Summary 47
  Key Terms 47
  Activities for Further Understanding 47

Chapter 3. Understanding Language Acquisition 49
  Interlanguage: The Journey From First Language to
    Second Language Proficiency 51
    Errors Found in Interlanguage 51
    The Developmental Sequence of Interlanguage 53
    Emotion and Interlanguage 56
    Restructuring and U-Shaped Learning 57
    Summary 58
  Second Language Acquisition Theories 59
    Natural Order Hypothesis 59
    Affective Filter Hypothesis 63
    Input Hypothesis 64
    Acquisition Versus Learning and Monitor Hypotheses 66
  Factors Affecting Second Language Acquisition 66
    First Language Foundation 67
    Motivation 68
    Social and Psychological Distance 69
  Summary 71
  Key Terms 72
  Activities for Further Understanding 72

Chapter 4. Understanding Fluency   75

Proficiency: What Does It Mean to Be
    "Fluent" in a Language?   77
Cummins's BICS and CALPS Model   78
    Student Acquisition of BICS and CALPS   79
    Questions to Explore Before Making a
        Special Education Referral   79
Canale and Swain's Four-Part Model
    of Communicative Competence   80
    Grammatical Competence   81
    Discourse Competence   88
    Sociolinguistic Competence   92
    Strategic Competence   100
Summary   103
Key Terms   104
Activities for Further Understanding   104

SECTION II. STRATEGIES FOR ASSESSMENT AND PLANNING FOR INSTRUCTION   107

Chapter 5. Strategies for the Assessment Process   109

The Instruction/Assessment Cycle in Special Education   111
    Eligibility for Special Education Services   113
    Eligibility for ELL Services   114
The Eligibility Process and CLDE Students   119
    Step 1. Noticing Difficulty in the Classroom   120
    Step 2. Teacher Interventions   121
    Step 3. Intervention Team   121
    Step 4. Acquiring Parental Permission   122
    Step 5. Multidisciplinary Evaluation   123
    Step 6. Multidisciplinary-IEP Meeting   125
    Step 7. Monitoring Progress   127
Tailoring Assessment Procedures for CLDE Students   128
    Discrepancy Model and CLDE Students   128
    Response to Intervention and CLDE Students   129
    Functional Behavior Assessments and CLDE Students   132
    Gifted and Talented CLDE Students   133

Summary   135
Key Terms   136
Activities for Further Understanding   136

Chapter 6. Collaboration Skills   139

Diversifying the Concept of Collaboration   141
Foundations of Collaboration   142
Creating a Collaborative School Culture   144
Co-Teaching as Collaboration   146
    Co-Teaching Model 1: Whole Group Teacher and
      Supporting Role Teacher   148
    Co-Teaching Model 2: Both Teachers Teach
      at the Same Time   150
    Co-Teaching Model 3: Group Facilitation
      by Both Teachers   153
    Strategies for Implementing Positive
      Co-Teaching Experiences   153
Working With Paraprofessionals   157
    The Role of Paraprofessionals in Schools   158
Summary   161
Key Terms   162
Activities for Further Understanding   162

Chapter 7. Planning Instruction   163

Planning for Instruction   165
A Philosophy of Differentiation   165
    Differentiation and CLDE Students   167
    Differentiating the Process   169
    Differentiating the Product   170
    Differentiating the Content   172
Universal Design for Learning   175
    Universal Design for Learning and CLDE Students   176
Application of Differentiation and UDL:
  Backward Design Planning   178
Instructional Planning Pyramid for Instruction and RTI   179
    Considerations for CLDE Students   183
Planning and Classroom Management   184
Summary   185

Key Terms   185
Activities for Further Understanding   185

Chapter 8. Culturally Relevant Pedagogy   187

Introduction and Definitions   188
Develop and Maintain Strong Teacher–Student
   Relationships   190
Emphasize Consistent Dialogical Interaction   193
Incorporate and Validate Space for
   Student Voice and Identity   195
Make Content Relevant to All Students in the Classroom   196
Summary   197
Key Terms   198
Activities for Further Understanding   198

Section III. Strategies for Content and Language Acquisition   199

Chapter 9. Teaching Strategies: An Integrated Content–Language Approach   201

Strategy 9.1 Making the Content Comprehensible
With the 3-Way Model   205
   Perspective From the Field
      of Language Acquisition   205
   Perspective From the Field of Special Education   208
   Putting It All Together   209
   Summary   209
Strategy 9.2 Front-Loading and Emphasizing the
Academic Language and Key Concepts of the Lesson   210
   Perspective From the Field of Language Acquisition   210
   Perspective From the Field of Special Education   214
   Putting It All Together   216
   Summary   217
Strategy 9.3 Accessing and Explicitly Teaching the Cultural
and Content Schemata for the Lesson   217
   Perspective From the Field of Language Acquisition   217
   Perspective From the Field of Special Education   219

Putting It All Together   219
Summary   220
Strategy 9.4 Allowing Students Time to Clarify
in the First Language   220
Perspective From the Field of Language Acquisition   220
Perspective From the Field of Special Education   221
Putting It All Together   222
Summary   222
Strategy 9.5 Helping Students Organize and Access
Academic Information: Explicit Strategy Instruction   223
Perspective From the Field of Language Acquisition   223
Perspective From the Field of Special Education   225
Putting It All Together   227
Summary   228
Key Terms   229
Activities for Further Understanding   229

Chapter 10. Strategies for Promoting Participation   231

Strategy 10.1 Creating a Comfortable
Classroom Environment   234
Perspective From the Field of Language Acquisition   234
Perspective From the Field of Special Education   235
Putting It All Together   237
Summary   238
Strategy 10.2 Increasing Interaction in the Classroom:
Heterogeneous Groupings   238
Perspective From the Field of Language Acquisition   238
Perspective From the Field of Special Education   239
Putting It All Together   241
Summary   244
Strategy 10.3 Encourage Extended Participation
From CLDE Students   245
Perspective From the Field of Language Acquisition   245
Perspective From the Field of Special Education   249
Putting It All Together   250
Summary   251
Summary   252
Key Terms   253
Activities for Further Understanding   253

Chapter 11. Strategies for Explicit Grammar Instruction   255

Language Errors   257
    Origins of Language Errors   257
    Rationale Behind Oral Language Error Correction   258
    Types of Error Feedback   259
    Error Analysis   263
Form-Focused Instruction   263
Different Strategies for Teaching Grammar   264
    Teaching Grammar Through Text   265
    Teaching Grammar in Context   266
Summary   268
Key Terms   269
Activities for Further Understanding   269

SECTION IV. STRATEGIES FOR LITERACY INSTRUCTION   271

Chapter 12. Strategies for Teaching Reading   273

Reading Components and CLDE Students   275
Section 12.1 Language and Literacy   278
    Strategies to Increase Vocabulary
      and Oral Language Proficiency   278
    Strategies to Increase Comprehension
      of the Text Language   283
    Strategies for Language Study   284
Section 12.2 Activities to Increase Background Knowledge   285
Section 12.3 Reading Strategy Instruction   288
Section 12.4 Strategies to Help Students Analyze,
    Organize, and Interact With the Content   291
Summary   293
Key Terms   269
Activities for Further Understanding   296

Chapter 13. Strategies for Teaching the Writing Process   297

Written Expression Challenges for Students With Special Needs   299
Written Expression Challenges for CLDE Students   301
Explicit Instruction of the Writing Process   302
    Step 1. Building Background Knowledge   303
    Step 2. Organizing the Information   304
    Step 3. Choosing an Appropriate Genre   305

Step 4. Discerning the Audience   306
Step 5. Analyzing the Genre's Features   306
Step 6. Modeling the Step-by-Step Process   307
Step 7. Independent Writing   309
Step 8. Editing and Revising   309
Example of Explicit Instruction of the Writing Process   310
Summary   315
Key Terms   315
Activities for Further Understanding   315

Chapter 14. Challenges When Teaching Writing   317
Specific Writing Challenges for CLDE Students   320
Challenges at the Grammatical Level   321
Challenges at the Orthographic Level   324
Challenges at the Cultural Level   330
Summary   333
Key Terms   333
Activities for Further Understanding   334

Chapter 15. Strategies for Written Error Correction   335
Considerations When Correcting CLDE Students' Writing   337
Error Correction   340
Steps to Error Correction   340
Examples of Error Correction   342
Summary   347
Key Terms   348
Activities for Further Understanding   348

SECTION V. NEW DIRECTIONS IN THE EDUCATION OF CLDE STUDENTS

Chapter 16. Policy Considerations for Working With CLDE Students

Glossary   349

References   359

Index   373

About the Authors   399

This section can be found in PDF at www.sage pub.com/grassi

Education for Culturally and Linguistically Diverse Exceptional Students

A Matter of Justice for All

A REFLECTION ON JUSTICE

My youngest brother, Barry, was born with brain damage. My parents spent years trying to provide the best learning opportunities available for Barry. My mother worked politically to help increase services for children with special needs. Today Barry lives in a group home and works at Goodwill Industries in a sheltered workshop. He is a wonderful man and generally very happy. When I discuss the meaning of justice, I often refer to Barry.

For several years, I have defined justice as the relationship that allows all life to flourish according to its nature and ability. The issue of justice is always relational: Every outcome depends on the quality and commitment within relationships. I believe this is true for both personal and international relations. Barry and I are very different people with different needs and abilities. The application of justice allows us both to prosper as full human beings. In simple terms, the language of justice is translated as fairness or equality. When we consider justice as equality it is clear that I don't mean that Barry and I are the same. I do mean that we both deserve treatment that will allow us to achieve our potential according to our abilities. Equality requires that each of us has access to the resources necessary for a healthy life. The relational aspect of justice means that individuals as well as groups must know each other well enough to identify basic needs, and that there is a commitment to meeting those needs so that all flourish.

I teach in a Jesuit university. In 2000, Fr. Peter-Hans Kolvenbach, SJ, Superior General of the Jesuit order worldwide, spoke at Santa Clara University about "Justice Education." He clarified that all 28 Jesuit colleges and universities in the United States must educate the whole person as a matter of justice. As teachers, we are challenged to educate the whole person, which means we must nurture the emotional, spiritual, and psychological development of students as well as contribute to intellectual growth. This charge requires that teachers know the identity of students as fully as possible.

Respect for the full identity of each person is essential so teachers know the needs of their students in order to apply best practices and effective learning strategies. The unique identity of each child must influence our educational approach. In my college classroom, I ask students to write a brief autobiography at the beginning of each semester. I want to know each student's background and how she or he identifies the primary influences that have shaped each student's worldview. In the special needs classroom, it is essential to know the influences and behaviors that have been foundational in the child's life as well as the specific extraordinary need that challenges the child.

What does it mean to guarantee justice for all in the context of multicultural or multilingual special needs education? This question opens the discussion of human and civil rights. As a society, we guarantee every child the right to an education. When that right includes circumstances beyond the norm, though, the guarantee fails. The extraordinary needs of some children simply are not met. The discussions of human rights and justice are especially challenging when "preferential treatment" is necessary for any group or individual. Every group needs attention and resources to serve its particular needs and abilities. There is a maxim that suggests that a civilized society will be judged according to how it treats those who are the most vulnerable. Children who enter our educational system with a cultural background other than "American," or whose first language (L1) is not English, or those who have special learning needs beyond what is deemed normal, are all vulnerable. Will we guarantee the basic rights of all our children?

The expression, "justice for all," is woven into the fabric of the United States. School children across the country repeat the phrase in classrooms each morning as they recite the Pledge of Allegiance. Most citizens would claim "justice" as an American value. The application of justice in our educational system requires a commitment to national priorities that provide the necessary resources to meet the needs of *all* children.

PRIORITIES AND POLITICAL WILL

When I consider the distribution of resources for education, it is clear that education is not a top priority in the United States. The guiding question in my evaluation of national priorities is, "Where does our security lie?" If the federal budget is an indication of U.S. priorities, it is clear that the U.S. government believes that military spending is the top priority for national security. In the federal discretionary budget for 2008, military spending is $481.4 billion with a $141.7 supplemental for the "war on terror." Health care is $70 billion, and education is $56 billion. Does this budget foster security? In 1967, at Riverside Church, Dr. Martin Luther King, Jr. told us, "A nation that continues year after year to spend more money on military defense than on programs of social uplift is approaching spiritual death."

Ironically, our security depends on healthy relationships, and lies in guaranteeing basic human rights and needs for all. Essentially, if we want peace and security in our lives we must do the work of justice. The means we use must be consistent with the ends we want to achieve. There must be a paradigm shift in our thinking about the nature of security to guarantee a commitment to full human development.

A paradigm shift will help create an awareness of the importance of children with special needs in our lives. We will recognize the value of interdependence as we make human needs a top priority in the United States and extend that priority to the global family. This spirit and commitment to interdependence is necessary to help us see the importance of creating relationships that allow all life to flourish. We are all part of a fragile web of life. We need each other. That may be new learning for some of us.

This raises the question of what we might learn from a child with special needs. What can we learn from those who are most vulnerable in our world? Parents and teachers of children with special needs can answer this immediately: We learn to see differently through the lens of someone whose worldview is other than our own. We learn how to receive the gift of diversity. We learn new ways to communicate. We learn compassion and the power of love to transform our lives.

To base our security in human rights and needs we have to believe that a commitment to the common good will ultimately serve the needs of each person as well. Whatever we do for the most fragile part of our society, we do for ourselves. Our security is relational.

Making education a funding priority is a critical part of our security. There cannot be a competition for resources between a classroom with children with autism, children with learning disabilities, children with Down syndrome, or children who speak languages other than English that forces the principal to choose where to assign one paraprofessional classroom aide. Our current distribution of resources fails to serve those who are most vulnerable. Without the commitment to the basic needs of all children, we are unraveling the fundamental rights that form the foundation of the United States.

LEADERSHIP AND POLICY

Passion for justice is characteristic of leaders who bring social justice into their classrooms and schools. Fortunately, there are educators who recognize the promotion of justice as a fundamental element of their leadership role. In a recent article (Woven in Deeply: Identity and Leadership of Urban Social Justice Principals, 2008, *Education and Urban Society, 41,* 1, 3–25), George Theoharis identifies leadership traits of school principals committed to social justice, saying, "Social justice leadership is a calling, not just a position for which you apply." For the principals he interviewed, the value of social justice leadership is woven into their lives.

Leadership characteristics that promote social justice include the importance of team building, invitations to participation and dialogue, and the fundamental principle of inclusion. Inclusion promotes dignity for marginalized children and, as Jill Bevan-Brown puts it (Beyond Policy and Good Intentions, 2006, *International Journal of Inclusive Education, 10,* 2–3, 221–234), "the right to be regarded and treated as equally valued members of society."

Educational leaders for social justice have the worldview and the lens that creates educational policy for the common good. Policy must be developed with the belief that justice for each child will be beneficial to the whole community. We are all part of a web. Whatever we do to any part of the web impacts all of us. Inclusive social justice policies in our educational system will ultimately guarantee that every student has the basic right to flourish.

TIME TO ACT

There is great value in the work that Elizabeth Grassi and Heidi Barker have done in this text to illustrate the integration of theory and practice for multicultural or multilingual special needs education. The missing link is the commitment and political will to provide the resources needed for full implementation of these educational approaches. Nobel Peace Prize Laureate Al Gore often mentions that political will is a renewable resource. The renewal must begin at the grassroots as citizens demand justice for all children within the educational system and through full funding for the best practices that can bring effective strategies to all classrooms.

It is time to renew the resource of political engagement in our society. We must get involved in issues of national priorities. Education is one of those issues that will make a fundamental difference in transforming our country, both in how we treat each other and in how we treat the global community. Culturally and linguistically diverse exceptional children will teach us humility, and help us move beyond arrogance to have minds and hearts without defenses or boundaries. We need all our children to teach us how to love.

Dr. Byron Plumley
Director of Peace and Justice Studies
Regis University, Denver, CO

Preface

INTRODUCTION AND PURPOSE FOR THE BOOK

We are both professors in the education department at a small liberal arts college. While we teach different subject matters—linguistically diverse education and special education—we found our students continually telling us that the strategies we presented were similar. Our conversations led to discussions of what those commonalities are, where the strategies differ, and why and where they overlap. It was at this point that we decided to undertake the writing of a book on the intersection between special education and linguistically diverse education. While the approaches to the two types of students can be similar, the reasoning behind the strategies we use differ, and the labels students are given make a difference in how teachers approach the student. There are also differences in assessment practices and in the services children receive as a result of the labels.

Our conversations with each other inspired many questions, and this book is an attempt to answer some of those questions.

1. What are the assessment practices for English as a second language, or bilingual education, and special education and are they effective at discerning between the language acquisition process and special education? How do you know if a child is experiencing the second language acquisition process, or has a learning disability, or is both an English language learner and exceptional?

2. What is the difference between sheltering in an English as a second language or bilingual classroom and scaffolding for students with special needs? What are the most effective teaching strategies to reach all students in every classroom?

3. How can school professionals better collaborate to meet the needs of students who are both learning English and have special needs?

4. How do we involve families of culturally and linguistically diverse exceptional students in the education process?

5. How do new laws and policies impact special education and bilingual education?

Our own wonderings led us to look for answers beyond what our own conversations and experiences could provide. We looked for ideas through research of the literature on second language acquisition, special education, teaching strategies for ELL students and students with special needs, and bilingual special education, and also through observations of teachers and other school experts in the field. We began to talk with everyone we knew in schools and conducted informal and formal interviews with practicing teachers.

Those interviews informed us that teachers shared the questions we had formulated. They were eager for us to put together ideas of how to work with the students in their classrooms. The teachers are frustrated by many points:

1. Teachers are frustrated with the assessment practices and the labeling of children as either English language learners or special needs—not looking at the whole child and allowing the teacher to get a more holistic picture of the child. Once labeled, children are tracked and the track in which they are placed is not often one that meets all their needs.

2. Teachers are frustrated by lack of knowledge of what to do with students who are labeled as either English language learners or special needs but who exhibit behaviors from both labels. Teachers report desperately needing strategies to meet the needs of students who are both second language learners and have special needs.

3. Teachers are frustrated by the lack of communication and collaboration between special education teachers and English as a second language or bilingual teachers.

The frustrations expressed by the teachers we have interviewed show the changing reality of classrooms. Today, many teachers have classrooms full of English language learners, many of whom also have special needs. Federal laws such as the *No Child Left Behind Act of 2001* and the *Individuals with Disabilities Education Improvement Act* now hold teachers accountable for *all* children, regardless of their labels. Teachers are truly desperate for strategies to help all children. Likewise, the philosophy of special education has evolved to encourage teachers to meet the needs of most students with special needs in the general education classroom, rather than in a separate special education classroom.

Talking to our students, each other, and teachers in the field, as well as reading the recent literature and spending time in classrooms, has encouraged us to write this book. We hope to provide classroom teachers of any subject and any grade level a clear description and examples of the philosophies, theories, and practices that meet the needs of culturally and linguistically diverse exceptional (CLDE) students.

INTENDED AUDIENCE

This text is designed for undergraduate, preservice, elementary, and secondary teachers, and for graduate-level practicing elementary and secondary teachers who are studying special education, or the education of CLDE students. This text is also meant for ELL teachers who have CLDE students in their classrooms. This text is meant to bring together foundational information from both the special education and the English as a second language or bilingual field to target the specific needs of CLDE students. This text also serves as a resource for schools or school districts as they conduct professional development in the area of assessment and instruction for CLDE students.

ORGANIZATION OF THE BOOK

The book is organized into five main sections: (1) Understanding Student Backgrounds, (2) Strategies for Assessment and Planning for Instruction, (3) Strategies for Content and Language Acquisition, (4) Strategies for Literacy Instruction, and (5) Policy Considerations. We know that assessment and instruction are not linear processes and hope that the reader will find connections between all the chapters and sections of the book.

The introduction chapter sets the context and need for the book. Chapter 1 gives a description of the demographics of the students in today's classrooms, descriptions of the types of programs available to linguistically diverse students, and the placement options that schools offer to students with special needs. Chapter 1 also discusses the policy behind program decisions and the philosophies that underpin the education of CLDE students and students with exceptionalities.

Section I includes collaborating with families and two chapters about the language acquisition process. These topics give insight into CLDE student backgrounds and provide foundational understandings for working with CLDE students. This section discusses topics such as creating relationships with and empowering culturally and linguistically diverse families, describes the language acquisition process, and examines different theories that provide a definition of "proficiency" in a language.

Section II focuses on the strategies for assessment and planning for instruction. Included in this section are procedures used to determine eligibility for special education services and English as a second language services, and a focus on broadening existing assessment practices to more fully support the needs of CLDE learners.

Sections III and IV focus on content-area instructional strategies and literacy strategies to support the diverse needs of CLDE students. We examine the literature on "best practices" for linguistically diverse students and for students with exceptionalities, and analyze how these strategies intersect for CLDE students.

Section V includes the final chapter that focuses on policy implications for working with CLDE students. This chapter is on the Web, and includes ideas for teacher education programs, teacher training, administrative support, and school climate. This chapter includes a case study that pulls the main ideas from the book together, as a series of questions guide teachers to their next steps in providing CLDE learner support.

Throughout the book, you will notice that we use the term "culturally and linguistically diverse exceptional students" (CLDE students). While we realize that the term "CLDE students" does not exhibit people first language, we chose to use this term because it is used in the current literature addressing the needs of students who are learning English and also have special needs. Our intention in writing this book is to address the needs of CLDE students as a group (through the institutional processes and laws) and as individuals (through assessment, planning, instruction, and eligibility decisions). We also use the term English language learners, or ELL students. Again, while this term does not exhibit people first language, it is the term used in current literature on students learning English.

ORGANIZATIONAL AND PEDAGOGICAL FEATURES OF THE TEXT

In our own experience, we have found that there is often a mismatch between theory and practice. Research on education does not often include the voice of teachers or reach the level of public school educators. We have specifically organized this book to address this mismatch. Each chapter begins with a list of **key points** covered in the chapter and ends with **activities for further understanding** that review the key points and **connect theory to classroom practice.** We also have included throughout the book personal narratives in the form of **case studies** from teachers, parents, and students. These case studies allow teachers, parents, and learners to describe the personal challenges involved in learning and teaching a new language and culture. We also have included samples of **authentic student language** and writing throughout the chapters to illustrate the concepts described and make connections to the research discussed in the text. **Research** is infused throughout the book to show the complexity of the issues, but given in the context of examples, stories from classrooms and experiences, and in case studies. We have tried to write so the book is **accessible and readable.** Our hope is that these ideas are implemented in classrooms.

Another feature, in particular, makes explicit bridges between **theory and practice.** We have included **video clip examples** from actual classrooms. Strategy chapters have video clips and rubrics with which to observe the teacher and evaluate the strategy on a Web site that is linked with the text. These video clips illustrate, in real classrooms, teachers who are exemplifying the practices described.

Ancillaries and Technology Accompaniments

We have tried to create a strong connection between the text and the accompanying Web site by placing a **Web icon** within sections of text where a direct link should be made to ancillary materials. The ancillary materials include video clips of teachers implementing strategies described in the text, rubrics for observing the teacher and evaluating the strategy, further examples of concepts and strategies described in the text, example forms and assessments, and more case studies. Students can go to the open access portion of the site at **www.sagepub.com/grassi.**

Instructor resources are included on a password-protected portion of the Web site, and include an extensive selection of useful tools that can be implemented in the classroom such as teaching tips, sample syllabi, PowerPoint slides for each chapter, and a variety of useful Web resources. Instructors can register to receive access to the site at **www.sagepub.com/grassi.**

Acknowledgments

Writing this book was a great personal and professional learning journey, supported by many people.

Many people were willing to tell us their stories. Not all the stories made it into the final editing of this book, but all of them informed this text. Many teachers and professionals offered their time, their expertise, and examples of student work to include in this book. Thank you to all of you:

Risschie Aran, Bev Addington, Jana Babcock Jessica Bass, Elizabeth Bucci, Traci and Jeff Bushnell, Linda Kazim Davis, Jillian Deganhart, Erika Erikson, Jamie Erickson, Joanie Esparza, Melissa Fogel, Rebecca Ford, Marie-Do Franco, Terry Garcia, Luke Grein, Kelly Grossnickle, Susan Harbor, D. J. Ida, Tonia Johnson, Brandon Jones, Sheila Karpan, Elizabeth Kean, Frank Kim, Amelia Koopman, Mary Kuhn, Erika Lee, Felicia Leist, Amanda Lewis, Nuria Linares, Harmony Looper, Denise Lopez, Haley MacNeil, Rebecca Marquez-Guerrero, Teresa Martinez, Caitlin Mergendahl, Thao Nguyen, Kathy Nutting, Isa Pineda, Mary Preston, Cari Reidlin, Jennifer Scovel, Erin Warner, and Laura Zoromski.

We also would like to thank the students from the ED 485 class Fall 2008 and the EDSP 403 class Fall 2008 for your careful editing and suggestions.

We thank the following professors for offering their expertise in the form of research articles: Obdulia Castro, Joan Armon, Anthony Ortega, Byron Plumley, and Sandra Mitchel.

Thank you to Nanci White. You know all that you do.

A special thank you to media specialists from Regis University for their expert filming and suggestions: Andy Dorfman, David Devine, and Todd Novosad.

Thank you to the professionals at SAGE who guided us through the process with patience: Deya Saoud, Diane McDaniel, Ashley Conlon, Taryn Bigelow, and Alison Hope.

Thank you to the reviewers. We appreciate the time you took to provide us with thoughtful feedback:

Lisa Aaroe, Grand Canyon University

José Luis Alvarado, San Diego State University

Leonard Baca, University of Colorado-Boulder

Beverly Barkon, Carlow University

Ji-Mei Chang, San José State University

EunMi Cho, California State University, Sacramento

Mary Friehe, University of Nebraska at Omaha

Anne Y. Gallegos, New Mexico State University

Diana M. Limón, Loyola Marymount University

Janet Medina, McDaniel College

Oneyda M. Paneque, Barry University

Tess Reid, California State University, Northridge

Diane Rodriguez, East Carolina University

Laura M. Sáenz, The University of Texas Pan American

Diane Torres-Velasquez, The University of New Mexico

Dr. Jan E. Waggoner, Southern Illinois University, Carbondale

Gwendolyn Webb-Johnson, Texas A&M University

Chapter 1

INTRODUCTION

Key Points

✦ How the changing demographics of students in today's classrooms create challenges with the identification and placement of CLDE students

✦ What laws and policies shape the educational programs available to English language learners, students with special needs, and CLDE students

✦ Why it is important for all teachers to be prepared to work with CLDE students

CASE STUDY 1.1 — Impact of Cultural and Linguistic Diversity on Academics

I was born in the United States. Both my parents are from Sri Lanka. They are Tamil and speak Tamil. I also lived with my grandmother who spoke to me in Tamil and English.

In second grade, I was said to have slow processing skills with reading comprehension. In order to address this issue, the teacher encouraged my parents to use only English in the house. From that moment on, I did not hear Tamil. At the time, I really did not mind whether I interacted with my language or not. But now, looking back, I wish my parents hadn't stopped speaking to me in Tamil, because I feel that I lost a part of my heritage. However, my parents did what the teacher told them to do. My parents' culture dictated that they not get involved in school and that they leave the schooling to the teacher, the student, and no one else. Therefore, my parents followed the teacher's advice because in Sri Lanka we believe that the teacher knows best for the student.

In middle school, I was still placed in lower-division classes. I was mainstreamed for math and science but was not mainstreamed for English classes. In the basic English classes, we learned how to make sentences and learned basic grammar. This placement made me feel incompetent. In the eighth grade, I transferred to a different school. I was put in all general education classes for the first time. At this school, they realized that I did not have a reading disability and I became more confident in my academic abilities.

It is nice to have parents like mine who just say "yes" to teachers, who trust even if they don't understand what the school is actually doing. In this case, the parents may not be able to communicate the proper information for the benefit of their child. In Sri Lankan culture, families do not talk back out of respect to the teacher. I was always told by my parents that the teacher is never wrong and she or he is always correct. This puts a strain on the relationship between student and parent because if there is a conflict, who is going to side with who? Teachers should recognize that they have more power than they think, and some of their decisions can put students on the wrong path for a long time. Teachers must attempt to know the culture and language of the student first.

—Bilingual, bicultural student

Consider the case study above:

- How does this student reflect the demographics of today's schools?
- What program or placement options would have been an effective learning environment for this student?
- What recent changes in legislation would have served this student?
- What training could teachers have benefited from in order to better meet the needs of this student?

SOURCE: Used by permission.

Case Study 1.1 illustrates the complexity of learning in U.S. schools as a bilingual, bicultural person and the mislabeling that can occur when teachers do not understand the culture or language acquisition process. When the student was first labeled as having reading comprehension issues, he was still working in two languages and two cultures. His reading issues may have been part of the normal language acquisition process or cultural mismatch, not necessarily a learning disability. School literacy activities can sometimes presuppose cultural knowledge and language that children and their families may not have acquired (Klinger, Artiles, & Barletta, 2006; Trueba, 1988).

Identification of English language learners with special needs continues to be a significant issue in education. It is often unclear whether the English language and culture acquisition process is interfering with learning or is masking a learning disability (Wagner, Francis, & Morris, 2005). Because the number of **culturally and linguistically diverse exceptional (CLDE) students** is increasing, educational practitioners must understand the cultural complexities, the linguistic complexities, the learning process complexities, and the laws and placement options pertaining to both English as a second language and bilingual education, and special education.

This chapter will begin with a review of the demographics of the students in today's schools. We will examine the numbers of students who are learning English as a second language (ESL), the percentages of students who have special needs, and the growing numbers of CLDE students. We will discuss the laws concerning the education of English language learners and students with special needs and examine program options for CLDE students. We also consider the least restrictive environment for CLDE students, and discuss the philosophical underpinnings of these placement options.

ESTABLISHING THE RATIONALE: DEMOGRAPHICS OF STUDENTS IN OUR CLASSROOMS

Demographics of English Language Learners

Today, approximately 19.5% of the U.S. population speaks languages other than English. The majority language spoken among immigrants today is Spanish, followed by French, Chinese, and German (Modern Language Association [MLA], 2006) (see Figure 1.1). Nearly 65% of bilingual people living in the United States speak Spanish as a first language, and Hispanics, who may be of any race, showed a 57.9% growth rate from 1990–2000, making Hispanics the fastest-growing population in the United States today (U.S. Census Bureau, 2000).

The U.S. public school population reflects this general population growth and an estimated 19% of school-aged children (ages 5–17) speak a language other

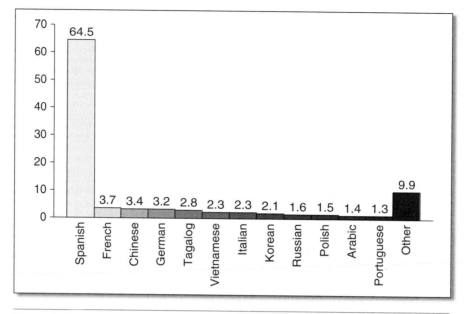

Figure 1.1   Percentages of Those Speaking Languages Other Than English in the United States

SOURCE: MLA, 2006.

than English (National Center for Education Statistics [NCES], 2006). By 2030, the number of school-aged children who speak a language other than English is expected to grow to 40% (U.S. Department of Education [USDOE] & National Institute of Child Health and Human Development [NICHD], 2003). It is estimated that 12.8% of the school-aged population speaks Spanish as a first language, and although students designated as **English language learners (ELLs)** speak a variety of languages, Spanish-speaking students represent over 79.2% of ELL students, followed by Vietnamese (2%), Hmong (1.6%), Cantonese (1%), and Korean (1%) (Kindler, 2002; MLA, 2006; Zehler, Fleischman, Hopstock, Stephenson, Pendzick, & Sapru, 2003).

The majority of ELL students preK–12 are concentrated in the western part of the United States. All states in the nation, however, have preK–12 ELL students enrolled in their schools and some states in particular have seen tremendous growth in the ELL student population over the last 10 years. Nevada, Nebraska, Arkansas, Indiana, Kentucky, Tennessee, Alabama, Georgia, South Carolina, North Carolina, and Colorado have all experienced over 200% growth in ELL student population since 1994 (National Clearinghouse for English Language Acquisition and Language Instruction Education Programs, 2006).

While demographic data indicate that Hispanic students make up the majority of ELL students in U.S. schools, Hispanic students continue to be more at risk than any other student population. The educational attainment rate of the Hispanic population is significantly behind the educational attainment rate of other foreign-born and native-born individuals. In 2006, only 59.3% of the Hispanic population 25 and over had completed high school as compared to 86.1% for whites, 80.7% of blacks, and 87.2% of Asian Pacific Islanders (U.S. Census Bureau, 2008). Data indicate that Mexican students have the lowest educational attainment rate of all Hispanic populations.

Demographics of CLDE Students

There are few studies that have begun to approximate the numbers of CLDE students in our schools. Presently, data indicate that 13.7% of the general school-age population is identified as having special needs (Office of Special Education and Rehabilitation Services [OSERS], 2003). National survey studies estimate that 9% of ELL students are also designated as having special education eligibility, and it is estimated that CLDE students account for 8.2% of all special education students (Zehler, Fleischman, Hopstock, Pendzick, & Stephenson, 2003). Spanish-speaking students make up the great majority of CLDE students and approximately 80.4% of students identified as CLDE speak Spanish as a first language (Zehler, Fleischman, Hopstock, Pendzick, et al., 2003).

While we are able to approximate the numbers of CLDE students in U.S. schools, accurate identification of CLDE students remains a concern. There is currently no uniform method for identifying CLDE students across the nation's school districts and large discrepancies across districts have been reported in the manner of their classification (Abedi, 2004, 2005; McCardle, Mele-McCarthy, Cutting, Leos, & D'Emilio, 2005; USDOE & NICHD, 2003). A 2003 survey distributed to a national sample of districts noted concern with the challenge of distinguishing between difficulties due to the second language acquisition process and ones due to learning disabilities. Most school districts do not identify CLDE students as a separate category and therefore must consult with both the ESL–bilingual coordinator and the special education coordinator to receive an approximate count of CLDE students (Zehler, Fleischman, Hopstock, Stephenson et al., 2003). Of greatest concern are ELL students with lower proficiency levels of English. Studies have found that these students are most often misidentified or mislabeled (Artiles, Rueda, Salazar, & Higareda, 2005). Labels impact how students are served in schools and therefore it is important that an accurate system for identification of CLDE students be in place.

Looking at Labels: Overrepresentation and Underrepresentation

Many districts are trying to address identification of students by bringing in the expertise of both the ESL–bilingual specialist and the special education specialist. Unfortunately, this system is not infallible and students are still mislabeled—especially students who fall within specific ethnic or racial categories. Table 1.1 delineates the over- and underrepresentation of specific racial or ethnic categories receiving special education services.

The overrepresentation and underrepresentation are especially seen in particular groups of students. OSERS (2003) found that the percentages of American Indian or Alaska Native (56%) and Hispanics (58.9%) with specific learning disabilities are overrepresented when compared to the percentage of all students with disabilities (49.2%). Asian or Pacific Islanders, who represent 4.4% of the

Table 1.1   Students Labeled as Disabled by Race or Ethnicity as a Proportion of the General Student Population

	General Student Population	All Students With Disabilities	Students Labeled as Specific Learning Disability	Students Labeled as Emotionally Disturbed	Students Labeled as Speech–Language Disability	Students Labeled as Mentally Retarded
American Indian or Alaska Native	1.2%	1.31%	1.47%	1.24%	1.19%	1.06%
Asian or Pacific Islander	4.4%	1.87%	1.56%	1.17%	2.58%	1.73%
Black	17.2%	20.28%	18.72%	28.23%	15.92%	34.08%
Hispanic	18.5%	15.42%	18.48%	9.50%	14.63%	12.08%
White	58.7%	61.13%	59.77%	59.86%	65.67%	51.05%

SOURCES: Office of Special Education Programs (OSEP), 2003; U.S. Census Bureau, 2006.

NOTE: Percentages are for students ages 6–21 served under the Individuals with Disabilities Education Act (IDEA).

general student population, are underrepresented in almost all disability categories. Black students, who make up 17.2% of the general student population, are overrepresented in almost all disability categories (18.72% of black students are labeled as specific learning disabled, 28.23% as emotionally disturbed, and 34.08% as mentally retarded). A black student is 2.21 times more likely to be labeled as emotionally disturbed than any other ethnic group (OSERS, 2003).

For charts of disability categories and race or ethnicity distributions see the following Web site: **www.sagepub.com/grassi.**

1.1

Overrepresentation of ELL students in specific disability categories occurs as well. When ELL students are identified as having a learning disability, they are most likely to be labeled as specific learning disabilities (5.16%) and speech or language impairments (2.17%), and data indicate that most CLDE students carry these labels (Macswan & Rolstad, 2006; McCardle, Mele-Mccarthy, Cutting, et al., 2005; Zehler, Fleischman, Hopstock, Stephenson et al., 2003).

The behaviors of students who are acquiring English as a second language may look similar to the behaviors of students who are learning disabled or have speech or language impairments—but the core issues that determine this behavior are different. For example, a student with a learning disability may be slower to respond during whole class discussions because this child requires longer processing time. Likewise, a child who is learning English may be slower to respond in whole class discussion because this child requires time to process between two or more languages, not because the child has a learning disability. A student who is learning disabled may read below grade level. A child who is learning English may also read below grade level, not because of a learning disability, but because the student has not fully acquired the English language. This child may have full knowledge of the reading process in the first language, but is not yet able to express this knowledge in the second language.[1]

Even though children with learning disabilities and children who are acquiring English may exhibit behaviors that appear similar in a classroom setting, the causes are very different, and it is important for teachers to distinguish between the two. With such rapidly growing numbers of ELL students, it

REFER TO CASE STUDY 1.1

How does this student represent the demographics discussed in this chapter? Was the student misdiagnosed? Why? How could mislabeling of this student have been prevented? How could the teachers have acquired a more thorough picture of the student?

is imperative that educational professionals begin to receive the proper training in both ESL–bilingual education and special education to avoid mislabeling, over-representation, and underrepresentation.

SETTING THE CONTEXT: LAWS THAT IMPACT PROGRAM OPTIONS FOR CLDE STUDENTS

CLDE students do not have specific laws or program options delineated for them. These students are often labeled as either ELL students who need special education support or as students with special needs who need ESL or bilingual support. To best meet the needs of CLDE students, educational practitioners must understand bilingual law and program options as well as special education law and placement options. When a student who is learning English is diagnosed as having special needs, we advocate that the multidisciplinary team carefully consider the current laws, service delivery, and placement that will most support the student's primary educational needs.

Bilingual Education Laws

ESL or bilingual education in the United States is based on the Civil Rights Act of 1964, which "prohibits discrimination on the grounds of race, color, or national origin in programs or activities receiving federal financial assistance" (Wiese & Garcia, 1998, p. 3). Equal access to the educational curriculum for ELL students (including education in the student's stronger language) is often considered a civil rights issue. Funding of bilingual education at the federal level began in the 1960s as it became clear to policymakers that students living in poverty, especially Mexican American students in the Southwest, were failing to make academic progress.

The first federal Bilingual Education Act (BEA) was passed in 1968 (Title VII of the Elementary and Secondary Education Act [ESEA]). The focus of the BEA was to create equal educational opportunities for low-income ELL students (Wiese & Garcia, 1998). Although not mandated through the act, the BEA provided opportunity to use the student's native language in instruction to increase academic achievement. However, the BEA did not require any specific methodology or instructional programs, and it was not until the reauthorization of 1974 that "native language instruction" was included in the definition of bilingual education (Wiese & Garcia, 1998). Grants under the BEA were typically awarded to plan, develop, and maintain programs that met the educational needs of language minority students and provided preservice training to teachers and paraprofessionals (Wiese & Garcia, 1998).

From 1975 on, the Bilingual Education Act was reauthorized several times and helped to identify different types of bilingual programs available to students, but it still did not consistently mandate native language instruction for language minority students. The amount of instruction in native languages under this act was encouraged (or discouraged) through the distribution of federal funds.

The reauthorization of the Bilingual Education Act in 1994 (BEA) finally addressed the importance of bilingual and bicultural competencies. For the first time, the BEA funded dual-language programs that encouraged bilingualism, biculturalism, and biliteracy for ELL students and English-only students as well.

It was not until the 1970s that the plight of ELL students enrolled in general education classrooms without bilingual services was addressed. A class action suit filed by a San Francisco student of Chinese origin forced the issue. The complaint argued that ELL students did not have equal educational opportunities because instruction in content areas was not specifically suited to the needs of students who were learning English. In 1974, in the landmark *Lau v. Nichols* case, the court ruled that equivalent instructional materials and strategies did not constitute equal educational opportunity, and that teachers must make **modifications** for students who did not speak English as a first language. Although Lau v. Nichols established the right of students to receive specialized instruction, Lau v. Nichols did not require a specific instructional methodology (Wiese & Garcia, 1998). In 1975, the Office of Civil Rights issued the "Lau remedies," which required more specific specialized instruction for English language learners, specified manners of identifying ELL students, specified manners of determining students' levels of English language proficiency, and created standards for bilingual education teachers (Ovando, 2003, p. 10). The Lau remedies also required bilingual education (home language instruction as well as ESL instruction) at all schools that had at least 20 ELL students of the same language (Ovando, 2003). In 1981, the *Casteneda v. Pickard* case established further guidelines for appropriate educational programs. This case established three criteria for developing effective educational programs for language minority students: (1) The educational program must be grounded in sound educational theory; (2) adequate personnel and services must be provided; and (3) the program must provide sound practices and results in all content areas (Ovando, 2003, p. 10).

In the 1990s, a recurring pattern in the political climate promoting English-only instruction gained the popular vote in some states (the English-only movement was launched in 1983 and continued from there on out). In 1998, California voters passed Proposition 227, which limited second language learners to only one year of specialized English language instruction before their placement in the general education classroom. Similar propositions passed in Arizona (Proposition 203) and Massachusetts in 2002. The English-only movement was ultimately enshrined in federal policy in 2001, when the **No Child Left Behind (NCLB) Act** completely removed all language encouraging bilingual education and eliminated the Bilingual Education Act (Crawford, 2002). At this point, federal policy placed full emphasis on English language acquisition as the academic goal for immigrant children. While NCLB does not prohibit bilingual education, all children, including those learning English, are required to show growth in English literacy and language skills. The same requirement for native language literacy and language skills is not delineated under NCLB.

NCLB and policy supporting English-only language instruction continue to encourage removal of all first language supports and transition to the general education, English-speaking classroom as soon as possible—many times before the second language is fully acquired. While we want all ELL students to learn English, research does not support early transition and swift removal of first language supports. As will be discussed in the section on bilingual or bicultural program options, bilingual education still remains a positive factor for academic achievement. Table 1.2 presents a summary of laws relating to the education of English language learners.

REFER TO CASE STUDY 1.1

Which ESL–bilingual laws would have benefited the student, had they been in place when he was attending school?

Table 1.2   Timeline of Legislation and Litigation Pertaining to the Education of English Language Learners

Year	Legislation and Litigation	Description
1954	*Brown v. Board of Education*	Determined that separate is not equal and the segregation of schools becomes unconstitutional.
1964	*Civil Rights Act*	Prohibited race, sex, and national origin discrimination in public places.
1965	*Elementary and Secondary Education Act (ESEA)*	Government funds became available to meet the educational needs of children from low social economic status and "educationally deprived children."

Year	Legislation and Litigation	Description
1968	*Elementary and Secondary Education Act Amendment: The Bilingual Education Act Title VII*	Provided school districts with federal funds to establish educational programs for students who do not speak English as a first language and who are from low socioeconomic status. Under this act, schools could, but were not required to, provide bilingual programs.
1974	*Lau v. Nichols*	Established that specialized language programs for ELL students were necessary to provide equal educational opportunities.
1974	*Equal Education Opportunity Act (EEOA)*	Organized the *Lau v. Nichols* decision and required school districts to take appropriate steps to help ELL students overcome language barriers that impeded equal participation in instructional programs.
1974	*Reauthorization of Bilingual Education Act Title VII*	Native language instruction required as a condition for receiving bilingual education grants. Bilingual education was defined as transitional bilingual education, where students are transitioned to monolingual English classes as soon as possible (usually by the third or sixth grade).
1975	*Lau remedies*	Provided informal guidelines for schools to effectively work with ELL students. Required districts to provide bilingual education in situations where the civil rights of bilingual students had been violated.
1978	*Reauthorization of the Bilingual Education Act Title VII*	Funding was provided for native language instruction only to the extent necessary to allow a child to achieve competence in English. Bilingual maintenance programs became ineligible for funding. The focus became transitional bilingual education programs and transitioning the child to monolingual English classes as soon as possible.
1980	*Lau regulations*	An attempt to make the Lau remedies official and to require bilingual instruction for students who are limited English proficient. The Reagan administration withdrew this proposal, leaving uncertainty about a school's obligation to meet the needs of ELL students.

(Continued)

Table 1.2 (Continued)

Year	Legislation and Litigation	Description
1981	*Castaneda v. Pickard*	An appeals court decision that established three criteria for programs serving ELL students: (1) based on sound educational theory, (2) implemented effectively with adequate resources, and (3) evaluated and proven effective.
1983	*U.S. English-only movement launched*	Debates concerning English as the dominant language to be used in law, society, and education.
1984	*Reauthorization of the Bilingual Education Act Title VII*	Most funding reserved for transitional bilingual education programs, with some funding reserved for bilingual maintenance programs, and English-only special alternative programs.
1988	*Reauthorization of the Bilingual Education Act Title VII*	The same provisions as 1984 existed, but 25% of the funding was reserved for English-only special alternative programs.
1994	*Reauthorization of the Bilingual Education Act Title VII*	Funding for dual language programs available for the first time. The quota for funding English-only programs was lifted.
1998	*Proposition 227 passed in California*	ELL students are limited to only one year of specialized English instruction before their placement in the mainstream, general education classroom.
2001	*No Child Left Behind (NCLB) Repeal of the Bilingual Education Act*	Emphasis on English-only instruction and removal of all language encouraging native language instruction. **Accountability** 1. Requires all teachers of ELL students to be proficient in the English language. 2. Established annual achievement objectives for ELL students. 3. Set English language proficiency as an objective. 4. Annual achievement objectives were required to relate to gains in English proficiency.

Year	Legislation and Litigation	Description
		5. Required reading and language arts assessment in English of any ELL student who had attended school in the United States for three consecutive years.
		6. Schools responsible for making adequate yearly progress as described in Title 1.
		7. Notification to parents about program placement and explanation concerning why their child needs a specialized language instruction program was required.
		Options for Student Success
		1. Parents had the right to choose among instructional programs if more than one type was available.
		2. Parents had the right to remove their child from a program designed for English language learners.
		Research-Based Teaching Methods
		1. Required that all curricula used to teach ELL students be tied to scientifically based research and demonstrated to be effective.

SOURCES: Baker, 2001, pp. 190–191; Crawford, 2004, pp. 124–125; data retrieved September 15, 2008, from the Lau Web site: http://www.stanford.edu/~kenro/LAU/index.htm; data retrieved September 15, 2008, from the No Child Left Behind Web site: http://www.ed.gov/nclb/landing.jhtml?src=pb.

Program Placement of ELL Students

When a student enrolls in a school, the school is required to find out if the student needs to learn English. By asking the parents what language is spoken at home, the school begins the process of determining the educational placement for a bilingual child.

Bilingual children are placed in programs depending on

1. a home language survey,

2. language proficiency tests to determine if the student needs language services,

3. program availability, and

4. parent choice under NCLB.

Once a student is identified as needing to learn English, program placement options become available. There are several different program models designed to meet the educational needs of ELL students. These models vary from state to state and are influenced by federal policy, which, depending on the current political climate, either encourages the use of native language instruction or the use of English-only. Figure 1.2 shows the trajectory of programs available to ELL students.

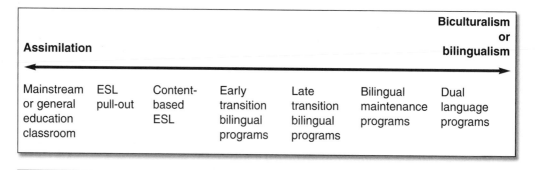

Figure 1.2   Trajectory of Programs Available to ELL Students

Bilingual or Bicultural Program Options

Two-way immersion or dual language programs work to develop bilingualism, biliteracy, and biculturalism in both ELL students and native-English-speaking children. In an effective dual language program, the curriculum is presented in two languages and is culturally relevant to the cultures represented in the classroom.

There are a variety of dual language program models. Some programs switch days, where some days of the week the content is presented in English and other days of the week the content is presented in the other language. Some programs switch languages throughout the day, where half of the day is in English while the other half is in the other language. And some programs switch languages according to the content, where, for example, science is conducted in English, while history and math are conducted in another language.

Bilingual maintenance programs are another form of program designed to maintain the student's first language and culture while simultaneously developing

English language and literacy skills. These programs are usually (but not always) designed in a 90:10 model where 90% of the instruction is in the child's native language and 10% in English in the first year. Slowly, the classroom transitions to 50:50, where (usually by the sixth grade) 50% of instruction is in the home language and 50% of the instruction is in English. The manner in which these programs are implemented and the actual strategies used in these programs can vary significantly from classroom to classroom and school to school.

The effectiveness of both dual language and bilingual maintenance programs are well supported by research. Rolstad, Mahoney, and Glass (2005) conducted a meta-analysis of bilingual education studies after 1985. This analysis found that the use of students' native language for content instruction increases measures of students' academic achievement. They also found that students in long-term bilingual education programs (such as maintenance programs) performed better academically than students in short-term bilingual education programs. Thomas and Collier (2002) found that the strongest indicator of academic achievement in the second language is the amount of formal instruction in the first language. ELL students immersed in general education, English-only classes, showed significant decreases in math and reading achievement by the fifth grade. This group also showed the largest rate of drop-out. Students in dual language programs and bilingual maintenance programs were able to fully reach at least the 50th percentile in both first and second languages in all subjects and showed the fewest dropouts (Thomas & Collier, 2002).

Programs Designed to Develop English-Only Skills and Assimilation

Transitional bilingual educational programs are designed with English acquisition and assimilation into the majority culture as the main goal. These programs aim to develop English language and literacy skills as soon as possible so that children can be placed in general education English-speaking classrooms (usually within two to three years). Content is often taught through the home language until the students are thought to be proficient enough in the target language to be transferred to the mainstream classroom. Transitional programs usually take two forms—late transition and early transition. Late transition programs are geared to move students to all English instruction by the sixth grade. Early transition programs are geared to move students to all English instruction by the third grade.

English as a second language (ESL) programs are designed to develop English language and literacy skills as soon as possible. These programs are considered a subtractive approach to bilingual education because their goal is to replace the native language with the majority language (Baker, 2001). There are many different forms of ESL programs. These include sheltered English (also called SDAIE [Specially Designed Academic Instruction in English], or content-based ESL), where the academic content is provided in a modified manner to make it more comprehensible to ELL students, and ESL pull-out, where students are pulled out of the general education classroom for specialized English instruction. ESL programs are a common option for schools where many different languages and cultures are involved, and bilingual teachers who represent the variety of languages are not available.

English submersion is where the child receives no special services but is expected to either "sink or swim" in the general education, English-only, content-area classroom. The goal of this program is assimilation into the majority culture and replacement of the native language with the majority language. This is the least effective program for English language acquisition. For example, Artiles et al. (2005) found that ELL students placed in English immersion classes (submersion) were more likely to be referred for special education services than were ELL students placed in bilingual education programs or specialized English language programs (ESL).

> **REFER TO CASE STUDY 1.1**
>
> What program placement would have benefited the student and perhaps avoided mislabeling?

Special Education Laws

Special education's history grew out of the civil rights movement. Like other minority groups, people with disabilities were prone to discrimination and had no laws to protect them. It was not until 1973 when **Section 504** of the Rehabilitation Act granted basic civil rights to people with disabilities. Then, in 1975, the Education for All Handicapped Children Act, **Public Law 94-142** passed, which granted a free and appropriate public education (FAPE) for all students, and provided the groundwork for the services that all students with special education needs are guaranteed today (see Table 1.3).

The **Individuals with Disabilities Education Act (IDEA)** is the follow-up law to Public Law 94-142. IDEA was passed first in 1990, revised in 1997, reauthorized again in 2004, and continues the movement to provide access to an equal and individualized education for students with disabilities. Each reauthorization takes into account the growing needs of particular disabilities, and, through different reauthorizations, has included autism, TBI (traumatic brain injury), behavior issues, and transitions for students with disabilities.

Table 1.3   Central Principles and Provisions Included in Special Education Law

FAPE	Every student has the right to an education in a public school, or if the public school cannot provide needed services then the school district must provide funding for the services.
Categories of disability	There are currently 13 categories of disability specified in IDEA. Only students with the disabilities defined in the law are eligible for special education services.
Least restrictive environment (LRE)	Every student must be educated in an environment that (1) provides the most access to the general education setting while (2) providing needed educational support and services. Current law states that the general education classroom should be considered first as the LRE for all students.
Individualized education	Every student who is eligible to receive special education services, must have an Individualized Education Plan (IEP) that designates specific learning goals, objectives, and how those will be met.
Nondiscriminatory evaluations and reevaluations	Schools must provide tests in the child's native language, tests that are appropriate for the age and characteristics of the child, and more than one test must be used. Assessments should be given and interpreted by a knowledgeable professional, and assessments must occur in all areas of the suspected disability (Yell, 1998).
Due process	Parents and students have the right to object if any educational service or practice designated in the IEP is not being followed. At this point, the school district must provide mediation services to remedy the situation.
Zero reject or child find	Every child, despite the nature or severity of his or her disability, must receive FAPE (even those enrolled in private schools). Each state has a *child find* system in place to let the public know about services available for students with disabilities. This concept also ensures that students who have communicable diseases are educated and guides school policies related to long-term suspension or expulsion.
Parent participation	Parents must be informed (in their home language) of all processes involved in special education testing, the IEP, and services, and must be informed of their rights and roles in this process.

1.2

For a list and description of these 13 disability categories, see the following Web link: **www .sagepub.com/grassi.**

(Continued)

Table 1.3 (Continued)

Transition services or early intervention	At age 14 and beyond, schools must help students transition to life after public school. This includes life skills training, educational plans, living independently, and community integration. A transition plan must be included in all IEPs. School districts are required to provide services to families who have students between the ages of 3 and 5 with special education needs.
Discipline	The student's exceptionalities must be taken into account when administering disciplinary action. If a child's disability will interfere with following the school's regular discipline policy, then a discipline plan must be written into the IEP.
Related services	Services that support educational success, such as occupational therapy, physical therapy, speech therapy, counseling, and transportation.

SOURCES: PL 94-142; IDEA.

The 2004 reauthorization of IDEA included several major changes of significance to give schools more freedom in how funds are used to support students. It stipulates that before referring students for special education services, schools may use up to 15% of their special education budgets to provide professional development in scientifically based interventions and educational support for students. As Response to Intervention is being implemented, special education funds can be used to support the training of teachers in intervention strategies. These are strategies that will support all students, including ELL students, who are struggling in the classroom. IDEA (2004) also acknowledges that **limited English proficiency (LEP)** could be a factor that impacts academic and behavioral achievement. The law requires that the **process** of acquiring a second language must be ruled out as the primary reason for lower academic achievement before the child can be labeled as needing special services. While this addition to the law is important when working with ELL students, there are still no specific provisions for placement or teaching strategies when addressing the needs of CLDE students.

Another important aspect of the 2004 IDEA was its provision of an alternative to the **discrepancy model** for determining specific learning disability eligibility. Previously, specific learning disabilities were determined by examining the "discrepancy" between IQ and achievement levels. Today, IDEA allows an IEP (Individualized Education Plan) team to determine eligibility for specific learning disability if the team has determined that the child is not making academic progress in an appropriate educational setting. At that point, the

Response to Intervention (RTI)[2] process is utilized to determine specific learning disability eligibility. Under the most recent IDEA, research-based strategies mirror the language utilized in NCLB, which delineates "research" as "scientifically research-based strategies." That means schools must rely on data to make all decisions regarding the education of students with disabilities.

RTI could greatly benefit CLDE students if the consulting child study team were diversified to include members who are familiar with the first language and culture of the child; familiar with the second language and culture acquisition process; and who will advocate for ESL or bilingual and culturally relevant teaching practices as research-based strategies that could benefit CLDE students. That said, the new IDEA regulations (as well as NCLB) still do not stipulate "research-based strategies" for CLDE students and there is still no specific delineation for meeting the placement needs of CLDE students. Table 1.4 presents a summary of special education laws and litigation.

Table 1.4   Special Education Legislation and Litigation

Year	Legislation or Litigation	Description
1954	*Brown v. Board of Education*	Basis for future rulings that children with disabilities cannot be excluded from school.
1972	*Pennsylvania Association for Retarded Children v. The Commonwealth of Pennsylvania*	Determined that no child with mental retardation can be denied a public education in Pennsylvania.
1972	*Mills v. Board of Education of the District of Columbia*	Determined that all students with disabilities have a right to free public education.
1973	*Section 504 of the Rehabilitation Act*	Guaranteed basic civil rights to people with disabilities. Required accommodations in schools and in society.
1975	*Education for All Handicapped Children Act (PL 94-142)*	Guaranteed a FAPE in the least restrictive environment for all children with disabilities.
1986	*Reauthorization of the Education for All Handicapped Children Act (PL 99-457)*	Added infants and toddlers to the act—birth to 3; provided for an individualized family service plan.
1990	*Reauthorization of the Individuals with Disabilities Education Act (IDEA) (PL 94-142)*	Added transition plans; added autism; added traumatic brain injury to the act.

(Continued)

Table 1.4 (Continued)

Year	Legislation or Litigation	Description
1990	*Americans With Disabilities Act (ADA)*	Barred discrimination in employment, transportation, public accommodations, and telecommunications. Implemented the concept of "normalization" across American life. Required phased in accessibility in schools.
1997	*Reauthorization of the Individuals with Disabilities Education Act (IDEA)*	Added ADHD to other health impairments; added functional behavior assessments and behavior intervention plans; made transition plans a component of the IEP.
2001	*No Child Left Behind Act (NCLB)*	Requires all children to participate in state and district testing. Requires 100% proficiency of all students in reading and math by 2012.
2004	*Reauthorization of the Individuals with Disabilities Education Act (IDEA)*	Includes the following additions (see text for complete descriptions): • Limited English proficient • Specific learning disability eligibility • Early intervening services (EIS) • Data-based decision making • Research-based strategies

SOURCES: Friend & Bursuck, 2009; Wright & Wright, 2007.

Photo 1.2 Students' language, culture, and special education needs should be addressed when making placement decisions.

Placement Options for Students With Special Needs

Students who are labeled with exceptionalities receive an **Individualized Education Plan (IEP).**[3] An integral part of an IEP is deciding where and how the students' needs should be met. Placement should not be decided by the types of programs available, but should be a decision based on the *needs* of the child (see Photo 1.2).

As part of the IEP, the **least restrictive environment (LRE)** must be determined. LRE is defined as the place where a student with special needs will be least restricted by his or her disability and will have the most access to the full general education curriculum. Before Public Law 94-142, students with disabilities were segregated from the general education classroom—often in separate schools, facilities, and classrooms. The current special education law takes into consideration this history of segregation and promotes inclusion and access to the general education curriculum. Current law states that the general education classroom should be considered first as the LRE for all students with special needs, although any of the placement options in the **continuum of services** can be considered as the LRE if it best suits the needs of the particular student. The committee determining placement weighs each of the options on the continuum of services, looking at possible negative influences as well as benefits from each placement. Figure 1.3 shows a trajectory of placement options from those that are most like a classroom for typical learners to those that are least like a classroom for typical learners.

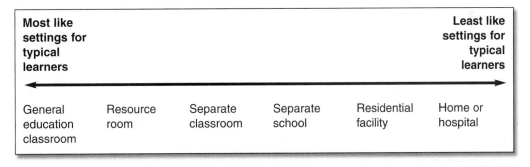

Figure 1.3   Continuum of Services for Students With Special Needs

General Education Classroom. The student is placed in general education classes with modified curriculum or teaching strategies as described on the student's IEP. The IEP goals might be reached with consultation with the general education teacher, with paraprofessional assistance in the general education classroom, or with some instruction (less than 20%) in another setting with a specialist.

Resource Room. Students receive 21% to 60% of their instruction in the general education classroom, but may be pulled out for instruction in particular subject areas or related services for the remaining portion of the school day. This placement option may be met by similar arrangements as described above, but the time spent out of the general education classroom is increased.

Separate Classroom. Less than 40% of the school day is spent in the general education classroom. Students receive the majority of instruction in a special education classroom. They may attend a "homeroom" for the beginning of the day, lunch, or other subjects for social interaction and instruction with peers in the general education setting.

Separate School. Only a small number of students with disabilities (3%) require this type of placement. These students may have very complex physical or cognitive disabilities or severe emotional disabilities that require a specialized setting for transitions, for learning skills for independent living, for safety, for structure, or for specialized programs that support a variety of complex needs. For example, some states have schools for students with visual impairments and students with severe hearing loss. When a placement of this type is considered as the LRE, the multidisciplinary team must consider the lack of interaction with typical peers and lack of access to a rich general education curriculum.

Residential Facility. A placement option outside the public school setting. This type of placement includes treatment facilities, detention services, state-funded schools for the blind, or schools for those with behavior disabilities. Residential facilities treat similar types of disabilities as those treated in a separate school setting, but provide structure, safety, and supervision 24 hours a day. Less than 1% of students with disabilities receive their education in this type of placement.

Home or Hospital. For a very small number of students (less than 0.5%), their home or a hospital is deemed the LRE for learning. For example, a student who is unable to leave the home for health or safety reasons, is medically fragile, or may be hospitalized for some length of time may be tutored or visited by a teacher for a few hours each week, providing for the goals and services designated by the IEP.

The Least Restrictive Environment for CLDE Students

What is most interesting about the concept of LRE is the perception of "least restrictive" for CLDE students. Not only does the student require special education services, but also requires support for learning English, for maintaining his or her home language, and requires an environment that is culturally appropriate. Program options for CLDE students have not been clearly delineated in any law. NCLB and IDEA only consider the second language acquisition process as an element in the eligibility for services but do not specify placement options. Although individual students who are learning English could have goals and objectives on their IEP that focus on the language acquisition process, this is not delineated in law as a required component of the IEP. As a result, special education teachers who are not trained in ESL or bilingual education may not even consider placements that support bilingualism and biculturalism.

Professionals must consider which environment will offer the most support for the student—a bilingual, bicultural classroom where the students' home language and culture are valued and can be used as a medium for instruction, or a special education classroom where the teacher has a deeper understanding of the child's special education needs. The philosophical underpinnings surrounding these two placements can be at odds. For example, the general education classroom can be considered both the most restrictive environment and the least restrictive environment for a CLDE student. If the general education placement has no language or cultural supports, it could be considered restrictive for CLDE students. On the other hand, if the general education placement gives the CLDE student access to the full and rich curriculum, then it can be considered the least restrictive. In Table 1.5, a comparison is made between the

Table 1.5   Comparison Between the LRE for Special Education Placement Options and ESL or Bilingual Placement Options

Special Education Placement Options	ESL or Bilingual Education Placement Options
General education class	Mainstream or general education submersion
General education with paraprofessional support	Mainstream or general education submersion with paraprofessional support
Special education pull-out	ESL pull-out
Special education classroom in a regular school	ESL content-area classroom in regular school
Center program within regular school	Bilingual program within a regular school (transitional early exit and late exit bilingual programs)
Special school	Bilingual school or dual language school

Most Restrictive to Least Restrictive (left axis, pointing up)

Most Restrictive to Least Restrictive (right axis, pointing down)

LRE for students who are learning English and students who have special needs. Because the educational placement is a critical component of a child's education, it is important for both ESL or bilingual professionals and special education professionals to be a part of the team that makes placement decisions for the CLDE child.

Recent Trends in Placement

The present placement trend in special education determines that the LRE for most students with special needs is within the general education school and the general education classroom (Sands, Kozleski, & French, 2000). Comparison data from 1990–2000 illustrate this trend. The percentage of students who spend the majority of their school day in the general education classroom (less than 21% of the day outside the general education classroom) increased from 33% in 1990 to 46% in 2000. The percentage of students who spent 21%–60% of the school day outside the general education classroom decreased from 36% in 1990 to 30% in 2000 (OSEP, 2003). A greater proportion of students with special needs now receive instruction for most of the day within a general education classroom.

The trend in placement for CLDE students also indicates that a majority of these students are placed in the general education, monolingual English-speaking classroom. A 2003 national survey of districts specifies that, compared to ELL students who do not have special needs, CLDE students receive very little native language or ESL services and are more likely to receive instruction all in English (Zehler, Fleischman, Hopstock, Stephenson et al., 2003). For example, only 27.7% of CLDE students in all disability categories received extensive ESL services and only 13.1% of CLDE students in all disability categories received extensive native language services. In fact, a full 63% of CLDE students in all disability categories received no native language services whatsoever (Zehler, Fleischman, Hopstock, Stephenson et al., 2003).

REFER TO CASE STUDY 1.1

How could the reauthorization of IDEA (2004) have benefited the student? How about RTI? What would have been the LRE for the student—taking into consideration his language and learning needs?

The increasing tendency to place CLDE students in monolingual English, general education classrooms illustrates a lack of understanding of the English language acquisition process and the supports needed to fully acquire a second language. If you place a child who is learning English in an environment where language acquisition is not emphasized or understood, and proper adaptations are not implemented, then this child may continue to struggle in school. Teachers may interpret this struggle as a special education need when, in fact, the child simply lacks the proper access or support to acquire the language of instruction and perform at grade level.

NEW DIRECTIONS IN TEACHER TRAINING

CASE STUDY 1.2 | **Teacher Training**

Sadly, few teacher education programs include classes that help teachers focus deeply on "transforming curriculum." New teachers report they have been taught the important progression of skills within each content area, but not how to modify their approaches for the wide range of student talents and abilities that arrive in their classrooms each year. Similarly, few programs offer courses designed to help teachers learn concrete ways to work more effectively with diverse family structures, cultures, languages, values, and more. Finally, few offer courses that address in detail how to establish a compassionate learning community, one that encourages, recognizes, and values the contributions of each of its members. These are the supports that teachers need to help them "increase accessibility" for all students and all families.

—Jeff and Traci Bushnell

Consider the view expressed above:

- How did your teacher education program prepare you to work with CLDE students?
- How do you increase accessibility for all students and families?
- What changes need to take place in teacher education to prepare teachers for the changing demographics of today's classrooms?

SOURCE: Used by permission.

It remains a small minority of teachers who are knowledgeable in both ESL or bilingual education and special education and can truly differentiate between a learning disability and the second language acquisition process. While 43% of the nation's general education teachers have at least one ELL student in their classrooms (USDOE & NICHD, 2003), only 12% of teachers nationwide have received introductory training (8 hours or more) in ESL or bilingual education (NCES, 2002; USDOE, 2002). Most general education teachers report that they do not feel equipped to teach the second language learners in their classrooms (Tharp, 2004), and many general education teachers are hesitant to refer ELL students to special education because they are unable to distinguish if a student's reading or academic difficulty is due to the language acquisition process or a learning disability (USDOE & NICHD, 2003).

Teacher preparation programs typically provide only one class for general education teachers to learn about students with special needs. Fully 59% of beginning classroom teachers surveyed in a Public Agenda study reported feeling unprepared to work with students who were doing poorly in their classes (Farkas, Johnson, & Foleno, 2000). Only one in five general education teachers responding to a survey by the National Center for Educational Statistics report that they are well prepared to work with students with special needs (NCES, 2006).

Following a 2003 survey distributed to a national sample of districts, it was reported that materials and training for instructing CLDE students were lacking in comparison to other types of training (Zehler, Fleischman, Hopstock, Stephenson et al., 2003). Only 32.2% of districts reported providing training for instructing CLDE students, in comparison to 41.7% that reported training for instructing ELL students, and 82.7% that reported training for classroom instruction in general (Zehler, Fleischman, Hopstock, Stephenson et al., 2003). Seventy-five percent of districts sampled reported a deficit in the number of teachers qualified to work with CLDE students (Zehler, Fleischman, Hopstock, Stephenson et al., 2003).

Because there is a nationwide gap in experts with foundational understandings of second language acquisition and special education, a majority of schools cannot provide services specifically designed for CLDE students. Rather, schools tend to provide services for these students by combining the separate efforts of ESL or bilingual staff and special education staff (Zehler, Fleischman, Hopstock, Stephenson et al., 2003). New directions in teacher training must include a more thorough and mandatory curriculum in both ESL or bilingual education and special education for all teachers. Until we have professionals who are trained to fully understand and work with the language and cultural acquisition process, as well as special education needs, then the effective education of CLDE students will remain at risk.

REFER TO CASE STUDY 1.1

What training would have helped the student's teachers better understand his needs? What training did the student's teachers appear to be lacking?

Summary

- With the number of ELL students expected to double in the next 20 years, schools must refine methods to distinguish between difficulties related to second language acquisition and those related to learning disabilities.

- The challenges of identifying and placing CLDE students are compounded by the lack of specific laws and programs designed to address their unique needs.

- Proper teacher preparation will be vital to the educational success of the increasing number of students from diverse backgrounds, including those with special needs.

Key Terms

Bilingual maintenance program

Continuum of services

Culturally and linguistically diverse exceptional (CLDE) students

Discrepancy model

English as a second language (ESL) program

English language learners (ELLs)

English submersion

Individualized Education Plan (IEP)

Individuals with Disabilities Education Act (IDEA)

Least restrictive environment (LRE)

Limited English proficiency (LEP)

Modifications

No Child Left Behind (NCLB) Act

Process

Public Law 94-142

Response to Intervention (RTI)

Section 504

Transitional bilingual educational program

Two-way immersion or dual language program

Activities for Further Understanding

1. Review the laws that impact special education services and the laws that impact students who are learning English. What similarities do you notice? What differences do you notice?

2. Observe placements for CLDE students at your school or at another school. Where are the majority of these students placed? Does this placement meet student needs? Why or why not?

3. Interview teachers of CLDE students. Where does the majority of their training lie—with special education or with ESL or bilingual? What gaps in training does the teacher notice in regard to educating CLDE students? What further training would the teacher like to receive?

4. Examine the demographics of students in your school. What is the percentage of students in special education? What is the percentage of special education students who are also learning English? Is there overrepresentation or underrepresentation of one ethnic or racial group of students in special education? What special education labels have been applied to CLDE students?

5. Explore the relationships between special education and ESL or bilingual teachers at your school. Do the two fields collaborate on IEP meetings and program or placement decisions for students? How do they collaborate?

Notes

1. A more detailed discussion of the process of second language acquisition will be presented in Chapters 3–4.

2. The concept of Response to Intervention will be discussed fully in Chapter 5. Scientific research-based interventions will be discussed in Chapters 9–15.

3. An IEP is instituted if a child qualifies for special education services as the result of the assessment eligibility process. See Chapter 5.

Visit the Student Study Site at **www.sagepub.com/grassi** for chapter-specific study resources.

SECTION I
Understanding Student Backgrounds

Chapter 2. Collaborating With Families

Chapter 3. Understanding Language Acquisition

Chapter 4. Understanding Fluency

Chapter 2

COLLABORATING WITH FAMILIES

Key Points

- ✦ Why it is critical for teachers to gain the trust of CLD families
- ✦ How to minimize cultural misunderstandings when working with CLD families
- ✦ What the MAPs process can do to empower CLD families

CASE STUDY 2.1 **Parent Letter to Teacher**

Imagine the following: For as long as you can remember, nearly everything you do is observed, evaluated, scored, and categorized. All of the things that you are "good at" are put in one column. All of the things that "need work" are in another.

Now imagine that all of the things you are good at, and perhaps even enjoy doing, are considered nonessential because "you can already do them." Everything else, all the things that are difficult for you, that create stress or pain (either physical or emotional), become the major focus of nearly everything that goes on in your life.

This, in many ways, is the life of a special needs child if they are lucky enough to be receiving "services" in the community or in the school setting. And as the parent of a disabled child, it feels on so many levels the right way to go. Because we are afraid. We are afraid our children will not get what they need. That they will not be "OK." So you go along with this pathologizing approach to parenting where your child is looked at as a set of challenges, problems, or in nicer terms, goals to be met. There is an underlying sense of urgency and hypervigilance that surpasses that of typical parenting. You don't buy a toy because it will be fun; you buy it because it will be "meaningful" or "therapeutic." You don't pick activities solely for the love of the thing, but also for the "benefits" it can bring. Through it all you try to remain hopeful yet realistic about your child's future. And the message that is covertly being communicated to your child is "if you were just less disabled things would be better around here."

And in the midst of all of this, you are dealing with professionals who you desperately want to trust because you hope with all of your heart that they know more than you. You want to keep them on your side because you fear any possible fallout toward your child. But you don't want to hand over all of your control because you have had to give up so much control already. You spend your life trying to celebrate milestones that come easily and naturally to other children. Who else has to celebrate these simple little accomplishments? But to not express gratitude seems even worse, and many people live in that place of being grateful for every little step. I admire them and sometimes can even be like them. But mostly what I am is tired. Tired of the struggles, the sadness, the pain, the constant thoughts and machinations that go into figuring out and finding what is best for my child.

To those of you to whom I entrust my precious child, I ask this: Please be patient. See the child, not the list of "issues." Trust that I know my child better than you. Do YOUR homework. Find out more about my specific child and her needs than just any special needs child. If she has a diagnosis, read about it, learn the best ways to help her, don't try to fit her into what you assume, what you have done before, or what you may think is best. Ten years into your career, please don't assume that things are still done the same way; stay current. Our knowledge base is constantly developing; things that were a given when you were in school may be seen completely differently at this point. Understand that I know you want the best for her but partner with me about how to accomplish that. Don't tell me what we are doing, discuss it with me. Honor my input. Don't label my child or me based on limited information. If we have a difficult interaction or even several of them, understand that no matter how fierce I may appear, or how timid, I want the best for my child. And I spend more time and energy on taking care of her and trying to make sure others do than you can ever, ever imagine. And please work with us from a place of caring and compassion, not just "what the district" says, does, or requires. I don't care what the district says. I only care about what my child needs. If you try to see everything from that perspective, we will probably get along just fine. Oh, and don't feel pressure to be "the one" who will figure everything out and make it all better. That isn't going to happen—this is a complex, lifelong journey and it is minimizing to think any one person is going to wave a magic wand or find a perfect plan without a REAL team approach. And finally, I would ask that you do two things: Take this very seriously—there is a life at stake. And at the same time, for the same reason, lead with your heart.

—Linda Kazim Davis, Bilingual parent
of a child with special needs

Consider the case study above:

- What collaborative strategies would have helped Linda be a part of the special educational process?
- What skills do teachers need to be able to collaborate effectively with diverse families?
- What insight can families provide that the teacher may not be able to assess in the classroom?

SOURCE: Used by permission.

For a case study from Erika, a parent of a child with special needs, see the following Web link: **www.sagepub.com/grassi.**

2.1

Formulating and instituting strategies for family involvement is one of the foundational skills for working with CLDE students. The latest authorization of IDEA (2004) stresses the importance of the role of families in the special education process. The Individuals with Disabilities Education Act states that parents are expected to be involved in the eligibility process to provide critical information about their children. When working with culturally and linguistically diverse (CLD) families, parents can provide information such as the educational background of the child in the home country, access the child has had to effective language acquisition programs, strengths or challenges in the child's **first language (L1),** culturally appropriate behaviors, and any mismatch between home and school life.

Working with families is a complex process. When you add cultural and linguistic differences to the complexity of what a disability brings to a family's dynamic, the role of collaborating becomes increasingly important. This chapter will discuss how collaboration with CLD families can be done in a manner in which parents feel welcome to participate, feel that their voices are heard, and are able to contribute valuable information that will lead to the academic success of their child.

CREATING RELATIONSHIPS WITH CLD FAMILIES

When working with families of CLDE students, creating trusting relationships is the first and most critical step in the process. Some CLD families have a long history of trust issues with schools in the United States. CLD families often distrust school personnel, they believe school assessments are culturally biased, and, to compound these trust issues, studies have indicated that schools tend to make fewer contacts with CLD families than with middle to upper class white families (Harry, 1992, as cited in Cartledge, Gardner, & Ford, 2009). Unless teachers build trusting relationships with the families, openly discussing academic, social, or special education issues will become increasingly difficult. We advocate for frequent meetings (both informal and formal) with parents to establish a trusting relationship and to gain as much information as possible about the child.

Informal Meetings

When a teacher contacts parents frequently to share achievements, not just concerns, the teacher shows that he or she cares about the student (Cartledge et al., 2009). Because the teacher is in a position of power, it is up to the teacher to initiate the relationship with parents. A good place to start is through informal contact such as quick check-ins or small talk during drop off or pick up from school. Positive telephone conversations are also helpful, where teachers call home to report the progress of the child (Al-Hassan & Gardner, 2002).

Home visits are another excellent manner of getting to know CLD families (Al-Hassan & Gardner, 2002). For most families, it is an honor to have a teacher visit and these visits can provide insight into the family's culture, the family dynamics, the living situation, and references that the child makes about home. Home visits also help build trusting relationships because they show respect for the family. By visiting the home, teachers show a willingness to get to know the family and their culture, and to acknowledge the importance of the family structure to the student's success.

It is a rare family that does not welcome the presence of a teacher in their home. There are some guidelines that teachers should adhere to during home visits, however:

1. In many cultures, it is considered very respectful to have a teacher come to the house. Dress and act accordingly.

2. If you bring somebody with you, make sure they have a defined role and the parents understand why the person is there as well.

3. Make sure you know why you are conducting the home visit. Have some specific questions prepared. This shows that you have a purpose and are professional.

4. Make sure this visit does not address "problems." Make this an informational visit in which you attempt to learn about the family and build relationships.

When making home visits to families from cultures other than your own, there will be a "cultural dance" you will need to negotiate. Until you are comfortable with the pragmatics (or cultural rules) of the families you visit, we recommend you go to home visits with a **cultural liaison.** If a liaison is not available, we recommend you approach the visit knowing that **cultural mismatches** may occur. Your good intentions, however, will be interpreted as such, and a sense of humor and an open mind can help negotiate issues. People are usually happy to share about their culture and a focus of your visit can be learning about the culture of your students. Don't be afraid to ask questions about how things are negotiated in that culture. Polite curiosity can be a manner of expressing respect.

> For examples of where there may be cultural mismatches on a home visit, and questions to consider, see the following Web link: **www.sagepub.com/grassi.**

2.2

Case Study 2.2 presents a description of a home visit with a Hispanic family. Consider how the teacher negotiated a successful visit to a home culture other than her own.

Formal Meetings

Once relationships are established with CLD families through informal means, the families will usually become more comfortable attending formal meetings such as open houses, IEP meetings, or conferences. When organizing formal meetings, there are guidelines that teachers should adhere to in order to make the meetings productive, to increase attendance, and to create a comfortable environment for CLD families.

CASE STUDY 2.2 | Home Visit With a Hispanic Family

Photo 2.2   Home visits are an effective way of building bridges with families.

It is 7:00 on a cold Tuesday evening in January. My two companions for this home visit are Mrs. Birch, our ESL teacher, and Ms. Scott, one of our district's Community Outreach Workers or Translators. A translator is needed because the family we are visiting speaks Spanish with minimal English.

We find the Alvarin home and park outside. We walk up the stairs and knock on the door. Berta, the mother, greets us at the door with *"Buenos noches."* Alicia, my student, and her younger sister, Kara, are standing in the front room. The home is beautiful and there are many photographs displayed around the room.

As we sit down, José, the father, comes out of another room and pulls up a chair. Berta, Kara, and I sit on the couch. At first, Alicia sits at the bar but I say, "Alicia, do you want to sit here next to me?" and she comes over to sit by me. The first thing that we talk about is how Alicia is doing in school. The translator repeats all of my comments in Spanish. Berta and José agree that Alicia is doing well in math but they, too, are concerned with her reading progress. We talk about the possibility of summer school for Alicia.

The next part of our conversation is about Berta's pregnancy: The baby is due in early May. Then, the discussion turns to where Alicia will go to school next year. She can continue at her present school but no bus transportation will be provided. Berta and José would like Alicia to stay at her school but transportation is an issue.

Alicia takes me on a tour of her room next. It is a girl's room, pink and white with lots of books and stuffed animals. Alicia and Kara show me a tea set that their uncle had brought them back from Mexico. When I asked Alicia why she did not go with them to Mexico, she tells me that they are afraid that if she went she would not be allowed to come back to the United States because she does not have the right papers. We go back out into the front room and rejoin the others.

As the conversation comes to an end, Ms. Scott asks José if he has any more questions. José gets very quiet and then proceeds to ask some questions in Spanish. The first thing he asks is "Do all teachers do these visits?" As I am listening to his question, I am wondering if he does not like the home visits. Mrs. Birch and I are starting to get a little worried. I answer him, through the translator, that all teachers do not do home visits. In addition, I tell him that I wanted to do them with all of my families. He is quiet for a moment and then replies in Spanish, "These visits are a good idea (pause). It means a lot to me that you not only care for my child (pause) but also for my family." This statement not only warms my heart, but also impresses on me the fact that he sees this visit as a matter of showing respect.

Alicia tells us that she and her mother have made enchiladas for us. We sit at the kitchen table and eat delicious enchiladas made with *"mole"* and *"queso de Mexico."* After we eat, Alicia wants to show Mrs. Birch and Ms. Scott her room, also. So, while they go on the tour, Berta, José, and I have a lovely conversation. We struggle as I speak only a small amount of Spanish and they speak very little English. However, that doesn't seem to matter to any of us. We talk about our extended families and California. California is a link between us as that is where I grew up and they had an opportunity to move to California at one point and declined. We agree that it is too busy there and that our state is very nice.

Mrs. Birch and Ms. Scott rejoin us in the front room. As we put our coats on, I am reluctant to leave the warmth and hospitality of this lovely home for the cold outdoors. This evening had brought family and school together in a comfortable and relaxed setting. During the visit, language barriers seemed to disappear and all of us were willing to "try" with the other's primary language. This visit served as a "window" into another culture, dissolved some preconceived ideas that I had about people who live in mobile home parks, and gave me some insight into the struggles that immigrant families face in our society.

—Beverly A., Excerpt from field notes, March 2007

Consider the case study above:

- What was the purpose of the visit in this case study?
- What did the teacher do to foster a relationship with the student and the family?
- What did the teacher learn from this visit?
- How do you think the teacher prepared for the visit?
- What would be the next steps the teacher should take after this visit?

SOURCE: Used by permission.

To read case studies about Beverly's home visits with a Russian family and a Japanese-Chinese family, see the following Web link: **www.sagepub.com/grassi.**

2.3

To begin, teachers should make information about school meetings available in the first language of families. If translators are not available, contact community centers or parents to help translate meeting notices. It is important not to directly translate from the L1 to the **second language (L2),** as some words or phrases do not translate appropriately. To increase attendance, the notices should be written in a linguistically and culturally appropriate manner.

Once notices are created, the teacher should consider advertising the meetings in community centers, churches, temples, or places where information is best disseminated in that culture. In order to determine how to best advertise for the families represented in your classroom, the teacher can contact the district liaison, parents of students, or the students themselves can provide this information.

Once the teacher has established the meeting time and place, make sure there are interpreters available who are cultural brokers as well. Children should not be used as interpreters. **Direct translation** from English to the home language is also not a good idea since many ideas are not directly translatable and direct translation could cause cultural misunderstandings. The interpreter should be fluent in the language *and* the culture of the families present.

When considering interpreters for meetings, make sure *all* languages are represented. Even though the classroom may have a majority language, if not all languages are represented, then some parents can feel left out or not respected. Unfortunately, many districts do not have adequate funds for translators. In this case, it may be necessary to get a head count of which parents plan to attend and attempt to procure translators for these parents. The students can help with this, but it is best to plan for everyone to attend and prepare as best you can. As your relationship with your students' families becomes more trusting, the communication will become more open and the teacher can directly contact parents to determine whether or not they will attend meetings.

During the meeting, the teacher should consider having a nice spread of food available. Food often shows respect for the families and creates a welcoming atmosphere.

Also, make sure the meeting is family friendly (all family members welcome, including young children) and announce this to families prior to the meeting. Many parents will not leave their children with a sitter and do not have family support to help with childcare. It is important that families be allowed to bring everyone to meetings if needed. In such cases, the teacher should have activities for younger children such as paper and crayons, chalk to draw on the board, child-friendly food, balls to play with outside, or an open gym area.

During the meeting, it is important that the teacher assume a professional demeanor. Professionalism must be reflected in behavior, attitude, dress, and actions. Professional does not mean "cold." It means respect with warmth. In many cultures, parents see the teacher as an authority figure—a person who provides guidance. The parents will expect the teacher to talk to them about their child's education and give specific examples about their particular child. When addressing parents, call them by their formal title (Mr. and Mrs., for example) and introduce yourself using your formal title. This also means that the teacher is not "friends" with the family, but works collaboratively and professionally with the families.

Before the meeting officially begins, allow time to engage in socialization. In many cultures, "talk story" is an important aspect of meetings. Ask families about themselves, their children, and their country of origin. Show the family where the student sits and who sits next to him or her before getting down to business.

When it is time for "business," make sure there is a clear purpose to the meeting. Important matters to discuss include any issue pertaining to the education of the child, for example, the curriculum, school rules, school policies, homework policies, and expectations. The teacher should be perceived as the leader of the meeting. Once the business has been conducted, leave time at the end for families to get to know one another. Many immigrant families feel isolated and this can be an opportunity for them to make connections with families from similar situations.

Finally, make sure your intentions come from your heart. Most people will forgive cultural mistakes that you make. Don't hesitate to ask questions. Ask families about their culture and let them guide you. The teacher does not need to know everything about every culture—that is impossible. But the teacher must be open-minded and understand that cultures are different and that these differences can lead to misunderstandings about expected school behaviors. If the teacher is perceived as arrogant, cruel, or disrespectful, the teacher will not be able to build relationships.

> **REFER TO CASE STUDY 2.1**
>
> How would Linda have benefited from both informal and formal meetings? What could the school and teachers have done to better build a trusting relationship with her?

CONSIDERATIONS OF CULTURE WHEN WORKING WITH CLD FAMILIES

When working with CLD parents, it is important to minimize misunderstandings and confusion due to culture and language. Therefore, teachers must have a basic understanding of the **cultural discontinuities** that can occur when working with CLD families. Below, we discuss three areas of cultural discontinuity we have observed in IEP meetings: perceptions of disability, perceptions of goal setting, and understandings of the process.

Perceptions of Disability

When a child is diagnosed with a disability, there are a series of stages or states of emotion parents experience as they begin to understand the issues involved. These stages progress from shock at the initial information to acceptance of the situation, with a variety of emotional states in between—anger, depression, sadness, rejection. These stages have been compared to the grief cycle any person may experience after a loss.

Sands et al. (2000) give a clear overview of the literature on these stages and how the complexity of the issues has led many authorities to question the validity of the **stage theory approach.** The emotional response to a child's disability can be impacted by gender, experience, the particular age and situation of the child, the type of disability, transition points during schooling and childhood, and by culture. Many of these aspects are fluid, and the emotional responses to the child's disability will change as the child and family change. In other words, the stages do not flow systematically from one stage to another and end nicely in "acceptance." Emotional responses to disability will depend on circumstances and situations that can be fluid and complex.

Among CLD families, cultural perceptions of disability and reactions to disability may differ from the school's and the teacher's view. For example, Harry (2002) found that African American and Hispanic families tended to show greater resilience in coping with disabilities, and perceived "normalcy" on a much broader scale than did middle to upper class Americans of European heritage. Huang (1997) found that Asian Americans tended to attribute learning disabilities to a lack of effort or motivation, rather than seeing them as a "disability" (as cited in Cartledge et al., 2009). While the above literature speaks in generalizations, the main point to consider is that the perception of what constitutes a "disability" can differ across cultures and across families.

Thus, when working with CLD families, we must take into consideration their perception of "disability." In American culture, the special education system is defined as a **"deficit system"** (i.e., we have found something wrong with a child [a deficit] and now are going to work to "fix" it). This is a very negative viewpoint of the child and should be taken into account when establishing goals and a plan for the child. It is important to consider the strengths of the child and the strengths of the family. This needs to be established first and needs to be established genuinely. A cultural liaison can be of tremendous support in this situation. Consulting with an expert of the same culture and language of the family will help inform the teachers and professionals about the family's perception of the disability, how to approach the family about the disability, and how to best involve the family in the process. The liaison can also help to establish a conversation, in a culturally appropriate manner, about the need to build on the child's strengths to support his or her needs. Schools and professionals must move away from a deficit model for CLD families and move toward a model of empowerment (Cartledge et al., 2009; Turnbull & Turnbull, 2001). Schools must look for family strengths and find ways to involve families in the decision-making process.

Perceptions of Goal Setting

Many times, the goals that are negotiated on the IEP differ from the desired goals of the family. For example, an IEP goal of "independence" usually stems from a middle class European American perspective in which schools work to transition the child with special needs to a more independent lifestyle. When working with CLD families, however, a goal of "independence from the family" may not be as important. Many CLD families are extended families and children are expected to live with parents until marriage—and after marriage as well. Often, an extended family will join to care for a child with severe special needs and independence from the family is not a relevant issue. In such cases, couching the concept of "independence" in terms of "academic readiness" or "social readiness for work," rather than emphasizing independence from the family, might be a better fit with the cultural norms of CLD families.

Understandings of the Process

Finding the time to become involved in the school and the special education process can be difficult for many families. For CLD families, understanding the school and special education process can be complicated by cultural differences. Families may not know when it is appropriate to ask questions, how to negotiate meeting times and places that work for the parents' schedule, and may not understand that the process is meant to be collaborative. In these cases, it is important that the school personnel take the initiative to guide the parents through the process. Scheduling meetings to open the communication process is one important step. In order to encourage collaboration with families, teachers, and other professionals may need

> **REFER TO CASE STUDY 2.1**
>
> How did Linda perceive disability? How does her perception differ from perceptions of parents you've worked with? What do you think Linda's goals are for her child? How do these goals differ from goals other parents may have?

to look for meeting times "outside the box." If meeting within school hours does not work, what are the alternatives? Can the teacher come to the family's house? Can the teacher meet at times other than during school hours? Can the school provide food so that the meeting can be held over a meal? Can childcare be provided so that both parents (or the single parent) can attend? When working with CLD families, it is important to research the schedule that works best for the families and try to accommodate this so that families can be involved.

EMPOWERING FAMILIES

To this point in the chapter, we have discussed ways to build relationships with families and ways to prevent miscommunication with families. These are the first steps to fully collaborating with CLD families. If teachers focus on building relationships and inviting families into the school process, CLD families will have the opportunity to play a meaningful role in the education of their children.

Many research studies have indicated that CLD families want to be involved in the decision-making process for their children and for their school—they are just not given access to involvement in a meaningful way (Cartledge et al., 2009). School personnel must provide the opportunity for true involvement and voice in the full spirit of the mandates put forward in IDEA.

MAPs: Gaining the Family Story

It is important to gather the family story as a source of rich data that can help inform instruction, social growth, and appropriate assessments for the child. One way to understand a family's story is by using the **Making Action Plans Process (MAPs)** (Forest & Pearpoint, 1992; Forest, Pearpoint, & O'Brien, 1996). The MAPs process can be adapted to work with CLD families and is a good starting point for gaining insight into situations such as

1. length of time in the United States,

2. the educational and health background of the child,

3. the learning style of the child,

4. the child's level of proficiency in the L1,

5. the family's perception of the disability,

6. the support for the family and student at home,

7. the family's perspective of education and the role of the teacher,

8. the work schedule of the family and the manners in which the family can support their children's education,

9. the work schedule of the student or how the student is expected to help out in the family, and

10. trauma when coming to the United States or when leaving the country of origin (especially pertinent with refugee students).

The MAPs process involves a gathering with family members, students, teachers, and other people who have an interest in the student. A facilitator guides the discussion, which is aimed at understanding the past, present, and future story of the child and the family. Questions are asked, and all participants contribute and brainstorm answers. It is important that the participants understand the process and its intent, and having the support of a cultural liaison and interpreter may be helpful during a MAPs session.

When using MAPs with CLD families, one consideration is the manner in which families talk about their family situations and their children. Some parents come from cultures where personal problems are not openly shared or fear "losing face" when confiding about their children (Taylor & Whittaker, 2003, as cited in Cartledge et al., 2009). These families would benefit from the presence of a cultural liaison to negotiate the MAPs process.

The way in which the discussion is conducted should also be considered. While U.S. culture is considered a low-context culture, where communication is stressed through words more than nonverbal signals, many parents are from high-context cultures and nonverbal communication can play a significant role in communication. Again, a cultural liaison should be present at meetings with families from high-context cultures to help the teacher interpret the nonverbal clues.

For a detailed description of high- and low-context cultures and the manner of communicating within these cultures, see the following Web link: **www.sagepub.com/grassi**.

2.4

Following is a typical sequence from a MAPs session and the questions used to facilitate a discussion with parents about the child:

1. *What is the student's history?* This question is designed to understand the past educational, social, and family history of the child. For

example, how did the family discover the child has a disability: Did the family know at birth or was it later discovered in school? How did the school handle the disability? How did the school's communication impact the family? How does the child's disability impact other family members?

2. *What is your dream for the student?* This question is designed to create goals for the child. For example, what kind of life does the family want for the child? What are the child's goals? What are the parents' educational goals for the child? What do other participants hope for the child?

3. *What are your fears for the child?* This question is designed to understand challenges the child may face. For example, what kinds of things worry the participants about the child? What types of things may the child not be able to accomplish?

4. *Who is the student?* This question is designed to get a general description of the student.

5. *What are the student's strengths, gifts, and abilities?* This question is designed to gather specific information about the student and his or her capabilities and interests.

6. *What are the student's needs?* This question is designed to gather information about the challenges, struggles, and issues the family and the child face. For example, does the child need to attend school with his or her siblings? Does the child need medication at school? Does the child need academic or behavior interventions? Does the child need a specific skill to contribute to the family?

7. *What would the student's ideal day look like and what must be done to make this happen?* This question is designed to get at challenges the student faces daily and how these challenges can be addressed.

REFER TO CASE STUDY 2.1

Using the MAPs protocol, what information about Linda's child can you gain from her story?

Case Study 2.3 is a family story as told by Luke, the brother of a young man with cerebral palsy. As you read the story, consider the MAPs questions and how the insight provided by the brother could help teachers when working with Jacob.

CASE STUDY 2.3   My Brother

Jacob was born two months premature, very healthy besides the cyst attached to his kidney. Jacob underwent surgery immediately following birth to remove the cyst and then complications began. After surgery, Jacob's kidney failed and doctors were forced to use medicines and techniques to save his life, but that also gave him all the "problems" he has today. My brother has severe cerebral palsy, severe hearing loss, cannot walk, bad eyes, and we just recently found that the medicine he has been taking all his life has given him severe osteoporosis (brittle bones). His sign language is very limited and he has the education of a first grader and would be considered "retarded" by many.

My name is Luke and I'm 21 years old, very athletic, love school, music, food, and hanging out. Right now, I'm studying to be a math teacher, playing soccer in college and hope to try out for a professional team someday.

Having a brother with cerebral palsy has changed my life dramatically. Every part of the day changes. Mom, Dad, the sisters, and I are all involved in getting Jacob ready for the day. He becomes more and more independent every day but still needs a lot of help. I set out clothes for him, help him shower, help him put on his leg braces, put on his shoes, give him his morning medicine, and make sure he eats breakfast. The whole family puts in a joint effort in taking care of him.

Jacob has really changed the way we all think. I pay attention to details and find myself thinking about so many things that everyone takes for granted. Using the restroom is especially difficult. It is very hard for Jacob to maneuver in the stalls and I have to clean the pot off for him because he won't do it. I help him sit down and stand him up. Because he can't stand, I pull his pants up, secure his pants, zip his zipper up, tuck his shirt in, and fasten his belt. All these things he can't do, but need to have done for him.

All my life I have wondered what it would be like to have a "normal" brother. A guy I can tell anything, wrestle with, be known as the brothers who are unstoppable. I wish I could be the best man in his wedding, be Uncle Luke to his kids, get in a fistfight, and have the exhilaration of finally beating him in a race. I guess one could say our relationship has been one that is very different from the stereotypical brother-to-brother relationship.

I used the word "retarded" earlier to describe Jacob and this word is one that is anything but him. I often try to put myself in his position and find myself wondering how the heck he does it. Jacob has become the single most influential person in my life. If it were possible, I would trade lives with him so that he would know what it feels like to run, talk, hear, dance to music, throw a baseball, and so much more. Jacob's ability to find happiness in life is beyond my comprehension.

(Continued)

(Continued)

Jacob has grown up watching every athletic game I've been in; hundreds of times he has been reminded that his legs don't work because of my ability to run. On top of that, he sees my passion and love for the game of soccer and I can only imagine what that does to him internally. I can go on and on about the way life has been unfair to him and think of scenario upon scenario where he had be the spectator to his siblings. I know for a fact that what I've just described doesn't fog his mind; it doesn't drag him down. Every home game he has been to during my college career he comes "running" out onto the field with his walker and gives me the biggest hug. You can tell he is proud of me, loves me, and enjoys coming to my games.

Every once in a while Jacob gets really frustrated, can't express himself, and just screams, hits, fights, sobs uncontrollable tears, and just wants to be held in someone's arms. This happens very rarely and his attitude, demeanor, and spirit do a 180-degree turn minutes later as if nothing happened. He has faced death so many times and is a living miracle. He is the most sensitive man I know. He has great compassion for anyone who is hurt and will give him or her a very warm hug. His hug and the way he acts is his language. With a hug, he identifies with a person on a level that is untouchable. He understands pain, disappointment, adversity, and hardship more than anyone I know. His ability to look beyond circumstances, to see beyond the superficial, to look into a realm, a realm of what is really important and what really matters is an ability few people have and live in every day of their life. Jacob's capability to find the good in situation after situation is his strength—it is strength that I learn from day after day.

—Lucas G.

Consider the case study above:

- What challenges does Jacob face?
- What are his strengths?
- How does the family view the disability?
- What do you think their dreams are for Jacob?
- How have they been supported? In what other ways could they have been supported?
- How can the information be used to support Jacob and his family?

SOURCE: Used by permission.

By empowering families to contribute to the conversations and data collection about the child, the intervention team can move forward with a more complete picture of the child. If the team decides at any point to complete a full assessment and referral for special education, the relationship has already been established with the family and the partnership can continue from the initial interventions to establishing an IEP if needed.

Summary

- Collaboration with families is the foundation for the success of CLDE students in the classroom.

- Informal encounters, home visits, and formal meetings are all means for teachers to surmount cultural and language barriers.

- Empowering families by building relationships, and inviting them to contribute to the process, can give powerful insight into student strengths and needs.

Key Terms

Cultural discontinuities

Cultural liaison

Cultural mismatch

Deficit system

Direct translation

First language (L1)

Making Action Plans Process (MAPs)

Second language (L2)

Stage theory approach

Activities for Further Understanding

1. Make a home visit to a family of a CLDE student. Describe the visit. What did you learn from the visit that you had not previously learned in the classroom?

2. Attempt informal communication with your CLD families for three weeks. What did you observe in these communications? What was the outcome of your attempts to communicate with the families?

3. Invite your CLD families to an event at your school. Follow the protocol for formal meetings listed in this chapter. How many parents attended? What was the outcome of your meeting? What challenges did you face? What would you do differently?

4. Interview a CLD parent, aide, or community member about his or her perception of disability and the goals he or she would have for a child with special needs. How do these perceptions differ from your own or from parents you have worked with in the past?

5. Interview a CLD parent about their child using the MAPs protocol. What did you learn about the child that you had not previously learned in the classroom?

Visit the Student Study Site at **www.sagepub.com/grassi** for chapter-specific study resources.

Chapter 3

UNDERSTANDING LANGUAGE ACQUISITION

CASE STUDY 3.1   My Journey to the United States

When I started school in America I did not know one word of English. I did not know what to say to my teacher and I did not understand what my teacher was telling or asking me. I felt lost and confused but still very excited about starting school. During my first year of school, I was one of three ESL students. The teacher worked to help me assimilate into the American academic life better and faster. After only two years of ESL instruction, I was mainstreamed and no other support was given to me.

I am from Vietnam, and teachers in Vietnam have a lot of prestige and are highly regarded in society, so of course, I had nothing but the utmost respect for my teachers, but sometimes I was treated unfairly.

In fourth grade I was punished for going through the process of learning English—forgetting to put the plural "s" on the end of nouns. I was writing stories for my book. I meticulously wrote until I completed my piece of writing. I showed my teacher the work that I had done. But instead of getting the response that I had hoped for, my teacher scolded, "How many times do I have to tell you to put an 's' on? You are going to sit down and fix this now!" Terrified, I went and sat down at my desk as the other kids headed out to recess. But instead of correcting my paper, I started to cry. The one person in school that I needed to help me thrive just crushed my love for writing and curiosity of learning. On my paper I wrote *the two cat* instead of *the two cats*. My teacher yelled at me as if I purposely didn't put the "s" on my noun just to rebel against her and all of her teachings. But the truth is, in Vietnamese we don't have plural forms for nouns. We say, "one cat, two cat, three cat." I had no reference for forming a plural noun and needed more than two years to acquire this. From this point on, I hated writing. I especially despised it when I had to hand in papers because I always had this self doubt that the piece I write will never be good enough no matter how hard I work at it and how much effort I put into it. This self-doubt still lingers with me today and I have yet to escape from it.

—Vietnamese student

Consider the case study above:

- How might her teachers have supported the student's language acquisition process in a more positive manner?
- How would her teachers know if she were acquiring English in an appropriate manner and at an appropriate pace?
- Were the language errors she made part of the normal process of acquiring a second language, or could they indicate a possible disability?

SOURCE: Used by permission.

3.1
For the rest of this case study, including a description of the struggles experienced in Vietnam and the student's challenges on first arrival to the United States, see the following Web link:
www.sage pub.com/grassi.

Foundational knowledge for working with CLDE students and their families includes an understanding of language acquisition. Because CLDE students not only have special needs, but are learning a new language, the process of language acquisition must be clearly understood by the teachers and professionals. When a CLDE student has an IEP, the student's special needs and the academic and social goals are delineated for the teacher. Rarely, however, does the IEP explicitly state at which stage of language acquisition the student is, the types of language errors the teachers should expect, how the language acquisition process might develop, and other pertinent information. To address this gap in information, we dedicate two chapters to language acquisition. In this chapter, we will look at the language acquisition process and discuss student characteristics as they journey from fluency in their first language (L1) to fluency in their second language (L2). In the next chapter, we will discuss what "fluency" or proficiency in a language really means and help teachers determine the difference between a learning disability and the language acquisition process.

INTERLANGUAGE: THE JOURNEY FROM FIRST LANGUAGE TO SECOND LANGUAGE PROFICIENCY

Larry Selinker (1972) coined the term **"interlanguage"** (also referred to as "learner language") to describe the language students use when moving from their first language to developing fluency in the **second language.** This is depicted in Figure 3.1.

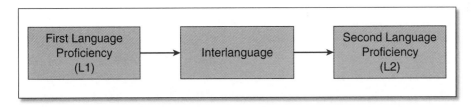

Figure 3.1   Interlanguage Is the Language Produced When a Student Journeys From First Language Fluency to Proficiency in the Second Language

Errors Found in Interlanguage

Interlanguage can be influenced by the learner's first language, the learner's exposure to and understanding of the second language, and other developmental characteristics evident in the interlanguage of all second language learners.

Interlanguage is often wrought with errors (Brown, 2007; Gass & Selinker, 2008; Lightbown & Spada, 1999), and these include (see Table 3.1):

- *Interlingual transfer errors*—transferring grammatical patterns, vocabulary items, and phonology from the first language to the second language. For example, if the sentence structure in the first language follows a noun-adjective sequence, the student applies this same grammatical sequence to the second language: "The *ball red* on table."

- *Intralingual transfer errors*—transferring learned rules in the second language to similar grammatical situations in the second language—also referred to as **overgeneralization.** For example, if the student has learned to add *'s* to words to show possession, the student adds *'s* to all words to show possession: "That *she's* ball."

- *Incorrect hypotheses about the language*—receiving incorrect information concerning a grammar point, a vocabulary item, or an idiomatic expression, or incorrectly using phrases heard in the media, on the playground, or in the classroom. For example, if the student was taught that *digestion* is the action indicating the breaking down of food, the student may mistakenly assume *digestion* is a verb and produce a sentence such as "He *digestion* the food."

- *Developmental errors*—language errors similar to those of young children developing their first language.

Table 3.1 Examples of Types of Errors Found in Interlanguage

	Interlingual Transfer	**Intralingual Transfer**	**Incorrect Hypotheses About the Language**	**Developmental Errors**
Types of errors found in this category	Using first language grammar, vocabulary, or pronunciation when speaking or writing in the second language	Overgeneralization: Applying one rule from the target language to all aspects of the target language	Hypothesizing about how to use idiomatic expressions or vocabulary terms learned from textbooks, media, or the classroom	Language errors that are similar to errors a child might make when acquiring the first language

	Interlingual Transfer	Intralingual Transfer	Incorrect Hypotheses About the Language	Developmental Errors
Example of student error	Using *no* to form all negatives because *no* is used in the first language to form negatives • She *no want* to go. • He *no can* do this.	Using *-ed* to form the past tense of all verbs in English • He *taked* the book. • He *goed* to the park.	Incorrect formation of expressions • We live in a *safety* place. • He *digestion* the food.	Using the present tense verb form to discuss all time periods • I *go* to the store yesterday. • My dad, he *eat* ice cream tomorrow.

SOURCES: Adapted from Brown, 2007; Gass & Selinker, 2008; Lightbown & Spada, 1999; Thornbury, 2007.

The Developmental Sequence of Interlanguage

REFER TO CASE STUDY 3.1

Which types of errors did the student produce? Were these errors part of interlanguage?

Teachers have reported frustration over students who do not acquire certain grammatical rules taught in class. Regardless of how many times the teacher instructs students to use *doesn't* to form the negative for the third person singular (she *doesn't* like), students still produce sentences such as "My mom *don't* like TV." This is because students learning English acquire many grammatical features in a developmental sequence, independent of the order in which the grammar rules are taught in class. The third person singular -s is a feature that is often acquired later and students will sometimes not acquire this grammatical feature until they have passed through earlier stages (Dulay & Burt, 1974). These developmental sequences, however, are not hard and fast—the student's first language, their level of motivation, and prior instruction, among other factors, can influence second language acquisition. Although most students will flow through the same developmental sequence, the way they do it and the time they spend on the grammatical feature can vary (Lightbown & Spada, 1999; see Tables 3.2, 3.3, 3.4, and 3.5).

Table 3.2 Developmental Sequence for Negation

	Description	Examples
Stage 1	The learner uses *no* or *not* before the verb.	• She *not* like this. • She *no* like candy.
Stage 2	*No* and *not* are intermittently used with *don't*. However, *don't* is not changed for tense or person (*She don't* instead of *she didn't* or *she doesn't*), and *don't* may also be used before verbs that should take *not* (such as *can, is,* and *may*).	• She *don't* like candy. • He *don't* can run. • He *don't* go there yesterday.
Stage 3	Learners begin to correctly determine between verbs that take *not* and verbs that take *don't*. However, *don't* is still not changed for person or tense.	• He *is not* happy. • She *cannot* dance. • He *don't* eat fish.
Stage 4	*Do* is correctly marked for person and tense. Frequently, however, learners mark both the auxiliary and the main verb for person and tense.	• She *didn't went* there. • He *doesn't likes* the food.

SOURCES: Adapted from Lightbown & Spada, 1999, pp. 77–78; Schumann, 1976b.

Table 3.3 Developmental Sequence for Questions

	Description	Examples
Stage 1	Learners use single words or sentence fragments with rising intonation at the end of the sentence.	• Two dogs? • I go?
Stage 2	Learners use a declarative word order with rising intonation at the end of the sentence.	• You go to the store? • She drive the car?
Stage 3	Learners begin to use fronting but still do not correctly invert the subject and the verb.	*Wh-* fronting with no inversion • Where the dog go? • What the man is saying? *Do-* fronting • Do he go now? • Does she have pencil?

	Description	Examples
Stage 4	Learners begin to use subject-verb inversions in *wh-* + copula, and yes/no questions.	• Where is the sun? • Is there a plate in the closet?

Stage 5	Learners use inversion in most *wh-* questions.	Inverted *wh-* questions with *do*
		  • Why do you think that?
		  • Where do you go?
		Inverted *wh-* questions with auxiliaries other than *do*
		  • Where is the man going?
		  • Why could she do that?

Stage 6	Learners begin to form more complex questions.	Question tags
		  • He left, didn't he?
		Questions in the negative
		  • Why don't you like this?
		Embedded questions
		  • Can you tell me where the bathroom is?

SOURCE: Adapted from Lightbown & Spada, 1999.

Table 3.4   Developmental Sequence for References to the Past

	Description	Examples
Stage 1	Learners use the present tense to refer to all events but may use a time or place to show that the event occurred in the past.	• My dad *sick* yesterday. • In June, we *go* to China.
Stage 2	Learners attach *-ed* to show reference to the past.	• She *worked* for two hours. • He *taked* the trash.
Stage 3	Learners begin to use the irregular past tense but continue to overgeneralize the *-ed*—sometimes mixing the two forms.	• She *eated* the spinach and went to bed. • We *sawed* the movie.

SOURCE: Adapted from Lightbown & Spada, 1999.

Table 3.5 Developmental Sequence for Grammatical Morphemes

	Description	**Examples**
Morpheme 1	Pronoun case (he/him, she/her, they/them)	• *He* doesn't like *him*.
Morpheme 2	Article (a/the)	• *The* boy has *a* toy.
Morpheme 3	Copula (is/are)	• He *is* tall. • They *are* happy.
Morpheme 4	-ing (be + V + -ing)	• She *is dancing*. • They coming.
Morpheme 5	Plural (s)	• The windows.
Morpheme 6	Auxiliary (is/are)	• They *are* dancing.
Morpheme 7	Regular past (-ed)	• He *walked* there.
Morpheme 8	Irregular past	• She *went* to the store. • He *ate* a cookie.
Morpheme 9	Long plural (-es)	• *Houses* • *Fishes*
Morpheme 10	Possessive ('s)	• Sarah's book.
Morpheme 11	Third person singular (-s)	• She *looks* at you.

SOURCE: Adapted from Dulay & Burt, 1974, p. 51.

Emotion and Interlanguage

When children in the interlanguage stage are stressed, excited, or under pressure, they will often attend more to the content, meaning, and truth value of the sentence than to the grammatical correctness of the sentence (Lightbown & Spada, 1999). As a result, students will continue to make the same error—even when corrected. For example, if a student comes running to the teacher to state that "Ali hurted he's hand," and the teacher answers back with the grammatically correct form, "You mean Ali hurt his hand?" the student, who is more concerned with getting the message across than the grammatical correctness of the sentence, will often answer back with a sentence such as, "Yes, Ali hurted he's hand!"

Producing ungrammatical sentences in times of stress does not mean that the student is unaware of the grammatical rules. It means that during stressful times, students will attend to the meaning of the sentence and often resort to ungrammatical features that have not yet become automatic in their second language.

Restructuring and U-Shaped Learning

While in the interlanguage phase, students can also produce inconsistent language forms. For example, it is not unusual that students move two steps forward and one step back—a phenomenon also referred to as **backsliding** (Brown, 2007; Lightbown & Spada, 1999). After students acquire new grammatical forms, they sometimes resort back to incorrectly formed features they had previously acquired. As frustrating as it may be for teachers, incorrect performance in the second language can signify the learner's emerging understanding of a new grammatical rule (McLaughlin, 1990b). When students are introduced to new information about the language (either through formal instruction or through input from peers), they do not simply place the new information into their existing English language repertoire and begin to use the new information correctly. Rather, students restructure their existing system to reflect the new learning, thus creating a slightly new English language system. As McLaughlin (1990b) states, "Restructuring is characterized by discontinuous, or qualitative change as the child moves from stage to stage in development. Each new stage constitutes a new internal organization and not merely the addition of new structural elements" (p. 117).

Restructuring, in turn, can cause students to produce **U-shaped learning** (Brown, 2007; Gass & Selinker, 2008; Lightbown, 1985). U-shaped learning has three phases. The first phase involves a correct grammatical form. The second phase involves an incorrect form—the learner appears to lose what he or she knew at the first phase. The third phase involves the correct form once again. For example, an English language learner may produce the following trajectory:

Phase 1: She *went* to the movie last week.

Phase 2: She *goed* to the movie last week.

Phase 3: She *went* to the movie last week.

Studies in second language acquisition (Lightbown, 1983, as cited in Gass & Selinker, 2008; McLaughlin, 1990b) indicate that perhaps a trajectory such as the one above reflects a student who was either initially introduced to, or took notice of, the irregular past tense (went—Phase 1). At a later time, the student was introduced to the regular past tense (add -ed to the verb). Once the new learning was introduced, the student had to integrate the new verb form into the existing English language system. This integration, or restructuring, involves learning the new verb form, comparing the new form to the existing knowledge of English, and readjusting the hypothesis about forming the past tense (Phase 2). As a result, the student made errors with both the irregular past and the regular until the student was able to restructure the English language system and correctly integrate both the regular and irregular forms (Phase 3).

On this same note, a learner's language can indicate progress in many different grammar points at many different stages. Incorrect forms of language can be expressed in conjunction with correct forms until, with time, the incorrect versions disappear (Brown, 2007). For example, when a high school student speaks a sentence such as, "My brother went to her's house," this could indicate that the learner has acquired the rules for forming the possessive adjective (her) and is either hypothesizing about forming the possessive by adding 's to the noun, or has recently learned the 's and is restructuring the existing system (McLaughlin, 1990b). Within this stage of restructuring, learners can make intralingual errors, or overgeneralize, rules. In the above case, the learner overgeneralized the rule for forming the possessive, and rather than just use the adjective (her) or just adding an 's to the noun, the learner did both. At the same time, the learner correctly used the past tense of to go (went), and correctly formed the possessive in the first part of the sentence (my brother). Correct versions in conjunction with incorrect versions of the language are common occurrences in interlanguage.

Summary

In sum, interlanguage, or learner language, is part of the normal process of acquiring a second language. It is important for teachers to recognize the types of errors students make and to note that these errors could be transfer errors, developmental errors, or errors that suggest restructuring of the existing L2. While it is crucial that teachers address language errors, it is also important to keep in mind that errors are a normal part of the language acquisition process. Patience is key as is explicit and prolonged instruction in the L2 to ultimately help students acquire a more accurate language.

> **REFER TO CASE STUDY 3.1**
>
> In grade school, when the student wrote *two cat* instead of *two cats*, what was happening? If you were to explain the student's language to another teacher, how would you explain her errors?

SECOND LANGUAGE ACQUISITION THEORIES

Over the years, there have been many theories of **second language acquisition (SLA)** that attempt to describe how children and adults acquire a second language. Many of these theories are discussed throughout the book, in particular in the methods section where we discuss the influence of the particular theory on the development of the methods we propose. One of the most influential of these, however, is Krashen's input hypothesis (1981, 1982, 1985). Krashen's input hypothesis involves a set of five interrelated hypotheses: the natural order hypothesis, the affective filter hypothesis, the input hypothesis, the acquisition versus learning hypothesis, and the monitor hypothesis.

Natural Order Hypothesis

Krashen's **natural order hypothesis** suggests that second language learners acquire some features of English grammar in a predictable order (Dulay & Burt, 1974). Based on this hypothesis, many schools have adapted charts illustrating **stages of SLA** that can be used as checkpoints for teachers to help them determine the language stages of their students. Each stage is a progression, providing guidelines for the language characteristics of a student and how long the student typically exhibits behavior in the particular stage. However, there are numerous factors that contribute to second language acquisition and the amount of time a student spends in each stage is dependent on various situations, such as

- the student's access to quality instruction in the **target language,**

- the student's access to communicative situations with native speakers of the target language inside and outside of the classroom,

- the student's oral language and literacy skills in the first language,

- the student's academic background in the first language,

- the student's access to support for passing through the acculturation process, and

- the student's access to academic support in the target language.

The stages listed in Table 3.6 are a general guideline and are not meant to be adhered to as firm and fast rules of the language development process.

REFER TO CASE STUDY 3.1

In which stage of language acquisition would you place the student?

Table 3.6 Stages of Language Acquisition

	Preproduction	Early Production	Speech Emergence	Intermediate Fluency	Advanced Fluency
Student's relative timeline in the stage	1–3 months	2–12 months	1–2 years	3–5 years	5 years and beyond
Learner characteristics	1. Silent period—very little speech production. 2. Student is building receptive language. Student may have up to 500 receptive words. 3. Student uses memorized phrases, or chunk learning, to communicate. The student understands the phrase's holistic meaning, but is unable to unpack the parts into anything meaningful (Gass & Selinker, 2008). 4. Student depends heavily on context for understanding. 5. Sometimes students are able to produce very little of the second language at this stage and will show comprehension through gestures, pointing, drawing pictures, or one-word answers.	1. Student produces one- to two-word responses: *He no like. She go? Bathroom?* 2. Student uses memorized phrases, or chunk learning, to communicate: *Check this out. Please be quiet! Everyone sit down.* 3. Student has a vocabulary of up to 1,000 receptive/active words. 4. Student is developing social language skills (language used to communicate with peers).	1. Student is able to string words together—simple sentence responses: *Today, I didn't went to swimming. She don't like the new boy. Why my dad not go?* 2. Student has fairly good comprehension and can communicate using creative sentences. 3. Student has a vocabulary of up to 3,000 receptive or active terms. 4. Student is actively building social and academic language skills.	1. Student speaks in sentences and can converse more fluently. 2. Student can communicate using verb tenses such as regular past, future, present. 3. Student begins to form correct questions. 4. Student still makes grammatical errors. *The boy who live downstairs, he don't play soccer. Did you really liked the movie?* 5. Student has a vocabulary of more than 6,000 active or receptive words. 6. Student is ready to actively acquire academic language skills.	1. Student is usually designated as FEP (Fluent English Proficient) and is placed in general education content-area classrooms. 2. Student is able to converse on almost any topic. 3. Student is able to write on almost any topic, but will still have spelling and grammatical errors. 4. Student still needs support with the acquisition of academic language.

Preproduction	Early Production	Speech Emergence	Intermediate Fluency	Advanced Fluency
6. Students may have a very strong base in the first language and are able to show comprehension through the first language.	5. Student transfers first language pronunciation, grammar, and cultural understandings to spoken and written second language.	5. Student is beginning to acquire verb tenses (past, future).	7. Student appears to be fluent in social language skills (although is still developing these skills).	5. Student requires advanced-level grammatical and writing instruction.
7. Student transfers first language pronunciation, grammar, and cultural understandings to spoken and written second language.	6. Student exhibits overgeneralization of many grammar rules: *He goed there.*	6. Student continues to overgeneralize grammar rules.	8. When pointed out, student should be able to correct many errors—some errors will still need explicit instruction.	
8. Students are extremely tired at this stage and will fall asleep at the desk or ask to use the bathroom numerous times.		7. Student still transfers first language pronunciation and grammar to the second language.	9. Students will attempt more complex writing usually following their first language writing norms.	
		8. Student begins to notice errors and, if pointed out, can sometimes self-correct.		

SOURCES: Haynes, 2006; Reed & Railsback, 2003.

CASE STUDY 3.2 | My Work With a Preproduction Student

Marian would smile at everything I would say to her (mostly because she did not understand me and didn't know what else to do). She had recently come from Mexico and had had no formal schooling. Marian had a sister in kindergarten and they absolutely adored each other. In Marian's draft book, she drew picture after picture of her sister, and sometimes herself, along with countless hearts, but with no letters or attempts at writing letters. It was September, and her progress was right on track for a preproduction student. Four weeks into school, she was finally comfortable with me as a teacher, knew the basic routines of the classroom, and seemed willing to learn.

As we sat down together at the back table, Marian placed her draft book down and opened up her empty resource folder as she had seen many other classmates do. I kindly asked her with a smile and a gesture, "Can you open your draft book to what you want to look at together?" She took a cue from my opening motion and opened to a picture of two girls by a tree and a swing. I tried not to assume that this was Marian and her sister, because I wanted to see what Marian could tell me about this scene. "Who is this?" I said, pointing to the girl with a ponytail and using questioning facial features and pose. Marian pointed to herself. I said, "Marian?" She nodded yes. From watching her over the last couple of weeks, I knew that she was still learning to write her name, so I started writing and verbally spelling it above the picture of her. "M-A-R-I-A-N. Marian." She beamed at me. I said to her, "Who is this?" as I pointed to the drawing of herself again. She looked at me and I answered, "Marian." I repeated, "Who is this?" We said together, "Marian." I saw the biggest smile yet on her face. I moved on to the next little girl in the picture with pigtails. After pointing to her and saying "Who is this?" Marian opened up and said, "Theresa." I smiled and put the name Theresa above the picture of her. I then moved on to the rest of the picture. Since Marian could not produce any language, I was the one verbalizing what she drew and hoped to get responses if what I was assuming was right. I looked at the swing and said while producing a swinging motion with my arms and body, "Marian and Theresa are swinging?" She madly nodded yes and smiled. I wrote swing above the swing in the picture while saying it very slowly. I pointed to the swing and said, "This is a swing. Marian and Theresa are swinging." I then wrote and said each sound very slowly, "Marian and Theresa are swinging." I took her hand and manipulated her fingers so the pointer finger stuck out and the rest curled in. With my guidance, I moved her hand across the sentence as we read, lifting her hand after each word. We did this two more times, and then it was her turn to try on her own. She read it beautifully with only a hesitation around the "ing" at the end. I congratulated her by saying "Great reading!" and gave her a high five. She was beaming once again from ear to ear. However, this time it was not out of confusion, but out of understanding and accomplishment.

—Amelia Koopman, First grade teacher

Consider the case study above:

- At which stage of language acquisition was Marian?
- How did the teacher adapt instruction to work with Marian's stage of language acquisition?

SOURCE: Used by permission.

Affective Filter Hypothesis

As noted in Case Study 3.2, in order to work effectively with Marian, Amelia realized that Marian's level of comfort in the classroom was an important factor in the language acquisition process. Krashen's (1982) **affective filter hypothesis** suggests that all learners have an "affective filter" that rises when students are stressed and can block language from being acquired, and lowers when students are relaxed and allows language to be acquired. Most of us can remember a situation—either in classroom instruction or when traveling to a country that does not speak our first language—where we were so stressed, anxious, or angry that we shut down and could not understand or produce the target language. Krashen would describe this situation as having a high affective filter.

When we compare the environments in which small children learn to those in which adolescents or adults learn, we can see where Krashen's (1982) affective filter hypothesis plays an obvious role in language acquisition. Our interviews with teachers have indicated that small children are often forgiven for their language errors. Most kindergarten and first grade teachers are accustomed to addressing language errors in both first and second language learners and usually approach these errors in a calm, comfortable manner. The higher the grade, however, the less likely it is that language errors will be tolerated, especially when the ELL student has attended school in the United States for a few years. Often teachers assume the language acquisition process should proceed more quickly than it does and do not understand why older students have not obtained proficiency in either the written or spoken language after attending school for a few years. Upper elementary, middle school, and secondary teachers need to keep in mind that regardless of the years spent attending schools, many students are not proficient due to many factors, including lack of access to speakers of the language,

REFER TO CASE STUDY 3.2

In Case Study 3.2, what did Amelia do to make Marian feel comfortable? How long did Amelia wait before attempting explicit English instruction with Marian? Why did she wait this long?

lack of effective instruction in the language, or lack of culturally relevant pedagogy. By expecting language performance beyond the **stage of second language
acquisition** of the student, a stressful environment is created. It is important that
all teachers instruct in environments that are comfortable and allow for risk taking with the language.

Input Hypothesis

In Case Study 3.2, Amelia also noted that she needed to try different techniques
to make her lesson comprehensible to Marian. These techniques stem from
Krashen's **input hypothesis** (1985). Krashen noted that in order for students to
acquire the target language, the language input they receive must be made
comprehensible—through visual support, gestures, context, drama, stories,
movies, modeling, and written instructions. Amelia made the writing lesson comprehensible to Marian by using Marian's pictures as visual support for the new
vocabulary. If Amelia had simply handed Marian a list of vocabulary words,
then Marian may have had trouble understanding and retaining the words.

Krashen's input hypothesis also includes the concept of i + 1—the input
must be at the acquisition level of the student (i), while continually adding new
concepts or challenges (1). The input must not be too challenging for the student (i + 2), and should also not remain at the current level of the student's
ability (i + 0). Amelia started with the language acquisition level of the student
(names and pictures) and added on to this level by introducing new vocabulary
to match the interest of the student.

Krashen's input hypothesis claims that all that is needed for language
acquisition to occur is **comprehensible input.** While comprehensible input is
crucial to understanding and acquiring the second language, some studies
have indicated that comprehensible input alone is not sufficient (see Photo 3.2).
Sharwood Smith (1991) noted that L2 learners often ignore grammatical evidence from the input they receive—comprehensible or not—and continue to
make grammatical errors in the target language. Sharwood Smith thus developed the input enhancement hypothesis in which input was enhanced, or
improved to the point where learners could *notice* the input. Enhanced input
is created through elaboration (duration with the linguistic point) and explicit-
ness of the linguistic point (metalinguistic depth). For example, a one-time,
in-depth explanation of a grammar point would not be considered elaborate,
but would be considered explicit. On the other hand, continuous repetition of
a grammatical form in casual conversation would be considered elaborate,
but not explicit.

Photo 3.2   Making the input comprehensible through the use of visuals, stories, and read-alouds increases academic achievement with CLDE students.

Studies on output and social interaction have also determined that more than just comprehensible input is required for language acquisition. Social interaction with speakers of the target language and **output** of the target language are also needed to fully develop the second language (Lantolf, 2005; Long, 1996; Swain, 2005). Students given a chance to output language and interact with native speakers experience benefits in several areas. To begin, native speakers will often modify their language to make it comprehensible to the learner, thus increasing the learner's ability to acquire the language (Long, 1983). Learners are also able to test their hypotheses about the language and culture during interaction and begin to *notice* gaps in their language or cultural learning (Swain, 2005). For example, when learners encounter confusion on the part of an interlocutor, learners notice that their output is not meeting target language norms and will try to adjust their output until the interlocutor's communicative expectations are met. Once *noticing* occurs, students more readily attend to gaps in their language learning. Finally, Lantolf (2005) found that learners achieve higher levels of proficiency when they collaborate and interact with more knowledgeable speakers of the target language.

When we compare lower elementary grades to higher grades, we see how Krashen's input hypothesis can impact L2 acquisition. Often, the higher the grade level, the less comprehensible the input becomes. While lower elementary children enjoy storybooks with lots of visual context and colorful classrooms that provide visuals for most key vocabulary and key concepts, older learners are usually faced with less context-based, more cognitively demanding lessons (i.e., lectures, worksheets based on textbook readings). The fewer contexts provided, the more difficult it is for ELL students to understand and acquire the language and the content. It is important, regardless of grade level, that teachers provide comprehensible input and opportunities for interaction.

Acquisition Versus Learning and Monitor Hypotheses

The **acquisition versus learning hypothesis** claims that acquisition (the subconscious and intuitive process of "picking up" a language) is far more effective in acquiring fluency in the L2 than is just learning (the process in which students attend to the form and rules of the language). Krashen claims that when students learn a language, they invoke the "monitor"—a manner of closely watching one's output for errors and mistakes (the **monitor hypothesis**), which, in turn, can hamper acquisition. Many studies, however, have indicated that **form-focused instruction** or explicit grammar teaching can enhance the communicative abilities of students, and a combination of learning and acquisition can be beneficial (Doughty, 1991; Lightbown & Spada, 1999). As Amelia noted in her narrative, four weeks of "acquisition" or trying to "pick up" the language was not productive for Marian and direct teaching of vocabulary words encouraged Marian's further development in the language.

> **REFER TO CASE STUDY 3.2**
>
> What aspects of Krashen's theory did the student's teacher practice? If you had the student in your class while she was still developing English, how would you change instruction to meet her language needs?

FACTORS AFFECTING SECOND LANGUAGE ACQUISITION

> **CASE STUDY 3.3 | My English Journey**
>
> I started learning English from zero and the first months in this country were like hell. I missed my family, and I missed myself. I had become a scared person. I hid from people; at my host family's place I spent most of my time in my room. At school, I would avoid interacting with others. I just wanted everybody to leave me alone, and all I truly wanted was to go home. I hated it because not being able to communicate and speak turned me into an insecure, quiet,

antisocial person. I felt lost. I felt angry with myself because I wanted to understand and I could not. I wanted to scream but there was no point in doing so, so I suppressed my feelings and I ended up living in my mind. I thought that I was not ever going to learn this new language. I felt like a failure. But then I became so tired of hiding, so tired of being mute, and so tired of not being myself. I realized that I had not given up everything for nothing. And I gave myself two choices: (1) to learn the language or (2) to learn the language. And that's how my English Journey began. Every time I felt sad I took out my book to study. Every time I felt upset I took out my dictionary to make a list of new words. Every time I missed my family I practiced writing and pronouncing new words. Somewhere I heard that listening to the radio helped, so I slept with the radio on every night. Someone said that kid shows on television could help, so I watched TV with my host family's kids. In my room I had sticky notes all over the walls and all over the ceiling with the words I wanted to learn. I placed a new word in front of my bed so that that word was the last thing I saw when I went to sleep and it was the first thing I saw when I woke up.

—Nuria, Math teacher, Salvadoran immigrant

3.2

For the rest of this case study describing Nuria's journey to the United States and the various challenges she experienced, see the following Web link: **www.sagepub .com/grassi.**

There are many factors that influence SLA—and Nuria exhibits many of them in her case study. As you read the following section, consider Nuria's story:

- Do you think Nuria has a strong first language foundation? What is your evidence?
- Was she motivated to learn English?
- What social or psychological factors contributed to her learning?

SOURCE: Used by permission.

First Language Foundation

Cummins (1981, 2000, 2001; Cummins et al., 2005) hypothesized that the acquisition of first and second languages are interrelated—the development of the first language can influence and facilitate the development of the second language, and when students have a strong base in their first language, they can acquire higher levels of proficiency in the second language. Cummins (2000) further states that academic skills (particularly literacy) learned in the first language can directly transfer to the learning of academic skills in the second language.

Cummins's theory makes intuitive sense, especially when applied to the content-area classroom. For example, if a student already knows how to read in the first language, those literacy skills can transfer to the second language to assist with literacy development in the L2. The student will already understand that letters form sounds, that words form sentences, that punctuation has meaning. If the student comes from a language that reads left to right and up to down, then these tracking skills will also assist with literacy in English. In science class, if an ELL student has already studied planets in his or her first language, then that student can reference the first language background knowledge to better understand the lesson in the second language. When the teacher displays pictures of the planets, the student can connect, for example, the vocabulary words around planets to his or her knowledge of *planetas* (Spanish). And finally, when students are old enough to have developed metalinguistic awareness (the ability to look at language as a system of rules), then they will understand that all languages have a grammar and will try to "break the grammatical code" of the second language. They will actively search for words in the L2 to discuss the present, past, and future, among other language aspects.

The National Literacy Panel on Language-Minority Children and Youth (August & Shanahan, 2006) examined various studies that attempted to discern the relationship between first and second language literacy development. Their findings indicated that "certain aspects of second language oral proficiency and literacy are related in some important ways to performance on similar (or identical) constructs in the first language" (p. 161). However, the findings also indicated that although transfer can positively influence second language oral and literacy proficiency, "transfer was not the sole source of influence in second language oral proficiency and literacy development" (p. 161). Second language acquisition involves a complex set of skills, and although proficiency in the first language can benefit acquisition of the second, there are many other factors that also contribute to the acquisition of the L2.

REFER TO CASE STUDY 3.3

What level of L1 foundation did she come to the United States with? What is your evidence for this?

Motivation

There have been a number of studies concerning learner motivation and the impact of motivation on second language acquisition. Most studies point to motivation as a positive contributor to language acquisition—regardless of the type of motivation the learner possesses. Gardner and Lambert (1972) categorized motivation into two areas: **integrative orientation** and **instrumental orientation.** Integrative orientation involves obtaining proficiency in the target language in order to integrate within the culture and society. Instrumental motivation involves obtaining proficiency in the language for instrumental purposes—to get a job, to study in higher education, or to receive a promotion. Both integrative and instrumental orientations have been shown to positively impact the language acquisition process (Lamb, 2004).

Two other types of motivation have been discussed in the literature—extrinsic and intrinsic. **Extrinsic motivation** is when an external factor encourages the student to gain proficiency in the language (when a teacher gives candy for a correct answer, when the student studies harder to make parents happy). **Intrinsic motivation** is when a student studies the language for his or her own happiness or gain—not for external rewards. When working with ELL students in our schools today, it is important to note where their motivation (or lack thereof) stems from. Table 3.7 delineates examples of the different types of orientations.

Table 3.7 Orientations or Motivations for Learning Language

	Integrative	Instrumental
Intrinsic	The student wants to learn English to better "fit in" with peers in his or her classroom.	The student is determined to attend college in the United States and works to learn English to obtain this goal.
Extrinsic	Students are discouraged from speaking their L1 at school, and are expected to integrate into the target culture as quickly as possible.	Parents wish the child to learn English to better help them negotiate the culture and system—child is often called upon to translate.

SOURCE: Brown (2007).

As noted in Table 3.7, all orientations or motivations can influence the learning of English—some more positively than others. When considering motivation as a factor for L2 acquisition, it is important that teachers examine the types of orientations expressed by students, especially students who lack motivation. If a student is learning only to please someone else or for other external factors, then the teacher can assist this student by helping the student explore intrinsic (integrative and instrumental) reasons for learning the target language.

REFER TO CASE STUDY 3.3

What type(s) of motivation did Nuria exhibit?

Social and Psychological Distance

Another factor closely related to motivation is Schumann's (1976a) pidginization hypothesis (in later works referred to as the acculturation model [Schumann, 1978]). In this theory, Schumann explores the social and psychological distance the ELL student has from the target culture as a factor in L2 acquisition. The greater the distance, the harder it is to acquire the L2. Table 3.8 delineates the eight factors of social distance (Schumann, 1976b), with positive and negative factors for SLA.

Table 3.8   Eight Factors of Social Distance

Factor	Positive	Negative
Social dominance	The second language learner's cultural group feels dominant or of equal status to the target language group.	The second language learner's group feels subordinate to the target language group.
Integration pattern	The second language learner desires assimilation or acculturation into the target language group.	The second language learner desires preservation of his or her own cultural identity.
Cohesiveness	The second language learner's cultural group encourages ample contact with the target language group.	The second language learner's group is cohesive and tends to discourage contact with the target language group.
Enclosure	The second language learner's group requires contact with the target language group to go about daily life.	The second language learner's group has its own churches, newspapers, and leaders and is not dependent on the target culture for daily living.
Size	The second language learner's group is small and encourages intergroup relations.	The second language learner's group is large and tends to facilitate only intragroup relations.
Cultural congruence	The target language group and the second language group are culturally congruent (similar).	The target language group and the second language group are incongruent (dissimilar).
Attitude	The attitude of the two groups toward each other is positive.	The attitude of the two groups toward each other is negative.
Length of residence	The second language learner intends to reside within the target culture for an extended period of time.	The second language learner only intends to reside within the target culture for a limited period of time.

SOURCE: Schumann, 1976b.

While social distance applies to the ELL students' cultural group, Schumann's psychological distance refers to the individual learner and his or her relationship to the target language group. Table 3.9 delineates psychological factors that can negatively impact SLA (Schumann, 1976b).

> **REFER TO CASE STUDY 3.3**
>
> What types of social and psychological factors impacted Nuria's language acquisition?

Table 3.9   Psychological Factors That Impact SLA

Factor	Description
Language shock	The learner has lost the ability to communicate fully and fluently as he or she did in his or her native language. The learner is hesitant to communicate with speakers of the target language for fear of appearing childlike, unintelligent, or comical.
Culture shock	The problem-solving and coping mechanisms used in the L1 do not work in the new language and culture. The learner experiences fear, stress, and anxiety. In an attempt to find a cause for his or her disorientation, the learner rejects the new culture and language.
Motivation	Schumann considers integrative motivation—the desire to integrate into the target culture—as a positive psychological factor. Schumann considered instrumental motivation—the desire to learn the L2 for instrumental purposes—to be less effective for SLA. If the learner's instrumental goals are merely survival, for example, the learner may find great psychological distance between himself and the target culture.
Ego permeability	Schumann found that learners who have ego permeability—are willing to temporarily give up their separateness of identity—are better language learners. Learners who have rigid egos are not good language learners.

SOURCE: Schumann, 1976b.

Summary

- An understanding of interlanguage—the language students use on their journey from first language to second language proficiency—is vital for working with CLDE students and their families.

- Theories of second language acquisition can provide checkpoints for teachers to help pinpoint the language development status of their students.

- Foundational skills in the first language, the motivation(s) for learning the second language, and the student's relationship to a new culture all impact the second language acquisition process.

Key Terms

Affective filter hypothesis	Intrinsic motivation
Acquisition versus learning hypothesis	Monitor hypothesis
Backsliding	Natural order hypothesis
Comprehensible input	Output
Extrinsic motivation	Overgeneralization
Form-focused instruction	Second language acquisition (SLA)
Input hypothesis	Stages of second language acquisition
Instrumental orientation	Target language
Integrative orientation	U-shaped learning
Interlanguage	

Activities for Further Understanding

1. Record a number of samples of a student's language. What types of errors does the student make—intralingual transfer, interlingual transfer, developmental, or faulty hypotheses about the language? Does the student exhibit any U-shaped learning? At what stage of language acquisition is the student?

2. Observe a teacher instructing students who are learning English. Which aspects of Krashen's hypotheses does the teacher implement? What would you change about the lesson to make it more conducive to the language acquisition process?

3. Interview a student who is learning English. Ask this student about his or her feelings about the language and the culture. Where does this student fit in Schumann's acculturation model? Does the student have positive or negative social factors? How about psychological factors?

4. Interview a student about his or her motivation to learn English. Why is the student learning the language? What are the student's future goals? After

interviewing the student, determine what type of motivation the student has. Where would the teacher need to work further with this student to make sure the student remains motivated to learn the target language?

5. Observe a student who struggles with learning English. Take note of the types of language errors the student produces. Then investigate the L1 background of the student. Does the student have a strong L1 language base? Does the student have continuing access to the L1? Where? How?

Visit the Student Study Site at **www.sagepub.com/grassi** for chapter-specific study resources.

Note

1. Dulay and Burt (1974) conducted a study of the morpheme acquisition order of 60 Spanish as a first language students and 55 Chinese as a first language students, ranging in age from 6 to 8 years old. Dulay and Burt concluded that students learning a second language—regardless of the first language background—could pass through a similar sequence in morpheme acquisition. Further studies on the topic have indicated possible reasons for this order. VanPatten (1984) suggests that "semantic clout" lies behind the acquisition of a particular order of morphemes (also see Wei, 2000). The learner starts with morphemes that are most essential for communication—morphemes that have the heaviest impact on meaning. Morphemes that are acquired later are those that are deemed necessary due to the grammatical structure of the language, not necessarily for communication purposes.

Chapter 4

UNDERSTANDING FLUENCY

Key Points

◆ What it means to be "fluent" or proficient in a language

◆ How to use Cummins's BICS/CALPS model of language proficiency to avoid misclassification of English language learners

◆ Why Canale and Swain's model of communicative competence is useful for identifying specific supports needed by English language learners

CASE STUDY 4.1   Academic English

My family and I came to the United States to learn English and go to college. After six months of ESL classes, I was ready for college! I sat in the first row so I could hear the professor and not get distracted. At the end of class I was exhausted! And I felt as if I did not get anything, or very little, from what the professor had taught.

Academic language is hard and it does not become part of our brain in a second language that easily. I worked very hard in order to accomplish my learning. I would put my children to bed at 8:00 P.M. and study until at least 2:00 A.M., with a dictionary by my side, trying to understand and learn. Sometimes, I was discriminated against in classes because I was a foreigner. For example, I was taking a speech class and even though I did an excellent job in each presentation, the professor only gave me a C because of my accent.

I have to say that despite many hard times, I feel my children and I were privileged learners because we were educated and literate in our first language. Coming here with a strong first language foundation, being able to speak properly, write, read, and communicate in the first language with fluency is an advantage. Why? Because we were able to transfer concepts and the common sounds of the first language into the learning of the second language. This made learning a second language a more pleasant and easier experience. Children that come here with a strong first language base and have parents who are literate in their first language and have high expectations, not only for their children but for themselves as parents too, have a much better possibility of being successful in learning the new language and culture. However, being an adult second language learner has been hard. No matter what, English will always be my second language, and even now, after being in the USA for more than 20 years, there are moments and situations when I feel lost. I am working on a master's degree and the readings that I am assigned take me at least twice as long as my native-English-speaking friends. When taking the many standardized tests that any student is expected to take through his or her lifetime in this country, it is nerve-racking to me. When I think of our second language learners having to take standardized exams after being here one, two, or three years, I think it is inhumane. I do not believe that students can show accurate growth in a second language when they have not had the opportunity to be immersed long enough in this new culture and language.

—Isa, Bilingual teacher, Venezuelan immigrant

Consider the case study above:

- How is academic language different from conversational language?
- What gaps in language proficiency did Isa experience in her academic studies?
- How did Isa's proficiency in her first language impact the learning of English?
- How do native English speakers perceive "accents"? Are accents related to proficiency?

4.1
For the rest of this case study, see the following Web link: **www.sagepub.com/grassi.**

SOURCE: Used by permission.

In this chapter, we continue our discussion of language acquisition as part of the foundational knowledge needed to work effectively with CLDE students and their families. We will take a deeper look at "proficiency" and will define proficiency in English from the perspective of two theories: Cummins's Basic Interpersonal Communication Skills (BICS) and Cognitive Academic Language Proficiency Skills (CALPS), and Canale and Swain's four-part model of communicative competence.

PROFICIENCY: WHAT DOES IT MEAN TO BE "FLUENT" IN A LANGUAGE?

There continues to be discussion among practitioners and researchers concerning the definition of "language proficiency." The U.S. Department of Education (2006) defines proficiency as

> The degree to which the student exhibits control over the use of language, including the measurement of expressive and receptive language skills in the areas of phonology, syntax, vocabulary, and semantics and including the areas of pragmatics or language use within various domains or social circumstances.

Valdés and Figueroa (1994, p. 34) delve a little deeper when they write

> What it means to know a language goes beyond simplistic views of good pronunciation, "correct" grammar, and even mastery of rules of politeness. Knowing a language and knowing how to use a language involves a mastery and control of a large number of interdependent components and elements that interact with one another and that are affected by the nature of the situation in which communication takes place.

Such definitions, however, are of marginal use to educators trying to help students in the process of learning a second language. What teachers need are practical benchmarks with which to evaluate the language proficiency of their students. Generally, schools measure language proficiency based on student performance on language assessments or academic achievement tests (see Chapter 5 for lists of these assessments). But tests can only tell us so much, and teachers often need a more thorough picture of language proficiency to pinpoint the language strengths and challenges of their students. In this chapter, we present two theories of language proficiency as guidelines for teachers: Cummins's (1979) Basic Interpersonal Communication Skills (BICS) and Cognitive Academic Language Proficiency Skills (CALPS), and Canale and Swain's (1980) four-part model of communicative competence.

CUMMINS'S **BICS** AND **CALPS** MODEL

BICS (Basic Interpersonal Communication Skills) is the language students acquire when speaking informally with peers and others (Cummins, 1979). BICS is social communication language, the language used to "fit in" with peers, or the language needed to successfully complete daily activities such as shopping, ordering at a restaurant, or opening a bank account. It typically takes a student three to five years to become fluent in BICS.

Students who are proficient in BICS are able to converse "fluently" on many different subjects—a trait that can sometimes lead teachers to believe that these students are fluent in all aspects of the English language. However, these "fluent" students often fail academic content exams and perform below grade level in academic writing and reading. That is because **CALPS (Cognitive Academic Language Proficiency Skills)**, the language of school and academic subjects, has yet to be developed in these otherwise "fluent" students (Cummins, 1979). CALPS includes any terms or manners of expression (both verbal and written) that people experience in the content area. For example, in a high school biology class, a student fluent in CALPS would be familiar with terms such as Fahrenheit, chemical reaction, and Bunsen burner, and would know how to express himself or herself, both verbally and in writing, in a scientific context. This student would be familiar with the scientific method and how to report a scientific experiment. This student would know how to examine a problem from several angles and would know how to acquire the information to do so. This student would know how to verbalize a scientific argument and would have a wide range of resources from which to draw.

ELL students will not be able to employ CALPS unless they are explicitly taught academic vocabulary and are instructed in how to deploy the vocabulary in arguments, essays, and test answers. It usually takes a student between seven and ten years to fully develop CALPS. Characteristics of BICS and CALPS are summarized in Table 4.1.

Table 4.1   Characteristics of BICS and CALPS

BICS	CALPS
<ul><li>Playground vocabulary</li><li>Language for social interaction</li><li>Language to "get by" (shopping, banking, filling up on gas)</li><li>3–5 years to acquire proficiency</li></ul>	<ul><li>Academic vocabulary</li><li>Language for communicating in academic subjects</li><li>Language for writing academic papers</li><li>7–10 years to acquire proficiency</li></ul>

Student Acquisition of BICS and CALPS

Students' main source for acquiring BICS is through meaningful, social conversations with native-English-speaking peers, teachers, and others. As long as students have the opportunity to interact in meaningful ways with native English speakers in and out of the classroom, they will eventually acquire BICS.

Students' main source for acquiring CALPS, however, is through school. Academic terms, sentence structure, and writing formats must be stressed and explicitly taught in a comprehensible manner for students to acquire fluency in CALPS.

Questions to Explore Before Making a Special Education Referral

A student who is proficient in BICS but not in CALPS can sometimes be mislabeled as learning disabled. The student appears to be fluent in English and can converse on a number of topics in a grammatically correct format; yet, when faced with academic reading or writing, the student performs below grade level. Before referring the student for special education services, it is important that the teacher consider the following questions:

- What level of CALPS does the student have in his or her first language?

As Isa discusses in Case Study 4.1, first language skills—especially academic skills—can be transferred to a second language. If a student has a high level of CALPS in his or her first language, then learning CALPS in the second language will be easier. If a student does not have CALPS in his or her first language, then not only will the concepts of the content matter be new to the student, but the English terminology for the content matter concepts will be new as well. Such a student needs extra help and more time to acquire CALPS. This student would benefit from content-area instruction in the first and second languages to develop CALPS in both L1 and L2.

- Has the student been given explicit and comprehensible instruction on the vocabulary terms for the content matter and the reading and writing style of the content matter?

Not all students can "pick up" academic terms (reading and writing styles) in content areas by reading textbooks or listening to classroom lessons. Many students need focused, explicit instruction to acquire CALPS. Thus, teachers need to explicitly point out the key terms and key concepts of the lessons and review these key components often. Bilingual instruction in the content matter is beneficial to the learning of CALPS as well.

- Is the student able to receive any CALPS assistance at home?

The teacher needs to determine if caregivers can assist the child with academic content matter in either the first or second language. If caregivers are unable to assist the child, then teachers should consider securing extra help for the student—especially bilingual assistance—in completing homework and assignments.

Tools to help teachers address these questions are presented in Table 4.2.

> **REFER TO CASE STUDY 4.1**
>
> Was six months of ESL instruction sufficient for Isa to gain enough CALPS to compete academically at the college level? Where and how did she learn English CALPS? What helped Isa in her acquisition of CALPS?

Table 4.2 Tools for Assessing Students' BICS/CALPS Status

Questions	Data-Gathering Tools
What level of CALPS does the student have in his or her first language?	1. State standardized academic achievement exams in the L1. 2. Past content-area exams in the student's L1. 3. Student records from the home country schools.
Has the student been given explicit and comprehensible instruction in CALPS?	1. Refer to Chapters 9–15. Are the strategies discussed consistently employed? 2. Videotape yourself teaching to examine the level of strategy implementation. 3. Gather data on the student's educational history and the type of programs that served the student in the past.
Is the student able to receive English or first language CALPS assistance at home?	1. Parent interview. 2. Student interview.

CANALE AND SWAIN'S FOUR-PART MODEL OF COMMUNICATIVE COMPETENCE

If a student is not proficient in BICS or CALPS, then teachers must look more closely at the language the student does have. Canale and Swain's (1980) four-part model of communicative competence (summarized in Table 4.3) is useful for identifying strengths and gaps in a student's language proficiency.[1]

Table 4.3   Canale and Swain's (1980) Four-Part Model of Communicative Competence

1. Grammatical Competence "Knowledge of lexical items and of rules of morphology, syntax, sentence-grammar semantics, and phonology" (Canale & Swain, 1980, p. 29)
2. Discourse Competence The ability to connect sentences into meaningful discourse—from spoken conversations to written texts in different genres
3. Sociolinguistic Competence Knowledge of the sociocultural rules of language and communicative interactions
4. Strategic Competence "The verbal and non-verbal communication strategies that are called into action to compensate for breakdowns in communication due to performance variables or to insufficient competence" (Canale & Swain, 1980, p. 30)

Grammatical Competence

Grammatical competence involves the ability to communicate in the target language (both orally and in writing) in a grammatically correct manner. A student who has grammatical competence is able to master the morphology, syntax, and phonology of the second language (see Table 4.4).

Table 4.4   Components of Grammatical Competence

Morphology	Syntax	Phonology
How words are put together by combining root words, prefixes, and suffixes	Grammatical structure of the language; the way word classes (nouns, verbs, adjectives) are combined to form sentences	The sound system of the language

ELL students can make grammatical mistakes in any area of the language and often produce creative and interesting sentences. Table 4.5 presents some of the types of grammatical errors found in ELL students' speech and writing.

Table 4.5   Grammatical Competence Errors and Examples

Grammatical Area	Types of Errors	Examples of Errors
Forming the possessive	1. Confusing subject pronouns for possessive pronouns (using "she" instead of "her") and adding an 's to these pronouns	She likes *she's* car. A daddy love of *he's* wife is good.
	2. Forgetting to add the 's to form the possessive	That *woman* book is red. My *friend* bike is new.
	3. Adding the possessive 's to the wrong word in the sentence	My family *dog's* is black.
	4. Using the incorrect possessive pronoun for the sentence	A dad is trying to fix *their* bike. She have *his* book in the bag.
	5. Mapping the first language possessive rules onto the second language	The room of my cousin.
	6. Using no possessive where one is needed	He hurt *the* leg.
The use of articles (the, a, an)	1. Use of the definite article *the* where none is needed	*The* Atlantic City is really big. *The* truth is *the* beauty.
	2. Lack of an article where one is needed	She is professor. He go movie theater.
	3. Using the indefinite article (a/an) instead of the definite article (the)	*A* sun is very hot today.
	4. Use of the indefinite article (a/an) where no article is needed	He left *a* bread in the plate. I didn't have *a* dinner yesterday. It was *a* good fun. We play *a* tennis on Sunday.

Grammatical Area	Types of Errors	Examples of Errors
	5. Using an article before a possessive pronoun	Sarah has *the* his book.
	6. Using *one* instead of an article	We went to *one* football game yesterday.
Subject-verb agreement	1. Omitting the third person singular -*s*	He *have* a lot of money. The boy *don't* like my sister.
	2. Using the third person singular -*s* where one is not needed	We *goes* to the park. I *haves* too many friends.
	3. Omitting a subject where one is needed or omitting a "dummy subject" (*it* or *there*)	Is a good thing. Is raining. No have money. Is a boy in my class.
	4. Omitting a verb where one is needed—especially the copula or the auxiliary *to be*	You a good people. He black and white. She running.
Verb tense and aspect	1. Use of the present simple for all situations	Yesterday I *go* to the park. Tomorrow he *write* me.
	2. Mixing up tenses within the same sentence	Joslyn *did* tell me that you *see* her last week.
	3. Overgeneralization of the -*ed* to form all past tense verbs	She *goed* a party. They *tolded* me that.
Prepositions with verbs and nouns	1. The use of an incorrect preposition with a verb or noun	I can count *in* him. I rely *in* him. He gave *out* on the project.
	2. The use of a preposition where none is needed	My next project will be connecting *to* the whole nation together. She remember *to* my dad.
Forming questions	1. Not inverting subject-verb order to form a question	The girl is talking on the phone? What my mom is thinking?

(Continued)

Table 4.5 (Continued)

Grammatical Area	Types of Errors	Examples of Errors
	2. Using a *wh-* question, but omitting the verb *to be* when forming a question	What they talking about? Why he going to my home see my mom?
	3. Incorrect use of a *wh-* question word	Why she talking about? Why is he remember?
	4. Omitting the verb *do* to form a question	Why the boy who live next door call her? What carry the women?
Forming the negative	2. Using *not* or *no* instead of *don't* or *doesn't* before the verb	All my family there, *not* know how my brother look like.
	3. Incorrectly forming a negative question	Why *is she don't* remember my dad? Why my dad *don't* go to my home?
	4. Use of double negatives	My dad *don't* go to my home *never* again.
	5. Use of double auxiliary to form the negative	My dad *is don't* go to my game.
	6. Keeping the tense and person with the main verb, rather than showing tense and person in the auxiliary verb *do*	She don't *goes* there. He don't *saw* the movie.
	7. Forgetting to add the third person singular -s to the negative verb	She *don't* know me. He *don't* read that book.

Grammatical competence also includes the sound system or **phonology** of the language. When students are first learning the second language, they will map their first language pronunciation onto the second language and pronounce words as if they were words in their native language (Tarone, 2005). This transference of the first language sound system occurs in all areas of spoken English—casual conversations, classroom discussions, and reading aloud from printed materials. Likewise, when students attempt to write in the second language, they will use their first language phonology to sound out words in English (see Table 4.6). For example, when a Spanish-speaking, second grade student attempted to write, "Pumpkins are orange and green and have candy," the sentence, when sounded out with the Spanish phonological system, looked like this:

The pumpkins are oring and grin and habe cande.

When an eighth grade ELL student attempted to write, "I doing my job," using her first language phonological system, the sentence looked like this:

I duing may job.

Table 4.6 Phonological Errors and Examples

Types of Errors	Examples of Errors
Transferring L1 pronunciation to L2 written or spoken words	May broder no hav baycicl.
Trouble discerning the difference between pairs of words (English phonemes)	The ship graze in the filds.
L1 pronunciation of some words while maintaining L2 grammatical correctness	I am watching the *telayveesion.*

Depending on the sound system of the student's first language, students may also have trouble discerning the difference between English phonemes (Rost, 2005). For example, many students will struggle with discerning the difference between pairs of words such as *lettuce* and *lattice, sheep* and *ship, soup* and *soap,* and *cat* and *caught.*

Age can also factor into the acquisition of the phonological system of the second language. Studies have determined that authentic (native-like) pronunciation is hard to acquire after the brain has lateralized, which happens around puberty (Scovel, 1988). Therefore, older English language learners may not ever master native-like pronunciation in the second language. Age does not affect overall proficiency, however, and, regardless of the accent and pronunciation of the second language, if the environment is conducive to learning, most students can acquire grammatical fluency in the second language. A point to consider is that as English becomes a prominent world language and is spoken in many different countries, perhaps the goal should be mutual intelligibility, rather than a focus on native-like pronunciation (Jenkins, 2000; Kachru, 2005; Tarone, 2005).

Student Access to Grammatical Competence

Grammatical competence is often modeled in secondary and elementary content-area classes, thus providing students with resources to acquire this competence. That said, although teachers, textbooks, and peers provide excellent language models, sometimes students need explicit instruction in the grammar and pronunciation of the language in order to acquire grammatical competence (Brown, 2007; Fillmore & Snow, 2000; Thornbury, 2007). Fillmore and Snow (2000) found that students who were not given explicit grammar explanations had difficulty reaching native-like grammatical fluency in written English before college. It is important for teachers to understand the grammatical rules of the English language so that, when needed, teachers can explain to the child why the sentence is incorrect.

Questions to Explore Before Making a Special Education Referral

All students learning English will make grammatical and phonological errors, regardless of the amount of time of instruction in the grammar or phonological point. Before considering an ELL student for special education services, it is important that the following questions be researched:

- Did the child receive explicit and comprehensible instruction in the grammar of the language?

Many ELL students can "pick up" the grammar of the language simply by listening and being immersed in the language. But, at the same time, many cannot. Research has shown that many learners need explicit instruction in grammar and frequent reinforcement to acquire a high level of proficiency in the second language (Brown, 2007; Doughty, 2003).

- Has the student had consistent schooling in the second language?

Many ELL students have moved from school to school and missed substantial classroom time in the process. This also means these students may have lost months of language training. If schooling in the second language has been interrupted or intermittent, the child may simply need more time to master the grammar of the language they are working to acquire.

- Are the parents fluent in the second language and can they assist the child with the grammar and pronunciation of the second language?

Many native-English-speaking children receive help at home in speaking correctly and in forming grammatically correct writing. Students learning English, however, may come from homes where the parents are not fluent in the second language and will not be able to assist their children with the grammar of the new language. In this case, the teacher should secure extra assistance for the child. It is also important to note that most parents of students learning English are fluent in the first language. As Isa describes in Case Study 4.1, if parents continue to build a strong base in the child's first language, then the child's grammatical competence in the first language can assist the child in gaining grammatical competence in the second language (Cummins, 1981, 2000, 2001; Cummins et al., 2005). Thus, be sure to encourage parents to continue to work with their children in the first language.

- Is the issue a phonological transfer?

When dealing with possible transference of the first language phonological system onto second language writing, it is important to understand that an English sentence spelled according to the sound system of a students' first language could be unrecognizable as English. A good first step in such cases is to ask students to read their sentences aloud. If the sentence makes sense when read aloud, then it is possible that the student has mapped his or her first language sound system onto the second language writing. At this point, the teacher should investigate the first language sound system of the child to determine whether a mapping has occurred. If the child is mapping the first language phonological system onto the second language, this child may need extra help in English phonics and phonemic awareness.

Tools to help teachers address these questions are presented in Table 4.7.

> ### REFER TO CASE STUDY 4.1
>
> Where did Isa learn grammatical competence in English? How was she able to rely on her L1 to assist her in acquiring the L2? What role did phonology play in her academic studies?

Table 4.7 Tools for Assessing Students' Grammatical Competence

Questions	Data-Gathering Tools
Did the child receive explicit and comprehensible instruction in the grammar of the language?	1. Gather data on the past educational programs the child has experienced. Did the student have access to high quality ESL or bilingual instruction? 2. Refer to Chapters 9–15. Are you consistently implementing the strategies discussed in these chapters? 3. Videotape yourself teaching. Are you making all new vocabulary words, grammar structures, and key concepts of the lesson comprehensible? 4. Determine your level of comfort with teaching grammar. Are there grammar points that you are unsure of how to explain? How can you get assistance in discovering the rules for those points?

(Continued)

Table 4.7 (Continued)

Questions	Data-Gathering Tools
Has the child had consistent schooling in the second language?	1. Gather the educational history and past records of the child. 2. Parent interview.
Are the parents of the child fluent in the second language and can they assist the child with the grammar and pronunciation of the second language?	1. Home visit with cultural liaison. 2. Parent interview.
Is the issue a phonological transfer?	1. Determine the child's first language sound system. Enlist the assistance of bilingual school aides or teachers, or parent, church, or community volunteers who speak the first language of the child. 2. Have the child read a text aloud. Determine whether the child is sounding out words according to his or her first language system.

Discourse Competence

Discourse competence involves the ability to connect words and sentences into stretches of comprehensible written and oral language. This competence concerns not only the ability to converse inside and outside the classroom, but also the ability to write lengthy texts such as essays, letters, and reports. Students who have discourse competence are able to produce comprehensible written texts in different genres. Table 4.8 presents some of the typical types of errors made by ELL students who are struggling with discourse competence. Most examples come from texts written by ELL students in the fourth grade through college.

Student Acquisition of Discourse Competence

In order to develop *social* discourse competence, students must interact with native English speakers (Hatch, 1992; Lantolf, 2005; Long, 1983; Pica, 1994). A supportive interactive environment where students have ample opportunities to practice the language assists students in moving to higher levels of social discourse competence.

Table 4.8 Discourse Competence Errors and Examples

Types of Errors	Examples of Errors
Punctuation: • Lack of punctuation • Overgeneralization of punctuation • Using L1 punctuation • Using *and* in place of punctuation	We are going to our swimming pool. it has a bathroom. and a har drayr. and shers in the bathroom. and the door dusint have a key to opin you need a pass waord to one and if you get it rong the peepl will come and you will get out of the pool.
Misuse of memorized phrases or idioms	It's hailing cats and dogs. She's highly poor.
Substituting words from the L1 to replace words in the L2 that the student does not know	In my primer day of the school, teacher is muy simpatico.
Direct translation from the L1 to the L2, usually using a dictionary to directly translate	The reasoning is being definition by world and contextual character in generic terms.
Transferring L1 discourse competence to the L2 (the way a letter is written, the way a story is formed, the way an essay is organized)	Business letter example from ELL student: Esteemed Sirs, It is great pleasure I write you this letter to discuss the electricity in my home. I hope this letter find you and family enjoying the summer. I enjoy my summer but my electricity not functioning and my family experience heat during hot season.

However, social interaction is not always so easy to come by. Many ELL students living in the United States do not have opportunity to interact with native-English-speaking peers. ELL students often go home to families or neighborhoods where the first language is spoken exclusively. Students can also be hesitant about approaching English-speaking peers in school—especially when they are new to this country. Therefore, ELL students are highly dependent upon their teacher to create environments where they can practice with native-English-speaking peers (see Photo 4.2).

Developing *academic* discourse competence is an entirely different skill. In order to develop academic discourse competence, teachers need to provide explicit instruction in CALPS vocabulary for the content area and they need to provide instruction on how to connect discourse to write competently in the content area. While spoken English is context embedded and can be assisted by the facial expressions and gestures often present in verbal conversations, written

Photo 4.2   Having opportunities to brainstorm ideas in groups can improve discourse competence.

text must create the context through the written words. Students should not be expected to know the parts of an essay, the expected length of an essay, what constitutes a sentence versus a paragraph, or what constitutes a "flowing" or "well-written" essay in English. "Good" writing differs dramatically across cultures and unless teachers explicitly instruct students in the expectations of the target language, it is likely that academic success will be delayed.[2] Likewise, students should not be expected to know how to speak using key academic terms and how to keep the flow of an academic discourse. Rather, students need multiple examples of the expected speaking style.

Questions to Explore Before Making a Special Education Referral

Discourse competence is often a daunting linguistic task for English language learners and it can take students years to acquire fluent English academic writing. Students will often resort to their first language writing system and write essays in English according to how they should look in their first language. ELL students also have difficulty in discerning the difference between spoken English and written English. Most students will begin their English writing in the same way that they speak on the playground with peers. Students need explicit instruction in how to write academically in order to master discourse competence.

Before recommending a student who demonstrates a lack of discourse competence for special education services, consider the following:

- How many consistent years of schooling has the student had?

If the student has lacked consistent schooling in either the first or second language, then the ability to master discourse competence has been jeopardized. It is important that the teacher spend time with this student, explicitly instructing the student on how to write and speak academically in the second language.

- Does the student have discourse competence in the first language?

As mentioned in Case Study 4.1, any competence that the student has in the first language will transfer to the second and assist the student in the acquisition process. If the student does not have discourse competence in the first language, then the student may have few literacy skills from which to draw. This student would benefit from bilingual instruction and gaining a foundation in the first language. If bilingual instruction is not available, than this student needs explicit instruction in the second language and adequate time to acquire discourse competence.

- Do the student's caregivers have discourse competence in the first or second language?

Again, if the caregivers can assist the student in gaining a foundation of written discourse competence in the first language, this will assist the student in the acquisition process. If caregivers also have discourse competence in the second language, then this can also assist the student in the acquisition process. If the caregivers do not have written discourse competence in either the first or second language, then this student will need extra assistance in gaining discourse competence but not necessarily special education.

- Has the student had access to comprehensible and explicit instruction in forming academic written discourse in the second language?

Unless the instruction the student has received has been comprehensible—either through use of the first language or other appropriate techniques—then it can be assumed that the student may lack discourse competence. In this case, the first step should be explicit and repeated instruction in the written or spoken genre.

Tools to help teachers address these questions are presented in Table 4.9.

REFER TO CASE STUDY 4.1

What struggles with discourse competence did Isa experience? How did she compensate?

Table 4.9 Tools for Assessing Students' Discourse Competence

Questions	Data-Gathering Tools
Has the student had access to comprehensible and explicit instruction in forming academic written discourse in the second language?	1. Gather data on the past educational programs the child has experienced. Did the student have access to high-quality ESL or bilingual instruction? 2. Interview the student. What does the student know about discourse competence in English? What does the student know about English writing? 3. Refer to Chapters 9–15. Are you consistently implementing the strategies discussed in these chapters? 4. Videotape yourself teaching. Are you making all new vocabulary words, grammar structures, and key concepts of the lesson comprehensible?
How many consistent years of schooling has the student had?	1. Gather data on the past educational history. 2. Student and parent interviews.
Does the student have discourse competence in the first language?	1. Gather the educational history and past records of the child. 2. State standardized test in the L1. 3. Have the student write a sample in the L1 and enlist the help of a cultural liaison, parent, or community member to determine the level of discourse competence in the L1.
Do the students' family members or caregivers have written discourse competence in the first or second language?	1. Home visit with cultural liaison. 2. Parent interview.

Sociolinguistic Competence

Sociolinguistic competence, or pragmatics, involves the ability to understand the deep cultural rules associated with a language. Having sociolinguistic competence means that the student is able to do the following:

- *Use the correct language for the situation.* How does a student verbally show respect to the teacher? How does a student appropriately get the teacher's attention? How does a student participate in a manner that makes him or her sound intelligent? How does the language a student uses with peers differ from the language a student must use with teachers?

- *Correctly interpret the contextual cues that trigger specific speech and behaviors.* What does it mean when a teacher walks past you and states, "Hi, how are you?" Is that an opening for an extended conversation or is it just a greeting? What does it mean when a peer walks by, raises his chin, and states, "What's up?" Does a student know what to do in each of these situations?

- *Engage in the correct proxemics for the situation* (determine how close or far one should be from the speaker and listener). How close should a student stand next to the teacher when discussing a homework assignment? How close should a student sit next to a peer when working in groups?

- *Engage in appropriate nonverbal behaviors for the situation.* How should a student show respect to the teacher? Should the student look the teacher in the eye or look down? Should the student smile or look sad? Should the student speak up or say nothing? How should a student show affection toward peers? Does one kiss or hug others in this culture?

- *Dress appropriately for the situation.* What does one wear to school? How do clothes represent respect for or affiliation with certain groups in the target culture?

- *Determine how men and women perform these sociocultural factors differently.* Do male students behave and show respect differently from female students?

Sociolinguistic competence has a tremendous impact on the acquisition of the second language. Language and culture are deeply intertwined and students must learn the culture and the language simultaneously to function in the new social setting. Sociolinguistic competence is one of the first competencies students will attempt to acquire—especially school-aged children—in order to "fit in," but it is one of the most difficult aspects of language to acquire. Because many cultural rules are "hidden" (difficult to articulate for a native-born citizen), the effort needed to discern the cultural rules often exhausts students and makes classroom learning difficult. And even when students have acquired a high level of sociolinguistic competence, when placed in stressful situations, students will often fall back on their first language sociolinguistic competences and will act according to their first language culture. Unless the teacher understands that a student's behavior can often be attributed to their first language culture, the student can find himself or herself in a cultural mismatch situation where his or her actions are interpreted negatively (Gass & Selinker, 2008). Table 4.10 presents some of the types of errors ELL students make with sociolinguistic competence.

Table 4.10 Sociolinguistic Competence Errors and Examples

Types of Errors	Examples of Errors
Incorrect use of language for the situation • ELL student learns slang or curse words and does not know the appropriate situation in which to use the language • ELL student learns formal English and uses this in all situations • The ELL student uses titles or greetings from the L1 • The ELL student falls back on polite conversation and questions from the L1 and uses these in the L2	• An ELL student is called into the principal's office and addresses the principal in the following manner, "Hey, what's up, man?" • An ELL student uses curse words while speaking to the teacher. • An adult ELL student addresses peers in the following manner, "So good to see you. How are you this fine morning?" • An ELL student refers to the teacher as "teacher" instead of using the teacher's name. • An ELL student asks the teacher numerous personal questions: How old are you? How much money do you make? Do you have children? Are you married?
Incorrect interpretation of the speaker's meaning or incorrect reading of the contextual clues, and a response based on the incorrect understanding	ELL student's response to U.S. professor's greeting: Professor quickly walks past the student in the hallway and states, "Hi, how are you." The ELL student stops and responds, "Well, I'm not doing too well, my English is poor, I am having trouble on exams. I find studying in this country to be difficult." The professor is visibly uncomfortable and states, "That's too bad," and walks away.
Incorrect proxemics for the situation	• ELL students stand "too" close to the teacher when they come for help. • ELL students hold hands at recess. • ELL student (or the family members) attempt to hug and kiss the teacher when they see the teacher outside of class.
Incorrect use of nonverbal behaviors for the situation	• When the ELL student is addressed by the teacher, the student looks down instead of making eye contact. • ELL students attempt to imitate U.S. peers by putting feet up on desk and speaking loudly in the classroom. The ELL students are not clear when to do this behavior and when not to. • The ELL student does not participate in class by raising her hand, but waits for the teacher to call on her.

Types of Errors	Examples of Errors
	• The ELL student appears not to be a self-directed learner. The student asks for direction in every aspect of the assignment and will not continue until he or she has direction from the teacher (where should I put my name, what color should I make the map, where should I write the description). • The ELL student invites the teacher over for dinner. When the teacher comes, the family serves the teacher first and watches the teacher eat. When the teacher is finished, the family eats.
Dressing appropriately according to the cultural norms of the student's country of origin	The ELL student comes to school dressed up formally for the first day.
Not sure about the appropriate gender roles	When called to the office, a male ELL student insists on speaking only to the male assistant principal.

To read a case study from an ESL teacher describing a cultural mismatch situation between a student and teacher, including accompanying analysis and questions, see the following Web link: **www.sagepub.com/grassi.**

4.2

Student Acquisition of Sociolinguistic Competence

When second language learners are going through the process of acquiring sociolinguistic competence, they pass through what is called **cultural acquisition.** The four stages of cultural acquisition are as follows (adapted from Brown, 2007, p. 195) (see Figure 4.1):

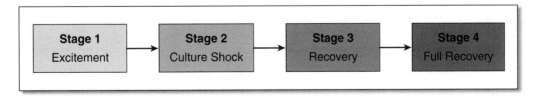

Figure 4.1 Stages of Cultural Acquisition

Stage 1—Excitement over the newness of the surroundings. At this stage, children are happy to be in school. They are ready to learn with bright eyes and smiles on their faces.

Stage 2—Culture shock. Students strongly feel the cultural differences and begin to question their sense of self. In this stage, students experience high levels of stress, frustration, anger, and sadness. Students will seek out the support of other students from their home country. Some of the behaviors teachers have observed from students in this stage include the following:[3]

a. Dropping out of school (middle school and above)

b. Constantly asking to go to the bathroom or to the school nurse

c. Crying, depression

d. Throwing chairs or books across the room

e. Inability to stay focused on the task

f. Falling asleep during class

g. Inability to complete homework or schoolwork

h. Outbursts of anger, violence, frustration, sadness

i. Getting into fights at recess

j. Leaving the classroom or asking to go home

k. Out sick from school for many days

Students whose first culture is greatly different from the target culture, or whose first culture is perceived as having less status than the target culture can experience even higher levels of stress (Schumann, 1976b, 1978). While students in the culture shock stage could use constant support, often the whole family is experiencing culture shock at the same time. Parents are trying to find work, figure out the system, and ensure that their children are safe. Sometimes, the families do not have contacts to help them negotiate the new culture and the parents and other relations struggle as much as the children. If the family members are refugees, the trauma experienced in the country of origin or in the journey to the United States adds even more stress to the situation. Children come home from school to families that are angry, frustrated, sad, and depressed.

Stage 3—Recovery. Students slowly begin to accept the cultural differences and begin to understand people in the new culture. In this stage, students begin to lose their ties to their native culture. They can feel regret as well as anxiety over "fitting in" and becoming part of the new culture. Students do not feel completely a part of the new culture, and, at the same time, no longer feel deeply tied with their native culture.

Stage 4—Full recovery. Students either assimilate or adapt to the new culture. If assimilation occurs, students leave behind their first culture and language and fully adopt the culture and language of the second language. If adaptation occurs, students develop a bicultural identity, a "new person" that maintains many aspects of the first culture, while also developing characteristics of the new culture and language.

Student Access to Sociolinguistic Competence

Sociolinguistic competence is rarely taught to students. Rather, students are expected to acquire sociolinguistic competence simply by living in the culture. While students can acquire some of the sociocultural rules by immersion in the target culture, every culture has rules that are less apparent and often difficult for students and their families to ascertain.

When ELL students and their families behave in ways that feel different from the cultural norms the teacher is accustomed to, it is helpful if the teacher assumes a cultural mismatch before assuming rudeness. More often than not, the student and family are acting appropriately according to their cultural norms. Additionally, the students' transition into the new culture can be smoothed if teachers explore the cultures of the students represented in their classroom. This will not only help teachers better understand their students, but also better understand where cultural mismatches are most likely to occur.

In order for students to be successful in the academic setting, they must learn the cultural rules for that setting. This does not mean that teachers should erase or devalue the students' first culture. Rather, while respecting, valuing, and encouraging the first culture of students in the classroom, teachers must assist students in acquiring the cultural rules of the new language (Kasper & Roever, 2005). Explicit instruction in the cultural rules of the language, in combination with practice opportunities, result in increased sociolinguistic competence.

Questions to Explore Before Making a Special Education Referral

Students who are undergoing culture shock often engage in behaviors that appear similar to children with special needs. Their attention wanders during class and they have trouble concentrating on the material. They appear to not understand the content presented. They can exhibit violent and aggressive behavior, or can become quiet, sad, and depressed.

Before referring a student for special education services, it is important to consider the following:

- How long has the student been living in the target country?

The acculturation process can take years—especially if the student and family do not have support through the acculturation process. Thus, teachers must investigate the length of time the student has been in the country and the type of support system the student has. If the student is struggling with acculturation, then teachers should provide support for the student first, such as cross-cultural counseling or acculturation assistance by a parent liaison or cultural broker.

- Do the student and family have a strong support system?

If a student's family does not have a strong support system to help negotiate the new culture, then it is possible that the student and family have not reached recovery stage. In this case, it would be beneficial to the student and the family to be provided with support in the new culture.

- What is the level of English language proficiency of the student?

The level of English language proficiency and the ability of the student to communicate in the target language are key components of the acculturation process. If the student is struggling with the English language, then giving the student more time to acquire English and helping the student to learn survival skills in English will help the acculturation process.

- Has the student had access to bilingual education or bilingual supports?

Having support in the first language and culture will help a student acculturate to the second culture. If the student has experienced only English immersion or submersion, then providing the student with first language and cultural support will help with the acculturation process.

Tools to help teachers address these questions are presented in Table 4.11.

4.3

To read a case study from Sheila, a school social worker who discusses the cultural challenges students and families face, and includes suggestions for teachers, see the following Web link: **www.sagepub.com/grassi.**

Table 4.11   Tools for Assessing Students' Sociolinguistic Competence

Questions	Data-Gathering Tools
How long has the student been living in the target country?	1. Gather student records and past educational history. 2. Parent, student interviews.
Do the student and family have a strong support system?	1. Parent, student interviews. 2. Home visit with cultural liaison.
What is the level of English language proficiency of the student?	1. District English language proficiency exam. 2. Student interview. 3. Teacher observations. 4. School records. 5. Student work samples. 6. Parent interviews.
Has the student had access to bilingual education or bilingual supports?	1. Gather student records and past educational history. 2. Parent, student interviews.

Resources for Support in the New Culture

Teachers and schools often serve as the first, and perhaps most important, culture broker for students and their families. Families will come to the school for help with non-school-related issues such as health care, resume writing, finding work, issues with immigration, or difficult family decisions. It is very helpful if the school or the teacher has a list of community resources to which they can refer families. Teachers can also engage in the following to help support students and their families:

1. Schedule regular *parent gatherings* at the school. Parent gatherings are extremely beneficial because they provide an opportunity for parents to meet others from the same culture, or the same situation, and begin to build a system of support.

2. Solicit assistance from *teachers* or *aides* who are from the first culture of the student. Teachers or aides can provide ideas to help the student adapt to the new culture and provide opportunities for the student to discuss their difficulties using their first language.

3. Solicit assistance from the school's *parent* or *community liaison*. The parent liaison can provide an excellent resource for first language assistance and to help families negotiate the new culture.

4. Call upon *parent volunteers* from the first culture of students to work with them in their first language. Parents are usually more than willing to volunteer in the classroom. If a parent does not speak English, that parent can help children in their L1 or provide other resources such as the presentation of cultural customs from their country.

5. Contact *community centers* or *churches* that sometimes provide cultural broker volunteers from the student's first culture who can work with families and help them negotiate the new culture.

Strategic Competence

Strategic competence is the ability to enact verbal and nonverbal communication strategies to avoid communication breakdowns. Strategic competence is vital in developing the second language; the longer students can keep a conversation going, the greater their opportunity to practice the new language.

Students who have not developed strategic competence will find ways to avoid or stop the conversation. According to Dörnyei (1995, p. 58), avoidance strategies include these:

- Message abandonment: The student stops speaking because of language difficulties or a lack of language skills to continue with the communication (e.g., My friend go to get . . .).

- Topic avoidance: The student avoids subjects that present language difficulties.

Students who have developed strategic competence will keep the conversation going by using compensatory strategies. Dörnyei (1995, p. 58) identifies a number of compensatory strategies:

- Circumlocution. Rather than articulating the correct word, the student describes the word by talking "around it." For example, if the student does not know the word for "nail clippers," he or she can state, "the thing that you use to cut your nails."

- Approximation. The student uses an alternative word that approximates the meaning of the target word as closely as possible (e.g., *eyelenses* for *eyeglasses*).

- Use of all-purpose words. The student uses a general filler in the place of a specific word (e.g., *thing, stuff, what-do-you-call-it?*).

- Word coinage. The student creates a new word in the second language based on a supposed rule (e.g., *drummerist* for *drummer*).

- Foreignizing. The student uses a first language word but states it using second language pronunciation.

- Using memorized phrases (e.g., *Where is the . . . ? How do you say . . . ?*).

- Use of nonlinguistic means. The student mimes, gestures, or uses facial expressions to get the message across.

- Translating literally from the first language to the second language (e.g., the *"opening wine bottles machine"*).

- Code switching. The student uses a first language word with first language pronunciation while speaking the second language (e.g., *The other day I went to the tienda to find platanos*).

- Appealing for help. The student asks for aid from the listener either directly (e.g., *What do you call . . . ?*) or indirectly (e.g., rising intonation, pause, eye contact, puzzled expression).

- Stalling or time-gaining strategies. The student uses fillers or hesitation devices to fill pauses and to gain time to think (e.g., *like, let's see, um, well actually*).

Many teachers have also noted that students seek out a translator, that is, the student looks for someone who is fluent in both the L1 and the L2 to translate the conversation and will not engage in conversation if there is no translator available. See Table 4.12 for ELL student examples of challenges with strategic competence.

Student Access to Strategic Competence

Teachers need to instruct students on communicative strategies—especially strategies that will help ELL students participate in the classroom. Dörnyei (1995, p. 80) suggests the following:

- Encourage students to take risks and use communication strategies.

- Provide L2 models of communication strategies (lists of questions: *How do you say? Could you repeat that please? What is the name of . . . ?*; how to draw a picture of the word if the student is stuck, how to use circumlocution, and how to approximate words from the student's L1).

- Provide opportunities for practice in strategy use.

Table 4.12 Strategic Competence Errors and Examples

Types of Errors	Examples of Errors
Having no strategies to continue the conversation	• The ELL student stops talking. • The ELL student suddenly changes the subject. • The ELL student stops making eye contact. • The ELL student looks for a friend to translate.
Not understanding the conversation and having no strategies to gain comprehension or clarification	• The ELL student "smiles and nods." • The ELL student looks interested but makes no verbal responses. • The ELL student stops making eye contact. • The ELL student talks about a subject different from the topic of the conversation. • The ELL student pauses for long periods of time before answering. Sometimes the student does not answer the question but will say something such as, "yes, yes." • The ELL student attempts to politely remove himself or herself from the conversation.

Questions to Explore Before Making a Special Education Referral

When students do not have strategic competence, they can exhibit behaviors that seem to indicate a problem with the language process. Teachers have reported that students will

- speak to the teacher only in the first language;

- refuse to answer a question;

- start talking, then say, "never mind" and walk away;

- get angry or frustrated when trying to communicate;

- cry when trying to speak with the teacher; and

- always communicate with a friend who can interpret for the student.

When a student stops communicating, it makes it difficult for the teacher or the assessor to gain a sufficient picture of the student's language proficiency. Before referring a student to special education services because of a lack of performance, teachers should consider the following:

- How does the student typically get out of communication breakdowns?

If the student cries, gets frustrated or angry, stops communicating, or tries to avoid the conversation, it could indicate that the student does not have strategic competence. This student may benefit from instruction in communication strategies.

- Does the student have ample opportunities for interaction and practice in the second language?

One of the best ways to acquire strategic competence is through social interaction with peers or teachers who are patient and willing to work with the student in communicating in the second language. If the student has limited access to interactions, then the student may not have opportunities to practice strategic competence.

Tools to help teachers address these questions are presented in Table 4.13.

> **REFER TO CASE STUDY 4.1**
>
> What strategic competencies did Isa employ? How did these help with her English acquisition?

Table 4.13 Tools for Assessing Students' Strategic Competence

Questions	Data-Gathering Tools
How does the student typically get out of communication breakdowns?	1. Parent, student interview. 2. Teacher observations.
Does the student have ample opportunities for interaction and practice in the second language?	1. Parent, student interview. 2. Home visit with cultural liaison. 3. Teacher observations.

For an article detailing the differences between language acquisition and learning disabilities by O. Castro, go to the following Web link: **www.sagepub.com/grassi.**

4.4

Summary

- Learning a language is a complex process, and teachers must be able to pinpoint the strengths and challenges that students exhibit as they develop language fluency so that supports for acquisition can be put into place.

- Cummins's BICS and CALPS model of language proficiency involves distinguishing social communication from the language of school and academic communication.

- Canale and Swain's four-part model of communicative competence is a vital tool to understanding the specific characteristics of students who are passing through the normal process of acquiring another language.

Key Terms

Basic Interpersonal Communication Skills (BICS)

Cognitive Academic Language Proficiency Skills (CALPS)

Cultural acquisition

Discourse competence

Grammatical competence

Phonology

Sociolinguistic competence

Strategic competence

Activities for Further Understanding

1. Gather spoken and written language samples from an ELL student. Observe this same student in academic and social interactions. In a group of your peers, analyze the student's language. What does the student know? What does the student still need to acquire? In what stage of cultural acquisition is the student? Which language proficiencies has the student mastered? What are the next steps you would take with the student?

2. See the acculturation quick screen tool (Collier, 1998). Implement the quick screen with one of your ELL students. Does the quick screen give an accurate description of the cultural acquisition stage of the student? What modifications need to be made in the classroom to help this student through the cultural acquisition process?

3. Audiotape an English language learner speaking. Analyze the language. What grammatical rules has the student acquired? What grammatical rules is the student still working on? How is the student's pronunciation? Does the student communicate in a culturally appropriate manner? Could this student be mislabeled as a student with special needs due to the language and behaviors the student produces?

4. Find an ELL parent to interview. Ask that parent about the struggles he or she has faced with language and culture. What does the parent need to better his or her English? What sort of cultural "instruction" would the parent desire at this point in acquisition? What challenges have the parent's children faced in school? How did the school or teacher help this parent? What further assistance could the parent have used?

5. Interview the ESL specialist in your school. What does he or she consider to be "proficient English?" How does the school measure proficiency? Is this an accurate measure? What aspects of proficiency are missing? How could you gather a more complete picture of students' strengths and gaps in language acquisition?

6. Interview a parent liaison or cultural broker from a school. What is the most important aspect of their job? What is the most crucial assistance that most ELL children and families need? How could a teacher better help ELL children and families?

Visit the Student Study Site at **www.sagepub.com/grassi** for chapter-specific study resources.

Notes

1. Although there have been more recent models of communicative competence in the literature (e.g., Bachman, 1990), Canale and Swain provide a model that can be easily navigated to assess an ELL student's language status.

2. For detailed description of strategies to teach writing, see Chapters 13–15.

3. Derived from a focus group interview with practicing teachers, K–12, in September 2006.

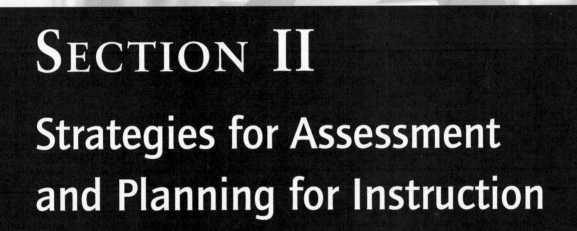

SECTION II

Strategies for Assessment and Planning for Instruction

Chapter 5. Strategies for the Assessment Process

Chapter 6. Collaboration Skills

Chapter 7. Planning Instruction

Chapter 8. Culturally Relevant Pedagogy

Chapter 5

STRATEGIES FOR THE ASSESSMENT PROCESS

CASE STUDY 5.1   Intervention Team Process

It is often a difficult task to identify the needs of ELL students and determine whether a student has a learning disability or experiences difficulty due to the language acquisition process. The ESL teacher and the cultural liaison are critical members of intervention teams when the needs of ELL students are discussed.

José, a first grader, was referred to the intervention team by his classroom teacher. She had concerns regarding his academic skills in all areas. José was having difficulty retaining information, processing, and following directions. He had not yet learned all of his letters and was struggling to learn letter sounds, even though his teacher worked with him daily on letters and sounds. José had also been working with the ESL teacher on a daily basis.

The ESL teacher contacted José's mother and invited her to come to the intervention team meeting. At the meeting, the ESL teacher sat next to the mother and acted as her advocate. She translated everything that was said by the team and by the mother.

From the discussion, the team learned that José was not yet fluent in English and was still relying heavily on the Spanish language. José still required a lot of wait time to process the English language. The ESL teacher explained the stages of language acquisition and described José's present stage.

According to his mother, José seemed slow to process information, follow directions, and remember things in Spanish as well. José's mother reported that he did not yet know how to read in Spanish and that also he was experiencing difficulty with the letters and sounds of his native language.

Based on the information gathered from the intervention team (which included the interview with the mother, advice from the ESL specialist, a list of the interventions implemented by the teacher, and supporting data collected by the teacher), a referral was made for José to have a special education evaluation. The Multilingual Assessment Team (MAST) was involved in the testing process so that José could be tested in Spanish and English.

After the evaluations were complete, the team met with José's mother and the ESL teacher again to review the results. According to the results, José was struggling due to executive functioning deficits in processing speed and working memory, in both English and Spanish. José showed severe deficits in his expressive and receptive language skills in both languages. It was determined that José qualified for special education services as a student with a speech or language disability who also needed academic support. Strategies were discussed to help José with the processing and memory difficulties that he was experiencing.

Without the knowledge, expertise, and experience of the ESL teacher, the parent, and the Multilingual Assessment Team, it would have been difficult to determine whether José was experiencing difficulty because of his second language acquisition or a special education need. Their involvement helped the team gather information about his native language and understand the typical patterns of second language acquisition.

—Becky Ford, Special Education teacher

Consider the case study above:

- What steps occurred to provide the support José needed in school?
- What kinds of informal and formal data were gathered?
- Who was a part of the assessment process and what were their roles?

SOURCE: Used by permission.

Generally, in the existing bureaucracies of school systems, students who are struggling academically either are referred as needing support from language acquisition programs or are referred through the existing special education system. These systems were set up for special education or for English language learners, not for students who need support from both systems. Because these systems are not set up for the complex needs of CLDE learners, we suggest adaptations to the current systems to address the needs of CLDE learners. First, we describe the current systems for referral for special education services and the existing system of eligibility for ELL students, and then we discuss how to enhance the current systems to include the needs of CLDE students.

THE INSTRUCTION/ASSESSMENT CYCLE IN SPECIAL EDUCATION

Assessment in special education involves an instruction/assessment cycle that determines student strengths and needs and provides for interventions. The term "instruction" is used in a broad sense to include placement decisions, strategy use, professional support, and behavioral support. The term "assessment" refers to the process of ascertaining, in a systematic way, the child's learning status (Popham, 2007). Thus, assessment is explicitly and completely linked to instructional strategies and interventions.

The **instruction/assessment cycle** is a circular process used to continually evaluate decisions related to instruction of all students (see Figure 5.1). When a student has been assessed formally, and qualifies for special education services, the assessment data are used not only for daily instructional decisions, but also to develop overall goals, short-term objectives, and placement decisions on an IEP. Within the instruction/assessment cycle, teachers and others who work with special education students must remember that the goal of assessment is to learn about one particular student and provide the best instructional plan and support for that individual. This is particularly critical for those who are culturally and linguistically diverse.

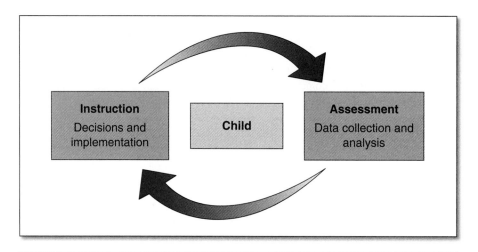

Figure 5.1   The Instruction/Assessment Cycle

It is through the instruction/assessment cycle that school professionals determine how to address a student's needs. Special education law spells out the framework of this process, but teachers can fully embrace the spirit of the law and better address the needs of CLDE learners by the following:

1. *Fully including all stakeholders in the process*—parents, students, general education teachers, ESL/bilingual teachers, special education teachers, support staff, and related services all need to play a part in the development and follow-through of the IEP.

2. *Holding the child's needs at the center of the process*—programs and placements should not be the driving force in how services are implemented; teachers and school staff need to work collaboratively to ensure that the student's needs and strengths are supported by the placement decisions (see Chapter 6 for more details on collaboration).

3. *Making the IEP a living document*—the IEP needs to be more than just a place to record strengths, weaknesses, assessment results, and goals. The information listed must also provide guidelines for instruction and support. All stakeholders need to fully understand and be committed to the interventions. They must also be willing to discuss those interventions if they are not successful. The IEP should not only document what happens in a meeting once a year, but also should be used in planning instruction and monitoring progress along the way.

These three topics will be discussed in detail under the section, "The Eligibility Process and CLDE Students," with additional information on how to broaden these steps to include the specific language and cultural needs of CLDE students.

Eligibility for Special Education Services

For a child to be eligible for special education services, he or she must be determined to have a special education need. The Individuals with Disabilities Education Act (IDEA) of 2004 uses 13 categories for defining disabilities and determining special education need (see Table 5.1). The federal government uses these **disability categories** to determine eligibility and to fund the costs of educating students with special needs.[1]

See Web Link 1.2 for a list and full definitions of the 13 disability categories at **www.sagepub.com/grassi.**

5.1

Table 5.1   Disability Categories in Federal Special Education Law

1. Learning disability
2. Speech or language impairment
3. Mental retardation
4. Emotional disturbance
5. Autism
6. Hearing impairment
7. Visual impairment
8. Deaf-blindness
9. Orthopedic impairment
10. Traumatic brain injury
11. Other health impairment
12. Multiple disabilities
13. Developmental delay

When students are given one of these labels, it protects their right to a **free and appropriate public education (FAPE)**. It also protects their civil rights and ensures support and protection throughout their lives. Labels also provide a diagnosis, which can lead to specific treatments (Sands et al., 2000). But teachers must also remember that labels have repercussions. Foremost among these is the stereotyping and stigmatizing of children according to their labels, which can have negative effects on students' academic performance, socialization with peers and others, and teacher attitudes and expectations.

The instruction/assessment cycle is a problem-solving process that includes very specific steps, some of which are required by special education law. If a child is eligible for special education services and labeled with a special education disability, federal law as implemented through school district policies must be followed. These steps include the following:

1. The teacher notices a difficulty in the classroom.

2. The teacher implements interventions in the general education classroom to address the academic difficulty.

3. The intervention team uses data to plan and implement further interventions.

4. The team acquires parental permission for full multidisciplinary evaluation.

5. Multidisciplinary evaluations take place.

6. The Multidisciplinary Assessment Team–IEP meeting takes place to complete an IEP.

7. Progress is continually monitored.

> **REFER TO CASE STUDY 5.1**
>
> Which steps of the problem-solving process for special education eligibility were implemented? Who took part in those steps and what were their roles?

These steps are discussed in more detail later in this chapter in terms of their application to CLDE students.

Eligibility for ELL Services

The Individuals with Disabilities Education Act (2004) requires that language acquisition be ruled out as the reason for academic difficulties before a child can be eligible for special education services. Therefore, teachers and professionals must understand the eligibility process for ELL services when working with CLDE students.

Classification of English Language Learners

The English language proficiency of students is determined when a student enrolls in a new school. This usually involves a basic, two-step protocol (Kindler, 2002):

Step 1: The student's family is given a *home language survey*. If the parents or caregivers note on the survey that a language other than English is spoken at home at any time, then the school must follow up with Step 2.

For examples of home language surveys, see the following Web link: **www.sagepub.com/grassi.**

5.2

Step 2: The student is given an *English language proficiency test* to determine the level of spoken and written English. It is also advisable to give a *native language proficiency test* to determine the spoken and written language level in the native language.

To see a list of the types of English language assessments each state uses, see the following Web link: **www.sagepub.com/grassi.**

5.3

Figure 5.2 presents an example of a decision guide for how to assess and place ELL students who enter public school. Most districts across the nation follow a similar protocol.

Assessment of ELL Students and Interpreting the Results

The No Child Left Behind Act (NCLB, 2001) requires states to demonstrate that all students have reached the "proficient" level on the state's language arts and mathematics assessments by 2014. Even ELL students, after one year of residence in the United States, must meet the same academic progress goals as other students. States must demonstrate **adequate yearly progress (AYP)** toward this goal each year by showing that increasing percentages of students are reaching proficient achievement levels.

Under NCLB, states are required to assess students' oral language, reading, and writing skills in English each year to determine students' progress in learning English and whether they have attained English proficiency. Once English

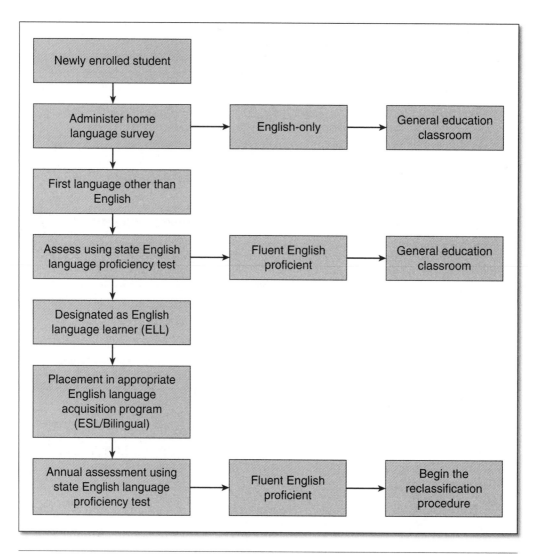

Figure 5.2 Sample Decision Guide for Assessment and Classification of ELL Students

language assessments are administered, the classroom teachers are informed of the language level(s) of the student. Most language proficiency tests are designed to measure how proficient a student is in English as compared to native-English-speaking peers of the same age or grade level. Teachers will receive results such as "Level A, B, C, D" (or Level 1, 2, 3, 4), "Fluent English Proficient," or "Exited" from language services. Most assessments also provide separate results for oral language, reading, and writing, to let the teacher know if the student is beginning, intermediate, or advanced in each skill area.

Unfortunately, language proficiency tests do not give teachers a complete picture of the student's language proficiency. To begin, these tests are generally *discrete point assessments,* which means that these tests attempt to measure the students' overall level of English language proficiency based only on an analysis of isolated components of the language (Baca & Cervantes, 2004). Additionally, these tests neglect to measure other significant aspects of language proficiency, such as precise levels of academic language or stages of cultural acquisition.

Under NCLB, states are also required to administer standardized academic achievement tests to ELL students on an annual basis (after one year of residency in the United States). Most standardized academic achievement tests require students to have specific culturally based information in order to perform well on the test. This is often referred to as **cultural bias** and many tests are heavily biased toward the mainstream—white, English-only, middle to upper class students. As a result, students can be mislabeled when they perform poorly on a test that is not geared toward their cultural knowledge base (Baca & Cervantes, 2004). And when students who are not fully proficient in English are given academic content knowledge tests only in English, the test can become an assessment of the student's English language skills, rather than an assessment of the student's content knowledge (Abedi, 2004). Once a state determines that ELL students have attained English proficiency, they are no longer included in the group of students considered limited English proficient (Government Accountability Office [GAO], 2006).

In general, assessments used to measure English proficiency level and content-area knowledge of students learning English can have issues that result in students receiving less than proficient scores. The GAO (2006) found that a lower percentage of students considered limited English proficient achieved proficient test scores than any other selected student group.

Reclassification of ELL Students

Once assessments of both language proficiency (upon entering and yearly from then on) and content knowledge (usually after the first year of exemption) have been administered, schools follow a protocol to determine if the student should still be labeled as LEP or should be reclassified as **Fluent English Proficient (FEP)** and exited from ELL services. Once students are exited from services, most districts continue to monitor these students for one to two years to make sure that they continue to achieve academically. Table 5.2 provides an example of a guide

Table 5.2   Sample Guide to Reclassification of a Student From English Language Learner to Fluent English Proficient

Step 1: Annual assessment of English language proficiency using state-designated assessment	If student scores at advanced or higher, then move to Step 2.
Step 2: Examine student results from state standardized academic achievement tests administered in English	If student meets the school district's criterion for reclassification (usually the 50th percentile or higher), then move to Step 3.
Step 3: Obtain teacher evaluation of student academic performance	If student meets the school district's academic performance indicators for reclassification, move to Step 4.
Step 4: Parent or guardian notification	Inform parents of their rights to participate in the reclassification process (preferably in the L1). Encourage parent participation.
Step 5: Reclassification	Reclassify student as Fluent English Proficient (update files). Notify parents or guardians of reclassification status (preferably in the L1). Monitor student's progress for two years to make sure student continues to achieve academically.

to reclassification of an ELL student to Fluent English Proficient. Most states follow a similar protocol.

Some schools use data sources beyond the tests to gain a more complete picture of the student's achievement on an annual basis as well as for reclassification purposes. Using data sources such as student interviews, teacher observations, student records, student portfolios, and student work can help give a more accurate description of the language and academic levels of the student. We advocate using *multiple assessment measures* (in both the first and second languages) in *multiple contexts* to obtain a more accurate assessment of the student's proficiency levels.

Regardless of the protocols used in your state, we recommend that all teachers use a case study approach and gather additional data to gain a more holistic picture of the student's strengths in both the first and second languages, as well as to gain knowledge of the areas where the child may need focused instruction or support. When exams do not appropriately measure all aspects of proficiency, students can be designated as Fluent English Proficient and exited from ELL services, even when they are not fully proficient. In such cases, the expectations for exited ELL students are similar to those of native-English-speaking students, and often the ELL students no longer receive appropriate supports. It is not uncommon at this point for educators to refer students for placement in special education (Ortiz, 1997). To prevent the mislabeling of ELL students as having

REFER TO CASE STUDY 5.1
What data from ELL assessments were included in the decision-making process? What further information could have been helpful to the intervention team?

special needs, it is important that teachers are clear as to what aspects of proficiency are measured by the tests administered, that they gather further evidence of proficiency beyond the assessments, and that they continue to provide supports—even for those students exited from ELL services.

THE ELIGIBILITY PROCESS AND CLDE STUDENTS

In this section, we will illustrate how the assessment procedures already used for special education eligibility, some of which are mandated by policy such as NCLB or IDEA, can be broadened to take into account the language and culture of CLDE students, to include CLD families in the process, and to assess in manners that help evaluators gain a more complete picture of the student.

There are gaps in the purposes, processes, and types of information gathered during the assessment of CLDE students. If we closely examine these gaps, we notice some distinct themes:

- Teachers lack the training to distinguish between a language and cultural acquisition process and a learning disability or emotional disability.

- Standardized assessments are unable to clearly pinpoint if a child is both ELL and has special needs and are not broad enough to include multiple contexts and multiple situations.

- The cultural and linguistic voices of parents, families, and children do not always play a role in the instruction/assessment cycle.

This section will show how the specific steps in the special education referral process and assessment procedures can be enhanced for CLDE students to address the gaps in assessment and instruction through meaningful, focused, and systematic collaboration (see Figure 5.3). An enhancement of the special education eligibility steps can better provide more comprehensive data for determining appropriate placement and instructional strategies to best meet the needs of CLDE students.

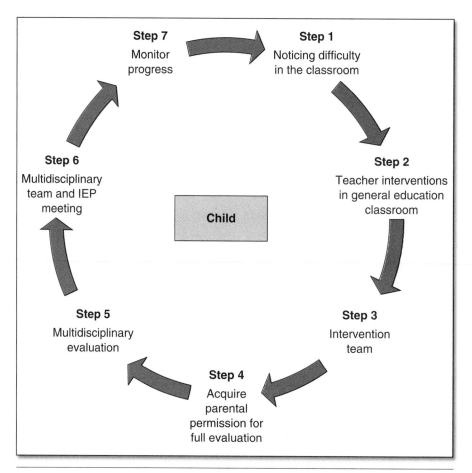

Figure 5.3   Steps in the Problem-Solving Process for Special Education Eligibility

For guiding questions for each step in this process, see the following Web link:
www.sagepub.com/grassi.

5.4

Step 1. Noticing Difficulty in the Classroom

In the conventional special education process, the teacher notices that the student is experiencing issues that impact his or her participation and progress in the general education curriculum. For example, the teacher notices that a student is not making age-appropriate progress in literacy or that a student's behavior affects his or her ability to complete assignments. The issues are not just noticed on one project or one assignment; there are patterns.

When working with ELL students who may have a special education need, this step needs to be broadened to properly assess the core of the issues. For example, when analyzing difficulties with students who are learning English, teachers must consider whether the difficulties stem from the language acquisition process or the cultural acquisition process rather than from a special education need. For example, the student could still be developing English and, therefore, be unable to compete academically at grade level at the present time. It is also possible that the student does not have strong literacy skills in the L1 and, therefore, is unable to transfer these skills into the L2. The student could also be experiencing culture shock and be unable to concentrate at the level needed to compete academically.

In order to rule out a language or cultural acquisition issue at this step, it is imperative that teachers solicit parental input and observations from an ESL or bilingual specialist or cultural broker who is from the same culture and language as the student.

Step 2. Teacher Interventions

At this stage of the conventional special education process, the teacher attempts interventions with the student to increase academic progress. For example, if the student is having difficulty with reading achievement, the teacher might try some reading strategies that typically support struggling readers, such as small group instruction, word work, and vocabulary development. The teacher documents which strategies were tried and which worked (or did not work) so this can be communicated to the intervention team if needed.

When working with CLDE students at this stage, it is imperative that teachers gather information that can help inform whether the issue possibly (or partially) could stem from the language acquisition or cultural acquisition process. If the child has not fully developed the second language and culture, then teacher interventions for this student must include strategies to help with language and cultural acquisition. Interventions that are considered "best practice" in the ESL or bilingual field should be used (see Chapters 9–15 for more on best practice strategies).

Step 3. Intervention Team

During the conventional special education process, if teacher interventions do not make a positive impact on academic achievement, then the teacher can request that the student be studied as part of the pre-referral process for special education. The intervention team meets and discusses the teachers' concerns and the interventions attempted. The **intervention team** is a problem-solving committee that is required to create a more extensive plan, suggesting a variety of teaching strategies that will support student learning. This plan includes teaching interventions that differ from the ones already implemented by the teacher to better address the specific needs of the student, a timeline for implementation of the new interventions and assessment of student progress, and suggested ways in which the teacher will collect data to show evidence of progress. The intervention team generally meets on a regularly scheduled basis (weekly, bimonthly, monthly) to discuss student issues.

Federal law does not mandate the makeup of the intervention team. Rather, the team is developed at the school or district level and every school's configuration may be different. When working with ELL students, however, it is critical for the intervention team to include a cultural liaison, the parents or caregivers, and a professional trained in ESL or bilingual education strategies. The cultural liaison must be from the same culture and language as the child and should be an active participant in the process to explain the intervention team process to the parents and the student, help the parents and the student have voice during the process, and make sure the process is culturally appropriate. The ESL or bilingual professional should make recommendations to the student's general education or content-area teacher concerning teaching interventions that might increase the academic success of the student. These interventions may include changing the student's language acquisition support to include more instruction in the home language, or putting the student in a classroom with a teacher who is trained in ESL or bilingual techniques. These interventions may also include cultural acquisition support for both the student and the family. Finally, both the cultural liaison and the ESL or bilingual professional should advocate for multiple assessments in multiple contexts to gain a more accurate picture of the student's strengths and challenges.

Step 4. Acquiring Parental Permission

In the conventional special education process, if the teacher has implemented the intervention team plan from Step 3, and the student continues not to make academic progress, the student can then be referred for full special education evaluation. Before the special education evaluation can begin, however, the parents or caregivers must give written permission for the child to be evaluated. The parents or caregivers are also informed of their special education rights and procedural safeguards and must be informed of these rights before they give written permission for evaluation.

One of the major issues when implementing Step 4 with culturally and linguistically diverse students and their families is that parents often do not understand what they are signing, do not understand what the evaluation consists of or why it is being conducted, and do not fully understand their rights (Al-Hassan & Gardner, 2002). Here, it is imperative that a cultural liaison or interpreter be present and have ample time to explain the process and to answer questions. The cultural perceptions of "disability," discussed in Chapter 2, may become more apparent. Parents may not understand why their child needs testing, may not see the child's issues as a "disability," and, in many instances, will not understand why the teacher cannot simply address the issues in the general education classroom. If the intervention team deems it necessary to conduct a full evaluation of the child, then language and cultural interpretations and clear documentation become very important to gain the family's support (Al-Hassan & Gardner, 2002).

Step 5. Multidisciplinary Evaluation

If parental permission is procured, the **Multidisciplinary Assessment Team (MAST)** will conduct a full evaluation of the child. The multidisciplinary team consists of specialists who are trained to conduct evaluations in the following areas:

a. Cognitive functioning evaluation—designed to assess how the child learns and what he or she is capable of learning.

b. Speech and language evaluation—designed to assess speech production and expressive and receptive language skills.

c. Educational evaluation—designed to show the current academic level of the student.

d. Social or emotional evaluation (obtained from parent interviews and teacher observations)—designed to collect data about the child's social and emotional functioning in diverse settings such as in the academic classroom, on the playground, interacting with peers, or when following rules.

e. Health or physical condition evaluation—designed to review the child's health and whether his or her health situation affects development. This evaluation looks for milestones in child development such as premature birth, and walking and talking in the appropriate developmental sequence. This evaluation also includes hearing and vision screening.

f. Parent interview—conducted in order to obtain any other pertinent information and to give parents an opportunity to discuss their hopes, priorities, and concerns about their child.

When working with ELL students, the evaluations should be conducted in the student's strongest language (Al-Hassan & Gardner, 2002; McCardle, Mele-McCarthy, & Leos, 2005). If a version of the evaluation in the first language of the student is not available, then it is recommended that the student be given more time or other **modifications** to process the information and perform to his or her full capability. Remember that standardized test results may not be accurate due to bias and sometimes it is more helpful to disregard protocol and let the child have more time or modifications to see how far he or she can go. This information can be reported, not in a standardized fashion, but in a way that informs the teacher as to the learning style of the child and strategies that help the child learn. Sometimes the information from the test, rather than the score, can provide a richer description of the student.

It is also very important that those conducting evaluations understand the language acquisition process, for example, knowing the wait-time needed for students to process in more than one language. They should understand the types of grammatical, phonological, and discourse errors that ELL students make as well as the types of errors made in interlanguage (see Chapter 3). ELL students are not just acquiring the language; they are acquiring the culture as well. The evaluator should be able to differentiate between culturally appropriate and inappropriate behaviors in the child's first culture. The evaluator should also ask the parents and the child questions about their culture and culturally appropriate school behaviors (McCardle, Mele-McCarthy, & Leos, 2005).

The evaluator should also be familiar with the concept of culture shock and the behaviors students exhibit during this stage. When ELL students experience culture shock, their academic and social behavior often mirrors that of students with special needs. Therefore, we recommend including an *acculturation evaluation* in the multidisciplinary evaluation to determine the child's cultural acquisition status. This may help rule out a special education need.

We also recommend that the evaluators observe the child in multiple settings and multiple times. Students may perform differently according to their comfort level in different settings. The evaluators should take note of differences in behavior and achievement according to setting (McCardle, Mele-McCarthy, & Leos, 2005).

When conducting evaluations such as the health history or parent interviews, it is very important that a relationship has been previously established with the parents. Everything must be conducted in the home language and the interpreter should be accompanied by a cultural liaison who will understand and be able to interpret parents' answers and behaviors. In this manner, the evaluator is able to solicit maximum parent contribution.

Finally, one cannot discuss the evaluation of ELL students without mentioning test bias. Test bias exists when a test produces systematically differential performance among test takers of the *same ability* but from *different subgroups* (such as gender, age, race, or ethnicity). Test bias can be exhibited through the content of the test, the response format of the test, the implementation and scoring of the test, the test environment, and through student access to the testing situation (Kunnan, 2005). If differences in performance on a test between two or more subgroups (age, gender, race, or ethnicity) exist, this indicates test bias and this test should not be used for placement purposes, special education eligibility, or for any high-stakes situation.

> For a detailed discussion of test bias, see the following Web link: **www.sagepub .com/grassi.**

5.5

Step 6. Multidisciplinary–IEP Meeting

At this step in the instruction/assessment cycle, the multidisciplinary team has conducted a full evaluation of the student and meets to determine eligibility for special education services. If the student qualifies for special education, the team will develop an IEP and the family will be involved in an IEP meeting. Under IDEA, this meeting must include the parents, the general education teacher, the special education teacher, an administrative representative, the student (when appropriate), and other individuals (at the discretion of the parent or school) who have knowledge and expertise regarding the student. See Table 5.3 for a list of the elements that must be included in the IEP document.

Table 5.3   Required Elements in an IEP

Specific requirements and formats may vary somewhat between states and even school districts, but all IEP documents are required by federal law to contain the following elements:

- Present level of performance
- Annual goals and short-term objectives
- Extent of participation in general education
- Services and modifications needed
- Behavior intervention plan
- Date of initiation of services, frequency and duration of service and modifications
- Strategies for evaluation
- Transition plan (16 years or older)
- Signatures of participants in the development of IEP (including parents)
- Justification of the placement decision

When working with ELL students and their families, there are several points to consider before and during an IEP meeting (adapted from Cartledge et al., 2009).

Before the IEP Meeting

1. Placement—if there is not a bilingual special education setting, the team must decide on the most appropriate setting that (a) gives access to language acquisition development, (b) provides the least restrictive environment, (c) provides culturally relevant strategies and environment, and (d) provides support for the child's disability.

2. Make sure you have established a solid relationship with the family or caregivers first. Make time for informal conversations about the student and parent expectations for school.

3. Meet with the family before the IEP meeting and carefully explain the process: who will be there, what they will say, the tests that have been used and what they measure, questions the family can ask and how to ask them. Meeting with the caregivers first does not impede the collaboration of the IEP team; rather, this will encourage active participation from the family members and understanding of the IEP meeting (Al-Hassan & Gardner, 2002).

During the IEP Meeting

1. Make sure an interpreter, and a cultural broker or liaison, is present. Do not engage in direct translation (directly translating word for word). Most languages do not translate literally and the manner of speaking must be changed in order for the languages to be mutually comprehensible. Direct translation can result in cultural misunderstandings and should never be used (Al-Hassan & Gardner, 2002). In addition, it is not appropriate to use children to interpret. It is not uncommon for children who are translating for their parents to change the way they stand, their voice tone, and the sentence structure (as well as the content of the sentence) in order to make the message comprehensible and socially acceptable either to their parents, or to the person their parents are attempting to communicate with.

2. Involve all stakeholders in the decision-making process. Make sure that stakeholders are given voice by (a) having interpreters and cultural brokers or liaisons present; (b) cuing parents when it is appropriate to ask questions, provide information, and express opinions; and (c) using terms that are accessible to all present.

3. Make the focus of the meeting the functionality and the symptoms of the disorder. Do not use terms such as "disability," "disorder," or "problem." Explain the symptoms, how they affect academic achievement, and detail the steps that can be taken to increase academic achievement. Talk about the symptoms in a clinical, medical sense.

4. Consider running the IEP meeting in a different format. It is most common in IEP meetings for each professional to summarize and explain their assessment results. This may not be necessary. Some of the data collected on the child may not be relevant to the issues that the team deems most important. The team should bring forth data that support the creation of specific learning goals or provide evidence of the child's strengths, not data that emphasize the "problem."

Step 7. Monitoring Progress

The student's IEP must be reviewed annually and every three years the student must be reevaluated for eligibility. Every professional working with the student should be aware of the goals and objectives listed on the IEP. The teacher who is working with the student must also review and monitor progress toward the goals and objectives. If the goals are deemed inappropriate at any point by any member of the IEP team, the team can be reconvened to adjust the IEP.

When reviewing the goals and objectives of a CLDE student, the language and cultural acquisition process must be listed on the IEP and continually monitored. It is important that CLDE students continue to make progress in language and cultural acquisition and the IEP team must reevaluate this growth annually (at least). If progress in language and culture is not noted, then placement should be reconsidered. Teachers working with the CLDE child should be well versed in strategies to meet the particular needs of the student and the teacher's interventions should be adjusted to the growth of the student. The IEP should be a "living document" and used to guide instructional planning.

For sample IEP goals for a CLDE student, see the following Web link: **www.sage pub.com/grassi.**

5.6

For a flowchart detailing the steps of the special education referral process, see the following Web link: **www.sagepub.com/grassi.**

5.7

TAILORING ASSESSMENT PROCEDURES FOR **CLDE** STUDENTS

REFER TO CASE STUDY 5.1

Consider each step as described in page 110. What data were included and what information would be needed to make the best possible eligibility and placement decisions for José? What actions did the school take to include the parent perspective throughout the process? How else did the school ensure that cultural and language perspectives were included?

More than half of all students served under IDEA are labeled as learning disabled (OSERS, 2003). New regulations as part of the 2004 reauthorization of IDEA give an alternative to the manner in which "specific learning disability" eligibility can be determined. Eligibility processes for specific learning disabilities traditionally involved the discrepancy model. Now eligibility includes the option of Response to Intervention. Thus, schools can use evidence of the child's failure to respond to instructional interventions as part of the data documenting the presence of a specific learning disability (Brown-Chidsey & Steege, 2005).

5.8

To see specific regulations concerning learning disability eligibility, see the following Web link: **www.sagepub.com/grassi.**

Discrepancy Model and CLDE Students

Historically, the discrepancy model has been used to determine eligibility for special education for those with a learning disability. In this model, a student's academic achievement level (measured by tests such as the Woodcock–Johnson or other achievement tests) is compared to their intelligence level (measured by IQ tests). When there is a discrepancy between intelligence and achievement—and each state sets its own standards concerning the discrepancy level for eligibility—the child is determined to have a learning disability. For example, if Alfred has an IQ of 105 but only scores at an 80 level on the Woodcock–Johnson math subtest (which is normed in the same manner as the IQ test), then there is a discrepancy between his intellectual ability and his math achievement and Alfred would qualify for special education services in math. In other words, Alfred intellectually has the potential to score at or above 105 on the Woodcock–Johnson math subtest, but is achieving below that level.

The discrepancy model does not take into account the process of acquiring a second language and culture. When evaluating ELL students, it is important that both IQ and academic achievement tests are implemented in the stronger language of the student. It is also important that the evaluators are familiar with the culture of the student and understand the stages of cultural acquisition. If the assessment tools used exhibit cultural or linguistic bias, then the information gathered from these tests could be inaccurate and consequently lead to labeling a child with a learning disability that is not necessarily present (see the discussion of test bias earlier in this chapter).

For a comparison of RTI and discrepancy models, see the following Web link: **www.sagepub.com/grassi.**

5.9

Response to Intervention and CLDE Students

Taking the same scenario presented above, let us assume Alfred is not achieving in math classes. First steps under the Response to Intervention (RTI) model would be to have the RTI team collaboratively work with the teacher to implement research-based instructional strategies (see Chapters 9–15) that might benefit Alfred. These research-based strategies need to be implemented with fidelity and for enough time to impact the child's achievement (recommendations are generally from six to eight weeks). Once these strategies have been consistently implemented in the class, the teacher collects data on the child's achievement and the child's response to the intervention strategies. The data is then brought to the RTI team and analyzed to determine whether the student is responding positively to intervention or not. If the response is positive, the teacher should continue with the interventions. If the response is negative, then the team decides whether to try different instructional interventions or to implement a higher level of intervention such as a full multidisciplinary assessment or special education referral. For a depiction of this process, see Figure 5.4.

In most cases, the RTI model begins to address issues from the onset by providing opportunities for teachers to examine the strategies they are implementing to determine if, how, and why they are meeting the needs of a struggling learner in their classroom. Students are given an opportunity to access curriculum in a variety of ways before it is assumed that a disability exists. By focusing on teaching and by providing a framework for collecting and analyzing data about the impact of teaching strategies, RTI can provide support for struggling learners in the general education or secondary content-area classroom before special education professionals become fully involved.[2]

One of the benefits of RTI is that it gives power to stakeholders (such as teachers) to make decisions based on children's needs and not necessarily based on numbers from test results. RTI puts the onus on the teachers to solve the

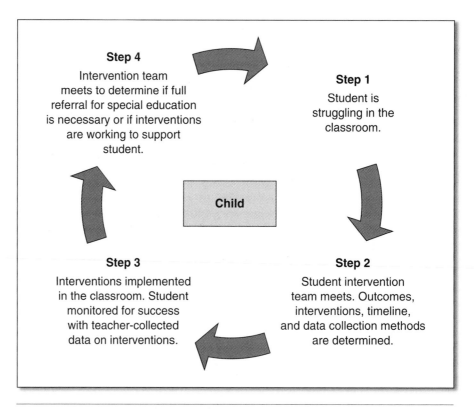

Figure 5.4   The Problem-Solving Cycle in Response to Intervention

problem and promotes access to good instruction for all students. Because intervention suggestions are implemented immediately when a child is having trouble in the classroom (rather than having to wait until a certain age or grade for testing), RTI can also support students with learning disabilities earlier in their academic career before the discrepancy grows and students get farther behind in schooling.

While RTI can be a positive support for students, there are shortcomings when considering the education of CLDE students. To begin, research-based strategies for the general education or content-area classroom do not necessarily take into account modifications or strategies specifically designed for students learning English (such as bilingual education or ESL instruction). Very few general education, content-area teachers, or special education teachers are trained in ESL or bilingual strategies and if the RTI team does not include professionals from the second language field, then the "best" strategies may still be ineffective with ELL students.

Another issue involves consistency. Every teacher will interpret and implement "research-based" strategies in a different manner. Therefore, when students are educated by many different teachers, consistency across curriculum (especially at the secondary level) is difficult to achieve, and academic success may be apparent in one class but not necessarily in another. It is important for teachers to have consistent training and coaching in strategies to best meet the needs of struggling students, including the needs of students learning English.

Finally, teachers are often not trained in how to collect pertinent data to monitor the student's progress and to determine the effectiveness of strategies. And the gathering of pertinent data, when working with ELL students, requires the teacher to monitor the student with many different tools and in many different contexts. In order to determine if the academic and behavioral problems stem from the linguistic or cultural acquisition process or from a true learning disability, multiple measures in multiple contexts, as well as full involvement from parents or cultural liaisons is imperative when conducting an RTI cycle. For example, let's say the teacher has implemented many different strategies with an ELL student, and the student continues to struggle in the classroom. When the teacher monitors the student in different contexts (such as when working in the first language or when working with people from his or her own culture), however, she or he notices a marked reduction in the child's behavioral or academic struggles (see Photo 5.2). This, then, would be an obvious indicator that the child's issues stem from the cultural and linguistic acquisition process. Possible monitoring measures to use when evaluating ELL students include observations in different contexts (playground, lunchroom, hallways, elective classes),

Photo 5.2 Tapping into student extracurricular activities can help students engage academically.

REFER TO CASE STUDY 5.1

Was José eligible for special education services by the RTI process or through the discrepancy model? Provide evidence to defend your ideas.

home visits and parent interviews, observations from cultural liaisons, and oral and written language assessments in both first and second languages.

Functional Behavior Assessments and CLDE Students

Functional behavior assessment (FBA) is used to analyze behavioral issues. When a child's behavior is disruptive to a classroom environment and to his or her own learning, a teacher needs to examine the function of that behavior. Most often, behavior is a way to communicate, and teachers should attempt to figure out what the behavior is indicating. In order to assess the function of the behavior, the following steps must be followed (see Figure 5.5):

1. Collect data on the types of behaviors exhibited.

2. Look at when, where, and how the behavior is exhibited. An ABC chart is effective: A—what is the *antecedent* to the behavior, B—what is the actual *behavior,* and C—what are the *consequences* of the behavior.

3. Try to analyze what function the behavior is serving for the student— what is the child gaining from this behavior?

4. The teacher and the intervention team must work to figure out an alternative or replacement behavior for the student.

A functional behavior assessment must be implemented as a part of a behavior plan if the student's behavior is due to disability.

One of the greatest issues with the functional behavior assessment and ELL students is that behavior is culturally determined. That is, what is deemed appropriate behavior in one culture may be deemed inappropriate in another culture. A functional behavior assessment assumes that the culture of the teacher, who is ultimately judging the behavior, is the norm. As a result, students who behave in a way that is uncomfortable for the teacher may be assumed to have behavioral issues when, in fact, these children may be behaving in a culturally appropriate manner. In order to prevent misdiagnosis of a culturally and linguistically diverse student as having behavioral issues, the intervention team should include a cultural interpreter who can carefully monitor the child for culturally appropriate and inappropriate behavior.

Another issue concerns culture shock or the process of cultural acquisition. When a child is learning English and the accompanying culture, the behaviors the student exhibits can be extreme (see Chapter 4). Therefore, it is imperative that culture shock be ruled out before the student is referred for special education services due to behavioral issues.

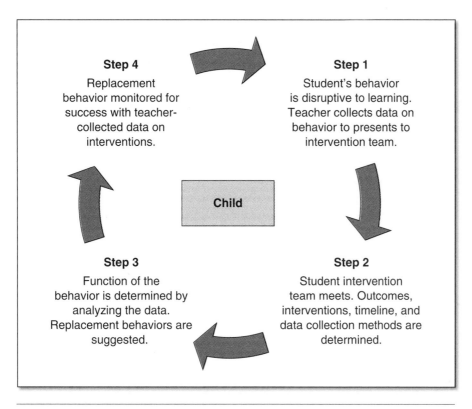

Figure 5.5   The Problem-Solving Cycle in Functional Behavior Assessment

Again, some of the most effective strategies for preventing misidentification due to cultural mismatch are to assess the child in multiple contexts, diversify the team to include professionals in second language acquisition and professionals from the same language and culture as the child, and actively seek the observations of the parents.

For a case study on conducting a functional behavior assessment, see the following Web link: **www.sagepub.com/grassi.**

5.10

Gifted and Talented CLDE Students

Although the label of gifted and talented (GT) does not fall under the federal guidelines of IDEA, it does warrant discussion, especially when considering the education of CLDE students.

The current definition of giftedness from the U.S. Department of Education is derived from the Jacob K. Javits Gifted and Talented Students Education Act of 1988 and was incorporated into the NCLB:

> Children and youth with outstanding talent perform or show the potential for performing at remarkably high levels of accomplishment when compared with others of their age, experience, or environment. These children and youth exhibit high performance capability in intellectual, creative, or artistic areas, possess an unusual leadership capacity, or excel in specific academic fields. They require services or activities not ordinarily provided by schools. Outstanding talents are present in children and youth from all cultural groups, across all economic strata, and in all areas of human endeavor. (USDOE, 1993, p. 3)

Every school district has a different manner of identifying and labeling gifted and talented learners; however, most often, general education teachers, secondary content-area teachers, or parents are instrumental in the initial stages of the process, for they are often the first people to recognize that a child may be gifted. When working with culturally and linguistically diverse students, this initial identification can be problematic, and CLDE students have been, and continue to be, underrepresented in gifted education (Cartledge et al., 2009).

To begin, many parents from cultures other than the dominant culture do not know the process for recommending their child. Some parents are from cultures that value group rather than individual achievement and would not make an effort for their child to "stand out." And, just as elaborated in Case Study 1.1, culturally diverse parents may not advocate for their child and bring the child's gifts to the attention of the teacher.

Many teachers do not recognize the culturally appropriate classroom behaviors of students from diverse cultures. As a result, these students may not be perceived as exhibiting behaviors most commonly cited as those "typically displayed by gifted students" (see Clark, 2002). Without proper training, teachers may fail to recognize behaviors of culturally and linguistically diverse students that exhibit giftedness (Cartledge et al., 2009). If students are developing the English language and the teacher is monolingual, it can be difficult for the teacher to recognize complex thinking and problem solving when the child does not have the language skills to express this in the second language.

If assessments such as formal test results, informal assessments, or student products are used to determine GT eligibility, these assessments can be biased—that is, they do not reflect the language variety or culture of the test taker, they do not account for multiple types of intelligence, and they may be heavily language based, which can cause difficulty for ELL students.

Finally, the strengths of bilingual, bicultural children are often not recognized in the dominant school system as "gifts" or "talents." As Valdés (2003) points out, the cognitive, linguistic, and creative compensatory strategies utilized by bilingual children to overcome linguistic shortcomings are higher-level cognitive skills and should be recognized as such. For example, translation and interpretation, which many bilingual children are involved in for family members, involve many complex cognitive processes. Students are expected to "retrieve words quickly, repeat a message while listening simultaneously, remember what has been said, and evaluate the target language by reflecting on language structure and the meaning it conveys" (Valdés, 2003, p. 30). Child translators are expected to exhibit excellent memory, abstract word knowledge, and abstract reasoning—all skills identified under most definitions of giftedness.

In order to promote equal consideration of the gifts and talents of diverse students, we advocate for schools to use multiple measures in multiple contexts to determine GT eligibility. Manifestations of giftedness may involve assessing the child from different perspectives, including those of cultural brokers and parents or caregivers. Cartledge et al. (2009) also recommend assessing students who are learning English with nonverbal intelligence tests such as the Naglieri Non-Verbal Abilities Test or Raven's Matrix Analogies Tests, in order to give these students an opportunity to show their strengths without heavy reliance on the English language. GT eligibility should also become a consideration of the school's student intervention team. Teachers need to assess carefully the achievement and behavior of diverse students by fully utilizing culturally sensitive tools, cultural liaisons, and parent perspectives to capture the full picture of the student. When working with ELL and CLDE students, achievement and behavioral issues can mask GT, as these students can also be low performing or have behavior issues in the classroom.

Summary

- Current assessment procedures and policies used to place students in special education or ESL or bilingual programs may not be adequate for students who need support in both areas.

- Teachers need to have a clear understanding of existing policy as well as how assessment procedures can be broadened to address the needs of CLDE students.

- Keys to improving services for CLDE students include diversifying the professionals involved, actively seeking the input of parents, and assessing the child in multiple contexts, all of which will help evaluators gain a more complete picture of the student.

Key Terms

Adequate yearly progress (AYP)

Cultural bias

Disability categories

Fluent English Proficient (FEP)

Free and appropriate public education (FAPE)

Functional behavior assessment (FBA)

Instruction/assessment cycle

Intervention team

Modifications

Multidisciplinary Assessment Team (MAST)

Activities for Further Understanding

1. Find out about the intervention team at your school. Who are the members? When do they meet? What process do they follow? How does this team compare to the suggestions put forward in this chapter?

2. Attend an intervention team meeting. Who is present? What is each person's role? What data is presented? What are the next steps for supporting the student? How did this meeting compare to the suggestions put forth in this chapter?

3. Look online at a local school district's Web site. Find out what the processes are for ELL eligibility, for special education eligibility, for behavior interventions, and for GT eligibility. Are CLDE students mentioned? Are language and cultural acquisition mentioned? What recommendations could you make to improve support for identifying the needs of CLDE learners in the district's processes?

4. Attend an IEP meeting for a CLDE student. Who is present? What is each person's role? What data is presented? What are the next steps for supporting the student? How did this process compare to the suggestions put forth in this chapter?

Notes

1. School districts and state educational agencies may describe the categories differently. Some of the more common terms used at the local and state levels are listed in the descriptions in Web Link 1.2. Teachers need to be aware of the terms their particular school or district uses.

2. Research on the effectiveness of RTI on culturally and linguistically diverse students is limited. Schools are still in the process of responding to changes in IDEA and are still developing full implementation of RTI in this context.

Visit the Student Study Site at **www.sagepub.com/grassi** for chapter-specific study resources.

Chapter 6

COLLABORATION SKILLS

CASE STUDY 6.1   **Interview With a Secondary Math Teacher**

Question—What do you perceive as the major issues teachers face when working with CLDE students?

Teacher—First, the departments are very separated, and we should be working together. But instead, it is more of a special education versus ELL super bowl championship. Second, it is hard for us to distinguish between the L2 acquisition process and special education needs, especially when we don't speak the native languages of our kids. We know from our studies in linguistics that a child cannot move or progress in their L2 acquisition if the cognitive piece isn't also being met in their L1. Third, we have a hard time providing services for a child if they don't have a label. There again, we can't give them a proper label until they can be tested. They can't be tested until they have been in the U.S. education system for quite some time, leaving the child behind and inadequately educated. Do you see now why the process is the biggest quagmire you will ever have to work with as an ELL teacher?

Question—What support do you get for working with CLDE students?

Teacher—The district won't evaluate the kids if they have had less than three years of educational history in the United States, so we don't get any support from the special education department. They won't even talk to us when it comes to this issue because they need to make sure it's not a language issue first. We have had students who have disabilities such as TBI and dyslexia and even though we go to the intervention team meeting with piles and piles of evidence, they won't even look at the students because they have been in the ESL program for less than three years. What it really boils down to is the fact that they need to consider the language issue first because years ago lots of ELL students were placed into special education classrooms and it was overdone. Now they are terrified to put any ELL student in a special education classroom—which is a good fear, but not the best for all children. We have the numbers to prove that something is needed and that this fits but we just can't get the support that we need.

—Middle school ELL math teacher interview, May 2007

Consider the case study above:

- How can school professionals utilize the expertise of one another to meet CLDE student needs?
- What skills are needed to foster professional relationships?
- What is the administrator's role in fostering a collaborative school culture?
- How can collaboration skills be utilized to facilitate relationships between and among departments within a school?

SOURCE: Used by permission.

Special education procedures are immersed in a problem-solving model—looking at the difficulties a student is experiencing and trying to find the right interventions to support the child. The eligibility process, the student intervention team process, and the functional behavior assessment all use a similar model that promotes the use of data, research-based strategies, and collaboration between a variety of school professionals and families. It is the expansion of "collaboration" that can make the most significant impact on these processes for CLDE students.

As noted in Case Study 6.1, there can be a lack of collaboration between language specialists and special education specialists. This lack of collaboration can stem from historical overrepresentation of ELL students in special education classrooms. Giving time for the language to be fully acquired is a wise caution to employ when working with ELL students. However, as we have discussed throughout the book, misidentification can possibly be avoided by incorporating strategies addressing language acquisition and cultural relevance during the instructional planning process, by assessing in multiple contexts with multiple measures, and by expanding and diversifying the intervention team.

DIVERSIFYING THE CONCEPT OF COLLABORATION

In today's data-driven school climates, where teams of educational professionals work together to find solutions and interventions to meet student needs, all teachers need to learn concepts of collaborative problem-solving skills to effectively work. A diversified intervention team can more fully evaluate the cultural and linguistic issues of the child and possibly help to distinguish between the language acquisition process and a special education need. Each member of the team brings a different viewpoint of the educational process and a unique view of the student:

1. The *general education* or *content-area teacher* promotes access to the general education curriculum and can often give insight to current functioning in the classroom.

2. The *ESL or bilingual specialist* helps access information to determine which school issues stem from a language acquisition process and which school issues stem from a special education need. The ESL or bilingual specialist also supports language and cultural acquisition and provides strategies that promote access to the general education curriculum for an ELL student.

3. The *special education professionals* support the classroom or content-area teacher in addressing the child's special education needs by providing appropriate accommodations and modifications.

4. The *cultural broker or interpreter* helps access information that will help determine which school issues stem from a language acquisition process or cultural difference. The cultural broker or interpreter also builds relationships between the teachers, family, and student.

5. The *family* provides crucial information concerning the cultural and linguistic background of the student, including insight as to how culture and language play a role in academic and social success, the strengths of the child in the first language and culture, and the health and educational history of the child.

Together, a collaborative group, including the members described above, can consider assessments that provide a more complete picture of the strengths of the student and interventions to help teachers build upon those strengths. When collaborating across disciplines and areas of expertise, teachers have more resources from which to choose in supporting *all* facets of a child's needs—academic, linguistic, cultural, and behavioral.

REFER TO CASE STUDY 6.1

How would collaboration with a variety of experts alleviate some of the teacher's frustrations and provide more complete services for the students?

FOUNDATIONS OF COLLABORATION

Collaboration is an interactive process that enables teachers with diverse expertise to provide quality instructional services to students with a wide range of needs (Idol, Nevin, & Paolucci-Whitcomb, 2000). What follows is a list of the defining characteristics of collaboration and how they apply to CLDE students (adapted from Friend & Cook, 2007; Texas Education Agency, 2000):

- *Collaboration is voluntary.* Even if teachers are assigned to an intervention team, they make choices about how much to participate and how invested in the process they will become. When working with CLDE students, schools need to make certain that all stakeholders understand how vital they are to a student's success.

- *Collaboration is based on parity.* In a true collaborative process, all members of the team have an equal voice. For CLDE students, that requires due consideration of both the linguistic and special education aspects of the child's learning needs. Expertise from both fields needs to have equal weight for effective instructional and placement interventions.

- *Collaboration requires a shared goal.* Team members must have an agreed understanding of the goal. For CLDE students, the goals should address the language acquisition process, the cultural acquisition process, and the special education issue.

- *Collaboration requires reciprocity* of ideas and teaching, that is, shared responsibility, shared accountability, and shared resources. Teachers maintain mutual responsibility for the students in the class; members of the team own the problem-solving process in all aspects—planning, instructing, evaluating, and decision making. Educational professionals should examine the supportive roles available in the school (paraprofessionals, specialists, and teachers) and the instructional resources and knowledge these professionals hold. By problem solving together, stakeholders can determine how resources can be used most effectively to meet the needs of the child. The accountability and responsibility for any action plans should be shared among the professionals involved. This means that all teachers and paraprofessionals—not just ESL or special education teachers—must adhere to a student's IEP or intervention plan, including any language or cultural acquisition issues addressed in the plan.

- *Collaboration is an emerging process.* To solve a problem together takes time, trust, and respect. Relationships must be built among the separate specialties, as well as with parents, and frequent, even short, meetings can help this process. Meetings should take place not only when there is a problem, but also to communicate about student successes, to explain the processes, to discuss issues and gain better comprehension from the perspectives of all involved, and to encourage input from all stakeholders.

- *Collaboration requires interactive communication.* Actively listening to each other and asking clarifying questions, speaking in language that is clear to all participants, and employing positive nonverbal communication is extremely important when working across fields and across cultures. Specialists must use language that is not laden with jargon so everyone can understand. If culturally and linguistically diverse parents are present, then removing idioms and specialized language will increase comprehension. It is important that school professionals consult with a cultural liaison, or have one present, to understand more deeply any cultural nuances in meetings.

- *Collaboration includes conflict resolution.* Allowing adequate time to discuss issues and differences that come up, and fostering open communication, can help avoid ongoing misunderstandings. Cultural awareness training can help assist in this situation and a cultural liaison should be present at all times, especially when professionals are working with families from cultures that differ from their own.

REFER TO CASE STUDY 6.1

Which aspects of collaboration are present? What would need to happen to include fully all aspects of collaboration?

CREATING A COLLABORATIVE SCHOOL CULTURE

If we are truly going to meet the complex needs of CLDE students, we need to utilize the expertise, the strategies, and the support of specialists in schools. Placement in the general education or content-area classroom provides CLDE students with access to the rich and full curriculum opportunities. This access is further supported when co-teaching or co-planning provides specialized instruction and planning that targets the special education and language needs of CLDE students. The benefits of two teachers working together go beyond the needs of the labeled students; the rest of the class also benefits as instructional goals can be more precisely targeted for everyone (see Photo 6.2).

Photo 6.2 Collaboration between teachers for CLDE student success.

That said, we realize that co-teaching and co-planning require resources to be successful—teachers must be provided time to plan, must have the administrative support to schedule their classes together, and the school must allocate funding for co-teaching opportunities. Training may be required for teachers to co-teach and co-plan in an effective manner. Some of this training will take place as the co-teaching relationship develops. For example, when an ESL specialist and a general education or content-area teacher work together, they learn content from each other, strategies to make the content accessible to various students, and they learn the philosophical background to each other's specialty. When collaboration is a part of the school culture, the sharing of ideas becomes the norm and learning begins to occur on many levels. Teachers learn from each other, share ideas, and a strong sense of community begins to develop where students are not "one teacher's problem" but are embraced by the school as a whole.

In order to collaborate effectively with all stakeholders in the process, school administrators must assume a pivotal role. Administrators need to support the philosophy of collaboration by fostering a culture within the school that promotes collaborative ideals. This can be done through schedule design, meeting time, room space, and resource allocation. Administrators should also take an active role in envisioning how to pull from the strengths of the entire faculty by breaking out of the "departmental boxes," looking at professionals individually, and examining what they can bring to the process. Table 6.1 lists additional ideas from a former school administrator for fostering a collaborative school culture. That being said, administrators can only start the process; stakeholders must take the responsibility for continued collaboration.

> **REFER TO CASE STUDY 6.1**
>
> Which aspects of a collaborative school culture are missing? What could the teacher suggest to the administrator of the school to better meet the needs of CLDE students?

Table 6.1   Top Ten Tips for Collaboration

1. Focus on the students—make decisions based on what is best for students as the primary focus.

2. Build trusting relationships that lay the foundation to make it through both the calm and troubled waters.

3. Expect the best from one another—make positive presuppositions the rule.

4. Set guidelines for how to work together and take collective responsibility—"our students" rather than "your students" or "my students."

(Continued)

Table 6.1 (Continued)

5. Promote the culture of sharing and learning from each other through open communication and by honoring the contributions of all team members.

6. Build team skills such as respectful listening, managing conflict, reaching consensus, and setting goals.

7. Make the best use of individual and team strengths.

8. Be intentional about building and sharing leadership.

9. Seek support for your collaborative efforts through professional growth opportunities and needed resources (especially time).

10. Recognize and celebrate your successes and efforts.

SOURCE: Kathleen S. Nutting, Former School Administrator.

CO-TEACHING AS COLLABORATION

CASE STUDY 6.2 | Co-Teaching

During my first year as a special education teacher, co-teaching opportunities were few and far between. Many of the general education teachers were not interested in co-teaching and other teachers did not like having another teacher in their classroom "disrupting" the flow. Having come directly out of a teacher education program that strongly encouraged co-teaching, I was baffled by this negative perspective of co-teaching. I decided that I had to work on changing teachers' perspectives of co-teaching, but how could *I* do this?

I went into my second year of teaching with the intention to focus on ways to increase co-teaching opportunities. By returning to the same school, I began to form stronger working relationships and developed more trust with all the teachers. I had an idea of how teachers ran their classrooms from student observations I had completed the previous year. This particular year I was fortunate to have the largest percentage of my caseload in fourth grade—the two fourth grade teachers happened to be the most open-minded and progressive teachers in the school. The fourth grade teachers and I began meeting regularly to discuss student needs and I kept mentioning co-teaching and how I could help in the classroom. Eventually, both fourth grade teachers agreed to co-teach math and writing with me.

At first, I must admit, I felt like a highly trained teacher's aide, but after a few months the teachers began to trust me more. As they became more comfortable with me in the class, the more opportunities I had to show them that I could teach as well. We began planning, teaching, and reflecting together—and we began to see better student achievement from all students in the class, not just the students with special needs. The fourth grade teachers liked the support I was offering and they began to talk to other teachers. Soon other teachers were interested in co-teaching and the principal, who previously saw co-teaching as a waste of resources, began to support the idea as well. The fourth grade teachers and I modeled what co-teaching could look like and this was a powerful way to increase buy in from other teachers and administration.

It was wonderful to finally put what I learned about co-teaching into practice. I realized how time-consuming co-teaching was, but that was outweighed by the benefit it had on student achievement. I know it is not realistic in most school settings to co-teach with all teachers or in all classes. Rather, special education teachers should choose to co-teach in the classes that best meet the needs of the students.

—Jamie Erickson, Special Education teacher

Consider the case study above:

- What learning advantages can co-teaching bring to the classroom?
- What are some of the challenges of implementing co-teaching?
- What steps can be taken to create a positive co-teaching relationship?

SOURCE: Used by permission.

Co-teaching occurs when two teachers work as partners. They collaboratively create solutions to identify and address instructional and student problems; they create units of study; they plan and modify lessons; they carry out classroom instruction; and they supervise student work (Sands et al., 2000). The main goal of co-teaching is to bring intense and individualized instruction to students in a general education, content-area setting, while also giving students access to the rich and full curriculum (Friend & Cook, 2007).

The advantages of co-teaching are many. Co-teaching can provide students with opportunities that would not be present otherwise. For example, all students receive more adult attention in co-taught classes. Students who are struggling in the classroom receive an extra instructional boost, and achievement and social skills can be enhanced. For students who are academically gifted, they may have more opportunities to complete alternative assignments and participate in enrichment activities (Friend & Cook, 2007). Co-teaching provides students with more individualized and diversified learning experiences; more innovative instruction through the sharing of ideas, energy, and materials; increased responsiveness to student needs during instruction; and increased exposure to diverse backgrounds, experience, and teaching styles when pulling from both teachers (Sands et al., 2000).

When administrators and faculty are considering schedules for co-teaching, the needs of the students in the class should be a part of that discussion. Would a class benefit from the expertise of an ESL or bilingual specialist? Does a student's IEP require the extra support of a special education teacher or a speech and language specialist? Could the student (and the class) benefit from a co-teaching situation in the general education or content-area classroom? How should the caseload of specialists be distributed to better meet students' needs? The concept of co-teaching works best when it is addressed intentionally in both short-term and long-term planning.

There are three foundational models for co-teaching a particular lesson or class, which are detailed below (adapted from Friend & Cook, 2007; Sands et al., 2000):

1. One teacher teaches the whole group and one teacher works in a supporting role

2. Both teachers teach at the same time

3. Group facilitation by both teachers

Co-Teaching Model 1: Whole Group Teacher and Supporting Role Teacher

There are basically two manners in which to implement this model. In the first, one teacher teaches the academic content, while the other takes on a supporting role. The supporting role can focus on particular students or can focus on the other teacher. For example, the supporting teacher can gather data by observing the student response to the teaching, the teaching strategies implemented, behavior issues, or student engagement. The purpose of the data gathering should be jointly decided by both teachers. Either person may take either role. These roles should be changed so that one teacher is not always in the supporting role.

One of the benefits of this manner of co-teaching is to provide opportunities that are not available when only one teacher is in the room. For example, this model is an effective way to implement the collaborative problem-solving cycle (Response to Intervention, functional behavior assessments, gifted and talented protocol, multiple measures in multiple contexts). Students who are in a co-teaching situation such as this, where one teacher collects and records data used to make instructional decisions, can often make better academic progress than students whose teachers do not follow progress-monitoring procedures (Fuchs, 1996).

The second manner of co-teaching under this model involves one person teaching a group while the other person teaches individuals. This can be especially effective for reteaching students, for giving guided practice or review to students who need more work with a particular concept, or for introducing concepts to students who need more individualized attention. This model is also effective when implementing projects, writing assignments, or other types of learning where students would benefit from individual conferencing or guidance from a teacher.

This manner of co-teaching allows for interventions to be implemented within the content or general education classroom as part of the collaborative problem-solving cycle. The supporting teacher can make adaptations to instruction or content, can give one-on-one or small group attention, can provide variations in approaches to the content, can slow down the speed, or can focus on vocabulary, grammar, or the main concepts of the lesson. These types of interventions may allow the student to continue to function in the least restrictive environment of the general education or content-area classroom with his or her peers.

When using Co-Teaching Model 1, it is important that the supporting teacher is not utilized to just "help where needed"—that is, walking around the classroom observing student work as the other teacher teaches. The purpose of a co-taught lesson is to intentionally plan for the needs of the class, the needs of individual students, and to provide more attention to students in ways that cannot happen with only one teacher. Helping only as needed does not constitute an intentionally planned lesson.

Another caution is related to the grouping of students. The particular groupings should be based on the specific content to be taught, not the overall academic ability of the students. In other words, group membership could change from day to day or from skill to skill. The students who work with the supporting teacher are students who need additional learning opportunities to master the content or skills required for the particular lesson being taught.

When co-teaching with CLDE students in the classroom, there are several considerations to take into account. To begin, the supporting teacher should be well versed in ESL or bilingual strategies so that time spent working with individuals who are learning English is comprehensible and appropriate. If the supporting teacher is observing, this person should be able to examine the depth of

ESL instructional strategies and suggest modifications to make the instruction more comprehensible and accessible to CLDE students.

Both teachers should also understand the language acquisition process so that the work provided to students is developmentally appropriate and adapted according to language acquisition level. Likewise, the person collecting data should be able to pinpoint oral and written language that is indicative of the language acquisition process versus a special education issue.

Both teachers should understand the cultural acquisition process so that appropriate support can be given to students who are experiencing culture shock or having difficulty adapting to a new culture. In this case, a co-teacher of the same culture and language of the student could be very beneficial.

Both the supporting teacher and the whole class teacher should make sure that there is no stigmatization of students who are pulled aside. The whole class teacher should provide opportunities for all types of students (GT, ESL or bilingual, individual students, students with IEPs, etc.) to work with the supporting teacher.

Co-Teaching Model 2: Both Teachers Teach at the Same Time

In this model, both teachers teach the content at the same time. They may be teaching half of the class, or they may be presenting the material at the same time together in front of the class. Below we provide three manners of teaching under this model—parallel and simultaneous teaching, team teaching, and speak and chart teaching.

Parallel and Simultaneous Teaching

In **parallel teaching**, the class is divided and both teachers present the same content to portions of the larger group of students. For example, both teachers prepare a science lesson together. They then split the class in half: One teacher implements the science lesson to one-half of the class, and the other teacher implements the science lesson to the other half of the class.

In **simultaneous teaching**, the content is divided and each teacher provides one part of the lesson to half the students. The students then switch places and the instructors provide the same content to the second half of the class. For example, teacher A instructs one-half of the class on a new novel, while teacher B works with the other half of the class on writing an expository essay. Halfway through the class time, the students switch teachers to gain the part of the content they were not previously exposed to.

In both parallel teaching and simultaneous teaching, the groupings can be heterogeneous or homogeneous. The students should be grouped according to the objectives of the lessons. Sometimes, it may be more appropriate to group students according to ability levels and other times, it may be appropriate to group with a variety of academic learning levels represented. When working with CLDE students, language acquisition needs should be considered as groups are formed.

Both parallel and simultaneous teaching provide more opportunities for a larger number of students to participate and interact with each other and with the teacher. The class is divided into smaller sections—which provides more opportunities to participate—and each small section receives the attention of both teachers. Because these models allow for smaller student to teacher ratio, they also allow the teachers to monitor individual student responses and knowledge more closely.

Student discussions will vary depending on the groupings. By bringing the class together for a whole group conclusion, summarizing skills can be reinforced and perspectives from the different discussions are synthesized. When students share what their group has learned, the whole group conclusion reinforces students' skills in summarizing key information (Texas Education Agency, 2000).

Team Teaching

Team teaching is a format in which both teachers teach the whole class together at the same time. Both teachers are leading the class, taking turns talking, leading class discussion, asking questions, and facilitating activities. They also monitor students working and can focus on individual student needs. One benefit of this format is the ability of teachers to model, to give examples, to role play, to debate, and to show the students the knowledge base of both teachers. One teacher may lead the lesson, while the other interjects with elaborations, comments, and questions to clarify the material. This model works well in any type of lesson format, including demonstrations, hands-on activities, shared projects, or independent or whole group work.

When team teaching, a great amount of trust is required and usually a shared philosophy of teaching and learning is needed. Teachers must truly understand the style of the other teacher and the two must work together so that their styles complement each other. Planning as well as reflecting on the teaching are integral aspects of this model. Teachers generally find this model one of the most rewarding ways to co-teach, despite the additional time required in planning, communicating, and reflecting. When teachers have worked together co-teaching and have formed a solid and effective co-teaching relationship, the following teacher behaviors are often present (adapted from University of Colorado at Denver, 2003):

- Both presenters talk.

- They alternate or finish sentences for one another.

- They use humor, examples, and knowledge of the content to fill in.

- They use physical proximity as a tool.

- They choreograph the physical space.

- They avoid blocking each other from speaking and subtly cue each other with looks, proximity, hand gestures, voice tempo, and intonation.

- They stay focused all the time, each attentive to the other and to the students.

Speak and Chart Teaching

This form of co-teaching specifies the role of the second teacher. One teacher presents the information, while the other charts key points and student responses. Both teachers are "on stage" at the same time, but one plays a supportive role by writing ideas on a chart, overhead projector, or whiteboard. This format can be especially effective for implementing content-based ESL strategies by highlighting key vocabulary and giving students a record of the key concepts that have been discussed during a lesson.

Considerations for CLDE Students With Co-Teaching Model 2

There are several considerations for teachers of CLDE students when implementing Co-Teaching Model 2. To begin, both teachers should understand how best to organize content to make it accessible to CLDE students. Both teachers should have the same philosophy concerning how to approach instruction for CLDE students. For example, are ESL strategies or bilingual strategies more effective? Should students be grouped by L1 or should mixed L1-L2 groupings be implemented? Are there more appropriate groupings for specific content or aspects of the lesson? If the two teachers disagree on the best strategies to meet the language and cultural needs of the CLDE students, that is fine, as long as students have access to both teacher's strategies.

It is important that both teachers are well versed and consistent with ESL or bilingual teaching strategies, and they should know how to adapt instruction to further comprehension of the content material (see Chapters 9–15). Both teachers need to understand the language and cultural acquisition process and should be skilled in adapting instruction to meet the language acquisition stage of the students. Both teachers should also understand the special education needs of CLDE students and be well versed in instructional strategies and modifications to meet the special education needs of the individual.

And finally, both teachers should be given time to plan together and to reflect together on strategies and modifications that best meet the needs of CLDE students. This is also a time for teachers to clarify learning outcomes and expectations.

Co-Teaching Model 3: Group Facilitation by Both Teachers

This model is often used during cooperative learning activities, for reading groups, and at learning centers or stations and is best used when there are varied activities occurring simultaneously in the classroom. Under this model, both teachers facilitate the various groups and activities within the classroom. Either teacher can work with a specific group, monitor group tasks, guide a specific station or activity, or teach a specific skill or content to a small group. The role of students in the model can vary as well. Students may move between stations or may be assigned to complete specific tasks. Students can work in groups or individually, in pairs or in small groups. The groups may be heterogeneous or homogeneous.

The variety of ways that teachers can plan for lessons with this model makes it interesting for teachers and for students, but also requires thoughtful collaborative conversations during planning. When setting up groupings, teachers must consider learning preferences, ability levels, skill or content gaps, interests, language acquisition levels, and other aspects of learning needs.

This co-teaching model can be very effective for CLDE students who require intensive small group instruction, which can be easily implemented in this format. Groupings must be appropriate to meet both the special education needs and the language or cultural needs of CLDE students. Both teachers should be well versed in ESL or bilingual strategies *and* understand the special education needs of the CLDE student and have interventions and adaptations available in the moment should students require them.

Strategies for Implementing Positive Co-Teaching Experiences

Regardless of the model of co-teaching implemented, co-teaching requires skills that take time to develop. These skills include interpersonal skills as well as instructional and assessment skills. Time to plan, time to build relationships, and time to practice co-teaching in the classroom are all needed to create a positive co-teaching experience. Below are some beginning strategies to provide guidance for co-teaching (adapted from Friend & Cook, 2007; Texas Education Agency, 2000; University of Colorado at Denver, 2003; Vaughn, Schumm, & Arguelles, 1997):

1. Create a collaborative co-teaching and working relationship. Before co-teaching, it is important that both teachers address the following questions in order to understand each other and determine whether a positive co-teaching relationship can be established (adapted from Walther-Thomas, Bryant, & Land, 1996):

   a. How do you organize your classroom?

   b. What are your basic classroom rules and consequences?

   c. What is your noise tolerance?

   d. Describe a typical lesson, assessment, how you plan, how you grade.

   e. How do you communicate with families?

   f. How can we share responsibilities?

   g. What are some of your pet peeves in the classroom?

   h. How will we communicate?

   i. How do you plan? How far ahead do you plan lessons, how closely do you follow your plans? How do you plan for language and special needs in the classroom? How do you differentiate instruction?

   j. What do you think is the most effective manner of instructing CLDE students?

   k. How will we give each other constructive feedback?

   l. What are some things that we can do to build trust?

   m. What are your expectations for students?

   n. What is your biggest fear about co-teaching?

   o. What do you hope can be gained from co-teaching?

2. The purpose of co-teaching is to best meet the needs of all students and teachers involved. When discussing the different co-teaching models, consider the modifications needed in order for all students to learn: What are the needs of students on IEPs? What are the needs of students

with learning and behavior problems? What are the language and cultural needs of CLDE students? Teachers should identify possible solutions to students' problems before they arise in the classroom. Table 6.2 gives an overview of the models of co-teaching, including benefits and considerations for working with CLDE students.

3. Designate time to plan. Co-planning is most effective when teachers set aside a designated time to plan.

4. Designate a workspace for both teachers who will be teaching in the classroom. Make sure that the "visiting" teacher has a place to put his or her materials so that he or she feels welcome in the classroom.

5. Co-teachers should communicate together with students and parents. Provide information for parents that explains how co-teaching arrangements will benefit students. Consider how you will communicate with parents—will both names appear on correspondence, and will there be a "primary" contact person?

6. Assign grades together whenever it is possible or appropriate. Also, make sure that assessment practices are planned together as part of the instruction/assessment cycle. By working together on all aspects of a co-taught course, communication, instruction, and assessment will be more clearly aligned.

Table 6.2 Summary of Co-Teaching Models

Name of Model	Description of the Model	Considerations of the Model With CLDE Students
Co-Teaching Model 1: Whole Group Teacher and Supporting Role Teacher		
One person teaches, one gathers data	One person takes responsibility for the class while the other person observes to collect data on student behavior and learning, or teacher strategies and interactions.	a. The person collecting data should understand the language acquisition and cultural acquisition process. b. Both teachers should have a strong foundation in ESL strategies. c. The observer can make sure adaptations listed on the IEP are met.

(Continued)

Table 6.2 (Continued)

Name of Model	Description of the Model	Considerations of the Model With CLDE Students
One person teaches group, one person teaches individuals	One person teaches the whole group while the other person works with individual students or small groups on specific skills, or behavioral or academic needs.	a. The supporting teacher should be well versed in ESL or bilingual strategies. b. The supporting teacher should understand the language and cultural acquisition process. A supporting teacher of the same culture and language of the student could be very beneficial. c. The supporting teacher should understand and be able to modify for the special needs of the student. d. The supporting teacher should make sure there is no stigmatization of students who are pulled aside.
Co-Teaching Model 2: Both Teachers Teach at the Same Time		
Parallel teaching and simultaneous teaching	Each teacher instructs one-half of the class. In parallel teaching, both teachers teach the same content to half the class. In simultaneous teaching, each teacher takes a piece of the content to teach to one-half of the class—the class then switches teachers to gain both pieces of the content.	a. Both parties should be well versed in language acquisition and cultural acquisition. b. Both parties should be well versed in ESL strategies. c. Both parties should be familiar with the IEP goals. d. Both teachers should be given time to plan together and to reflect together on strategies and modifications that best meet the needs of CLDE students.
Team teaching	Both teachers are active in the teaching of the lesson. They both teach at the same time to the whole group and take turns talking and clarifying the subject matter.	a. Both teachers need to understand the language and cultural acquisition process and be able to adapt instruction. b. Both teachers should have the same philosophy concerning how to approach instruction for CLDE students. c. Both teachers should be well versed in ESL or bilingual strategies and should implement these strategies continuously. d. Both teachers should have a clear understanding of the special education issues of the CLDE student and should be aware of necessary adaptations or modifications to meet the special education needs of the student.

Name of Model	Description of the Model	Considerations of the Model With CLDE Students
Speak and chart teaching	One teacher instructs the class while the other teacher writes key points, key vocabulary, and any other important information.	a. Both teachers must be clear as to what the key vocabulary and key points of the lesson are so that students are clear as to learning outcomes and expectations. b. Both teachers should understand how best to organize the content so that ELL students and students with special needs can effectively access the content. c. Even though one teacher is charting the content, it is still important that the other teacher is consistent with ESL strategies and further implements the 3-way model by providing visuals, repetition, graphic organizers, language objectives, and so on.
Co-Teaching Model 3: Group Facilitation by Both Teachers		
Cooperative grouping, pair work, or stations are facilitated by two teachers	Students are grouped and both teachers facilitate students as they move through group activities.	a. Stations must be appropriate for the language acquisition stage of CLDE students. b. Adaptations to stations must be available to meet the special education needs of CLDE students. c. Both teachers should be well versed in ESL or bilingual strategies and be able to provide adaptations in the moment should CLDE students require them. d. Both teachers should understand the special education needs of the CLDE student and have interventions available to meet the educational needs of the students.

WORKING WITH PARAPROFESSIONALS

CASE STUDY 6.3 | **Notes From a Former Paraprofessional**

I didn't realize how incredibly valuable paraprofessionals were until I became a teacher myself. Paras bring valuable experiences and knowledge to the classroom. They are often extremely caring individuals who just want to work with students. Having an extra set of hands that you can trust to work with your students on an ongoing basis not only helps you as a teacher, but the students benefit as well.

(Continued)

(Continued)

The following is a list of effective ways paraprofessionals can work in the classroom:

- Meeting with various small reading groups regularly.
- Working one-on-one with students while I teach a whole group lesson.
- Working with the larger group during math so I can work with students one-on-one.
- Giving tests to small groups.
- Leading extension math activities with groups of students.

I have found that students really enjoy working with paraprofessionals regularly. It has always seemed like such a waste of talent to put a paraprofessional in a copier room for the day and never tap into the other strengths he or she may have. Paraprofessionals are part of an intricate team for each child. They should be seen as professionals and used as such.

—Kelly, Elementary teacher and former paraprofessional

Consider the case study above:

- How can a paraprofessional contribute to a classroom?
- What collaborative skills are needed to foster positive working relationships with paraprofessionals?
- How can a paraprofessional support the learning needs of CLDE students?

SOURCE: Used by permission.

The Role of Paraprofessionals in Schools

As school districts are asked to meet the needs of a more diverse student body, teachers are also being asked to show that all students are learning through the use of standardized testing and adequate yearly progress (AYP). Data are used to support instructional decision making and differentiation becomes an integral part of planning instruction. At the same time, schools are faced with limited budgets.

One way that many schools save money while giving students the attention they need, and teachers the support they need to teach a wide variety of learners, is by hiring **paraprofessionals (or paraeducators)**.[1] Because of a shortage of special education teachers, an increase in ELL students, a trend toward inclusive practices, and a growing population of CLDE students, the need for paraprofessionals has increased dramatically (Chopra et al., 2004; Daniels &

McBride, 2001; Giangreco, Edelman, Broer, & Doyle, 2001; Giangreco, Edelman, Luiselli, & MacFarland, 1997).

Paraprofessionals are not required to be licensed teachers, but are individuals who must have at least two years of college if their role is primarily instructing students (NCLB, 2001). The 2004 IDEA further clarifies by stating that paraprofessionals should be used to assist in the provision of special education and related services, but are not primary service providers. They work in the schools to support students and teachers, but are under the supervision of a licensed teacher or professional. IDEA also states that paraprofessionals should be appropriately trained to meet the needs of students with whom they are assigned to work.

For many years, paraprofessionals performed mostly clerical work in schools. Today, that role has shifted. Paraeducators spend 85% to 90% of their time focused on instructional activities (OSEP, 2003). These instructional activities include working with individual students, working with small groups of students, gathering data, implementing behavior management plans, preparing materials, and meeting with teachers. Paraprofessionals also monitor students in hallways, during lunch, on the playground, and in other noninstructional situations.

Because of the changing role of paraprofessionals and the higher number of paraprofessionals in schools today, complex relationships are created. Teachers must change their perception of the collaborative relationship from "gracious host to engaged teacher partner" (Giangreco, 2003). Teachers should do their part in creating a collaborative relationship with a paraeducator (Friend & Cook, 2007). Teachers can provide paraeducators with detailed, clear instructional plans, clear expectations, and respect. Teachers can model respect for the paraeducator through their attitude and by the way in which they establish the paraeducator in the classroom. Simple ideas, such as providing a desk for the paraprofessional and listening to insight the paraprofessional can provide about students and instruction, can model a climate of respect for the paraeducator. In addition, the following list provides guidance for creating a participatory environment (adapted from Friend & Cook, 2007; Giangreco, 2003; OSEP, 2003):

- Explain the classroom discipline policies, instructional routines, and other important classroom information

- Encourage the paraprofessional to help all students in the class—not just the CLDE students—unless the para is a personal assistant to a student as stated in the IEP

- If the paraprofessional makes an error, make sure you discuss the error without the students present

- Create a systematic way to communicate and elicit the paraprofessional's ideas, opinions, and insights

- Demonstrate appreciation for the paraprofessional's work

- Consider the interests, preferences, and abilities of the paraprofessional when assigning tasks

- Invite the paraprofessional to participate in the intervention team meetings if they assist the child in instruction

- Adapt the co-teaching models to include a paraprofessional; make sure the roles are clear and that all parties understand the instructional tasks

Often, teachers are not trained in second language acquisition or integrated content-language approach and do not feel prepared to work with ELL students. ELL and CLDE students, therefore, commonly are assigned to work with a paraeducator—the teacher assumes this will take care of their language acquisition needs. However, a clear message is sent to ELL and CLDE students when this occurs as a regular practice. These students perceive that they are not a part of the classroom community and are not deserving of the teacher's attention. A better practice is for all involved—teachers and paraprofessionals—to be thoroughly trained in integrated content-language approach, and for a rotation of roles in the classroom (OSEP, 2003).

Paraprofessionals who are working with CLDE students also need to be versed in the disability of the student, behaviors that may occur, strategies to meet the learning needs, as well as actions to take for implementing behavior plans. This involves strategic hiring of paraeducators who have very clear roles and competencies in working with the children they are assigned. These paraeducators should receive initial and ongoing training that matches their roles in the classroom (Giangreco, 2003). The paraprofessional needs to feel comfortable enough to ask the teacher for assistance if he or she needs more clarification.

When a paraprofessional is assigned specifically to a CLDE student or a classroom with several CLDE students, the teacher is ultimately responsible for the instruction and well-being of these students. This can complicate the relationship because the paraprofessional often communicates or reports directly to the special education or ESL or bilingual teacher and not the general education or content-area teacher. This is an area where communication could be improved and the paraprofessional should feel comfortable directly reporting to the classroom teacher as well.

Teachers often use bilingual paraprofessionals for concurrent translation of the content material. Concurrent translation involves the teacher stating the lesson in English and the paraprofessional directly translating the lesson into the

L1. This is an ineffective strategy. It encourages ELL or CLDE students to disengage during the English portion of the lesson and wait for the translation in the L1. A better practice is for the paraprofessional to engage in "preview or review," where the paraeducator works with a group of ELL or CLDE students in their L1 to discuss the key concepts, the key vocabulary of the lesson, and students' background knowledge of the topic before the lesson. The students then participate fully in the lesson in English. After the lesson, the paraeducator reviews the key concepts, the key vocabulary, and also works on a cultural level by asking the students to relate the new concepts to their background knowledge. In this model, the paraeducator is still working with the assigned students; however, CLDE or ELL students are an integral part of the general classroom community as they participate in the main body of the lesson.

Another consideration is the cultural aspect of working with CLDE students. Many paraeducators are from the community in which the school is located. These professionals may have connections and cultural knowledge that is integral to the success of the students in the classroom. It is important to honor and integrate the cultural knowledge of the paraprofessionals to better meet the needs of CLDE students in the classroom. The teacher needs to be open and observant of paraprofessionals who are from the same culture and language of the students. The manner in which the paraprofessional works with the students can bring tremendous insight into culturally relevant teaching practices.

Summary

- A collaborative school culture allows the strengths and knowledge of various specialists and staff to be tapped for the benefit of CLDE students.

- Three models of co-teaching provide multiple options for meeting the needs of different groups of students, including those who may be CLDE.

- Teachers should encourage and learn from paraprofessionals, who often bring unique cultural and linguistic talents into today's increasingly diverse classrooms.

Key Terms

Collaboration

Co-teaching

Parallel teaching

Paraprofessionals (or paraeducators)

Simultaneous teaching

Team teaching

Activities for Further Understanding

1. Observe teachers planning together. What aspects of the collaboration model do you notice? Are all teacher voices heard equally? Are responsibility and accountability shared equally? Is everyone there voluntarily? Is there a mutual understanding of the goals of the meeting?

2. Observe teachers co-teaching. Which model do they use? How could they improve upon this model? Which students benefit from the model they are using?

3. Choose one model of co-teaching to apply to a lesson in your content area. Why did you pick the particular model? When you implemented the lesson, what worked? What did not work? What would you do differently next time?

4. Find a CLDE student who has a number of different teachers. How do the teachers collaborate to meet the student's needs?

5. Interview a paraeducator at your school. What is the paraeducator's role in the classroom and school? What training has he or she had? What types of collaboration does he or she have with the classroom teacher and other staff members at the school?

6. Observe a paraeducator working with a CLDE student. What does the paraeducator do well? How could the paraeducator improve his or her skills?

7. Observe a teacher-paraprofessional relationship. How is the paraprofessional utilized in the classroom? How could the strengths of the paraprofessional be better put to work with CLDE students?

8. Consider your relationship with a paraprofessional in your classroom. What strengths does the paraprofessional in your classroom have? How do you collaborate with your paraprofessional? How could you better utilize the paraprofessional in your classroom so that the needs of CLDE students are met?

 Visit the Student Study Site at **www.sagepub.com/grassi** for chapter-specific study resources.

Note

1. The terms paraprofessional and paraeducator are used interchangeably in this chapter.

Chapter 7

PLANNING INSTRUCTION

Key Points

✦ Why differentiating instruction and universal design for learning allow CLDE students to succeed in mainstream classrooms

✦ What practical strategies teachers can use to plan instruction for all levels of learners, including those who are CLDE

✦ How strategic planning helps to minimize management issues in today's diverse classrooms

---

CASE STUDY 7.1   **Support From the General Education Teacher**

My son's preschool teacher was the first person to tell me that my son was lagging behind in some essential skills and suggested that I get him tested through Child Find. Alex qualified for preschool services that would help him catch up to his peers. That was almost nine years ago. As he began kindergarten, I was so grateful that he had access to special education services. He was slowly starting to improve. When his three-year testing came around I was so nervous because I wanted the services to continue so he would have access to these teachers who had been so helpful. Unfortunately, he did not qualify by a very small margin. I understand the value of these tests, but I was so disheartened. How was he going to get the support he so desperately needed?

As I entered the room that held the seven people who had been such a wonderful support for both my son and I, I wanted to beg them not to abandon us! As each advocate gave their testimony of the test results, the determination was made that my son could move on without special education services. This was a great thing, right? That meant that he had "caught up" enough to function in the classroom with his peers without additional services. I should have felt proud of the accomplishments. Why did I feel so alone all of a sudden? They assured me that if I had any questions that I could always stop by the special education offices and they would be more than happy to help. After everyone left the room, my son's teacher stayed behind to talk with us. She seemed to know what we were feeling and said that we would now be a team to continue to help my son progress. She offered to meet with us and make a plan. These words made all the difference.

This wonderful general education teacher made sure there was a plan established for reading, writing, and math. She continued to consult with the teachers in the special education department. She and every teacher after that made sure that my son's needs were met, modifications were made, and most of all made sure he continued to love school in spite of his difficulties.

The special education teachers were incredible, but the classroom teachers were the ones that made sure everything was taken care of and communicated with me constantly about my son's learning.

—Kelly, Mother of middle school student

Consider the case study above:

- How did the classroom teacher validate and support the mother's concerns?
- How can classroom teachers support learners who may not be at grade level proficiency?
- How can general education or content-area teachers structure their classroom and plan for students who are struggling academically?

SOURCE: Used by permission.

The opening case study reminds us that general education or content-area teachers are largely responsible for educating students with special needs. Although Kelly's son did not continue to qualify for services, he continued to need extra support from the general education teacher. As Chapter 5 noted, the assessment/instruction cycle is the foundation for meeting student needs, and the general education teacher has an important role in the **process** by implementing interventions and choosing strategies to meet those needs. This chapter lays the foundation for planning instruction to include CLDE students and leads into implementation of the specific instructional strategies discussed in Chapters 9–15.

PLANNING FOR INSTRUCTION

When a teacher knows the needs of the students in his or her classroom, the teacher can more effectively plan instruction to make the curriculum accessible to all students. In order to better know one's students, teachers must understand how to interpret assessment data (assessment reports, both formal and informal, summative and formative) and also understand the learning styles of students and how these styles are influenced by culture, language acquisition, background experiences, and personal interests of students. All of this information gives teachers pathways to connect the material with the learner, to create opportunities for the child to take in the information and concepts, and to help students understand the ideas, knowledge, and content. By gathering as much information as possible about each student, teachers can better plan for instruction. One of the ways that both secondary and elementary teachers can effectively and thoughtfully plan for most of the students in their classrooms is to accept a philosophy of differentiation.

A PHILOSOPHY OF DIFFERENTIATION

Differentiating instruction (DI) is a way of approaching the planning and implementation of curriculum and instruction with an understanding that learners differ in a variety of ways (Sands & Barker, 2004). Based on the work of Tomlinson (1995, 1999, 2000), differentiating instruction responds to diverse learners by considering

1. *readiness levels,* by varying rates of instruction as well as the complexity of the targeted content;

2. *learning profiles,* by providing access to and interaction with information in numerous ways and across multiple dimensions; and

3. *interests,* by incorporating the learner's affinity, curiosity, and passion for a particular topic or skill.

These variables are attended to when teachers plan and thoughtfully vary the process, product, or content associated with a particular unit or lesson of instruction. When teachers utilize these variables in their planning and choose strategies that support a variety of learners, they are differentiating instruction.

In order for teachers to plan according to the readiness levels, the learning profiles, and the interests of their students, teachers must access information about a student from a variety of sources, some of which we described in Chapter 5 on assessment. To review, below are some information sources that help to give a complete picture of the learner (CLDE students in particular):

- Parent input
- Cultural background of student
- Learning style of student
- Interests of the student
- Language acquisition levels of the student (in both L1 and L2)
- Literacy levels of the student (in both L1 and L2)
- Samples of the student's work that "show" the challenges and strengths
- Information from student interviews
- Information from informal conversations with the student
- Classroom observations of what strategies work to support the student
- Past educational background (including past placement and program types)
- Past teachers' or schools' perspective of learning issues
- Any observations you have made in general
- Formal assessment reports
- Informal assessments
- Comparative work samples
- Teacher-made assessments

- Attendance records

- Transcripts, grades, and cumulative files

- Data from other teachers who work with the student

This list is by no means exhaustive, but by collecting a variety of information about students, teachers will better understand their students as learners and as individuals and will capture a more complete picture of students' readiness levels in academic areas. The information gathered about students is critical to building the best learning environment, and must be brought into lesson planning and implementation. A full picture of the student and the class is integral to the philosophy of differentiation.

> For examples of inventories for various student levels, see the following Web Link: **www.sagepub.com/grassi.**

7.1

Differentiation and CLDE Students

The philosophy of differentiation is a key component to preparing CLDE students for academic success. It is rare that a secondary or elementary general education teacher will have all CLDE students at the same level in terms of English language proficiency, first language proficiency, educational background, learning capability, or cultural background. The diversity in back-

> **REFER TO CASE STUDY 7.1**
>
> What information could the teacher use to plan instruction? Did she consider differentiation? What other steps could the teacher take to ensure that Kelly's son's needs are met?

ground experiences, past schooling, special education issues, and linguistic proficiencies requires effective teachers to differentiate instruction. Basic strategies for integrated content-language instruction (described in Chapters 9–15) must be adhered to for all CLDE students; however, the process, product, and content can all be differentiated to meet the needs of different CLDE students.

Teachers must consider student choice when differentiating instruction for CLDE students. Choice does not mean "choosing whether to do the work or not." Rather, choice is giving students options on how to access the same curriculum and how to demonstrate understanding of the learning objectives. When students are given choice, the teacher can observe what students choose and begin to better understand each student's strengths and challenges based on the choices they make.

Another aspect of differentiating instruction is to utilize different strategies for presenting and scaffolding the curriculum, especially strategies that make the content accessible to all (see Chapters 9–15), and observing student reaction to the various strategies. When using different strategies, teachers can observe which strategies CLDE students respond to best, thus beginning to understand students' learning styles, academic needs, and linguistic needs.

Once teachers are in a position to observe students and how they best access the content and demonstrate their understanding, teachers will begin to notice which students they need to focus on to better understand how that student learns. It is at this point when differentiation becomes a critical component of the classroom. Differentiation gives teachers a pathway to provide different manners of presenting the content and assessing understanding in order to better meet the learning needs of all students. While differentiated instruction is a philosophy of teaching that is based on the idea that "instructional approaches should vary and be adapted in relation to individual and diverse students in classrooms" (Hall, 2002), we would argue that these considerations also need to be implemented at the point of planning instruction in response to what teachers know about their students. In other words, differentiated instruction should begin when teachers plan instruction for their students. Case Study 7.2 describes how a middle school teacher differentiates instruction to meet the needs of diverse students in the classroom.

CASE STUDY 7.2   Differentiation

The sixth grade classroom is a "typical" middle school classroom. Twenty-five students have desks positioned in a U-shaped pattern. Some students are clustered at desks, some are working on the floor, some are working with a teacher, and others are working with a paraprofessional in the room. The students are finishing a writing project where they are creating a guide to the school for visitors. Each small group or individual is working on a different area of the school: the office, the art room, the cafeteria, the gym, and so on. Each group will prepare a description of the area, describe its purpose, and explain why a visitor might be interested in seeing that particular location. They are also including drawings of each location. When everyone is finished, the guide will be used in the office as a tool for welcoming visitors to the school. The teacher has asked bilingual parents to join in the project by working with some ELL students in their L1, and by helping students to translate the guide into various languages for any visitors who are culturally and linguistically diverse.

The students are engaged and excited about what they are doing. During the work time, six students come into the room. They have been with the English as a Second Language (ESL) specialist. Three of the students who are returning to the classroom are from Mexico, two are from African countries, and one child is from the Middle East. The teacher has already discussed the assignment with the ESL specialist so that the ELL students were supported in the project through their work with the specialist. The six ELL students take their writing folders and join their small groups. The class also has five students who are supported by the special education teacher, and seven students who are labeled gifted and talented.

Consider the case study above:

- Who are the students in this classroom and how might their learning needs differ?
- How is the teacher providing for these different learning needs?
- What kinds of activities in the lesson described above provide for different learning styles, different academic abilities, and varied interests?

Differentiating the Process

Differentiating the process is achieved by allowing for various ways to access the content. One of the ways teachers can differentiate the process is by setting up a classroom environment that encourages student-centered work. This is a classroom where students are not always doing the same thing concurrently. Take the example in Case Study 7.2. In this lesson, students are working on a group project with individual components. Some students are working individually and some are working in groups, some are working with a teacher or paraprofessional, some are working on their own. Some of the writing is very complex; some is at a simpler level of English. Some students use supports of pictures and vocabulary, others do not. Some students are working in two languages; others are just working in English. Most important, all students are working on the same curriculum. Every student is challenged to meet the common goal of writing for a purpose, of describing a part of the school and its usefulness to the students. When a teacher differentiates, he or she does not dilute the curriculum; rather, these modifications set a tone in the classroom that supports collective learning through individual needs.

Case Study 7.2 specifically describes differentiation of the process for CLDE students. Some CLDE students need time to clarify the content in their L1 and, if resources are available, providing the content in both the L1 and the L2 is a very effective manner of differentiating the process. In Case Study 7.2, this was achieved by allowing for flexible groupings throughout the lesson and by calling upon bilingual parents and paraprofessionals to help clarify the content in the L1 for students who needed this accommodation. CLDE students will also typically require instruction in English grammar and vocabulary for the lesson—usually to a deeper extent than native English speakers. This was achieved by allowing time for specialized language instruction with the ESL specialist. CLDE students will also need encouragement to actively participate in the lesson—by having discussion questions before the class, by having time to think-pair-share with peers before participating in whole group, and by participating in a written format or through drawing or acting. The teacher above provided ample opportunities for students to work in groups, share their ideas, and present materials in written and drawing format—all of which would help prepare students to participate in whole group activities around the writing process.

Case Study 7.2 provides a scenario that can be easily adapted to the secondary level. For example, science teachers can differentiate the process while simultaneously having all students work on the same experiment. If students are grouped in clusters that are supportive to all participants (socially, linguistically, academically), if CLDE students are allowed to participate orally (and complete the written portion later with assistance), or if they are given structured organizers to help them complete the written portion in the groups (such as note-taking guides, cloze outlines), then CLDE students can actively participate in the process because they have been given the differentiated supports they need to participate. And if the teacher uses integrated content-language methods (see Chapters 9–15)—such as modeling all steps of the experiment, providing students with a step-by-step instruction guide, and labeling instruments in the classroom so students can easily find them—then CLDE students can better access and succeed in the content-area task. Differentiating the process is a method that can be adapted to any grade level and to any subject matter.

> **REFER TO CASE STUDY 7.2**
>
> How did the teacher differentiate the process? How could you differentiate the process in your content area or general education classroom?

Differentiating the Product

Another component of a differentiated classroom is the idea of "choice" in the product. Choice gives students the ability to show more clearly what they know. In a classroom where differentiation is present, ideas are communicated through a variety of avenues. Teachers give students opportunities to "show-what-they-know" in different ways (telling, writing, drawing), or through different types of products (a speech, a report, a collage, an interview, a film, or an exam). Students need to have experiences in all of these genres, but there are times in a classroom when students need to be able to choose how they will show their knowledge. Today, all students must take the state standardized exams, and these exams show one area of comprehension. But when students are also given opportunities to choose the product that best demonstrates their understanding, teachers are more likely to see a more complete example of a student's comprehension. Students are apt to choose products that allow them to work within their linguistic and academic capabilities.

When a teacher has CLDE students who are performing at different linguistic levels in the classroom, differentiating the product becomes even more critical to academic success. What should a teacher expect from a student who is in the preproduction or early production language acquisition stage? Should the product expectations be different from those for a child at the intermediate or advanced fluency stage? If the class is assigned a three-page report, how can that be differentiated for the student who is not fluent in English writing? What other ways can a teacher encourage CLDE students to show their understanding of the content without heavily relying on their English proficiency skills? Teachers should consider different products such as art-based projects and drama, and teachers should have realistic expectations of the types of grammatical errors in products from CLDE students. Teachers should also consider products created in the student's L1.

Secondary students, in particular, can benefit greatly from differentiated products. Many students have skills and talents beyond what is expected in the curriculum and, given a chance to show their talents, usually become more motivated to learn the topic. For example, in a secondary history class the teacher can allow students to show their understanding of the general curricular topic through different products. Students can interview or film experts, attend a talk and write a report, read books on the topic and write reports, create poetry or a drama depicting an important issue, or create media or PowerPoint presentations (see Photo 7.2) from the perspective of a certain figure during the time. While it is expected at the secondary level that all students will take the same test, also allowing for choice can increase interest, expertise, and motivation around the topic. It is important to note here again that this does not mean that the teacher is "watering down" the curriculum. Rather, the teacher is finding ways to encourage output, to encourage learning, and to support each student's learning in content, process, and language acquisition.

Photo 7.2   Projects can be differentiated through technology.

Differentiating the Content

REFER TO CASE STUDY 7.2

How did the teacher differentiate the product? How could you differentiate the product in one of your lessons?

Differentiating the **content** is a way to make the content accessible to students, and to spark student interest in the content. Student choice is an excellent way to differentiate the content. For example, if the goal is to read a particular genre of literature, students can choose the piece of work that they want to read as long as it fits that genre. The characteristics of the books are all the same, but the students choose the topics. To further illustrate, if the assignment is to explore the genre of biographies, then biographies can be read about men or women, people of color, or immigrants to this country. All students are working on the same content focus, but choice helps to engage students. And in particular, when working with CLDE students, making the content relevant to the different cultures represented in the classroom is a key strategy for academic success. If students are given choice on the perspective to research, they will choose what is interesting and relevant to them and the variety of information gathered will make for a more complete picture of the academic concept for all the students. Likewise, using materials in different languages will allow students to examine perspectives and content material that provide linguistically and culturally diverse perspectives.

A teacher can also utilize differentiation of content to address diverse readiness levels. If students are studying the genre of poetry, for example, a variety of reading levels can be incorporated in the poetry reading that the class does together, or the class can be separated into groups for part of the lesson to make sure that all students are working at their readiness level. Some students may need to listen to the poetry on a tape. Some students may need to read the poetry in both the L1 and in English. Some students may need explicit instruction on the vocabulary, the grammar, the patterns included in the poem, and most students would appreciate visual context. Choice, in some of these cases, is set by the teacher, but the students in a classroom understand that everyone is getting what they need—and what they need is not always the same product or process. Case Study 7.3 presents an example where differentiation of content was not implemented systematically.

CASE STUDY 7.3   Mr. Jacobson

Mr. Jacobson's classroom is ready for their literacy instruction. Approximately one half of the 25 students in class are below grade level in reading, several students are English language learners, and several of the students have an IEP for other special education issues.

The students are gathered around the teacher who, yesterday, randomly assigned each small group of students a poem to summarize. The students were allowed to choose their own groups of five. The students worked in groups to prepare their summaries and have turned those in to the teacher. The students are now sitting in a half circle around the whiteboard, where across the board, the original poems the students had summarized are taped up. The whole class task is for students to guess which poem is being presented after the teacher has read aloud each group's summary.

The teacher reads the first group's summary. Five of the 25 students present are paying attention. Other students are tapping pencils, moving in their seats, slipping notes to each other, and looking to go to the bathroom. Regardless of this behavior, the teacher continues to read summaries—with no pausing, visual context, or written versions with which the students can follow along. As the 45-minute lesson progresses, the teacher becomes more and more frustrated with the students' behavior. He constantly asks students to be quiet, stop moving, and to put their pencils down. It is evident that the students are not engaged and many students are having trouble staying focused on the task.

(Continued)

(Continued)

Consider the case study above:

- Why are students not engaged in this lesson?
- In what ways could this lesson be differentiated to meet the diverse needs of the students in the classroom?
- How can differentiation of content better meet the needs of students?

In Case Study 7.3, content choice was limited. Students were assigned a poem that the teacher chose randomly—the poem did not necessarily reflect student interest, reading ability, or cultural perspective. Within the whole class activity, the teacher did not differentiate the process for students who were learning English, students who needed visual cues, or students who had attention issues. The students could not become involved in the learning because the content was not accessible.

On the secondary level, differentiating the content is an excellent way to engage students with the material. For example, in a history class, if the topic is World War I, then the content can be differentiated by perspectives (students choose a country's perspective to study, a soldier's perspective, a civilian's perspective, a leader's perspective), by job (who did what during the war), or by countries' decisions (which country decided what). Students choose what they would like to investigate and are required to bring their knowledge to the whole class. Teachers can also offer students choice in the process—they can access information off the computer, from interviewing experts, from reading books in any language, or from seeing movies. And teachers can differentiate the product—students can present their information to the class in PowerPoint format, in a written outline, by showing and explaining clips from movies, or in a poster presentation. By differentiating the content, process, and product, students will gather information that goes beyond the textbook, and the class as a whole will gain a fuller picture of the topic—while increasing their motivation to study the topic. See Table 7.1 for a summary of classroom applications for differentiating product, process, and content.

REFER TO CASE STUDY 7.3

How could Mr. Jacobson have differentiated the process to make it more accessible to students? How can you better differentiate the process in one of your classes to make the content more accessible to your students?

Table 7.1 Application of Differentiation[1]

Differentiating process	• Explicit instruction in vocabulary and key concepts • Group and individual work stations • Scaffolded projects • Use of technology to complete the project • Drawing, drama, and writing to learn about the content • Access to content through a variety of modalities (audiotapes, movies, Web sites, interviewing an expert) • Using different graphic organizers • Large print versions • Content at a variety of reading levels
Differentiating product	• Different types of assessment—written, interviews, art projects, dramatic productions • Use of portfolio to show learning over time • End products in either the L1 or the L2 • Culturally relevant products governed by student choice and experience • Products that reflect the linguistic level of the student
Differentiating content	• Culturally relevant—give students the choice of which perspective to study concerning a specific topic or time period • Different books within a particular genre • Different choices on research projects and topics • Different experiments to choose—using the scientific method • Connect content to students' background knowledge • Provide content materials in different languages

UNIVERSAL DESIGN FOR LEARNING

Another concept that shares the same philosophy as differentiation—that is, teachers must implement various ways to make the information accessible for all students—is the concept of **universal design for learning** (UDL). This is a term borrowed from architecture, where universal design is part of the process of making buildings accessible for all people from the moment the building is envisioned. For example, instead of adding on a ramp to make the building accessible, the ramps are incorporated in the design process to make them a part of the beauty and function of the building. The ramp is not an "add on" or an afterthought, but is part of the original design—a design that values access for everyone.

In teaching, the concept of universal design for learning is used to ensure that all students have access to the curriculum from the point of planning. We need to think about providing that access as part of the original lesson plan, not as an add-on or a modification midway through the lesson when we notice that students are struggling. Teachers are very good at making modifications "on the fly," or reteaching if needed, but we need to become better at thinking about our students' needs from the onset of our lesson planning. We can do this by incorporating the concept of universal design for learning, which promotes access to curriculum by providing the following (Center for Applied Special Technology [CAST], 2007; Orkwis & McLane, 1998):

- **Multiple means of representation,** to give learners various ways of acquiring information and knowledge,

- **Multiple means of expression,** to provide learners alternatives for demonstrating what they know, and

- **Multiple means of engagement,** to tap into learners' interests, offer appropriate challenges, and increase motivation.

UDL shares many of the same philosophical tenets of differentiating instruction, yet universal design for learning imagines that the multiple means of representation, expression, and engagement occur at the curriculum design level. Differentiated instruction often occurs during instruction (after the curriculum has already been designed) in response to learner needs (Hall, Strangman, & Meyer, 2003).

Universal Design for Learning and CLDE Students

Like DI, the concept of universal design for learning (UDL) is integral to planning for successful instruction for CLDE learners. Multiple means of representation is needed for CLDE students to understand the content. The teacher should provide all material using the 3-way model: spoken, written, and with visual context (see Chapter 9). Likewise, students will need time to work in groups to clarify the subject matter in their first language, and CLDE students will need specialized language instruction in grammatical concepts that native English speakers may not necessarily need (see Chapters 9–15).

When teachers are faced with various levels of English language proficiencies in both the secondary and elementary classroom, students must have multiple means of expression in order to communicate their knowledge of the topic. The teacher should consider allowing the students to use their L1, to draw pictures, to have time to think about the topic with their groups first, to create media representations of their knowledge, to design creative projects, or to act out the topic. When linguistic skills of CLDE students are at a beginning level (preproduction or early production stages), the teacher needs to consider different ways for the students to express themselves and their content knowledge without heavy reliance on English.

Finally, when teachers work with students from different cultures and educational backgrounds, teachers must find multiple ways to engage these students. When teachers at any grade level give students choice, students can engage in content that interests them. When teachers provide various models and various perspectives, they reach more students in the classroom (see Table 7.2 for a summary of instructional applications of universal design for learning).

> **REFER TO CASE STUDY 7.2**
>
> In what ways did the teacher incorporate UDL into the classroom? How can you better provide multiple means of representation and expression, and multiple ways to engage students in your classroom lessons?

Table 7.2 Applications of Universal Design for Learning[2]

Multiple means of representation	<ul><li>3-way model of instruction (Chapter 9)</li><li>Graphic organizers</li><li>Emphasizing key concepts and vocabulary</li><li>Providing access to content at appropriate reading levels</li><li>Group clarification</li></ul>
Multiple means of expression	<ul><li>Differentiated product</li><li>Requiring assessments that measure the content—not the language</li><li>Allowing for different means of showing comprehension</li></ul>
Multiple means of engagement	<ul><li>Activities that are culturally relevant to the students in the classroom</li><li>Technology</li><li>Experiential learning</li><li>Hands-on activities</li><li>Experiments</li></ul>

APPLICATION OF DIFFERENTIATION AND UDL: BACKWARD DESIGN PLANNING

A practical strategy for implementing the concepts of DI and UDL is the backward design model (Wiggins & McTighe, 1998). A backward design model requires teachers to start planning the lesson from the end by determining the desired results—What do I want my students to understand and be able to do after this lesson? Teachers then build their lesson from the endpoint working backwards to plan activities and lectures that will bring students to the desired outcomes. While planning activities, the teacher can keep in mind differentiation and UDL for individual students. How can the teacher adapt activities to meet the needs of particular students?

For example, if a math lesson involves adding and subtracting fractions, the teacher would start by identifying the desired results or learning outcomes. The teacher may want students to know the following by the end of the lesson:

1. Finding the least common denominator (finding the factors of numbers)

2. Changing the numerator of a fraction based on the least common denominator

3. Adding and subtracting fractions once they have a common denominator

Once the teacher has laid out all the learning outcomes, the teacher needs to determine the steps he or she will use to reach these outcomes with students. At this point, it is important to consider how to make the content accessible using either differentiation of process, or multiple means of representing the material. The graphic organizer in Table 7.3 is adapted from Wiggins and McTighe (1998, p. 186) to help guide teachers in determining the activities needed to reach their desired outcomes.

Once activities have been determined, teachers should consider the evidence they will gather to show that the students comprehended the lesson. Taking into account a philosophy of DI, evidence of understanding (or product or assessment) can be differentiated to include individual or group tests, projects, tasks, and informal observations of students.

When using the backward design model, teachers can also consider differentiation of process and think about the different ways in which students can all arrive at the same knowledge—but perhaps not through the same process. When students are given access to the content, are given opportunity to show their strengths, and when these strengths are valued, then students are more inclined to engage with the material.

Table 7.3 Utilizing Backward Design for Multiple Means of Representation or Differentiation of Process

Learning Objective	Description of Teacher Actions (What teaching and learning experiences will equip students to demonstrate the targeted understandings?)
Finding the least common denominator	1. Teacher draws all steps on the board. 2. Teacher uses colored markers to differentiate each step. 3. Teacher repeats the steps at least three times. 4. Teacher leaves the steps on the board for students to reference. 5. Teacher groups students and presents each small group with different fractions and has them find the LCD. 6. Teacher has steps written out on a worksheet for each student in the class. 7. Teacher works with specific groups. 8. Teacher checks in with all groups to make sure they understand.
Changing fractions once the LCD is determined	1. Teacher draws all steps on the board. 2. Teacher uses colored markers to differentiate each step. 3. Teacher repeats steps at least three times. 4. Teacher leaves the steps on the board for students to reference. 5. Teacher divides class into groups and each group attempts to change the fractions. 6. Teacher passes out a worksheet with the steps delineated for each member of the class. 7. Teacher works with specific groups.
Adding or subtracting fractions	1. Teacher writes on board and explains at least three times. 2. Students have the choice to work individually on worksheet, in small groups, or with the teacher. 3. A teacher station is set up at the back of the class for students who want more support.

INSTRUCTIONAL PLANNING PYRAMID FOR INSTRUCTION AND RTI

An **instructional planning pyramid** for instruction is one concrete application of the concepts of differentiated instruction and universal design for learning—process, product, and content, or multiple means of representation, expression, and engagement. An instructional planning pyramid can help organize the choices that teachers make for instruction when teaching in a diverse classroom. Teachers must purposefully select strategies, supports, and placements that best meet the needs of the specific students, especially when considering students who have an IEP. The pyramid consists of three levels that represent a way to think about planning for the diverse needs in a class (Marston, Reschly, Lau, Muyskens, & Canter, 2007; Sands et al., 2000; Schumm, Vaughn, & Leavell, 1994). This three-tiered pyramid is also used as a framework for implementing the Response to Intervention (RTI) model for identifying the presence of a specific learning disability (see Figure 7.1).

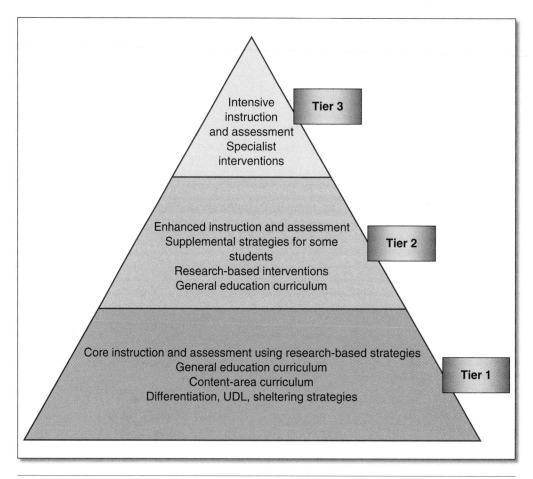

Figure 7.1 Intervention Levels Using a Planning Pyramid

Tier 1, represented by the biggest portion of the pyramid, consists of the general strategies that a teacher uses to reach most of the students in the classroom. The strategies that work best in one classroom for most of the students may be different from the strategies that work for most students in another classroom. For example, if a teacher is in a school where most of the students are learning English, the strategies utilized in the baseline planning will be different from those for a teacher who has no students who are learning English in his or her class. Tier 1 reflects strategies that will reach most of the students and make the content accessible to the majority in that classroom. In Tier I, all students receive research-based, high-quality core education. Interventions are preventative and proactive with the goal of meeting the needs of most students. Approximately 80% to 90% of students in the classroom should be successful with Tier 1 interventions (Hoover, Klinger, Baca, & Patton, 2008; Myers & Bieber, 2007).

The teacher in Case Study 7.2 implemented research-based strategies that best met the needs of most of the students in her classroom; that is, she first designed the lesson utilizing intervention supports from Tier 1 of the pyramid. Of course, all of the students are individuals and have diverse needs; but for planning purposes within Tier 1, the teacher can think about some of the students in distinct groups and the types of support that they will need. There is a group of students learning English, a group of gifted and talented students, and a group of students who are on IEPs for various reasons (but who all need extra support in reading and writing). The teacher has utilized groupings and students' interests, and has created an assignment that challenges students at their academic and English language levels and allows for a variety of outputs or products (writing, drawing, talking). Students are talking to each other, both in English and in their native languages. Students have access to vocabulary lists and pictures of the school areas. A teacher, parents, and a paraprofessional are also working with students on individual needs and goals. By constructing the core lesson at Tier 1, around the needs of groups of diverse children, and by using a backward planning model to provide supports within the lesson that meet the specific needs of those groups of children, the teacher is able to meet the learning needs of the majority of the children in the class. At the same time, when questions come up for individual students and further modifications are required, the teacher can then begin to implement strategies from Tier 2. In Case Study 7.4, the teacher moves from Tier 1 instruction with all students, to Tier 2 instruction for a select few. By scaffolding the instruction at the Tier 2 level, the teacher makes the content accessible to more students.

CASE STUDY 7.4 | Scaffolding Instruction

Miss Benson has a classroom of 30 ninth grade students. Twenty students in the class are ELL students and many of these students also have an IEP. As a result of the demographics in her class, Miss Benson has taken several professional development workshops on effective instruction for ELL students and incorporates these strategies into all of her math classes.

Today, Miss Benson is teaching students how to create a graph. Because Miss Benson has had training in culturally relevant pedagogy, she is concerned by the graphs presented in the students' textbook. She has a class with a majority of students of color, yet the graphs in the textbooks present statistics that illustrate either low academic achievement levels for students of color, or that have information that is not of interest to her students. Therefore, before beginning the lesson, Miss Benson reads up on leaders within the community from which her students come. She then calls many of these leaders and interviews them about facts from their life. Once she has collected all the data, she creates numbers and statistics that depict the average grade point average, salary, workweek, and so on for leaders and important figures from the community.

To teach the lesson on graphs, Miss Benson places students in groups of four that have access to different fact sheets about people from their community. Miss Benson has instructions for the day's activity on the board. She starts by reading Step 1 from the instructions to the class, "Read over the statistics and facts on your table and highlight the important points." She underlines several words from Step 1—*read over and highlight important points*. Miss Benson then picks up her fact sheets and models what she wants done. As she is reading her fact sheets, she asks students, where might I want to pause and highlight? What seems like important information? Students volunteer answers and Miss Benson writes their ideas on the board. Once Miss Benson is confident that students understand Step 1, she then reads Step 2 from the directions she has written on the board, "Record the important facts you have highlighted on the chart provided." Miss Benson holds up the chart that each student has at his or her desk and models for students by writing her important facts in the correct space. Miss Benson then tells the students to begin their work and sets her timer for 20 minutes. Immediately, five hands are raised—these are five students in the class who require extra scaffolding, regardless of the ESL strategies already implemented in the class. Miss Benson collects the five students in a group and repeats all directions and walks them through a couple of the facts step by step. Once Miss Benson has worked with these students on three more examples, they readily begin to work as a group without the assistance of their teacher.

Consider the case study above:

- Which Tier 1 strategies did Miss Benson utilize in the lesson?
- What other strategies did she need to implement to reach the five students who required more scaffolding?

Tier 2 interventions are represented by the five students in Case Study 7.4 who, regardless of the strategies the teacher employed at Tier 1, still required further adaptations to have access to the same core curriculum. Tier 2 includes research-based interventions that are designed to better scaffold for students who, for example, are at risk of academic or social challenges, are identified as underachieving, are at beginning stages of learning English, or require specific supports to make progress in the classroom. Approximately 5% to 15% of students in the general education or content-based classroom will require Tier 2 modifications (Hoover et al., 2008; Myers & Bieber, 2007). At this level of planning, teachers should consider strategies that will help these groups of students gain access to the content. This does not include diluting the curriculum, but providing research-based interventions that will support students in the content-area classroom. In Case Study 7.4, further repetition of directions and further modeling with the students provided enough scaffolding for the five students in the case study to begin work on their own.

In Tier 2, it is important that the teacher document strategies attempted and results of the modifications—especially when working through the RTI cycle as described in Chapter 5. If interventions do not yield satisfactory results, the RTI team can proceed with more focused interventions at Tier 3 (Hoover et al., 2008).

Tier 3 of the pyramid is designed for those individuals who need more support than can be provided by research-based modifications in the general education or content-based classroom. These students may require specialized individualized programs developed by specialists (such as special education teachers), they may be pulled from the classroom for small group instruction by a specialist (usually listed on the IEP), they may have a paraprofessional who works with the teachers to support the student's needs, or they may be working with a modified curriculum to reach goals listed on their IEP. Students in this group are generally labeled with a special education label (although some will also have an ELL label) and have gone through the special education identification process discussed in Chapter 5. For students in Tier 3 of the pyramid, support from the specialist, whether it is direct services or indirect consultation[3] should be provided. Approximately 1% to 5% of students in the general education or content-based classroom will require Tier 3 intervention (Hoover et al., 2008). These students may be several grade levels behind, and monitoring should occur more often to ensure that interventions are working (Myers & Bieber, 2007).

Considerations for CLDE Students

Many schools consider interventions for CLDE students to be at Tier 2 and 3, and pull these students out of the general education or content-based curriculum for specialized classes with the ESL or bilingual or special education specialist. However, because of the rapidly changing demographics of schools today, we advocate for strategies that meet the needs of CLDE students to be implemented in Tier 1 planning. Teachers need to utilize effective strategies for CLDE students at the planning stage and we advocate that *all* teachers are thoroughly trained in these strategies to meet the needs of all students in their classrooms. If effective strategies for making the content accessible and engaging to diverse students become a part of Tier 1 instruction, it is less likely that misdiagnosis based on language acquisition or cultural difference will occur. We want all students to be a part of the general education or content-based classroom and have access to the rich and full curriculum we require of our monolingual English-speaking students. This requires teachers to have knowledge of language acquisition, effective strategies for CLDE students, and culturally relevant pedagogy. It also requires teachers to implement these strategies in every class with culturally and linguistically diverse students.

PLANNING AND CLASSROOM MANAGEMENT

We are of the philosophy that if students are challenged, engaged—but not frustrated—and have strong student-teacher relationships, then discipline issues are minimalized. Effective classroom management at all grade levels stems from good planning and effective strategies. This means that teachers have clear goals and expectations and that lessons are focused on the learning needs of students in their classrooms.

Universal design for learning and differentiating instruction are manners of challenging and engaging students, while removing the barriers that cause undue frustration. When students are allowed choice, they take more ownership of the projects, and if students are given choice in how to exhibit their understanding, they can display their strengths to the teacher. Once students are comfortable in the classroom and feel that they can be successful, then the teacher can begin to introduce more challenging material that addresses students' particular barriers and can help students work on those barriers in a comfortable, safe environment.

UDL and differentiation strategies must be integral in Tier 1 planning. In other

REFER TO CASE STUDY 7.3

How could Mr. Jacobson differentiate instruction so that students can access the lesson and engage in their learning? Explain how behavior issues may have been lessened. Refer to Case Study 7.4. How did Miss Benson differentiate the lesson at Tier 1 and what were the behaviors of students in her class?

words, the teacher must be prepared to meet the individual linguistic, academic, social, and learning style needs of his or her students from the point of planning the lesson, thus addressing potential frustrations and barriers to learning before the lesson is implemented. Often, if students' needs are consciously and purposefully planned for, then frustration is reduced, engagement is increased, and classroom management issues are minimalized.

For detailed discussions of classroom management strategies with CLDE students, including Positive Behavior Intervention Supports (PBIS) and social skills instruction, see the following Web link: **www.sagepub.com/grassi.**

7.2

Summary

- Differentiating instruction and universal design for learning are approaches to teaching that ensure that all students, including those who are CLDE, have access to the curriculum.

- Backward design and the instructional planning pyramid are practical strategies that help teachers organize instructional choices when teaching in classrooms that include CLDE learners.

- Good planning and the use of effective strategies engage and challenge all learners and minimize discipline issues.

Key Terms

Backward design model

Content

Differentiating instruction (DI)

Instructional planning pyramid

Multiple means of engagement

Multiple means of expression

Multiple means of representation

Process

Product

Universal design for learning (UDL)

Activities for Further Understanding

1. Think of a lesson you have recently taught or observed in a classroom. Think of the students in the class. How could you better differentiate product, process, or content to meet their needs, interests, and abilities?

2. Observe a lesson in a classroom. Does the teacher provide a variety of access points for the students? Are there multiple means of representation, engagement, and expression in the lesson? How does the teacher address needs of CLDE learners in the class through instructional planning?

3. Interview a teacher to find out how he or she plans lessons and units. Is a backward design model used? How are needs of CLDE learners addressed in the planning process?

4. Pick a content-area subject and try the concept of backward planning with an upcoming topic. What were the results? How could you improve?

Visit the Student Study Site at **www.sagepub.com/grassi** for chapter-specific study resources.

Notes

1. Extensive discussion of specific strategies will be presented in Chapters 9–15.

2. Extensive discussion of specific strategies will be presented in Chapters 9–15.

3. This is only meant to be a framework to consider how to most effectively support students in the general education classroom. A student's IEP may place a student at any of the intervention levels in this framework—it is important for teachers to know what those plans entail and to follow through with the implementation of strategies, supports, and so on documented in the IEP.

Chapter 8

CULTURALLY RELEVANT PEDAGOGY

Sandra L. Mitchell

Key Points

◆ What classroom practices can exclude students who are culturally, linguistically, socially, or economically diverse

◆ How to build a positive classroom environment that includes students' lives and experiences in the learning process

CASE STUDY 8.1	**Discovery of America**

Mr. Robbins is teaching a lesson on the discovery of America. Along with facts that include names and dates, Mr. Robbins says, "and so Christopher Columbus discovered what he initially thought was India. That's why Native Americans are called Indians."

Jonathan, a usually quiet, but very attentive student in the class, interrupts Mr. Robbins, "But Mr. Robbins, how could he discover a place that people already lived. My family has been here way before that."

"OK. Where did you hear this?" Mr. Robbins asked.

"My grandfather. He told me that what we learn in the history books about our people is not true," Jonathan replied.

Mr. Robbins did not acknowledge Jonathan's comment and went on to finish the lesson. As the semester went on, Jonathan paid less attention in class, seemed less interested, and his performance in the class went from a "B" at mid-semester to a "C" at the end of the term.

Consider the case study above:

- How did the teacher respond to Jonathan's version of history?
- What message did this send to Jonathan?
- What might be a more effective way to respond to this student's comments?

> *To teach in a manner that respects and cares for the souls of our students is essential if we are to provide the necessary conditions where learning can most deeply and intimately begin.*
>
> –bell hooks

INTRODUCTION AND DEFINITIONS

Public education stands not only as a powerful tool to educate and expose students to various perspectives and cultures, but also, and perhaps most relevantly, as one of the great equalizing foundations of our democracy. While policies exist to help ensure that students have equal access to knowledge, there are practices that can inadvertently exclude some students or undermine learning. As educators, we want our students to be motivated to learn. The question remains, how do we position our classrooms as more inclusive learning environments? How do we take into account students' personal histories, perspectives, and experiences to enrich the learning environment for all students? Inclusive pedagogy, diversity pedagogy, equity pedagogy, culturally relevant teaching, responsive teaching, or inclusive teaching all provide one approach to achieve this. These terms, which are sometimes used interchangeably, share the same basic ideas as defined here:

- **Inclusive pedagogy** is an emerging body of literature that advocates teaching practices that embrace the whole student in the learning process (Tuitt, 2003).

- **Diversity pedagogy** is an ideology that views the relationship between culture and cognition as essential to understanding the teaching-learning process (Sheets, 2005).

- **Equity pedagogy** is the acknowledgment that students from different backgrounds may learn in different ways. Teachers need to be aware of this in order to write lessons that maximize every student's success (Banks, 1997).

- **Culturally responsive teaching** occurs when there is equal respect for the backgrounds and contemporary circumstances of all learners, and when there is a design of learning processes that embraces the range of needs, interests, and orientations to be found among them (Wlodkowski & Ginsberg, 1995).

All of these ideas, no matter what we call them, are a departure from the traditional one-size-fits-all approach to teaching. One-size-fits-all teaching can leave students who may not fit the model of "standard," such as students of color, students with special needs, or students who are learning English, to fend for their own learning. While the one-size-fits-all approach views cultural diversity as a "melting pot" in which the aim is to make all students the same, culturally relevant pedagogy is more of a "salad bowl" in which each member of the class (students and teacher) may add to and share in the teaching and learning process simply by being who they are.

Culturally relevant teaching emphasizes the following ideals:

1. Developing and maintaining strong teacher-student relationships.

2. Emphasizing consistent dialogical interaction.

3. Incorporating and validating space for student voice and identity.

4. Making content relevant to all students in the classroom.

DEVELOP AND MAINTAIN STRONG TEACHER-STUDENT RELATIONSHIPS

An important step to building positive relationships between teachers and students is to consider how a positive classroom environment is built. To begin, teachers should create an open and welcoming environment that is conducive to learning. While this is a complex issue, this may be done simply by displaying and utilizing artwork, books, and other publications in the classroom that reflect the cultural diversity of students.

In a positive classroom environment, teachers *maintain positive attitudes toward students*. If we perceive certain students as less likely to learn, they will be. When we treat students as competent, they are likely to demonstrate competence (Ladson-Billings, 1994).

In positive classroom environments, teachers *share power with students*. They allow students to provide, as well as gain, information. For example, if a student asks a question for which we do not know the answer, we might honestly tell the student that we "don't know" and invite him or her to answer along with us by researching it together. Students often have creative learning resources at their disposal (such as Jonathan's grandfather in Case Study 8.1). Students respond well to teachers who actively participate with students in co-construction of ideas (Sheets, 2005). In this kind of democratic classroom, students are free to express their value choices, determine how those choices conflict, examine alternatives, and consider the consequences of different value choices (Banks, 1997).

Positive classroom environments actively *make linkages between home and school knowledge*. Students are better motivated in classrooms where their home knowledge, not just their school knowledge, is honored. In a fourth grade math class, for example, a teacher can present the following scenario: Juan's sister Selena will celebrate her *Quinceañera* next month. The family is expecting 45 people to come to the celebration. They are buying gifts for the guests, but the gifts come in packages of 12. How many packages will they need to buy? In my own classes, I have made references to popular culture such as movies and music that are known favorites of students in the class, to add a point of reference for introducing and understanding material.

Positive classroom environments also *provide students with multiple forms of assistance or differentiated supports*. For example, as a learner I benefit from one-on-one interactions with the teacher. In these interactions, I can take the time that I need to express myself without the fear of embarrassment in front of my colleagues. Others may find that interactions with two or three peers, especially those who share a common language provide valuable learning. In order to best provide students with the supports they need, teachers must have a complete

understanding of students, including their
cultural backgrounds and histories (Ladson-
Billings, 1994). A complete understanding
also helps teachers interact with students in
multiple ways, which reflects the complexity
of student identity and interests, and prevents
the treatment of students as one-dimensional.

> **REFER TO CASE STUDY 8.1**
>
> Did Mr. Robbins create a positive classroom environment? How could he have improved upon this?

Another way of strengthening student-teacher relationships is for the teacher
to understand her or his own awareness of differences and how one responds to
these differences. As teachers we often respond, even if only at a visceral level,
to what we perceive a student to be and thus how she or he should be treated
as a learner.

CASE STUDY 8.2 | **Initial Stereotypes**

As a college instructor, I had a student, Chad, who entered the classroom on the first evening
of class wearing his baseball cap backwards, a pair of torn jeans through which could clearly
be seen his boxer shorts and a dirty T-shirt. He slouched in the front row of the classroom with
his legs outstretched and a soda can next to him into which he was discarding his chewing
tobacco. My initial thought, based on his appearance, posture, and behavior, was that he was
only in the class because it was required and I could expect minimal, at best, performance from
him. As the semester went on, however, and I had more opportunities to interact with him, I
found Chad to be one of the most engaged and conscientious students in the class, earning
one of very few "As" in the course. The important lesson for me was that by getting to know
this student who looked like a "slacker," I discovered he was far from it. I was remiss to "judge
the book by its cover."

As demonstrated in Case Study 8.2, the teacher's stereotypes influenced the
teacher's perception of the student. If the teacher had maintained her perceptions of Chad and treated him based on her stereotypes, she might have disre-
garded this student's true ability, "writing him off" before he was able to prove
himself. This happens quite frequently with students who are racial minorities,
are nonfluent English speakers, have special needs, or are in a different socio-
economic class than the majority of students.

There are several steps teachers can take to build their own cultural competence. Teachers can *examine their personal thinking habits especially with
regard to stereotypes.* We all have prejudices and we must examine how they

affect our interactions with others. Become aware of how you respond to differences in students' appearances, values, and behaviors. What are our "pet peeves," and how do we respond when faced with them?

Teachers should also *observe student response to instruction* and adapt instruction accordingly. If a student is not responding to a lecture, is there another means of instruction such as group activities or hands-on activities that may be more effective in facilitating learning? Cartledge et al. (2009) refer to this as equity pedagogy, which encourages teachers to match instruction to the learning styles of students.

Teachers should *assume responsibility for pedagogical knowledge*. As the students and contexts for learning change, teachers must be willing not only to acknowledge what they do not know, but make an effort to acquire knowledge and put it into effective practice. One of the most common errors teachers make is unconsciously to ask a student to speak for her or his entire race, which is often done by people who are well versed in work and theory on "white privilege,"[1] but have not effectively applied the concept to their classroom practice. Attending seminars and faculty development workshops can provide wonderful opportunities to acquire knowledge, but the responsibility for applying the knowledge lies with the teacher.

Teachers also need to *recognize, interpret, and respond to cultural displays* (Sheets, 2005). Cultural displays are manifestations of norms and values relevant in children's homes and communities. These displays can provide valuable insights to student identity, how they behave, and what they know. For example, reverence for authority is a common value in many homes, which can be observed in the way that children interact with teachers. Cultural displays can also be observed in the way that students and families of color perceive white teacher attitudes about race. For example, as an African American, when I step into the classroom, I assume that the teacher has a set of preconceived ideas about my cultural and personal background, as well as my ability as a student, based on my appearance. Even when I sit at the front of the room, arrive early, and fully engage in the class (behaviors that are manifestations of my desire to learn), I assume that this teacher believes that I am not as prepared academically because I came from a poor inner-city school where academics were not emphasized, and that I am likely to not be as "articulate" as my white colleagues because slang and improper language use are simply an accepted part of my culture. Right or wrong, I have been raised to believe this about teachers at all levels. Getting to know learners and their backgrounds and realistically acknowledging the fact that students also come into the classroom environment with preconceived ideas can help a teacher better facilitate learning. Beginning courses with reflective activities (such as writing) that allow students to talk about themselves help students develop confidence and provide the teacher with insight.

Finally, teachers will need to *change patterns of thinking and challenge stereotypes*. When students question, joke, or comment in class about sensitive topics such as race or ethnicity, religion, or gender, teachers need to continue the discussion, not ignore it as if it never occurred. When expressed biases can clearly isolate students, the teacher should certainly not let them go unnoticed as the failure to acknowledge such often implies that it is acceptable. Failure to address such issues also sends a message to students who are isolated by such comments that they are not cared for.

Angelica, a young Latina student, described a situation in a class in which students were discussing the achievement gap. The instructor asked, "What do underachieving students look like? What do you think of these stereotypes?" A classmate responded, "Clinch your purse and hide your stereo." Angelica and the other student of color in the class, an African American male, looked at each other and chuckled in disbelief. There was an audible gasp from other students in the room. "I was so angry I just couldn't speak," Angelica said. The students of color felt isolated. The instructor took advantage of this opportunity to talk to students about the negative consequences of stereotyping. As a result, Angelica and the other student of color did not have to say how they felt or bear the burden of addressing the issue (which may have further isolated them); rather, the entire class had an opportunity to engage in the discussion, including the classmate who made the comment. At the same time, this classmate was not isolated for her faux pas and the class learned a valuable lesson about ways that stereotypes, even used humorously, can be hurtful.

> ### REFER TO CASE STUDY 8.1
>
> What types of self-examination could benefit Mr. Robbins? How would a practice of self-examination help students of color in Mr. Robbins's classroom?

EMPHASIZE CONSISTENT DIALOGICAL INTERACTION

Inclusive classrooms are often best built through dialogical interactions and a sharing of power. Successful dialogical interactions value student voice as much as teacher expertise. Again, this is a departure from the traditional belief that the teacher imparts knowledge through one-way lecture without any sharing from students. Inclusive pedagogical models challenge the notion that only the teacher possesses knowledge and instead proposes that teachers and students are equally responsible for constructing knowledge (Tuitt, 2003). While dialogues are most comfortable when they simply "happen," sometimes such dialogues need to be encouraged. Use agreements or ground rules in encouraging open dialogue in the classroom, so that all students will feel comfortable in participating (see Table 8.1).

Table 8.1 Agreements for Open Dialogue in the Classroom

- Use "I" statements when speaking.
- No one is wrong. Everyone and their opinions are equal.
- Information shared and discussed in this dialogue should not leave this space. Confidentiality is to be respected at all times.
- Listen carefully and with respect to what another person is telling you. Don't formulate your response while someone is speaking but wait until they have completely finished.
- Listen to your inner voice. Become aware of when you are moved to speak and when you are not.
- Speak personally and specifically rather than generally and abstractly. No one can or should speak for an entire group of people, nor should they be expected to.

Of all of these agreements, understanding (and accepting) that an individual is not wrong despite their opinion can be very difficult. It is important to emphasize the humanity and dignity of the individual regardless of their views. For example, as an African American instructor, I must sometimes negotiate the lines between my own feelings about white supremacist views stated by a student about a particular topic or issue, my instinct to judge the student (and even disregard her or him completely) as a person, and to guard the safety of the learning environment. On such occasions, I must constantly remind myself that the student is sharing his or her views on a particular issue and that this is not necessarily a reflection of them as a person. I then ask the student where such ideas came from, and while it takes some extra time and energy to do so, we address some of the misconceptions that are often behind extreme views on many issues. I can also choose to respectfully disagree with that student and even let her or him know that I take offense to some of their stated views without saying that I take offense to them (i.e., the student personally).

REFER TO CASE STUDY 8.1

How did Mr. Robbins encourage or discourage dialogical interactions. How could he have improved on his response to Jonathan to encourage more dialogue?

INCORPORATE AND VALIDATE SPACE FOR STUDENT VOICE AND IDENTITY

A respectful learning environment means that the integrity of each person is valued in ways that welcome the worth and expression of one's true self without fear of threat or blame (Wlodkowski & Ginsberg, 1995). Each classroom has a wide range of student engagement and participation—from students like Jonathan, in Case Study 8.1, who are willing to make their voices and opinions known, to students who are afraid to utter a word. Each student brings both voice and personal identity to the learning environment. Respecting student voice and identity are crucial to inclusive pedagogy as it allows for diverse voices to be part of the dialogue (see Photo 8.2).

Individual differences may be influenced by culture (such as collective vs. individual goals) as well as personality (outgoing versus withdrawn). Teachers have to be sensitive to the diversity that exists and the multiple expressions of students and should consider questions such as the following (Barules & Rice, 1993):

Photo 8.2 Teachers need to foster an environment that encourages participation.

1. Who may feel unable to speak without fear of explicit or implicit retribution?

2. Who may want to speak but feels so demoralized or intimidated by the circumstances that they are silenced?

3. What rules of communication may be operating in the classroom that prohibit certain areas of concern or modes of speech?

Says one Latina student, "In middle school, I always raised my hand to answer questions. Now I'm intimidated, especially if I think I may be wrong. I'm afraid to speak my mind because I worry that I may be viewed as less intelligent because my classes are mostly white and I may be the only person of color." The most common solution to this concern would be to simply call on the student, which as most of us know, further adds to the isolation. Better solutions include putting students in pairs for discussion or activities, asking students to write reflections, and providing opportunities for individual student presentations.

The activation of student's voices in diverse classrooms needs to be accompanied by a sense of the context and personal histories that students bring to the classroom. At a minimum, knowledge of individual students helps the teacher distinguish between students whose voices are silenced and students who choose to be silent or choose to engage in ways other than dialogue. At best, this sense of individual differences helps to build strong teacher-student relationships that may in turn strengthen the learning process.

REFER TO CASE STUDY 8.1

How did Mr. Robbins make space for student voice and identity? What could he have done differently to better validate all students' voices?

As noted in Case Study 8.1, Jonathan's personal history informed the outlook that he brought to the history lesson (Tuitt, 2003). The lens that students bring to the classroom is impacted by their personal history and the teacher needs to consider each student's background.

MAKE CONTENT RELEVANT TO ALL STUDENTS IN THE CLASSROOM

Teachers know that if a student can apply meaning and value to content, they are more likely to retain what they have learned, apply what they have learned, and increase their motivation to continue learning. Culturally responsive teaching respects and incorporates the learner's deeper meaning to create joyful, absorbing, and challenging learning experiences (Wlodkowski & Ginsberg, 1995). Personalizing the subject by giving specific examples of value to students' life experiences is good for all learners. Students' real-life experiences are legitimized as they become part of the "official curriculum" (Ladson-Billings, 1994). Culturally responsive teaching enhances meaning and helps to increase the complexity of what is learned in ways that matter to learners. Teachers help students understand, investigate, and determine the implicit cultural assumptions and frames of reference and perspectives of the discipline they're teaching (Banks, 1997).

In order to best implement culturally relevant teaching, teachers need to know what matters to students so that students might apply what they are learning to their lives and values. Traditional teaching models often design instruction before the makeup of the class is even realized. A more inclusive pedagogy requires teachers to apply instructional design methods that include the learner in the design of instruction. The instructional design should consider not only what students learn, but the best ways for them to do so. This means the design should be student centered, placing the student at the center of the learning process, and instruction should be designed to include the cultural identities of students in the classroom. Teachers should realize that students bring great diversity and should build a repertoire of strategies to accommodate diversity (in social identity, cultural identity, as well as learning styles). Teachers should be aware of perceptual barriers between student and teacher and the negative consequences these perceptions can have on the learning process. Teachers should continually examine their own beliefs and value systems for biases that could create perceptual barriers, silence student voices, and have a negative impact on teacher-student relationships. And finally, while not expected to be experts in the various cultures represented in their classrooms, teachers should be responsible for learning as much as they can (by reading about cultures, attending community events, and participating in faculty development opportunities). Families who are willing to share information can be a tremendous resource for learning about cultures and filling in knowledge that the teacher may not have. One of the scarcest resources for classroom teachers is time. We realize that even suggesting that teachers have time to research cultures may be a bit idealistic. But, if teachers can draw out the voice of students and their families, then different cultures can be incorporated into the classroom. We also realize that much professional development revolves around increasing academic achievement and it is rare that the connection between culturally relevant pedagogy and increased academic achievement is considered. However, students are more motivated to learn and are more likely to retain the information that they acquire if it is relevant to them.

> **REFER TO CASE STUDY 8.1**
>
> How did Mr. Robbins make the content relevant to the students in his classroom? How do you make the content relevant to your students? How can you better increase cultural relevance in your classroom?

Summary

- Strong student-teacher relationships develop when teachers provide a positive classroom environment and build their own cultural competence.

- Inclusive classroom environments place as much value on student voice and identity as they do on teacher expertise.

- Culturally responsive teaching occurs in an environment of mutual respect where curriculum is designed in ways that matter to learners.

Key Terms

Culturally responsive teaching   Equity pedagogy

Diversity pedagogy   Inclusive pedagogy

Activities for Further Understanding

1. Observe a classroom in a diverse school. What aspects of culturally relevant pedagogy does the teacher employ? How does the teacher enhance student-teacher relationships? How does the teacher emphasize consistent dialogical interaction? How does the teacher incorporate and validate space for student voice and identity? And how does the teacher make the content relevant to all students in the classroom? Take notes on your observations, compare to suggestions in this chapter, and determine what aspects the teacher does well, and what aspects still need further development.

2. Examine professional development opportunities in your school or a school where you are observing. How many of these opportunities include training in culturally relevant pedagogy?

3. Attend or reflect on an in-service in cultural training or culturally relevant pedagogy. How does this in-service compare to recommendations in this chapter?

4. Consider a lesson in your content area. What can you do to make the content more relevant to the students in your classroom? How would you adapt the lesson?

5. Consider the relationship you have with students in your classroom. Which students do you need to get to know better? How can you go about doing this?

6. How do you make space for student voice in your classroom? How can you do this better?

 Visit the Student Study Site at **www.sagepub.com/grassi** for chapter-specific study resources.

Note

1. For more on white privilege, see McIntosh (1990).

SECTION III

Strategies for Content and Language Acquisition

Chapter 9. Teaching Strategies: An Integrated Content-Language Approach

Chapter 10. Strategies for Promoting Participation

Chapter 11. Strategies for Explicit Grammar Instruction

Chapter 9

TEACHING STRATEGIES

An Integrated Content-Language Approach

CASE STUDY 9.1 | Teaching CLDE Students

One of the most difficult things I have encountered as a teacher is how to effectively teach ELL students who have special needs. All my students are ELLs, and at least one-third of them have special needs. While their needs and strengths are unique, my struggles to teach them are similar, from one to the next. Learning how to teach Abigail has been one of my most significant, yet rewarding, challenges to date.

Abigail is an ELL student assigned to the eighth grade. Abigail performs around a third-grade level in her core subjects. Because we have not yet received the IEP from her previous school, we don't know what she has accomplished. She has low retention and remembers only about 15% to 20% of the new material I teach to her. She is unable to concentrate long enough to do homework or work independently. She is so far behind the other students that she is often left behind during discussions and lessons.

Throughout the year, I have employed a number of techniques and strategies to help Abigail grow academically. Some strategies have been successful or produced consistent results, while others have failed completely.

First, I dedicate a significant amount of time to working with her one on one several times a week after class. This one-on-one time has made a significant difference in her willingness to participate in class. She recalls learned material more easily in these individual settings, which carries over to group settings. I believe one-on-one time with teachers is very important for the growth of CLDE students.

When I am unable to work with her one on one during class time, I pair her with students that she trusts and who are strong in the content. She has built some good friendships and gets a lot done when she is working in groups.

I provide graphic organizers for her for everything we do. The graphic organizers are used for vocabulary, events, rules (in grammar, math, science), cause and effect, and so on. Having a mapped-out and structured visual in front of her has helped greatly in scaffolding her learning. I also have created places in the classroom where she can keep her materials. Helping her learn to be organized has helped increase the amount of work she can get done in a day.

All instructions are written down ahead of time and handed to her, read aloud to the class (with emphasis put on key words), and modeled before she is asked to complete the task. I always give examples. Whenever possible, I give her step-by-step written or drawn directions and examples for new concepts or information. Having instructions and examples modeled is essential for all of my ELL students, so they can better recall what is being asked of them. I use pictures throughout the lesson, and I draw examples or pictures on her work to help her.

Finally, the work and assessments I give Abigail are customized to be as specific and concrete as possible. Her tests have matching and multiple-choice questions, for example. I ask very specific questions instead of questions that could be answered with abstract explanations. She is able to participate in class, but her assessments are tailored to her abilities.

Abigail has made significant growth in her oral performance, organization, motivation, and reading comprehension. I know Abigail still has many struggles ahead of her, and she will be in need of differentiated lessons and materials for the length of her school career. However, the advancements she has made so far this year are worthy of cheer.

—Caitlin, Secondary social studies teacher

Consider the case study above:

- What challenges does this teacher face in her classroom?
- What strategies were most effective in working with Abigail? Would these strategies be effective with most CLDE students?
- Which of the strategies Caitlin describes do you incorporate in your classroom? Which could you better incorporate?

SOURCE: Used by permission.

In the best possible scenario, where schools are full of qualified bilingual teachers who can successfully teach academic subjects in both languages and provide culturally relevant pedagogy for all, we would advocate the placement of all CLDE students in these classrooms. However, reality dictates that the majority of teachers today are English monolingual, with little to no cultural training. In addition, policies such as NCLB encourage the use of English in the classroom and English proficiency as soon as possible. Therefore, as realists and pragmatists, we advocate that *all* teachers be thoroughly trained in ELL strategies (e.g., Dutro & Moran, 2003; Echevarria, Vogt, & Short, 2008; Short & Echevarria, 1999) and special education strategies (Friend, 2005; Marzano, Pickering, & Pollock, 2001; Tomlinson, 1999; Tomlinson & McTighe, 2006) in order to meet the needs of their CLDE students.

Many of the strategies based in English language acquisition are similar to the strategies used for students who have special needs—the difference lies in the *reasons why* teachers choose particular strategies. For example, if a student with special needs has trouble reading, the teacher will adapt the text to help the student access the reading. Likewise, if an ELL student has trouble reading in English, the teacher will adapt the text. Adaptations for both ELL and learners with special needs include strategies such as highlighting key vocabulary, providing visual context, reading the text aloud to the student, or giving the student time to process the readings—but the reasons behind each strategy differ. There also will be particular adaptations for the specific needs of the student.

Providing the text in the student's L1 or with modified English vocabulary will greatly benefit the ELL student. Providing text with a larger font or with fewer words on the page are scaffolds that can help some students with special needs.

These scaffolds need to be in place to support access to the text. Teachers need to pay particular attention to the stages of language acquisition of ELL students, and to remove scaffolds as the student progresses through the language acquisition process. For a student with special needs, goals need to be monitored as required by the student's IEP. Adjustments and modifications should be made as the student reaches the IEP goals. With CLDE students, the teacher cannot ignore one need in order to address another. Research-based strategies from the fields of *both* ESL or bilingual education and special education must be integrated for successful instruction. One of the many challenges of instructing CLDE students is that teachers must adopt two roles: content teacher and English language teacher. Both of these roles are vitally important to the academic success of CLDE students. When working with CLDE students, adaptations, scaffolding, and monitoring of progress need to take into account the content, the language acquisition process, and the special education issues.

In this chapter, we will discuss foundational strategies to make the content accessible to CLDE students, while concurrently supporting the language acquisition process. One of the guiding principles to an **integrated content–language approach** is that teachers maintain high expectations for *all* students. Teachers should not water down the curriculum or expect less from students because they do not speak English as an L1. Many of these students have a strong base in their L1, are highly motivated, and will work hard to meet expectations. Rather, teachers need to adapt their techniques to assist CLDE students in meeting high expectations and gaining access to the same rigorous content that is presented to students in general education.

The strategies discussed in this chapter are based on research in second language acquisition (Krashen, 1982; Long, 1996; McLaughlin, 1990a; Swain, 2005) and adapted from research in teaching (Dutro & Moran, 2003; Echevarria et al., 2008; Fillmore & Snow, 2000; Kame'enui, Carnine, Dixon, Simmons, & Coyne, 2002; Marzano et al., 2001; McGregor & Vogelsberg, 1998; Short & Echevarria, 1999; Tomlinson & McTighe, 2006). We will discuss the following strategies:

1. Making the content comprehensible using the 3-way model

2. Front-loading and emphasizing key academic vocabulary and key concepts of the lesson

3. Accessing and explicitly teaching the content and cultural schemata needed for the lesson

4. Allowing students to clarify the subject matter in their L1

5. Helping students organize and access academic information

While this chapter will generalize about students with special needs and not differentiate for each disability, we realize that there is a great variety in the needs of students with special education labels. The strategies we have chosen are generally effective for most students who require support in classroom learning. Nevertheless, it is also important to continually explore strategies that incorporate tenets of "best practice" and that meet the needs and strengths of the individual student. The students' IEPs will provide the strategies that work best for their particular learning needs.

> **REFER TO CASE STUDY 9.1**
>
> How did Caitlin address both the content and the language acquisition process of her students? Which strategies did she employ that address both the students' special needs and the language acquisition process?

STRATEGY 9.1 MAKING THE CONTENT COMPREHENSIBLE WITH THE 3-WAY MODEL

Perspective From the Field of Language Acquisition

As discussed in Chapter 3, Krashen's (1982) input hypothesis states that, in order for L2 acquisition to occur, students need access to input that is

a. comprehensible and

b. challenging $(i + 1)$.

In order to make the content matter comprehensible and challenging, the teacher will need to provide ample context to help students understand the material presented in the classroom. One way to ensure comprehension is to present all content following the **3-way model:**

Step 1. The content and directions for all activities are *spoken.*

Step 2. Key points from the content and directions for all activities are *written down.*

Step 3. Key points from the content and directions for all activities are presented with *visual context.*

Step 1. Speak Content and Directions

The content and directions must be *spoken* so that students can make connections to language they have heard. This is especially true for students who have high verbal comprehension skills and are able to follow the spoken word. Speaking the content and directions also appeals to those with an auditory learning style.

Not just any spoken words will do, however. In order for ELL students to comprehend the spoken word, teachers should simplify the vocabulary, use repetition, and paraphrase definitions (Chaudron, 1988, as cited in Rost, 2005). Rate of speech also can influence comprehension and word recognition. Slower speech rate and pauses at natural pause boundaries facilitate L2 listening comprehension (Rost, 2005).

Finally, to help ELL students process the information and prepare a response, increased teacher wait-time before expecting students to respond greatly assists students with speech production (Echevarria et al., 2008). When ELL students are asked to participate in class, they must tackle several steps before producing a response (adapted from Andrews, 1980):

1. They must comprehend the question (which often involves translating part or all the question into the L1).

2. They must search their memory for relevant facts or information.

3. They must select a response in either the L1 or L2.

4. If their response was formed in the L1, they must translate their response to the L2.

5. They must form the response so it is culturally acceptable in the U.S. classroom.

6. They must overcome any inhibitions about speaking in their L2 in front of a group.

Building in appropriate wait-time for processing is an important step in encouraging participation in the content area or general education classroom. Providing students with the discussion questions prior to the actual discussion will allow ELL students time to think about and prepare their responses so they can better participate in the discussion.

Step 2. Write Down Key Points From the Content and Directions

When key points are written down, students can take notes. This can be important if students are unable to understand everything that is spoken in the classroom.

They can refer to the notes later as a manner of reviewing the material and furthering comprehension of the material (Rost, 2005).

Depending on a student's prior experience with English, some might have literacy skills in English but not verbal skills, and might be able to read English but not understand English words spoken to them. When key points of the lesson and directions for activities are written down, they become accessible to these students. In addition, multiple directions given at one time can confuse ELL students. When instructions are written down step by step, students who were unable to process oral directions can refer to the written instructions. Written points and directions also assist visual learners in accessing the material.

The writing should be organized in some fashion to make the key points clear and concise. Teachers can organize the points they write down in a semantic web, in an outline, or some sort of **graphic organizer** that helps students categorize the new content.

The key points do not always have to be teacher generated. When students provide key answers to higher-level questions, it is important that teachers write the student responses as well. In this manner, ELL students and visual learners—who may have experienced a lapse in attention during the spoken word—can refocus their attention and stay attuned with the discussion.

Step 3. Use Visual Context to Teach Key Points From the Content and Directions

Visual context must be provided so that students who do not understand the spoken or written words or who are at beginning levels of the acquisition process can follow the discussion by making connections between the visual clue and the spoken or written words. Providing visual context also appeals to visual learners, assisting with their retention of the material. Examples of visual clues include the following ways to present the concept:

a. Holding up a picture

b. Drawing a picture on the chalkboard

c. Showing PowerPoint slides

d. Showing a film

e. Reading a picture book

f. Using maps, photos, and illustrations

g. Using realia—costumes, artifacts, authentic texts, and so on

h. Modeling directions for the activities

   i. Conducting demonstrations of the activities

   j. Modeling examples of finished products so students visualize the expected outcome

   k. Taking field trips

   l. Using manipulatives

  m. Using gestures and drama

The visual context provided must be connected to the written and spoken explanation so that students can begin to acquire the necessary academic vocabulary. Content area teachers who have ELL students in their classes will follow a sequence such as the following:

   a. The teacher explains a content point while showing a picture.

   b. The teacher tapes the picture next to a graphic organizer on the board (each individual student also has a copy on which to write) and reiterates the point by writing about it on the organizer.

   c. The teacher shows a video clip about the concept, again referring to notes written on the organizer.

   d. The students then read about the concept in the textbook, locating the key vocabulary and concepts already introduced.

When the teacher inserts several visual context clues into the regular lesson, the ELL student sees, hears, and writes about (takes notes about) the material.

To make the written word comprehensible to ELL students, the writing must be legible. Students might not be familiar with the words they hear, so they might misspell them and not be able to decipher them later. In addition, many ELL students have an L1 with an alphabet system quite different from English.

Content-area teachers with ELL students in their classes are accustomed to writing on the board or overhead projector as they speak, writing down all directions for students to follow along, writing down student responses, and displaying pictures or other visuals as they discuss key concepts. These teaching methods also ensure greater understanding of the content by native English speakers in the class.

Perspective From the Field of Special Education

Students who have special needs, like all students, learn best in different ways. For instance, a student who has a perceptual disability might have trouble understanding written directions, but can easily understand when the teacher reads the directions aloud. Likewise, a student with a learning disability might not be able to focus while the teacher is stating a complicated series of instructions, but can follow a list of written directions. When students are instructed in a variety of ways, or when the instruction is differentiated to meet the particular needs of students, teachers are more likely to capitalize on the variety of learning preferences within their classrooms (Dunn, 1996; Gardner, 1983; Sternberg, 1996 in McGregor & Vogelsberg, 1998). If the teacher provides instruction using all modalities—the 3-way model—students will have a better opportunity to access the information presented (Barbe & Swassing, 1979; Dunn & Dunn, 1975; Gregorc, 1982; Woolfolk, 2007).

Putting It All Together

When working with CLDE students, a key component to academic success is making the content comprehensible and accessible using multiple modalities (the 3-way model). From the English language acquisition standpoint, the student will need comprehensible input in order to acquire the content in English.

From the special education standpoint, the student will need access to the information in the learning preference best suited for the student's strengths and in a manner that best supports her special education needs. By providing the CLDE student with content instruction from various modalities, language acquisition and content understanding are enhanced and the special education needs supported.

> **REFER TO CASE STUDY 9.1**
>
> How did Caitlin use the 3-way model with her students? What further changes would you implement to meet more of the needs of her students?

Summary

1. All content points and directions are spoken.

2. Key content points, student answers, and directions for activities are written down and organized systematically.

3. Key content points and directions are presented with visual context, and the visual is connected to the written and spoken word.

9.1

> To access a video clip of a teacher making the content comprehensible using the 3-way model, and a rubric to observe the teacher and evaluate the strategy, see the following Web link: **www.sagepub.com/grassi.**

STRATEGY 9.2 FRONT-LOADING AND EMPHASIZING THE ACADEMIC LANGUAGE AND KEY CONCEPTS OF THE LESSON

Perspective From the Field of Language Acquisition

When ELL students are placed in general education or content area classes, they often are overwhelmed by the amount of information presented during a lesson. They are often unsure of which information is essential and which is nonessential to learning. It is not uncommon for ELL students to try to take notes of every word the teacher says, and then to become frustrated when they are unable to write fast enough, or unable to understand every spoken word.

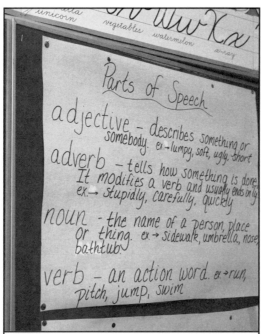

Photo 9.2   Writing down key concepts and key vocabulary of the lesson helps students understand what to look for.

Likewise, it is not uncommon for ELL students to memorize or copy down every word of the textbook because they are unable to differentiate between key concepts and superfluous information. In order to assist students in determining the key concepts and language of the lesson and to help develop English language skills that are necessary for understanding and participating in the lesson, the teacher must **front-load** (i.e., teach before the lesson begins) and emphasize the key academic language and the key concepts of the lesson (Dutro & Moran, 2003; Echevarria et al., 2008).

Key academic language consists of the language needed to understand, write about, and speak about the content. Key academic language is the language used in academic texts, in academic discussions, and in formal writing (see Photo 9.2). In simpler terms, academic language consists of two areas:

1. *The key vocabulary, phrases, or expressions* commonly used in the discipline—especially those that are needed to understand and participate in the present lesson

2. *The grammar* needed to participate actively in the lesson

Studies in language acquisition have found that explicit teaching of *key vocabulary, phrases, and expressions* is essential to comprehension of the subject matter (Dutro & Moran, 2003; Echevarria et al., 2008). ELL students often report that it is lack of "word recognition"—not knowing a word—that is one of the most difficult aspects of the acquisition process (Rost & Ross, 1991). Likewise, studies have indicated that when spoken or written vocabulary words or phrases are outside a student's knowledge, these unknown words or phrases can cause a "blip" in attention and prevent students from focusing on the immediate and successive discourse (Rost & Ross, 1991). Studies in L2 acquisition have indicated a strong relationship between vocabulary development, academic achievement, and comprehension (Echevarria et al., 2008). Thus, if students are not able to understand the key vocabulary and so try to wade through all that is said or read, they will miss the main points of the lesson.

The *key vocabulary* is determined through extracting the specialized content area words, terms, and phrases that are specific to the discipline. For example, key vocabulary words for social studies are government, constitution, conflict, politics; for science, they are hypothesis, invertebrate, cells, observe; for math, they are addition, multiplication, division, formulas; and for language arts, they are plot, character, summarize, and infer. Before beginning the lesson, the teacher should create and present a list of academic terms, expressions, and phrases that are key to understanding and participating in the lesson. Teachers should also include words, expressions, or phrases that students will encounter frequently in the lesson, that are new to students, or that students may have difficulty figuring out independently or through the context of the lesson (Graves, Juel, & Graves, 1998).

The teacher should be prepared to front-load this vocabulary so students will be able to participate orally and in writing.

Repetition is a key component to making the content comprehensible for ELL students. Once the teacher has emphasized the key vocabulary, the students need to implement strategies to encourage repetition and retention of the academic language learned. Below is a list of recommended strategies (adapted from Nation, 2005, pp. 589–593):

1. Learning from word cards

2. Guessing from context

3. Using word parts

4. Using word sorts

9.2

> For a detailed description of each of the strategies listed above, see the following Web link: **www.sagepub.com/grassi.**

Grammar of the Lesson

The grammar of the lesson consists of specific grammatical structures that will assist ELL students in successfully participating orally or in a written format. For example, to discuss the Civil War, students need to produce the past tense in English—"The war *took place* many years ago. The soldiers *were* ordinary citizens." Likewise, students may need to learn grammatical structures such as the past conditional to discuss possible scenarios of the war ("If I *had lived* in the North, I *would have fought* to free the slaves.").

Dutro and Moran (2003) define the grammar of the lesson as the structures needed to perform the academic task. For example, if the task involves comparing and contrasting the North to the South, then the teacher must determine the grammatical structures, vocabulary, and phrases most commonly used to contrast and compare these ideologies. A list of possible academic classroom tasks could include the following (adapted from Dutro & Moran, 2003, pp. 7–8):

- Asking and answering informational questions
- Asking and answering clarifying questions
- Relating information—such as past events
- Comparing and contrasting
- Explaining cause and effect
- Justifying ideas
- Drawing conclusions
- Summarizing
- Evaluating
- Persuading

The required language structures must be explicitly taught to students before and throughout the lesson, using one of the following strategies:

1. The teacher can pull aside a small group of ELL students and present them with a quick lesson of the structures that will be needed during the school day.

2. The teacher can present the necessary structures to the students the day before and provide them with homework to review the grammatical structures before the lesson begins.

In addition to explicitly teaching the structures in small group settings, the teacher should have the grammatical structures on the board under "language objectives" and quickly review them before beginning the lesson.

Often, teachers are unable to ascertain all the grammatical structures that students will need to participate in the class. In this case, the teacher can take advantage of "teachable moments" (Dutro & Moran, 2003). If students attempt to produce a grammatical structure to participate in the lesson and are inaccurate in their approximation, the teacher can give a grammatical explanation to the class about the structure, using the content to develop examples of that structure (Table 9.1). Alternatively, the teacher can take note of the structures students are attempting and give explicit grammatical quick lessons during later small-group time.

Regardless of the explicit and clear explanation of the grammar, students might continue to make the same grammatical mistake until they are ready to acquire the structure. The teacher must both provide accurate explanations and *repeat* these explanations numerous times over the long run until all students acquire the structure.

Table 9.1   Key Academic Language

Key Vocabulary, Expressions, and Phrases	Key Grammar
• Content-specific words, phrases, and expressions	• Structures needed to participate in the academic discussions • Structures needed to perform the task

Key Concepts of the Lesson

Key concepts involve clearly defining the learning outcomes of the lesson for students before the lesson begins. In order to determine these concepts, it is recommended that teachers follow a "backwards design model" (Wiggins &

McTighe, 1998). As discussed in Chapter 7, a backward design model requires teachers to start planning the lesson from the end by determining the desired results or key concepts of the lesson. Teachers then build their lesson from the endpoint working backward to plan activities that will bring students to the key concepts.

The key concepts must be explicitly pointed out to ELL students before the lesson begins so these students know where to focus their attention. These concepts should be highlighted as the teacher refers to them during the lesson. Students' comprehension of the key concepts should be evaluated at the end of the lesson to determine whether learning outcomes have been achieved.

9.3

For an example of a backward design lesson for the secondary science classroom, see the following Web link: **www.sagepub.com/grassi.**

Key concepts need to be reviewed often so that students can retain their learning of the concept. Teachers should review key concepts for at least 2 to 3 consecutive days to help students retain the information. There are many quick activities for reviewing material, such as

1. think–pair–share board work,

2. Round Robin,

3. white board work, and

4. graphic organizers.

9.4

For a detailed description of each of these strategies, see the following Web link: **www.sagepub.com/grassi.**

Perspective From the Field of Special Education

Emphasizing and Front-Loading Key Vocabulary

Emphasizing key academic language—including specific vocabulary instruction— is an important component for teaching students with special education needs, especially students who have reading difficulties or other issues related to language (Marzano, 2004). Many learners who have special needs lack vocabulary knowledge. That is, they do not have as broad a base of vocabulary knowledge as their peers, and thus retain and understand fewer words than do their peers (Swanborn & de Glopper, 1999). Most researchers who have studied vocabulary issues agree on the following points:

a. Average learners know more vocabulary words than students with learning issues do.

b. Average readers have a greater understanding of the words they read than students with learning issues do.

c. The more students read, the more they increase their vocabulary.

d. Students with reading difficulties, and who therefore read less, have a vocabulary that is less well developed.

e. Students with reading difficulties have less exposure to new words.

f. Over time, the vocabulary gap between average readers and those with learning issues increases (Kame'enui et al., 2002, p. 40; also in Marzano, 2004; Marzano et al., 2001).

The above points indicate that most students are exposed to greater vocabulary through their reading. They pick up the vocabulary because they are exposed to the vocabulary words a number of times through the text. However, if a student is not a good reader, he will become frustrated by the process and will become a "reluctant reader." Often, lower-level readers are given remedial texts with limited vocabulary exposure. Over time, the gap in vocabulary knowledge between proficient readers and students with reading difficulties increases.

Many students with exceptionalities have reading difficulties, so they need explicit vocabulary instruction. They may not have been exposed to academic vocabulary words enough times to learn the words, and also might have retention or memory issues. By highlighting the key vocabulary before a lesson and providing students with the meaning of key vocabulary through explicit instruction, students with special needs are given opportunities to focus on and retain key information. Furthermore, if the teacher includes strategies for practice and retention of the vocabulary, students will use that vocabulary in other contexts.

For a list of strategies to enhance vocabulary instruction for students with special needs, see the following Web link: **www.sagepub.com/grassi.**

9.5

Emphasizing and Front-Loading Grammar Structures

A student with special needs also might require instruction in the academic grammar or language needed for the lesson. Most native-English-speaking students with special needs will have already acquired grammatically correct spoken English. That said, the grammar expected in written academic English differs from spoken English and, if the student is not performing at grade level in written work, this student will need explicit grammar instruction and instruction on the language used for written English.

Emphasizing and Front-Loading Key Concepts

Students with special needs also require front-loading of the key concepts of the lesson in order to be attuned to the main ideas of the lesson. Students with special needs may not be able to "weed through" the content to gain understanding, or may not know what pieces of information are pertinent to the lesson. Students with special needs may be overwhelmed with the amount of information presented. These students will benefit from instruction that focuses on big ideas or concepts, that reviews and front-loads the most important conceptual knowledge of the lesson systematically, and that emphasizes explicit strategies for learning concepts from context (Kame'enui et al., 2002, p. 43).

Putting It All Together

When working with CLDE students, *front-loading and explicit instruction in key academic language and key concepts* are necessary components for academic success. From the perspective of language acquisition, this strategy increases access to the core curriculum and increases students' ability to participate by making the vocabulary, grammar, and key concepts of the lesson explicit and comprehensible. From the perspective of special education issues, this strategy helps students access the content by drawing attention to the key vocabulary and grammatical structures needed for comprehension and application of the content; by allowing students opportunity to practice the necessary vocabulary and thus increase retention; and by reducing the ambiguity of complex concepts by front-loading and emphasizing the pertinent concepts throughout the lesson.

When given explicit instruction on what is important to the lesson, CLDE students can focus on the essential points. These students, who are learning English *and* who have special needs, will be mentally tired from engaging in the learning process. They will expend an enormous amount of energy trying to keep up with their peers and comprehend the material. By helping CLDE students understand the key vocabulary, by giving them the grammatical structures needed to participate, by helping them understand the salient points of the lesson, and by drawing attention to these points when they are discussed, saturation point can be avoided and students' attention will likely be more focused when needed.

> **REFER TO CASE STUDY 9.1**
>
> How did Caitlin front-load and emphasize the key concepts and academic vocabulary for her students? How could she better employ this strategy to meet the needs of her CLDE students?

Summary

1. Determine the key vocabulary, expressions, and grammar for the lesson.

2. Front-load the key academic language before the lesson begins.

3. Highlight the key academic language throughout the lesson.

4. Instruct students in strategies to retain the key academic language.

5. Determine the learning outcomes or key concepts.

6. Front-load these concepts before beginning the lesson and highlight these concepts as they are discussed in class.

7. Implement strategies to review the key concepts with students.

> To watch a video clip of a teacher introducing key concepts and terms and to access a rubric with which to observe the teacher and evaluate the strategy, see the following Web link: **www.sagepub.com/grassi.**

9.6

STRATEGY **9.3** ACCESSING AND EXPLICITLY TEACHING THE CULTURAL AND CONTENT SCHEMATA FOR THE LESSON

Perspective From the Field of Language Acquisition

A student's ability to understand a speaker depends largely on shared sociocultural knowledge. Students come to the classroom already equipped with sociocultural knowledge obtained from their past learning, their home life, and their country of origin. This background knowledge or prior knowledge is often referred to as **content and cultural schemas.** Content and cultural schemas differ greatly across cultures. If the reader or listener is unfamiliar with the culture represented in the content material, then retention and recall of the material will be negatively affected (Abu-Akhel, 1999; Mandler & Johnson, 1977; Rost, 2005).

Many teachers assume all students have U.S. cultural knowledge that may be integral to understanding a lesson. However, many ELL students do not have this schema (although they often have ample cultural knowledge from their own country of origin). As a result, these students might perform poorly on the assignments. Teachers should ask themselves questions concerning schemata when preparing lessons such as, "If I were from X country, what information would I need to know in order to understand and perform well during this lesson?" "What cultural information is integral to understanding this lesson that students from cultures other than mine may not have?"

At the start of a lesson concerning a new concept or new reading material, teachers need to help all students access and connect to prior learning and background knowledge. In addition, the background knowledge that ELL students bring to the classroom are rich sources of information. Accessing this knowledge not only helps the individual student connect to the content, but also enriches the curriculum for all. It is important for teachers to access students' background knowledge and incorporate the individual histories present in the classroom as part of the curriculum. There are many techniques for achieving this, including the following:

1. Using KWL charts

2. Group brainstorming

3. Using semantic or concept webbing

9.7

For a detailed description of the strategies listed above, as well as examples of graphic organizers for the strategies, see the following Web link: **www.sagepub.com/grassi.**

If students do not have any content or cultural schemata pertaining to the subject matter, teachers must provide it. One effective method of providing schemata is the preview–review method. The teacher provides a preview to the lesson in which the cultural schemata needed for the lesson is introduced to the class in a comprehensible manner (i.e., using the 3-way model). After the lesson, the teacher reviews the lesson with the ELL students (or the class as a whole) so that students can make connections, comparisons, and contrasts between their L1 culture and the culture represented in the material.

Perspective From the Field of Special Education

In the area of special education, cultural and content schemata are referred to as **background knowledge or prior knowledge**. Students with special needs can have gaps in their academic background knowledge for various reasons: they might have missed part of the regular classroom curriculum when they received special education services, they might have processing or memory issues that prevent them from acquiring all the necessary content or making the necessary connections to their past learning, and they might have limited vocabulary knowledge in L1 or L2 or both. Teachers should not assume that students with special needs have the background knowledge necessary to fully understand new concepts. Preassessment of students' background knowledge is a critical first step when introducing a new concept. If students do not have this information, then teachers must explicitly teach it. The following are effective manners of teaching background knowledge (Marzano, 2004):

- KWL charts
- Opportunities for students to explore connections
- Direct vocabulary instruction
- Experiential learning

For detailed descriptions of the above strategies, see the following Web link: **www.sagepub.com/grassi.**

9.8

Putting It All Together

When working with CLDE students, explicit instruction in cultural and content schemata is doubly important. To begin, the CLDE student is usually coming from a culture and language different from most teachers in U.S. classrooms and has background knowledge that can differ significantly from curriculum presented in U.S. classrooms. The teacher cannot assume that the student's cultural background knowledge matches that of the concepts presented in class, and teachers must explicitly instruct students on the cultural and content schemata of the lesson, while concurrently honoring and incorporating the background knowledge of the student. The CLDE student also may have gaps in learning due to special education issues. CLDE students may have had learning issues that

REFER TO CASE STUDY 9.1

Did Caitlin help students access cultural and content schemata? How can you incorporate this strategy into your lessons?

were not addressed in prior classrooms. These students might have fallen farther and farther behind, incorporating less and less background material.

It is critical that teachers give CLDE students opportunity to relate the new concepts to their own background knowledge in order to increase comprehension and retention of new material. If there is a gap in background knowledge, then teachers must provide the schemata needed to understand the lesson.

9.9

To watch a video clip on a teacher accessing students' cultural and content schemata, and to access a rubric to observe the teacher and evaluate the strategy, see the following Web link: **www.sagepub.com/grassi.**

Summary

1. Access the schemata students already have about the subject matter through strategies such as KWL, group brainstorming, and semantic webbing.

2. Check students' work to make sure they have knowledge of the subject matter.

3. If students do not have any schemata or have limited schemata, implement strategies to provide schemata:

   • Determine what cultural and content aspects the students need to understand in order to grasp the content.

   • Explicitly teach these cultural and content aspects in a comprehensible manner.

STRATEGY 9.4 ALLOWING STUDENTS TIME TO CLARIFY IN THE FIRST LANGUAGE

Perspective From the Field of Language Acquisition

Making the lecture, oral presentation, reading, or writing content comprehensible also requires *time for students to clarify the material in their L1*. Giving students time to discuss the content in their L1 usually results in better performance in the final task in the L2. This is due, in part, to learners having the time to truly comprehend the ideas and to clarify the L2 vocabulary in a supportive context.

Sometimes teachers fear that ELL students grouped with other students who speak their L1 will socialize instead of focusing on the content. However, when students speak in their L1 during class time, most often they are clarifying the subject matter. When learning new concepts or skills in an L2, it is important to fully understand the content material or the academic skill. Working with someone who can help students clarify in their L1 will increase students' comprehension of the content or the skill and help them succeed academically in the classroom.

Allowing students to work in their L1 does not mean that teachers ask bilingual students to engage in **concurrent translation** of the material for ELL students with limited English skills. Concurrent translation involves introducing the content first in one language then immediately translating the content to the other language. This model can encourage students to focus on the translation of the content in their stronger language and limit their attention to the content in the language they are trying to learn. A far more effective model can be found by systematically providing time for L1 grouping during class. Teachers can assign tasks that help the groups clarify the content in their L1, such as these examples:

1. Have students fill out KWL charts.

2. Have students create a list of questions they would like answered about the content.

3. Have students create a list of how the content has affected the world.

4. Have students create a list of how students would use the content matter in their lives.

5. Group students with an L1-speaking paraprofessional to review the content with students.

6. Provide students with L1-content materials they can review to further their comprehension of the subject.

Perspective From the Field of Special Education

When monolingual English-speaking students have special needs, there is no rationale for use of this strategy. If students with special needs are bilingual or ELL students, then this strategy is appropriate.

Putting It All Together

Allowing for clarification in the L1 is an important strategy to assist CLDE students in gaining better access to the content. If students are academically behind due to issues related to their disability, clarification of the content material in their stronger language allows them to gain better access to content that is already difficult to acquire due to disability issues. Likewise, CLDE students are expected to not only compensate for their disability, but also to attempt to understand the content in a new language. If CLDE students have an opportunity to clarify with peers in their stronger language, then the challenge is lessened, and the student can concentrate better on the learning task.

REFER TO CASE STUDY 9.1

Did Caitlin give her students time to work in groups and clarify in the L1? What was the result of implementation of this strategy? How can you better incorporate this strategy into your lessons?

As noted above, it is important to have specific tasks accompany L1 grouping so that students can use their strengths. For example, in a specific L1 group, one student with stronger bilingual skills can help with the language and translation for another student. If one student understands the concepts better, that student can help with the content and explanations in the L1.

9.10

To watch a video clip of students working in L1 groups, and to access a rubric with which to observe the teacher and evaluate this strategy, see the following Web link: **www.sagepub.com/grassi.**

Summary

1. Systematically implement L1 groups during class time so students can clarify the subject matter.

2. Make sure the L1 groups have a task that will help students to clarify the content.

3. If available, use L1-speaking paraprofessionals and L1 content materials to help students better understand the content.

STRATEGY 9.5 HELPING STUDENTS ORGANIZE AND ACCESS ACADEMIC INFORMATION: EXPLICIT STRATEGY INSTRUCTION

Perspective From the Field of Language Acquisition

Helping students *organize and access academic information* is another foundational strategy for academic success. Many students who are from different cultural and educational backgrounds have very different experiences when it comes to "school" skills. Teachers should consider the following (Dutro & Moran, 2003):

a. Students may not know how to take notes.

b. Students may not know how to organize the content information presented in class—especially when the class is conducted in the student's L2.

c. Students may not know how to access information from various sources such as the Internet, dictionaries, indexes, thesauruses, or encyclopedias.

d. Students may not know how to study for a test.

e. Students may not know how to organize a written paper (see Chapters 13 and 14 for more details).

f. Students may not know how to organize information to begin a project (see Chapters 13 and 14 for more details).

Teaching Note-Taking Strategies

Note taking and organizing content can help students better access, categorize, and review the content material. In addition, notes are integral to assisting with comprehension, especially if the notes are "complete, accurate, and clear enough to support subsequent reconstruction of key ideas and information" (Rost, 2005, p. 519).

Not all students know how to take notes or how to organize the information given in class. In order to assist students, teachers should have graphic organizers for every concept presented, such as written outlines, note-taking charts, diagrams, flow charts, and semantic webs. Teachers should model how to use these graphic organizers and assist students by writing key points in the organizers for everyone to see.

Teaching Organization Strategies

When teachers assign students a project or written paper and instruct students to use the information gained from class and other resources, ELL students are often overwhelmed. Which information should they use? How much information should they use? In what order should they present the information? Many teachers have reported frustration with ELL students who focus on "irrelevant aspects of the content" and not the key points, or who "throw everything on the page" in a disorganized fashion. ELL students are often unsure of what information is pertinent or relevant, how to organize information in the new language and culture, or the teacher's expectations. It is important to remember that the concept of "important information" and "projects" differs across cultures. What may be acceptable in one country could be vastly different from what teachers expect in the United States. Before assigning a project or written paper, the teacher needs to help students organize the information they have gathered and point out the pertinent points. This can be done by modeling strategies such as

- outlining,
- graphing,
- flow charts, and
- cloze outlines or graphs for students with lower English levels.

Teaching Students How to Access Information From Different Sources

Some ELL students arrive at U.S. schools with little or no schooling, having had little opportunity to access different sources, especially those derived from technology. Some ELL students will come from disadvantaged schools without resources, and some ELL students will come from schools with plenty of high-quality resources. Even with the latter students, though, the way of finding information and the type of information that is considered valid and reliable can differ across cultures.

For students who come to the United States from different countries, explicit instructions on how to access information and instruction on which information is considered valid and reliable are integral to academic success. Depending on the educational background of the student, some ELL students will need explicit instruction on how to use sources such as indexes, dictionaries, encyclopedias, and the thesaurus, some students will need explicit instruction in how to use the computer and conduct Internet searches, and most students will need explicit directions in how to use the library's resources in the United States.

Once sources are accessed, most ELL students will need instruction on how to judge between valid and invalid information. Sources such as the Internet sometimes present all material as if it were factual. ELL students will not have the cultural schema to understand the difference between nonsense and fact, valid and invalid facts, and reliable and unreliable Internet sites. Therefore, it is important that teachers provide students with guidelines. Providing students with a checklist of what to look for during Internet or other resource searches will help tremendously.

Teaching Study Skills

ELL students, especially those who have had little or no schooling, will benefit from explicit instruction in how to study. Study skills will help ELL students perform better on assignments and exams. Some study strategies to include are

- highlighting important aspects of a text,
- using flashcards to memorize vocabulary or facts,
- rewriting notes or reorganizing notes as a form of review,
- outlining information, and
- categorizing and organizing information.

Perspective From the Field of Special Education

Teaching Students How to Organize Information

Teachers need to teach students with special needs how to organize the information they gather, and they need to teach this in an explicit way. Much like ELL students, many students with special needs are overwhelmed by a large quantity of information presented. Often, the goals and objectives on their IEPs may be related to organizing and accessing information.

In order to help students organize information, the teacher can provide tools such as note-taking guides, advanced organizers, and other graphic organizers. These types of tools will help students who have difficulty picking out main ideas, summarizing, or focusing on the text to learn the main concepts of a lesson. In order for these tools to be effective, however, teachers must explicitly teach the student the *purpose* of the tool and *how to use* the tool.

While we advocate for project-based learning, projects (or reports) usually require multiple steps and deeper thinking. The teacher needs to help students with special needs outline the steps involved, organize material for each step, and scaffold each step to the final project. The teacher should help students organize the project in realistic "chunks" and check off each step as it is completed.

Some students with special needs might also need a system of organizing homework and class notes. Some students may not remember what is assigned, may not write down the correct pages, might forget supplies such as the correct worksheet or textbook, or may even lose items between school and home. Assignment books, sets of texts at home, and a systematic way of communicating with the student such as a notebook, school day summary, or email are all ways of teaching organizational skills.

Teaching Students How to Access Information From Different Sources

When students with a variety of learning needs access academic information, it can help for them to differentiate the process. (See Chapter 7 for details of differentiating instruction.) Students may need to gather information from a variety of modalities. Some students may need to gather information from watching a video, listening to an audiotaped book, listening to a lecture, participating in an interview, or working in a group format. Teachers can highlight important information in a text so the student can identify pertinent concepts. Students also might need to access information from an appropriate developmental or academic level, which requires differentiating the process and the materials used (Tomlinson, 1999).

Teaching Study Skills

Students with special needs also might need explicit instruction in *how* to study the information gathered. Some students may not have memory of how to complete a task and will need explicit instruction on the processes and procedures that are needed to complete a task. This is called procedural knowledge (Sands et al., 2000). Steps to tasks should be explicitly taught and reviewed both orally and in written format. They also should be practiced in order to ensure that the student has learned and can remember the procedures for completing the learning task. Giving students specific questions to answer as they read a text helps to teach the process and procedures associated with that particular study skill. Unless students are taught systematically how to question and interpret texts, they will not learn those skills (Massey & Heafner, 2004). Questions such as the following can be posed for students to follow as they read and after they read to guide their thinking process (from Duplass, 2008, p. 189):

- Is the text fact or fiction?

- Is the meaning literal or figurative?

- Is the text accurate or inaccurate?

- Is the writing biased or objective?

- Are there inferred or explicit messages?

- Are the messages subtle or obvious?

- What is the purpose of the reading?

Putting It All Together

Systematically providing CLDE students with organization strategies, graphic organizers, study skills, and alternative ways of accessing information are integral to academic success. From the perspective of language acquisition, CLDE students need as many supports as possible to organize and access content material presented in the target language. Understanding the concepts in the L2 is difficult enough—organizing the information in a coherent manner can be even more difficult.

CLDE students may have issues that require differentiation to access the content material. For example, students might have processing issues, learning disabilities, or attention issues that necessitate different ways to access the material. Some students may need to see the material numerous times in different formats or at a slower pace. Some students also may be overwhelmed with the amount of the material or the academic level of the material and will need modifications based on their particular learning level and style. Students with attention issues often become distracted by the amount or type of stimuli and may require the information to be broken into chunks or presented in a way that is not overwhelming.

The special needs of CLDE students also may require strategies for organizing and studying the material presented. If the teacher provides the scaffolds to take efficient notes, graphic organizers or other tools to organize the material, and study skills to better review and retain the material, the CLDE student will have better access, understanding, and retention of the content material.

When working with CLDE students, we recommend that the teacher

- use the integrated content-language approach for instruction (especially the 3-way model);

- provide graphic organizers, note-taking strategies, and different manners to organize notes and content information;

- break down the information in chunks to make it more accessible;

- help students access resources; and

- explicitly teach study skills.

REFER TO CASE STUDY 9.1

How did Caitlin assist the student in organizing and accessing academic information? How can you better help your CLDE students organize and access academic information in your classroom?

All of these strategies must be taught explicitly for them to be effective. It is not sufficient to hand out a note-taking guide and expect students to effectively take notes on a lecture or movie. Instead, the teacher should discuss and model procedural knowledge step by step and should state explicitly the rationale behind using specific strategies or graphic organizers.

1. Provide graphic organizers and note-taking models.

2. Provide explicit instruction in using resources to gain information.

3. Provide instruction in study skills.

9.11

To watch a video of a teacher helping students organize and access academic information, and for a rubric to evaluate this strategy, see the following Web link: **www.sagepub.com/grassi.**

Summary

Instruction that integrates the content area and language acquisition involves many key strategies that are aimed at increasing comprehension of the content matter; increasing students' vocabulary, knowledge of grammar, ability to organize and work with the content; and creating an environment where students are comfortable, challenged, and able to learn both the content and the target language. After reading this chapter, you should know how to implement the following strategies:

- Make the content comprehensible, using the 3-way model.

- Emphasize key vocabulary and key concepts before, during, and after a lesson.

- Access students' background knowledge about the subject and provide cultural and content schemata.

- Allow students to clarify the content in their L1.

- Using explicit strategy instruction, help students organize the content information and study for exams.

To view tables that summarize the rationale and use of the strategies discussed in this chapter, see the following Web link: **www.sagepub.com/grassi.**

9.12

Key Terms

3-way model

Background knowledge, or prior knowledge

Concurrent translation

Content and cultural schemas

Front-load

Graphic organizer

Integrated content-language acquisition approach

Key academic language

Key concepts

Repetition

Visual context

Activities for Further Understanding

1. Implement the 3-way model in one of your classes. What were the results? How did students react? How did this model help your CLDE students better access the material?

2. Pick a lesson from your content area. What vocabulary and language structures do you need to front-load in order for your CLDE students to better understand the lesson? How can you front-load this language? Implement those strategies. What were the results?

3. Interview CLDE students in your classroom about the topic you are working on. What background knowledge do these students have about the topic? What knowledge are they missing? How could you provide cultural and content schemata for these students in an engaging manner?

4. Consider your students with an L1 other than English. Provide time in your lesson for these students to clarify the content in their L1. What strategies can you employ to make sure they are discussing the content? How have you planned for students who do not speak a different L1? What were the results of this strategy in your classroom?

5. Go to a Web site that provides free graphic organizers (e.g., freeology.com). Find a graphic organizer for at least two activities in your lesson. Explicitly instruct students on the organizer and integrate the organizer into your lessons. How did this help your students with the information presented? How would you do this activity differently next time?

6. Interview a student who speaks English as an L2. Ask about study skills the student learned in her country of origin. What are those skills? How do they differ from what is taught in U.S. schools?

7. Observe a lesson taught by one of your peers or colleagues. Which aspects of this chapter did the teacher incorporate into the lesson? What suggestions would you provide to make the content more accessible to CLDE students?

Visit the Student Study Site at **www.sagepub.com/grassi** for chapter-specific study resources.

Chapter 10

STRATEGIES FOR PROMOTING PARTICIPATION

CASE STUDY 10.1	Promoting Meaningful Participation in the Classroom

My classroom is a mélange of language, literacies, and cultures. My students come from million-dollar dwellings, low-income apartments, middle-class houses, and homeless shelters. There are six languages spoken in my classroom. After the hustle and bustle of busy morning routines, the clock hits 8:30 and one of my favorite parts of the day begins. The class walks, with purpose, to the classroom meeting area. This 25- to 30-minute period lets us check in with each other, work together, and appreciate our differences in a meaningful way. It allows the students to begin their day positively, leaving baggage that interferes with academics in a safe place; to acknowledge and support classmates through important events in their lives; and to participate in activities that acknowledge similarities and differences in the classroom.

Greeting

"Es salaam aleikom, Angel!" Cari says to Angel. They shake hands and make direct eye contact. Angel then turns to the student to his right to repeat the greeting. Each day, each student in the class extends a greeting to another student until every student has been acknowledged. Today the greeting is in Arabic, honoring the students from Saudi Arabia, Sudan, and Egypt. In the beginning of the year, we began with talks about appropriate hand shaking and why eye contact is important in our classroom. We honor all of the languages spoken in our classroom. This is an easy and meaningful way to connect culturally diverse students, and it always brings smiles.

Activity

Tre'Jhaun can barely hold the door open for himself with the three dodge balls he has borrowed from the gym teacher. It is time for group juggling, a favorite morning meeting activity. We begin this activity by choosing the order in which we will juggle—by alphabetical order, by age, or by birthdates. We practice one round of juggling using only one ball, and throw the ball as quickly and silently as possible. After we have mastered the task, we add a second, then a third. We strategize about what helps us and what doesn't. This kind of group communication is crucial to the classroom environment; it prepares the students for grouping that is even more meaningful, including guided reading and literature circles.

Share

We decided to have a share hour once a month. When I asked the students how we should manage it, they suggested a sharing of roses and thorns. I was wholeheartedly blown away by what evolved in my classroom. There were stories about family members hating each other, feeling ugly, being in trouble at home, serving in Iraq, battling with cancer, and feeling lonely. During this special time, we try our best just to listen, and to be a shoulder for each other to cry on.

One memorable moment was when Kiki revealed watching *America's Next Top Model* the night before, then going straight to the mirror and thinking, "I'm so ugly." She broke down sobbing. A rambunctious and notoriously impulsive student, Samuel jumped up from across the circle and yelled, "YOU ARE BEAUTIFUL!! You have to listen to the voice deep inside you, you know, the one that is strong, the one that tells you the right thing to do! You have to keep hearing it. It says you're smart. You're a good person. You are beautiful." Other students chimed in, telling the girl that Samuel was right. Simbate, an ELA student who has only been in the United States for a year, later added, "I don't understand, but when you cry, I cry." It is not always this intense, but our incredible school counselor is available for the deepest wounds. Sharing our lives together has made everything we do in the classroom more meaningful.

—Melissa Fogal, Classroom teacher

Consider the case study above:

- How are students welcomed and honored in the classroom?
- How is student voice a part of the morning routine?
- How are both language and culture a part of the activities?
- How are all levels of learners, native English speakers and nonnative speakers, encouraged to participate in the activities?

SOURCE: Used by permission.

This chapter will continue the discussion of the integrated content-language approach to include the voices of students and techniques to encourage participation from CLDE students.

CLDE students should be active, participatory members of the general education and content-area classrooms. Active participation in the academic discourse is a critical factor in retaining and understanding the content matter. If students are excluded due to language or special education issues, then their access becomes limited. When learners are passive recipients to the material, they do not own it, make the connections, or engage. In this chapter, we will provide specific strategies for encouraging student voice and extended academic participation from CLDE students:

- Creating a comfortable classroom environment

- Increasing interaction: group work with native and nonnative speakers of English

- Encouraging extended participation

Strategy 10.1 Creating a Comfortable Classroom Environment

Perspective From the Field of Language Acquisition

A comfortable environment is the foundation for promoting participation in the classroom. Krashen's (1982) **affective filter hypothesis** states that the lower the stress level, the more learners are able to receive linguistic input and to begin to process the language. If anxiety levels are high, learners will shut down and have trouble concentrating on the class content or listening to the lesson (Rost, 2005).

One of the most effective ways to lower anxiety for ELL students is to make sure the content is comprehensible to all students (using the methods described in Chapter 9). If students feel that they understand the content and are able to achieve academically, their anxiety levels will lower.

Another manner of ensuring low anxiety is to create a classroom environment where errors (especially those in spoken and written work) are viewed as part of the learning process, and where students are encouraged to take risks in their spoken and written English. There are many types of errors that ELL students will produce in interlanguage: these errors are a normal part of the language acquisition process. However, regardless of the errors students produce, it is important that teachers continue to push students to produce spoken and written English. Students' English **output** is integral to language acquisition (Swain, 2005; Swain & Lapkin, 1995). The key to output is for teachers to create a classroom environment where student errors are perceived as a normal process in language acquisition, and students are encouraged to produce—regardless of the errors they make.

Building relationships with students is another critical strategy for creating a comfortable classroom environment. Unless strong teacher–student relationships are built, students will not feel comfortable in the classroom to participate and take learning risks (Nieto & Bode, 2008).

A final method of ensuring a comfortable classroom environment is to represent equally all cultures and languages in the classroom, and to make the content relevant to students (Banks, 1997; Sheets, 2005; Tuitt, 2003). We can best provide the rationale for this strategy by presenting the reader with a story of a situation we experienced in a teacher education course:

During a preservice teacher course on Multicultural Education, one of our preservice teachers (who was a student in the university) approached us with the textbook he was required to use. He opened the book to a page that described George Washington in detail, including all the contributions he had made to the United States. On the same page, in a sidebar, was a picture of James Derham, the first African American to practice medicine. Rather than describe James

Derham's contributions in detail, however, the book had a picture of Derham with his name under the picture and a brief description of his life as a former slave and then doctor. The preservice teacher looked at us and said,

> If this were switched and George Washington were the side bar and James Derham were the main focus, then this chapter would be relevant to me. As it stands, this book has reinforced the perspective I've received all my life: that black people made insignificant contributions, that we were not important to the development of this country, and that any African American worth mentioning boils down to five people presented in the margins of textbooks—Martin Luther King, Harriet Tubman, Rosa Parks, Ruby Bridges, and Malcolm X.

> —Preservice teacher seminar, October 2003

This preservice teacher's story struck us as extremely relevant to all students from diverse cultures enrolled in U.S. classrooms. If students are overloaded in K–12 classrooms with images of monocultural and monolingual leaders (usually from the white, upper-class culture), and if scientists, authors, and musicians, and important figures from other cultures do not receive equal airtime, then students receive an ongoing subtle message: "Their culture is not as important or as valued as the white culture is." Students develop a higher self-esteem in classrooms that acknowledge the contributions and importance of all cultures represented and incorporate these cultures into the regular academic curriculum.

We know that many teachers and schools are becoming aware of the importance of incorporating varied cultural perspectives, but unless they do this on a regular basis, in a systematic fashion (not as an "add on"), then multicultural perspectives can be easily overlooked while teachers rely solely on the curriculum—which is vastly **monocultural**. We have noted that teachers who consciously and systematically include the perspectives and voices of all students create comfortable environments where students feel valued and are comfortable taking risks.

Perspective From the Field of Special Education

When working with students who have special needs, "comfort" is created by constructing a classroom where access to the content is purposefully planned (Friend, 2005; Tomlinson, 1999; Wehby, Symons, & Canale, 1998).

While all students are engaged in the same content material, the manner in which the student interacts with the material is adapted to his or her particular learning needs. It is important for teachers to establish a classroom atmosphere in which students understand the following concept: "Fair" does not mean everyone does the same thing—"fair" means everyone gets what they need. By incorporating a concept of "fairness" in the classroom, comfort is increased and students are more likely to take academic risks.

Part of taking academic risks involves participation. Students are less likely to participate, however, if they do not understand the material, are not prepared to participate, or believe that they are unable to keep up with the rest of the class (Smith, Polloway, Patton, & Dowdy 2007). Court and Givon (2003) note that "children and adolescents with learning disabilities have social difficulties when compared to their peers. They report feelings of loneliness, isolation, and lack of fulfillment in social situations. This social isolation deepens over time contributing to negative self-image and difficulty in social functioning" (p. 50). School is a social situation. If students do not feel comfortable in that atmosphere, they will not participate in the lesson or the academic discourse. To promote student participation, specific strategies can be implemented at both the secondary level and the elementary level:

- *Provide different kinds of opportunities for participation.* Allow students to observe, attempt, practice, listen, watch, take notes, ask questions, answer questions, write responses, explain responses, support others, and teach others (Wiggins & McTighe, 1998).

- *Create a community that accepts diverse learners.* If critical elements of creating a classroom community are overlooked, then "students who present various kinds of diversity will continue to be disenfranchised" (Schaffner & Buswell, 1996, p. 53). The teacher has a crucial role in creating situations that require cooperation between peers, planning positive learning groups, and helping students find potential friendships (Court & Givon, 2003). At the secondary level, "critical friends groups" or "research groups," where students are grouped to analyze, ponder, research, critique, and report on academic concepts provides structure for academic community building.

- *Promote cooperative rather than competitive goal structures in the classroom* (Johnson, Johnson-Holubec, & Johnson, 1984, as cited in Schaffner & Buswell, 1996, p. 53). Work with students to create their own individual learning goals and encourage students to work with one another toward meeting these goals in academic groupings.

- *Establish classroom rituals in which everyone is provided the support necessary to participate equally and fully* (Pearson, 1988, as cited in

Schaffner & Buswell, 1996, p. 53). Facilitate "community time," where students have the opportunity to share aspects of their lives and to participate in engaging topics and activities that encourage students to get to know one another.

- *With students who others perceive as being different, find opportunities throughout the school day to introduce them in a positive way to their peers and other adults in the school* (Schaffner & Buswell, 1996). Find ways to showcase students' strengths—post student work on classroom blogs and Web sites, and hang up and highlight student work on classroom walls.

- *Ensure that* **accommodations** *are made so that everyone, including students with challenging needs, can participate actively* (Schaffner & Buswell, 1996). Make sure that differentiation is a foundational aspect of all lessons. Give movement breaks, allow for different types of projects, give reading materials at different levels, make sure students have the opportunity to practice and understand concepts, skills, and vocabulary first so that they can participate actively in the lesson. Incorporate student choice as much as possible, allow for student voices in different languages and cultures, and make expectations clear to all students.

- *Infuse positive values of respect, appreciation of people who are different, and cooperation into the curriculum itself* (Noddings, 1995, as cited in Schaffner & Buswell, 1996, p. 53). Choose curriculum materials and topics that value diversity as well as support the skills and knowledge required by standards.

- *Involve students in decision making regarding classroom and school policies that support each student* (Villa & Thousand, 1992, as cited in Schaffner & Buswell, 1996, p. 53). Have students define "positive classroom community" and create rules to support the students' definition.

Putting It All Together

A comfortable academic environment for CLDE students means that the environment not only supports the language and cultural acquisition process, but also supports the special needs of all students. This means that the content is provided in a comprehensible manner, using foundational strategies from the content-language approach; that teachers incorporate culturally relevant teaching strategies to support the cultural background of the students; that instruction is adapted as listed in the IEP; and that planning for CLDE students takes place in the initial planning process. Creating a comfortable environment requires conscientious, deliberate planning. Without a comfortable environment, CLDE students might shut down, have trouble participating, struggle with the language and culture acquisition process, and fall behind academically.

The strategies listed on pages 236 and 237 for creating a comfortable environment for ELL students and students with special needs are all strategies that accommodate the needs of a CLDE student. Teachers should consider incorporating as many of the strategies as possible. Not only will these strategies help CLDE students, but also they will encourage *all* students to participate fully in the academic discussions and activities.

> **REFER TO CASE STUDY 10.1**
>
> How did the teacher create a comfortable environment? What strategies do you use in your classroom to create a comfortable environment?

10.1

> For a video clip of a teacher creating a comfortable environment, and for a rubric with which to observe the teacher and evaluate the strategy, see the following Web link: **www.sagepub.com/grassi.**

Summary

1. Make all the content and directions comprehensible.

2. Encourage risk taking and mistakes in English production.

3. Build strong teacher–student relationships.

4. Value (and systematically implement) the perspectives of all cultures and languages represented in the classroom.

5. Purposefully plan access to the content.

6. Adapt instruction as listed in IEP.

7. Use specific strategies to promote participation.

STRATEGY 10.2 INCREASING INTERACTION IN THE CLASSROOM: HETEROGENEOUS GROUPINGS

Perspective From the Field of Language Acquisition

While it is important to give students the opportunity to work with peers who speak their native language, it is equally important to diversify the groupings

Photo 10.2 Putting students in groups with varied abilities, cultures, and languages can increase learning for everyone.

so that students also work with peers who speak English as their native language (Dutro & Moran, 2003). Working in groups with both native speakers (NS) and nonnative speakers (NNS) of English is an essential component to academic success (see Photo 10.2). This type of group work allows ELL students to (1) clarify the subject matter in the L2, (2) gain further insight on the subject matter from peers, (3) discuss different perspectives on the subject matter, (4) hear more of the target language around the content matter, and (5) interact more with other speakers of the target language.

Perspective From the Field of Special Education

Many students with special needs have traditionally not done well in whole group direct instruction settings. Whole class instruction often has everyone in the class doing the exact same thing at exactly the same pace—for example, listening to a lecture, reading a passage and answering questions, or participating in whole group discussion. In these situations, if a student has processing issues and requires extended time to form answers, to understand the material, and to participate verbally, the pace of the class based on the average students can be very stressful. As well, when a student's learning style differs from the teacher's style in whole group activities, the student may tune out and have trouble following the lesson. Once this occurs, the student will hesitate to participate because he or she has missed key information.

By allowing for interaction in groups, situations such as diverse learning styles and processing and focusing issues can be accommodated more easily. Group work can enhance students' strengths, and learning needs can be supported by other learners. Group work, if implemented correctly, allows students to participate actively in the lesson without having to focus on the aspects of learning that are barriers to academic success.

For instance, if a student in the group is not a proficient writer and the group is asked to complete an experiment and write the results of the experiment, the student's strengths can be emphasized during the group work, and the student's challenges can be addressed after group work. In a lesson such as this, the outcomes for group work would be that all students understand the process, the experiment, and the results. The student for whom writing is a burden, but who has strong oral and social skills, can increase his or her understanding of the process, experiment, and results through conversations and work with peers in groups. Likewise, the student can fully and actively participate in the experiment and provide insight into the experiment without being hindered by the time needed to write out the process. After the group work is finished and the teacher is assured that comprehension is high, the student can access many options for writing up the results. The student can receive help with writing up the experiment during writing time, study hall, or after school. The student can dictate the steps of the experiment to the teacher, paraprofessional, or a peer. The student can draw the steps of the experiment and label with key vocabulary or sentences, or the student can work on the write-up of the lab during writing instruction, English, or special education class.

Group work also provides students with a very structured way to interact with peers. Some students with special needs do not understand social norms. For example, some students have difficulty fostering relationships with their peers, who might not be open to working with them. When students are given specific group roles, are instructed on the rules of the group, and are instructed on the tasks of the different roles, the social expectations are spelled out and students with special needs and their peers can focus on the academic outcome of the lesson, rather than on the complexities of social interaction (Johnson & Johnson, 1999).

Group work also has been shown to positively impact affect, self-esteem, peer relationships, and interactions (Johnson & Johnson, 1984). When students are surrounded by peers who are working together, positive social interactions can be reinforced. By teaching the social expectations explicitly, carefully structuring and planning the group tasks, and giving students the opportunity to practice social skills in peer grouping, goals related to social and emotional aspects of learning can be met within the general education or content area classroom.

Putting It All Together

When working with CLDE students, group work implementation has added challenges. To begin, CLDE students are struggling with interaction in their L2 and second culture. If the student has special needs related to cognitive or social issues, then the challenge to interact appropriately is increased.

With CLDE students, group work needs to focus on the language acquisition *and* the special needs of the students. Group work must be at the appropriate English language level, must provide opportunity for clarification in the students' L1 when possible, must be adequately sheltered, and must explicitly define the cognitive task and the social norms and expectations. While there are plenty of challenges to implementing group work with CLDE students, the benefits of peer grouping with CLDE students are numerous.

Peer group work allows CLDE students to practice the target language with native-English-speaking peers and to clarify the content in the L1 if grouped with students who share the same L1. Likewise, peer grouping allows CLDE students to gain and reinforce target cultural understandings from peers and gives native English speakers the opportunity to learn the cultural perspectives of the CLDE students. Finally, group work, when implemented appropriately, can allow CLDE students to participate fully in the process of learning without focusing on the barriers to learning.

As will be discussed in subsequent chapters, oral language development and verbalizing of the subject matter is often a first important step to literacy development. By systematically planning for group work and allowing CLDE students to work with peers to discuss the academic content, the student's ability to better understand and move on to the next developmental stages of literacy— reading and writing—is enhanced.

There are certain techniques to make group work successful with CLDE students, including the following (Gibbons, 2002, pp. 21–28):

1. *The teacher should provide clear and explicit instructions for the group work.* Successful group work depends on all students understanding and following the directions for the task. The 3-way model should be implemented when giving instructions for group work. If instructions are written, listed in checklist form (which also can contain the listed directions in the L1), and modeled, then students have a reference point and can access the key language and directions during the group task, if needed (Table 10.1).

Table 10.1   Example of Group Work Checklist

Instructions (Can be listed in more than one language)	Check Off When Completed
Step 1: Confirm every group member has a pencil, a textbook, a science notebook, safety glasses, and gloves.	
Step 2: Confirm *you* have the following chemicals on *your* table	
Step 3: Put two drops of Chemical #1 and three drops of Chemical #2 in a beaker.	
Step 4: Watch the reaction of the chemicals and either write down or draw what happens.	
Step 5: Add baking soda to the beaker.	
Step 6: Watch the reaction of the chemicals to the baking soda, and either write down or draw what happens.	

2. *The task should require oral language (talking), and all students should be involved in the task.* Many times, when CLDE students are grouped with native English speakers, the CLDE student is left to take on a passive role (such as time keeper) because he or she is perceived as "not as fluent in English," and, unfortunately, therefore "not as capable." Group activities are opportunities for CLDE students to become more fluent and gain more skills. It is important that the group task requires the active participation of all group members.

Tasks where all members of the group are required to provide an integral piece of information are referred to as *information gap tasks*. Information gap tasks are designed so that each member obtains, or is provided with, a piece of information that is integral to completing the task or solving the problem. For example, sequencing activities such as the construction of a timeline can be an information gap task. Each member is given a piece of history to study, after which the group comes together to place their pieces in a timeline or sequencing activity.

Information gap tasks are especially necessary when working with CLDE students. These tasks will give CLDE students opportunity to practice their

output, to review and work with the content, to work in the language surrounding the content, and to have an opportunity to interact with peers
appropriately. One note of caution: the information that the CLDE student is responsible for must be differentiated and accessible to the student.
This means the teacher needs to consider the language acquisition stage,
the reading level, the social goals, and other learning needs of the student.

For an example of instructions for a group "information gap" task at the secondary
level, see the following Web link: **www.sagepub.com/grassi.**

10.2

3. *The group work should have a clear and tangible outcome.* For CLDE
students, it is often beneficial to set up the task in intermediate steps so
that learners can effectively see their progress and understand the process
in completing the task. Likewise, the outcome should be explicitly
explained so that students are clear as to the goal of the group work task.

4. *The task should be linguistically and academically appropriate to the
learners.* It is important to consider Krashen's i + 1 hypothesis here: The
input should be at the student's linguistic level (i) and should provide a bit
of a challenge (1) (Krashen, 1982). This means that the teacher may need
to modify the linguistic skills required to complete the task for CLDE students. Again, this does not mean "watering down" the content. Instead, it
means providing scaffolds for the CLDE students to help them complete
the task regardless of their LEP. Additionally, the task should be designed
to meet the special education needs of the student. It is important to incorporate the goals of the IEP within the learning task, or to adapt the task
to meet the needs of the student.

5. *The task should be integrated within a broader curricular topic.* Group
work should be directly related to the subject discussed that day (or the
theme of the week, month, etc). Group work should be considered an integral part of the lesson and not an add-on activity. Students should be clear
as to how the outcome of the group work relates to the subject matter discussed in class.

6. *Students should have enough time to complete the task.* When working
with CLDE students, it is important to remember that these students will
require longer processing time because they are working in two or more
languages and have special needs. It is important to modify the task so that
the CLDE students can successfully complete their portion of the task in
the allotted time. Another effective strategy is to help CLDE students prepare for the group work prior to the activity taking place by giving them

the assignment or reading material a few days before. This gives them time to comprehend and begin to prepare their part in the task.

7. *Students should know how to work in groups before beginning group work.* Students from different cultures can perceive differently the concept of "group work." Therefore, it is important that the teacher be explicit about how to work in groups and the behavior expected of students. This is also an opportunity to explicitly teach social skills around academic tasks.

8. *The teacher needs to teach communication skills.* When students are working in groups or participating in class, and their English skills do not provide them with the vocabulary or structures they need, communication strategies give them a manner of continuing the discussion.

REFER TO CASE STUDY 10.1

How did the teacher encourage grouping? What grouping activities do you do in your class? How can these be improved?

Before grouping CLDE students, there are some factors to consider. To begin, heterogeneous L1/L2 groups should be encouraged. Clarification in the L1 is an important aspect of integrated content-language teaching, but students also need to practice the L2. In order to successfully implement L1/L2 groups, all content should be taught using the integrated content-language approach, and classmates should be trained in working in different ways to explain their ideas (i.e., students can draw their ideas, act out their ideas, speak their ideas, write their ideas, etc.). The social aspects of working in a group also need to be taught explicitly as an integral part of the lesson goals, and group work should be implemented purposefully and systematically.

10.3

For different grouping strategies for CLDE students at the secondary and elementary levels, see the following Web link: **www.sagepub.com/grassi**.

10.4

To view a video clip of a teacher incorporating group work, and to access a rubric to evaluate the strategy, see the following Web link: **www.sagepub.com/grassi**.

Summary

1. Give CLDE students the opportunity to interact with native and nonnative speakers and with students who have diverse academic and social needs.

2. Provide group work tasks so that all group members participate.

3. Be explicit about expectations for group outcomes and group behavior.

4. Ensure the task is linguistically and academically appropriate for all learners.

5. Make sure the students have enough time to finish the task: Present the task in intermediate steps so that students can progress one step at a time.

6. Make sure the group task is part of the curricular focus and not an add-on.

7. Teach students communication skills so they can contribute to the group, even if they have limited English skills.

STRATEGY 10.3 ENCOURAGE EXTENDED PARTICIPATION FROM CLDE STUDENTS

Perspective From the Field of Language Acquisition

Swain's (2005; Swain & Lapkin, 1995) **output hypothesis** states that student *output* and comprehensible *input* are both integral to L2 acquisition. In other words, students must be able to express their understanding of classroom content in order to increase their learning of the content.

When trying to convey a message, especially to a native English speaker, ELL students often need to make several attempts with the language to create a comprehensible message and to create grammatically accurate speech. Native English speakers will prompt these language attempts through verbal moves such as, "Sorry, I can't understand. Could you repeat that?" When ELL students are given cues to repeat or restate, they attempt a more-accurate utterance for the listener and thus practice their language. If students are only provided with comprehensible input, however, and never are forced to output, the learning involved in the construction of grammatically correct speech is lost.

Swain (2005) noted that when learners attempt to produce the target language (in either oral or written form), they begin to *notice* gaps where they do not know how to say or write the meaning they wish to convey. Noticing these gaps can motivate students to focus their attention on aspects of the language they need to improve upon.

Similarly, when learners produce the target language with other people, they are in a situation to *test their hypotheses* of how to correctly speak or write. When learners receive feedback from the interlocutor or the teacher, their hypotheses about the language are either proven or disproven by the feedback they receive. And research has indicated that learners will actively change their output based on feedback from teachers or interlocutors (Pica, Holliday, Lewis, & Morgenthaler, 1989; Swain, 2005).

Unfortunately, observations of content-area classrooms have noted that most general education teachers do not push ELL students to participate extensively in the classroom. Teachers often provide only limited opportunities for ELL student participation (Duff, 2001; Verplaetse, 1998).

One of the most common teacher practices in the classroom continues to be the three-part **IRF sequence** (Hall & Walsh, 2002; Wells, 1993). This sequence consists of a teacher-initiated question (I), a student response (R), and teacher feedback (F), which either corrects or judges the student response (such as "good," or "no, that's not quite it").

Teacher: Why did we engage in war with Japan? (I)

Student: Pearl Harbor? (R)

Teacher: Nice. And what was the repercussion for Japanese Americans? (F [Feedback])

Recent studies of teacher-student interactions reveal that a subtle but significant change to the third part of the IRF sequence encourages student participation that is more elaborate. Wells (1993) finds that some teachers, rather than provide *feedback* on student responses, provide *follow-up* to student responses by asking students to clarify, elaborate, or make connections to their own lives. As a result of this subtle change to the IRF pattern, teachers encourage more critical and enhanced dialogue and thus increase opportunities for students to learn.

Nassaji and Wells (2000) examine the practices of nine elementary and middle school teachers and their enactment of the IRF sequence. They find that the "feedback" portion of the IRF sequence actually suppressed student participation. On the other hand, "follow-up" moves, especially those that ask students to expand on their initial response, encourage further discussion.

Teacher: Why did we engage in war with Japan? (I)

Student: Pearl Harbor? (R)

Teacher: Tell me more about that. How exactly did Pearl Harbor contribute to our going to war with Japan? (F [Follow up]).

There are several ways to follow up on ELL students' responses to encourage extended participation. We have found the steps in Table 10.2 to be effective.

Table 10.2   Steps to Encourage Extended Participation With ELL Students

Step 1	Make the content comprehensible so that students understand the topic they are to discuss.
Step 2	Instruct students on the grammatical structures and the key academic language needed to participate.
Step 3	Begin by asking students an open-ended question around the topic, such as a question that does not require a scripted correct response or a yes/no answer. When working with ELL students, modify the question by simplifying the vocabulary or linguistic demands and not by simplifying the cognitive demand.
Step 4	Give the students plenty of processing time. Let students discuss the question first in groups; give the discussion questions to ELL students prior to the discussion to let them prepare; give students time to write their answers before answering orally; or give students ample wait-time to think about the question.
Step 5	Call on ELL students, being sure you call on both boys and girls equally. Implementing participation strategies such as randomly pulling students' names out of a hat or using popsicle sticks with students' names can increase equal participation.
Step 6	Scaffold the language, if needed. For example, the teacher can simplify vocabulary, help students find words, or start sentences in order to encourage participation.
Step 7	When a student answers, encourage the student to reflect on his or her answer through a "cue to improve" (Gall, 1970). A cue to improve is a teacher question or statement that prompts the student to clarify or expand upon the initial response, such as, "Tell me more about that," or "What do you mean?" The teacher can also continue to look at the student encouragingly in silence, giving the student more time to expand.
Step 8	Once the student has improved on the answer, encourage further discussion through the use of various strategies (Dillon, 1990): a. Continuers ("Hmm, yes, go on") b. Reflective statements ("So, are you saying that you disagree with this ideology?" "What I hear you saying is that you believe in this war.") c. Silence or wait-time d. A string of cues to improve (Gall, 1970)

Next we provide an example of a dialogue between a teacher and an ELL student that exemplifies steps to increasing student participation. This excerpt is from a general education science classroom (seventh grade) that enrolled a high percentage of ELL students (more than 50%). Before this excerpted dialogue took place, the teacher had taught the concept of energy conservation in a comprehensible manner. The teacher is working with a beginning-level ELL student to create a community survey on energy conservation that addresses three different energy topics (Grassi, 2003):

1. *T*   Hmmm. K. What are three possible topics . . . ? *(Starts with open-ended question.)*

2. *Sara* What are three?

3. *T*   Yeah, so three topics.

4. *Sara* Energy. (4)[1] Um. (10) *(Provides plenty of wait-time to process—4 seconds and 10 seconds.)*

5. *T*   More specific. What about energy? Would you ask people what they know about energy or . . . ? *(Follows up to student response with cues to improve.)*

6. *Sara* To see how many people. How much percent of city uses it.

7. *T*   Uses (3) Uses energy. To see what percentage of people uses energy for what? Like what? *(Follows up again with cues to improve.)*

8. *Sara* Um. (.) To brush his teeth.

9. *T*   OK. So maybe you were gonna think of a general category. What would you say that was for? Cause we're talking about using, like even the water running. What could be a general category for that? (2) To see . . . *(Follows up with more cues to improve, begins to scaffold the language by starting the sentence: "To see . . .")*

10. *Sara* Um. (.) To see how many people leaves it running and how many doesn't.

11. *T*   OK. Say that was one question. Say that was one of your questions. OK? What could the general category be that you're trying to figure out? *(Scaffolds again, trying to direct student to a general category.)*

12. *Sara* (2) Saving water.

13. *T*   Saving water!

The four follow-up moves in this case resulted in multiple learning opportunities for the student. She was able to practice her English through extended participation, she was able to develop a more appropriate response than her initial response of "energy," and she developed a question to place in her survey (i.e., "How many people leave the water running while brushing their teeth?"). In sum, not only was the student encouraged to stretch her language use, but she was encouraged to think more deeply and more critically about the steps involved in survey development.

Perspective From the Field of Special Education

Just as ELL students are sometimes hesitant to participate orally in class, so are students who tend to struggle with the academic content or with communication skills. Yet, these same students will have viewpoints or background knowledge that may contribute to the lesson. Talking about the content helps students to retain, better understand, and clarify the content—all critical first steps to further work in the content area. For students with speech and language disorders, the following strategies are recommended to help students practice their communication skills within the classroom (Friend & Bursuck, 2009, pp. 238–239):

- *Positive and accepting classroom atmosphere.* The classroom needs to be a place where students who have difficulty expressing their ideas feel comfortable to take the risk of participating. This acceptance can be encouraged by (1) modeling corrections instead of directly correcting the student, (2) giving more time for students to formulate and speak their answers, and (3) creating a calm and slower-paced discussion. If a student stutters, or has other fluency issues and is only able to communicate a partial response, then you may praise attempts to give a full answer. It is also important to continually model acceptance of students to minimize peer pressure.

- *Explicitly teach listening skills.* This is an important skill for all students, yet it is a skill that is not often taught to students (Lerner, 2006). Students who have communication issues need to know how to listen actively to students and teachers in the classroom, and students who have receptive language disorders or learning disabilities will benefit from being taught *how* to listen. Teach students to use and to listen for attention-getting phrases such as, "This is important," or, "You will want to know this." Give students specific information to listen for to encourage them to practice their listening skills. Make key information accessible for students to receive by using simple sentence structure, using simple vocabulary, and giving visuals. Make sure that there are minimal distracters in the classroom—this can reduce competitive stimuli by having only one activity going on at a time, by having only one person speaking at a time, and so on.

- *Model for students to expand their language.* If students contribute an incomplete answer or an answer that uses simple vocabulary or phrasing, the teacher can simultaneously model and praise the contribution. For example, if the teacher asks a question such as, "Why do you think it benefited China to enter this war?" and the student answers with a one-word or incomplete answer, the teacher can encourage the student to elaborate by modeling a longer response, giving further wait-time, then asking students to stop, think, and write their answers before contributing.

- *Provide meaningful contexts for practicing communicating.* Students need to practice communication in order to be academically and socially competent. The act of practicing communication can be integrated into the content-area curriculum and have meaning to the students. For example, students can work in groups with specific tasks for discussion, students can prepare speeches or other performances around the content material, and classroom activities can involve social aspects of communicating as well as practice of particular vocabulary and discussion of the content.

At times, it is not appropriate to push students with special needs to participate orally. It is important to consider self-concept and whether pushing a student to participate may cause more embarrassment than help. It is a fine line and requires that you know your students well in order to give appropriate academic and emotional support. Sometimes it may be necessary for teachers to give students opportunities to participate in ways that are not language dependent. For example, instead of participating in the group discussion to gain an understanding of the material, a student might read a book at his or her level or might watch a movie. Giving a student a variety of ways to access the information or to illustrate comprehension of the information lets the student use his or her strengths.

Putting It All Together

CLDE students can struggle on many different planes with classroom participation. CLDE students will struggle with the language and the culture when interacting. Because CLDE students also have exceptionalities, they can struggle with the language, communication, and social issues related to interaction. In order to address the needs of a CLDE student, the teacher needs to take into consideration many factors. To begin, a teacher should always allow for extra time for CLDE students to formulate answers. CLDE students are learning English and need time to process in two languages. Many CLDE students will have the added dimension of needing extra time for cognitive processing issues, for speech and language processing issues, or for attention issues. Wait-time is an important factor when trying to encourage extended participation with CLDE students.

As well, it is important to give students opportunities to practice their communication skills. CLDE students need ample opportunities for using the target language in order to increase proficiency. Likewise, practicing communication within the context of the target culture classroom increases cultural awareness and competence. CLDE students also may need opportunities to discuss the content in order to practice vocabulary, increase retention, and practice social interaction skills.

In order to best encourage extended participation, teachers should create a calm, comfortable environment in which students can safely make mistakes. CLDE students spend a good portion of their schooling in the interlanguage stage. As a result, they will make numerous pronunciation and grammatical mistakes when attempting to produce the target language. When the classroom allows for students to make errors in language production, students' stress will lower and they will move through the stages of L2 acquisition more easily.

CLDE students also may make mistakes in production of the language due to speech and language issues, lack of understanding of the content, or memory issues. Teachers will need not only to model the correct verbal utterance, but also will need to explain to students who are ready why this is the correct formulation of the utterance.

It is also important that teachers explicitly teach students how to listen as an integral part of participation. CLDE students who are at the beginning stages of language acquisition often panic when they hear the target language and so stop listening. It is important that these students be given

> **REFER TO CASE STUDY 10.1**
>
> How did the teacher encourage output? How can you better encourage extended participation in your class?

strategies to calm down and try to focus on the message. CLDE students may have the added dimension of shutting down when the content is too much or if they have attention disorders. These students also need to be taught to listen for key points so they can relax and absorb the content.

Summary

1. Make sure the content is understood by students and that students have the academic language forms to participate.

2. Create a comfortable classroom environment that allows for mistakes.

3. Ask open-ended questions and higher-level questions about the content.

4. Provide plenty of wait-time and processing time before expecting an answer.

5. If you are concerned about equal "air-time," make sure you have a participation strategy so you call on all students equally.

6. Encourage students to expand on their answer by following up with different strategies.

7. Teach listening skills.

8. Model language for students and provide students with instruction in communication strategies.

9. When appropriate, provide alternative ways to participate.

10. Provide meaningful contexts for practicing participation.

10.5

To view a video clip of a teacher encouraging extended output from CLDE students, and to access a rubric to evaluate the strategy, see the following Web link: **www.sagepub.com/grassi.**

Summary

CLDE students need to be active participants in the classroom in order to access and retain the content material. Teachers can employ strategies to encourage and promote participation. After reading this chapter, you should have a good understanding of the following:

- Strategies to promote participation of CLDE students in the academic discussion

- An understanding of how to create an environment conducive to active participation

- An understanding of the dynamics of group work and how to make group work effective for CLDE students

- Strategies for extending the participation of CLDE students in classroom discussions.

Key Terms

Accommodations

Affective filter hypothesis

IRF sequence

Monocultural

Output

Output hypothesis

Activities for Further Understanding

1. Observe a teacher in his or her classroom. How does this teacher create a comfortable environment? What evidence do you see for student comfort? What would you do differently?

2. Think of your classroom. What strategies from this chapter do you currently employ? Which strategies do you need to implement?

3. Observe a teacher implementing group work. Which steps presented in this chapter are present in the lesson? Which steps for group work are missing? What considerations have been made for CLDE students?

4. Consider the way you have implemented group work. Which strategies do you use? What strategies were successful with your CLDE students? How would you further adapt your group work to make it more successful for all students?

5. Observe a teacher during whole class discussion. How does the teacher interact with students? Does the teacher encourage extended participation? How? Who gets called on? Who is asked to extend their participation? How could this teacher improve on his or her practice?

6. Have someone film you while you are teaching. What participation strategies do you use? Do you equally call on all students? Do you ask students to extend their participation? How can you improve on your practice?

Visit the Student Study Site at **www.sagepub.com/grassi** for chapter-specific study resources.

Note

1. Silence is indicated by the amount of seconds or silence in parentheses. For example, (10) means 10 seconds of silence and (.) indicates a pause.

Chapter 11

STRATEGIES FOR EXPLICIT GRAMMAR INSTRUCTION

✦ Working with CLDE students with strategies for oral language error correction

✦ Using error analysis

✦ Focusing on form instruction with CLDE students

✦ Using strategies for explicit grammar instruction

CASE STUDY 11.1 | Explicit Grammar Instruction

As I learned more about the importance of explicitly teaching grammar to my students, I realized how much I have overlooked its role in teaching language learners. I have always focused on the importance of making meaning with my students, but I have neglected to specifically teach grammar. One of the biggest reasons is that I have not been sure how to do this consistently in context, because my previous training had a minimal focus on the instruction of grammar. I am still working toward finding a balance, but here is the story of one of my first attempts.

As I looked at my students' writing, I noticed that they had various issues with verb tense—especially understanding how and when to use words like "will" and "would" to express the future and conditional tenses. I read about an activity to teach verb tense. Modified, this activity would allow students to notice features within a text and begin to notice gaps in their own language learning.

I started by playing the Barenaked Ladies' song, "If I Had a $1,000,000," while I displayed the words and some pictures using PowerPoint slides. The song repeatedly states, "If I had a million dollars, I would . . ." After playing the song, I said, "I'm going to tell you about what I would do with a million dollars. As soon as I have finished, you will write down words or groups of words to try to remember what I have said." I told the students about six things that I would do with a million dollars. I memorized my script so that it would sound more natural but made sure to include the words that I wanted to teach. As I told the story, I used clip art images on PowerPoint to help the students remember the story. I told the story twice, then said, "Now it's your turn to write down what you remember about my story." After a short time of writing words or phrases, triads of students worked to reconstruct the text that they had heard. Then it was time for the fun part. I chose a student to scribe for the class. "Now you have a special job to do. Karen will write my story on this half piece of transparency, but you all must agree to what she should write. When you are all done, we will compare your text to mine and investigate what happens."

It was fascinating to watch my students work together to recreate my story. I had to referee a few times, but mostly I restrained myself from interfering. When they were done, their text was remarkably similar to mine. The result was precisely what research said would happen: The meaning was there, but there were differences in the syntax. They began the story using "would" just as I did, but as their story went on they increasingly used "will." As we compared their text with mine, they were able to notice this. This led perfectly to an authentic discussion of when we should use the word "would" and how the words "I'd" and "we'd" have "would" hidden in them.

For independent practice, the students then wrote their own "If I had a million dollars, I would . . ." paragraph. As I read through the students' paragraphs the next day, I noticed that, while most were inconsistent in their usage and used "will" at times, many were approximating the use of the words "would" and "I'd" to express what they might do.

—Harmony Looper, Literacy teacher

Consider the case study above:

- Why was teaching grammar and error correction important to this teacher?
- How does the teacher engage the students in the lesson?
- Why is it important to explicitly teach the concept?
- What would you add or change about the lesson to meet the needs of CLDE students?

SOURCE: Used by permission.

In a comfortable and safe classroom environment, students are able to take learning risks. Those risks, for CLDE students, include making language errors in English. It is important to remember that CLDE students are learning English as a second language. The process of error correction discussed in this chapter is appropriate to support CLDE students' language acquisition needs. While "oral error correction" is not generally a special education focus, it becomes a focus when working with CLDE students. CLDE students will make typical language acquisition errors that need to be addressed in order to progress in learning English, yet the student may not make the progress as readily as expected if they have memory, processing, or developmental disabilities that impede language learning. Therefore, it is important to keep the student's disability in mind when addressing oral language errors. The learning environment in the classroom must be such that students can have successes and can feel comfortable enough to take learning risks that might include a language error that can be discussed and corrected. The strategies addressed in this chapter can be effective if the teacher addresses language errors in a supportive manner, with expectations that include scaffolds to support the disability and the language acquisition process.

LANGUAGE ERRORS

Origins of Language Errors

As discussed in Chapter 3, CLDE students need to produce errors in order to learn the target language. CLDE oral English language errors stem from many factors (Brown, 2007; Gass & Selinker, 2008; Lightbown & Spada, 1999; Thornbury, 2007):

1. L1 transfers (*interlingual errors*) occur when the student transfers pronunciation, lexical items, grammatical structures, or culturally appropriate language use from the L1 to the target language (e.g., *The house of my uncle is in Cleveland*).

2. Overgeneralization transfers (*intralingual errors*) occur when the student overgeneralizes a grammatical rule in the target language and applies this rule to all situations (e.g., *She's book is up the stairs.*).

3. Developmental errors—part of a developmental sequence—often very similar to errors children make when they are learning their L1 (e.g., *He no like the candy.*).[1]

As discussed in Chapter 4, errors can appear at different levels: at the level of language pronunciation, at the lexical level (specific words or vocabulary terms), at the grammatical level (verb tenses, subject-verb agreement, adjective placement), at the discourse level (organizing sentences into a comprehensible flow of conversation or writing), and at the sociolinguistic level (the cultural rules of the language).

REFER TO CASE STUDY 11.1

What types of errors were the students producing? Where do you think these errors stem from?

It is important to note that CLDE students will produce errors that will usually not be produced by native speakers of English. For example, a high school–aged native English speaker will not say, "He no go there." Yet a high school–aged CLDE student will produce a sentence such as this on his or her trajectory toward fluent English. Therefore, elementary and secondary teachers need to become aware not only of the types of errors CLDE students will produce, but also of the grammatical rules for addressing these errors.

Rationale Behind Oral Language Error Correction

Many times teachers are told that if they correct students' errors, they will increase students' anxiety and will inhibit their fluency. Research has indicated otherwise for students who are learning English. Studies show that students need both positive and negative feedback in order to acquire the target language (Nassaji, 2007). Students' ultimate attainment in the L2 (as particularly measured by performance on discrete-point tests) can be enhanced through *explicit* error correction, grammar instruction, and focus on language (Doughty, 2003, as cited in Brown, 2007; Ellis, 2005; Thornbury, 2007). Explicit language instruction helps learners progress more rapidly through the stages of language acquisition (Ellis, 2005). In addition, the effect of grammar instruction can be durable or long term (Ellis, 2005; Norris & Ortega, 2000). If students receive error correction in context, in a comprehensible manner, through communication or functional tasks, and in a manner that does not impede the conversation flow or the meaning of the message, then explicit grammar instruction can help students progress toward a more accurate target language. There are individual learner needs that also warrant explicit grammar instruction (Thornbury, 2007, pp. 14–17):[2]

- Often, learners acquire a number of grammatical structures that enable them to communicate in the target language—but at a level that identifies them as nonnative speakers: "Yesterday, he bring me a few bread." While the message of the learner is understood, the manner of expressing the message is inaccurate, and not up to the standards of academic English. Explicit grammar instruction can serve to counteract less-than-proficient English grammar.

- While grammar instruction in and of itself does not create a fluent English speaker, just as Harmony discusses in Case Study 11.1, this instruction appears to help many students *notice* the grammatical structures as they attempt to use the language in a communicative setting (Brown, 2007; Schmidt, 1990).

- Once a student notices a grammatical structure, it appears to "stick" more readily.

- There are some learners who are comfortable with ambiguity, who are risk takers, and who have little problem experimenting with the new language. Other learners need structure and are assisted by knowing the rules of the language. Because grammar consists of a set of apparently finite rules, grammar instruction ultimately organizes the language into categories and makes the language more palatable for some learners.

> **REFER TO CASE STUDY 11.1**
>
> What rationale(s) does the teacher have for explicitly teaching the grammar point? Do you agree with the teacher's reasoning?

- Depending on cultural and educational backgrounds, some students will come to class with an expectation that the teacher's job is to correct errors and provide grammatical explanations.

Types of Error Feedback

There are many types of feedback teachers can give students when they produce an error, but there are certain factors to consider before choosing the type of feedback a teacher gives. Thornbury (2007, pp. 119–120) suggests teachers look at the following three factors before determining what type of feedback to give the learner:

1. *The type of error.* Does the error have a major effect on communication or meaning—often referred to as a *global error?* If so, then the teacher should provide explicit correction for this error. Is the error one that the learner could probably self-correct? If so, then the learner has acquired the rule for this error (although it has not yet become automatic in speech) and probably does not need explicit instruction on the rule.

2. *The type of activity.* Is the focus of the classroom activity more on form or on meaning? If the focus of the activity is on meaning (i.e., group work around the main ideas of an article), it is probably best to correct without interfering too much with the flow of communication. If the focus of the activity is on a grammar structure, then explicit grammar correction is appropriate.

3. *The type of learner.* Will the learner be discouraged or humiliated by overt correction? If so, then an indirect manner of feedback or individual work with the student may be best. Alternatively, will the learner feel short-changed if there is no correction? If so, this learner will benefit from explicit error correction.

When a student produces an error in spoken English, the teacher must determine the type of feedback to give the student and the timing of the feedback. It should be pointed out that if the student is stressed, excited, or anxious, or if the student has a speech disability or another disability that impacts communication, the student will probably produce more errors than usual. In that case, depending on the type of learner, it may be more beneficial to concentrate on the message than on the form. When students' communications are difficult to understand, teachers and peers need to ask in a respectful manner for them to repeat themselves, to clarify what they are saying. At the same time, listeners need to be aware of frustration that may occur when students are not able to make themselves understood in their speaking. Although with ELL students teachers can usually be direct in correcting a student's speaking errors—telling the student when he or she is making an error and how to correctly communicate the message—CLDE students may need to build confidence in the process of putting their thoughts together first. It will be necessary to make instructional decisions with CLDE students based on the IEP goals and the focus of the lesson. If the student is in a classroom situation where experimentation with language is encouraged, and where language correction is integrated into the lesson and is part of the normal classroom activities, then CLDE students will have more success with overt error correction. The following error correction strategies are effective with CLDE students (Brown, 2007; Nassaji, 2007; Thornbury, 2007; Williams, 2005):

- *Clarification requests* (Brown, 2007, p. 277; Nassaji, 2007). These are requests that ask students to repeat or restate what they had said— "Sorry?" "I didn't understand. Can you repeat that?" or, "What did you do yesterday?" When students reform their sentences after a clarification request, the sentence tends to improve, even if the student has not been told explicitly the type of error produced.

- *Recasting, modeling, or reformulating.* This is where the teacher repeats what the student said, but in a grammatically correct form and in a manner that does not disrupt the conversation flow:

Student: I go to the movies yesterday.

Teacher: Really? You *went* to the movies? What did you see?

Recasting, modeling, or reformulating is considered an indirect type of feedback since the teacher is not explicitly drawing students to the error, but instead is correcting the error in the reformulated response. This type of correction is beneficial in that it does not disrupt the flow of conversation. However, the drawback is that students may or may not notice the error in the reformulation. If the student does not notice the error, then the correction may not be beneficial (Williams, 2005).

- *Metalinguistic feedback or elicitation* (Brown, 2007, p. 277). This type of feedback encourages students to focus on the specific area where the error occurred and gives the student grammatical clues:

Student: Yesterday I go to the movies.

Teacher: Yes, remember that we talked about the past tense? How do you form "go" for yesterday?

The advantage of this type of feedback is that when learners are pushed to produce a more accurate language they may notice a gap between their language and the target language of the teacher (Nassaji, 2007; Swain, 2005).

- *Explicit correction* (Brown, 2007, p. 278). The teacher stops the student and explicitly corrects the error:

Student: Yesterday I go to the movies.

> *Teacher:* You did? Well before you tell me what you saw, remember that we don't use *go* when we talk about something that has already happened. We say, "Yesterday I *went* to the movies."

- *Future reference.* The teacher writes down the error for future reference to be taught in a grammar mini-lesson later. The teacher postpones the feedback so as not to disrupt the flow of conversation. While this type of error correction can be appropriate, often the most effective feedback is that which comes at the time the error is made. That said, this type of correction is beneficial if the teacher needs time to look up the rules for the error and prepare a mini-lesson to teach the rules to the students.

- *Teachable moment* (Dutro & Moran, 2003). This is where the teacher provides explicit mini-lessons at the time that the error occurs. The teacher uses the student's error to instruct the class (or the student) on the rules of the specific grammar point.

> *Student:* Yesterday I go to the movies.
>
> *Teacher:* Ah, yes. The movies can be fun. But quickly, let me tell you how you would say that sentence correctly. When we talk about *yesterday,* we are talking about the past. Therefore, we have to change the word *go* for the past tense of the verb. You have learned that we add "ed" to form the past tense, but that doesn't work with all verbs. The verb *to go* is irregular and does not use "ed" to form the past tense. The verb *to go* turns into *went* when we use it in the positive, declarative past. (Note: The teacher illustrates main points with visuals and examples.)

No one type of feedback is superior to another, generally. Rather, the teacher must consider the factors that contribute to the type of feedback one should give (the type of error, the type of activity, and the type of learner). Sometimes teachers will need to try more than one feedback method to find the one that is most effective with the student. The important point to remember is that feedback should be given to help students achieve a more proficient English, and that students usually respond well to feedback, especially if the teacher can give explicit instruction on the error produced.

REFER TO CASE STUDY 11.1

What types of errors were the students producing? What types of learners do you think her students were? What types of feedback did the teacher employ? Were they effective?

Error Analysis

Before giving explicit feedback on the error, it is important that the teacher classify the types of errors occurring. Steps to error analysis consist of the following (Gass & Selinker, 2008, p. 103):

1. *Collect data.* The teacher should take notes of errors performed by students and attempt to keep track of students' typical errors.

2. *Identify the errors.* What kind of error was performed (incorrect verb tense, incorrect subject–verb agreement, incorrect form of possessive, incorrect use of an article)?

3. *Quantify the errors.* How many errors of verb tense occurred? How many errors of possession?

4. *Concentrate on one error at a time.* Norris and Ortega (2000) found that a focus on form is more effective than a focus on forms. Consider one error that occurs most frequently or the error that most interferes with meaning. Provide an explanation for that error first.

5. *Ask the student to self-correct.* Using the feedback strategies above, if the teacher recasts or repeats the error, is the student able to *notice* the error and self-correct? If so, then the student has learned the rule—it has not become automatic yet, though. If the student cannot self-correct, then the teacher needs to provide explicit rule explanation.

While conducting error analysis, it is important to remember that when students are learning new forms, they will sometimes backslide (also known as U-shaped learning). For this reason, it is also important to note nonerrors as well to get a more complete picture of the development of the student's language (Gass & Selinker, 2008).

FORM-FOCUSED INSTRUCTION

Once an error has been identified, the teacher needs to provide explicit, clear, and concise instruction on the grammatical point. We have observed teachers giving grammatical explanations—some were accurate but many were not. Most of today's teachers have not been given grammar instruction

Photo 11.2   Explicitly pointing out grammar errors and providing explicit instruction in grammar rules can help many students with language acquisition.

in English, and certainly have not been trained in grammar instruction for CLDE students, yet we expect these teachers to have the skills to explain the grammar of English to students. Most teachers today are native English speakers and, therefore, intuitively "know" correct English grammar. However, "knowing" what correct English grammar sounds like does not give a teacher the needed skills to adequately explain the grammar point to the student. It is important that teachers know the rules of the English language and are able to articulate these rules in a comprehensible manner to help CLDE students reach a higher level of proficiency (see Photo 11.2). There is not room in the scope of this book to provide the rules for all the grammatical structures in English. We, therefore, recommend that all teachers who have CLDE students in their classes take a good teacher course in English grammar (such as grammar for TESOL teachers) or buy a good reference book on the grammar of English, or both. In the appendix, we list our favorite grammar books and Web sites for learning the grammar rules of English. We encourage teachers to attempt one small rule at a time and slowly incorporate grammar instruction into their subject matter.

DIFFERENT STRATEGIES FOR TEACHING GRAMMAR

There are numerous ways in which teachers can provide grammar lessons in the content-area or general education classroom, but there are two basic principles that should drive the grammar instruction in any classroom (Thornbury, 2007, pp. 25–27):

1. *Make the lesson concise, easy to set up, and efficient.* Today, teachers are faced with an enormous amount of content they must cover in order to prepare students for standardized tests required under NCLB. However, most of these tests also include English grammar. Taking the time to teach mini-lessons can be very beneficial. Because teacher time is limited, however, it is important that the grammar lesson be short, efficient, and easy for the teacher to implement.

   • Choose just one grammar point to teach at a time.

   • Know the rule accurately and be able to articulate the rule in a short period of time (5- to 10-minute lessons).

   • Present the grammar rule through an activity that is comprehensible (3-way model) and easy to set up.

2. *Make sure the grammar lesson is appropriate for the learners.* Different types of lessons must be implemented for students, depending on their age, their English proficiency level, their special needs, specifics from their IEPs, and their cultural and learning style factors.

Teaching Grammar Through Text

This strategy is adapted from Thornbury (2007, pp. 69–90) and involves the use of text for teaching the grammar point. *Authentic texts* can be used, such as newspaper articles, novel excerpts, textbook excerpts, and storybooks; *teacher-generated texts* can be used, such as teacher stories, or audiotaped dialogue; and *student-generated texts* can be used, such as journal entries, essays, reports, or narratives.

Basic steps for using text to teach grammar are the following:

1. The teacher chooses a type of text that is interesting to the students and has several examples of the grammar point.

2. The teacher has students read the text several times (teacher-fronted reading, silent reading, group reading).

3. While reading the text, the teacher asks students to *notice* the grammar point. For example, the teacher asks students, "How is the past spoken about in this text? What does the author do to mark verbs for the past?"

4. The teacher gives students time to extract examples of the grammar point. (Group work is beneficial here.)

5. The teacher lists the students' answers on the board.

6. The teacher and students then categorize the answers. For example, if the students pick out words from the text such as "yesterday, last week, a while ago, a long time ago, ran, jumped, looked, cooked, smiled, thought," the teacher can help students categorize the words into

   - regular verbs: jumped, looked, cooked, smiled
   - irregular verbs: ran, thought
   - adverbs and expressions of time: yesterday, last week, a while ago, a long time ago

7. The teacher and the students look for patterns in the categories. "What happens with regular verbs?" "What happens in the irregular verb category?" "Where does the author place the adverbs and why does she use them?"

8. After discerning the patterns, the teacher and students attempt to form a rule for the grammar point(s) from the examples.

9. This process is repeated as the teacher provides another text with examples of the same grammar point.

10. At the end of the activity, the teacher makes sure that the grammar rule has been correctly and explicitly stated so that there is no confusion around the grammar point.

Teaching Grammar in Context

REFER TO CASE STUDY 11.1

What aspects of teaching grammar through text did the teacher use? How effective was this strategy with her CLDE students? What would you change about the lesson to make it more effective with your students?

This strategy, also adapted from Thornbury (2007, pp. 29–68), requires the teacher to use the class content or students' language as the launching point for the grammar lesson. That is, the grammar is taught within the context of the lesson.

There are several ways the teacher can do this:

1. The teacher can "flood" students with examples—for instance, by writing down examples as they come up in class on the board, by underlining the grammar point when it is used to discuss the main points of the lesson, by underlining the grammar point as it is used in the textbook, and by underlining the grammar point as it is used in students' writing about the subject matter.

2. Once students are flooded, the teacher can either provide an inductive or deductive lesson on the grammar point.

  • An **inductive lesson** involves presenting examples first, then giving students time to "discover" the rule on their own. Similar to the text-based lesson, the teacher asks students to look for patterns in the examples and come up with a rule that explains the grammar point. Fotos (1993, as cited in Ellis, 2005) found that the "discovery" approach can be effective in that it allows opportunities for communication. Mohamed (2001, as cited in Ellis, 2005) found that this approach is more motivating to learners.

  • A **deductive lesson** involves the teacher giving an explicit explanation of the rule first, then providing examples. The teacher begins by explaining the rule, then asks students to renotice the grammar point that is underlined on the board, in textbooks, and in students' writing. The teacher then explains how the grammar point in each example follows the rule given earlier. Fotos (1993) found that this approach is effective in teaching the grammar rule.

To illustrate further, let us say the teacher is interested in teaching the different manners of expressing the future tense in English (which includes the use of "will + verb," "going to" + verb, and verb "to be" + ing). The teacher begins by flooding the students. Every time a future tense is used in either spoken or written English, the teacher writes the form on the board or has students highlight or underline the form in the text. Drawing attention to the form through highlighting, underlining, or writing on the board helps students *notice* the form, which has been shown to increase understanding of the grammar point (Ellis, 2005).

If the teacher has chosen an inductive approach, he or she would then group students and ask them to write down all the underlined sentences from the board and textbook. The teacher would then explain that these sentences are all used to express the future in English, but that they are different from each other (some use "will" + verb, some use "going to" + verb, some use the progressive + ing form). The teacher asks the groups to try to discover the rule for the different forms by looking at the sentences in context: How are they used in the textbook? How were they used in the lecture? What could be the difference in meaning between the different forms? Why is "will" used here, and "going to" used here? What is the difference?

Students come up with their own rules that the teacher writes on the board. The teacher then gives the correct rules and students compare their hypotheses with the accurate rules.

If the teacher were giving a deductive lesson, the teacher would ask students to write all the underlined sentences from the board and the textbook on a piece of paper. The teacher would then explain that these forms are used to express the future and would ask students to categorize the sentences according to the form used ("will," "going to," –ing). Once the sentences have been categorized, the teacher explains the rule for each category, how the point is formed, and the reason for using each form (the function of each form).

The teacher then asks students to reread the textbook or written text and to relisten to the lecture (if the lecture were tape-recorded or if the teacher repeats the lecture in a different manner). When students reach a future tense sentence, the teacher stops the reading (or the tape recorder) and asks students to articulate why the particular form was used in the sentence, according to the rules given earlier.

REFER TO CASE STUDY 11.1

Which aspects of teaching grammar through context did the teacher use? How effective was this approach? What would you change to make the lesson more effective with your students?

11.1

To read a case study from a kindergarten teacher, Erika Lee, which illustrates the teaching of grammar in context, see the following Web link: **www.sagepub.com/grassi.**

Summary

In conclusion, when correcting CLDE students' errors in English, there are several factors to take into consideration. To begin, the teacher must note where the error stems from: Is it part of the normal trajectory of learning English, or is it part of the special needs of the student? Once the source of the error is pinpointed, the teacher should determine what type of feedback is needed. Should the teacher overtly correct the error or let it go? What type of learner is the student? Is the learner one who shies away from correction or one who benefits from correction? The teacher must then investigate the type of error, the rules surrounding the grammar point, and the best way to instruct students on the grammar rules. Many repetitions of the rule are necessary before the form can become automatic in CLDE student speech and written work. After reading this chapter, you should know how to use the following in the classroom:

- Articulate the importance of error correction and focus on form instruction for CLDE students.

- Provide feedback to students when they produce errors.

- Choose the type of feedback according to the type of error produced, the type of activity students are involved in, and the type of learner the teacher is instructing.

- Be aware of the grammatical rule and be able to articulate the rule in a comprehensible manner, using a good grammar book as a necessary tool.

- Make the grammar lesson quick, efficient, and easy to implement.

To access a video clip of a teacher implementing a grammar lesson and to access a rubric with which to observe the teacher and evaluate the strategy, see the following Web link: **www.sagepub.com/grassi.**

11.2

Key Terms

Deductive lesson

Inductive lesson

Recasting, modeling, or reformulating

Activities for Further Understanding

1. Observe a teacher who works with CLDE students or ELL students. Does the teacher provide feedback to students when they make grammatical errors? What type of feedback does the teacher provide? Is it effective? What would you do differently?

2. Observe your students and the types of grammatical errors they make in English. Pick one error to address and design a grammar mini-lesson for your class (or small group of students). After teaching, reflect on the lesson. What worked? What didn't? What would you do differently next time?

3. Observe a teacher instructing ELL or CLDE students in grammar. What practices are effective? What practices are not? How would you change the lesson to better suit the students?

Visit the Student Study Site at **www.sagepub.com/grassi** for chapter-specific study resources.

Notes

1. See Chapter 4, Table 4.5 Grammatical Competence Errors and Examples for a chart depicting the different types of errors students will make when learning English.

2. In this book, we advocate for grammar instruction, and therefore do not provide the arguments against teaching grammar. For a concise and clear list of the reasons for not teaching grammar, see Thornbury 2007.

SECTION IV

Strategies for Literacy Instruction

Chapter 12. Strategies for Teaching Reading

Chapter 13. Strategies for Teaching the Writing Process

Chapter 14. Challenges When Teaching Writing

Chapter 15. Strategies for Written Error Correction

Chapter 12

STRATEGIES FOR TEACHING READING

CASE STUDY 12.1	Literacy Instruction at the Secondary Level

As an undergraduate, I trained to be a social studies teacher. I gave little thought to language or literacy. I assumed that literacy was "not my problem." Ironically, my first teaching job was as a high school reading teacher. I assumed that I would need to work mainly on comprehension and critical thinking skills with my students. I quickly realized, however, that while those types of exercises would benefit the few students reading two years below grade level, the rest of my students (who were reading at a fourth to seventh grade level) could access neither the content nor the concept. More than half of my students were learning English, and several had learning disabilities. Half of my students had never received any ESL or bilingual interventions. These students simply began speaking English upon entering kindergarten. The other students had been bounced in and out of unstable ESL classes for most of their school careers. None of my students lived in a language-rich environment. It seemed that most of my students were fossilized in BICS: They could survive at home, at work, and in the hallways with friends, but the coursework in high school proved to be a challenge. They were suddenly immersed in an environment where instructors forge through their language intensive content with little time for adaptations.

By my second year as a reading teacher, I realized the importance of teaching reading strategies, vocabulary, and grammar instruction: Few of my students could write a coherent paragraph. In my classes, I introduced a new academic vocabulary word each week. We also read texts and worked on comprehension skills and strategies. In the back of my mind, I knew there was still something missing. For instance, I couldn't read their papers without having to ask the students to read them to me. Not only was their handwriting bad, but their spelling was almost incomprehensible. I knew I had to do something with phonics and phonemic awareness, but I barely knew what these things were, let alone how to teach them. I put the idea off, thinking, "They feel dumb enough. How would they react to their teacher making them practice letter sounds and reviewing the alphabet?" No, I would not do that. A month into my battle, their English teacher came to me and begged me to do something about their spelling. I smiled and conceded.

I found a quick spelling assessment that would help me identify the level at which they were having their breakdowns. I found a list of words in another book that matched their level of spelling. I decided that I would teach phonemic awareness and the concept of sounds by approaching this as a "spelling" activity I called "phonemic analysis."

I picked key words from their textbooks based on the sound the vowel made, and chose either two different ways to spell that vowel or two different sounds associated with that vowel. There were about five words for each "category" and two "categories" a week. As students walked in for the day, I gave them a word that belonged in one of the categories. We went around the class and practiced how to say each word. Afterward, the students all came up to the board and put the words into different categories based on either their spelling or the way they sounded. When the class got all of the words sorted correctly, they wrote them on their "phonemic analysis" work sheet.

The next step was to work on predictions of why a letter sounded the way it did. As a class, we reached a consensus and created a rule that was made explicit to everyone. Then, we talked about the meaning of each word. Each student put the words into digital glossaries we made in PowerPoint. By the third day, we would use the words to write rhymes or plays that we would sometimes make into podcasts. At the end of each week, I tested the students on their words and their ability to transfer the rule to new words.

While the whole exercise felt awkward to me, I think that exposure to words and their sounds helped my students more than comprehension strategies could have at that point. Students are very aware when they are lacking something and they desperately want to learn the concept. I'm glad I finally conceded and started to give my students what they really needed.

—Tonia, High school social studies teacher

Consider the case study above:

- What did Tonia notice about her students' literacy skills?
- Have you noticed the same issues with students in your classes?
- What were the foundational literacy skills that she needed to teach?
- What foundational literacy skills do CLDE students need in order to be successful in the content-area classroom?

READING COMPONENTS AND CLDE STUDENTS

Reading can be a daunting task for many CLDE students.[1] CLDE students' reading abilities depend on their literacy and language skills in the L1, proficiency level in the L2, possible disability, past educational experience with literacy in the L2, the comprehensibility of the text, and the ability of the teacher to make the text readable and enjoyable (August & Shanahan, 2006; Eskey, 2005).

With the changing demographics in our school classrooms, preliterate and below-level readers are present not only in elementary classrooms, but also in middle level and high school classrooms, such as the classroom that Tonia describes. It becomes increasingly important that all teachers be trained, and that they understand how to implement literacy instruction in their content-area classrooms. Many elementary general education literacy methods can be adapted to teach reading skills to CLDE students, but with the increasing numbers of CLDE students coming to the secondary level—with little to no literacy instruction in the first or second language—it is important that secondary teachers know how to implement explicit literacy strategies within their content-area classrooms as well.

In writing this chapter, we assume that most teachers have been trained in basic literacy techniques in their preservice or ongoing education. However, in order for any literacy method to be fully effective with CLDE students, several other aspects of literacy should be taken into account. To begin, the five essential components of reading should be emphasized (Learning Point Associates, 2004; National Institute of Child Health and Human Development [NICHD], 2000; National Reading Panel, 2000):

1. **Phonemic awareness** is the understanding that words are made up of separate units of sound that are blended. For example, the word /cat/ consists of three sounds: /k/ /a/ /t/. Phonemes differ across languages; English phonemic awareness is an important step in literacy instruction for CLDE students. Phonemic awareness is also important for students with reading disabilities who often have difficulties in this area.

2. **Phonics** are the rules of how speech sounds are represented in written format. Phonics involves connecting the sounds students hear in spoken language to their alphabetic representation. For example, the sound /shun/ is usually represented as "tion" in English. However, in other languages, the /shun/ sound can be represented by differing letter combinations. If students have processing or perception disabilities, their phonetic understanding can be affected.

3. **Fluency** is the ability to recognize rapidly and accurately written words. Studies have found a connection between fluency and comprehension (NICHD, 2000). CLDE students typically are not fluent readers because they are both learning the new language and struggling with intellectual, developmental, or emotional needs that may impact their reading skills.

4. **Vocabulary** are the words used to communicate. Students depend heavily on their oral language proficiency to develop vocabulary. Students will use the pronunciation and meaning of words in their spoken language to help them recognize words they see in print (August & Shanahan, 2006). Even if children are good decoders, they can have difficulty understanding and recognizing a word if it is not part of their oral vocabulary. Vocabulary also is closely linked with comprehension: the larger the vocabulary, the more likely children will understand the text. It is important that teachers work to expand students' oral vocabulary first—especially the vocabulary words that will be found in the reading. Many of the disabilities present in CLDE students can impede vocabulary learning because of processing issues, perception issues, memory issues, developmental issues, behavioral needs, or educational history.

5. **Comprehension** is constructing meaning from and understanding what is read. Because CLDE students are reading in English as their L2 and have disabilities that can impact comprehension of a text, teachers must pay special attention to building comprehension of the text before, during, and after reading.

Most teachers are familiar with these five essential components of reading. When working with CLDE students, who are both learning an L2 and have a disability, these five essential components must be expanded to best meet the students' specific literacy needs. We consider five more components also to be essential literacy skills for CLDE students:

1. *Oral language proficiency in the L2.* The National Literacy Panel on Language-Minority Children and Youth found that success in L2 reading is directly related to proficiency in the L2 (August & Shanahan, 2006; Eskey, 2005, p. 566). Specifically, the level of oral language proficiency directly corresponds to reading comprehension.

2. *Language and literacy.* When working with CLDE students, the language acquisition process must be taken into consideration. Strategies to make the language of the text more comprehensible and strategies to help students study and use the language in context must be implemented.

3. *Explicit literacy instruction.* The literacy instruction for CLDE students must be explicit at all steps of the process, including explicit vocabulary instruction; explicit grammar instruction and language study; explicit connections to the students' background; explicit strategy instruction; and explicit instruction in how to analyze, summarize, and interact with the text.

4. *Cultural and linguistic background taken into consideration.* The students' cultural and linguistic backgrounds must be considered at every step of the process, including the influence of culture and language on the type of literacy chosen, the attitudes toward literacy, and the understanding of different literacies.

5. *Considering the special needs.* The student's special needs, including specific skills and needs addressed on the IEP, must be considered at every step of the process.

In sum, while basic literacy instruction is an important first step, further skills, such as the components above, are not easily acquired through basic literacy instruction. When working with CLDE students, basic literacy instruction must be enhanced with strategies to help students develop language around the text; build world knowledge around the topic; enhance the comprehensibility of the text to the point where students can summarize and analyze the information; help students actively interact with the text; and review, retain, and work with the information gained.

<table>
<tr><td>

REFER TO CASE STUDY 12.1

Which of the reading skills listed above did Tonia implement? Which reading skills would still need to be taught for her to have a complete literacy program? Which of the reading skills listed on pages 276 and 277 do you currently teach, and where could you expand your literacy instruction?
</td></tr>
</table>

In this chapter, we provide strategies for *prereading, during reading, and after reading* that will help teachers prepare CLDE students to gain required reading skills. We cannot present a complete literacy program within the scope of this chapter, but we do present foundational strategies that can be implemented immediately. These strategies can be adapted to either the elementary or the secondary level. The teacher needs to choose material that is developmentally and age appropriate for the students.

SECTION 12.1 LANGUAGE AND LITERACY

Strategies to Increase Vocabulary and Oral Language Proficiency

CASE STUDY 12.2 | Oral Language Proficiency

When I first started my coaching position, it became apparent that there was a need for classroom teachers to be able to work effectively with students who had both L2 needs and special education language needs. I started to ask questions about how the teachers worked with their CLDE students. In some cases, I found that they were doing the same thing over and over again and getting the same results, but we needed different results. Therefore, our school decided to do a book study specifically designed around oral language development. The first year I worked with a small group of teachers and we assessed students using an oral language assessment, and then discussed appropriate oral language development strategies to use with small groups, depending on their language acquisition stage and their special needs.

One of the teachers that joined the first year of our book study was a first-year teacher. She was frustrated because the traditional way of conducting a guided reading group was not producing any learning. The children continued with their avoidance reading behaviors and had limited understanding of the texts. After working on oral language development techniques—eliciting, restating, expanding, and refining the students' oral language, and then turning that language into charts and books the students could read—the students became highly interested and engaged in their reading and writing. She continued with this strategy, as well as many more from the oral language development program. These students developed their oral language skills. They became students who went from responding with one or two words to students who used complete and even complex sentences. Their oral language become highly successful; they were writing and reading at or near grade level because their oral language fluency drove their progress. They wanted to sit in the front of the class. They no longer tried to blend in so no one would ask them a question. They were a part of the learning process and would take part in classroom discussions throughout the day. Other teachers who worked with these students during music, art, or P.E. also noticed a change. One teacher said, "It is amazing. When students have language and the confidence to use it, what a difference it makes in their ability to learn and to be a part of a group."

Other teachers working with language learners, whether they were L2 learners or special education students, saw many of the same things happening in their classrooms. A third-grade teacher said to me, "I really thought that this student should be referred to special education." By giving the student the opportunity to understand and use oral language in a way that was meaningful and nonthreatening, though, the teacher was able to watch her grow into a reader and a writer. She was not at grade level at the end of the year, but the teacher said she wouldn't think of referring her for testing because of the huge growth that she had made.

I know the skill of using oral language is one of the most amazing skills for further enhancement of reading and writing. You can be a second language learner or special education learner and still be a language learner. Everyone benefits from oral language development.

—Joanie Esparza, Literacy coach

Consider the case study above:

- Did Tonia in Case Study 12.1 and Joanie in this case study notice the same issues with their students?
- Could oral language development have helped Tonia's students as well?
- What examples of reading improvement were noted after the teachers worked on oral language development?
- How can you implement oral language development in your primary or secondary classroom?

SOURCE: Used by permission.

Research has indicated a strong link between the level of oral language proficiency in the target language and success in reading in the target language (Aldridge, 2005; August & Shanahan, 2006; Dockrell, Stuart, & King, 2004; Peregoy & Boyle, 2005; Pollard-Durodola, Mathes, Vaughn, Cardenas-Hagen, & Linan-Thompson, 2006; Saracho & Spodek, 2007). The relationship between proficient reading comprehension and knowledge of L2 vocabulary is particularly strong. It has been well established that good comprehenders have higher levels of L2 vocabulary, and comprehension tends to improve with L2 vocabulary instruction (Beck, Perfetti, & McKeown, 1982; Brett, Rothlein, & Hurley, 1996; Pressley, 2008). Vocabulary instruction is particularly important with CLDE students. Studies such as that conducted by Fry (1981, as cited in Eskey, 2005) note that L2 readers who encountered more than one unknown word in 20 experienced great frustration and lower motivation to read.

One of the best ways to acquire a larger vocabulary in the L2 is through reading, while a prerequisite to enjoying reading in the L2 is an extensive oral vocabulary (Eskey, 2005; see Photo 12.2). The National Literacy Panel on Language-Minority Children and Youth found that English oral language proficiency was closely linked with reading comprehension skills in English (August & Shanahan, 2006). If a word found in print is not part of the child's oral vocabulary, the child could have difficulty recognizing and understanding the word.

Photo 12.2   Providing opportunities to develop oral language skills is a first step in literacy development.

If students can talk about the content first, using key vocabulary in context, then their ability to recognize the words in print will increase.

CASE STUDY 12.3 | **Increasing Talk Around the Topic**

I often use nonfiction books with my class. One of the books I use is about animal habitats. I frequently choose this book because all students have some background knowledge about animal habitats from their personal experiences or from trips to the zoo. The pictures in the book are photographs, and the text describes and matches the pictures. Nonfiction books are excellent for teaching vocabulary because they are full of "real" concrete information and pictures that usually match the words.

First, I introduce the text. Each student gets a copy of the book and we all look at the cover without opening the book. I always ask the same question before we read: "What do you think you might learn from this book?" Some of the students' answers are simple, but it gets them thinking about the topic and the text and the fact that we are reading this book to learn about habitats.

Next, we open the books and do a picture walk. We look at each page and I ask the students the same question for each page. "What do you think you are going to learn on this page?" I follow up with "Why?" When I ask these questions, I am teaching them several things:

- To use the picture as clues. Then, when they read the words, they can use those same pictures to check if what they are reading is making sense.
- To defend or support what they are saying by giving a reason for their thinking. This also encourages them to practice speaking and using words about and from the text.
- To continue to activate their background knowledge about habitats and to connect that knowledge to the book. I write the students' answers on the board so students can begin to connect the verbal language with the written word.

We still aren't ready to read the book. Next, I bring up unfamiliar and key vocabulary—such as rainforest, desert, biomes, habitat, and other words that I know are key to understanding the text. We locate the words in the book and talk about what they mean. I also write them on a chart, sometimes with a picture.

Now I have to give them a purpose for reading the book. I remind them that we are going to talk and write about what we learned when we are finished reading the book. Finally, it is their turn to read the book, which they do independently. I watch and listen to them reading the book on their own. I take notes on their understanding, their challenges, and their successes so that I know what needs to be taught next.

—Jessica Bass, Elementary reading teacher

(Continued)

(Continued)

Consider the case study above:

- What examples of vocabulary and oral language development strategies are present in this lesson?
- How do Jessica's strategies compare to Tonia's and Joanie's?
- How could Jessica's strategies be implemented in an upper elementary, middle, or high school classroom?

SOURCE: Used by permission.

12.1

For a case study example of the Language Experience Approach, see the following Web link: **www.sagepub.com/grassi.**

When discussing vocabulary development and oral language proficiency for CLDE students, emphasizing key vocabulary, front-loading, teaching the vocabulary words before the reading, and giving students an opportunity to develop their oral language proficiency around the topic (using the key vocabulary) will increase the overall comprehensibility of the text and will better prepare students to engage with the texts. Teachers should try to predict what the unfamiliar vocabulary will be for the students before they begin to read. It is important for students to understand the meaning of words they read if they are to learn content from the material (Nagy & Scott, 2000). As Jessica noted in Case Study 12.3, one of the most important features of her lesson was emphasizing key vocabulary and giving students the opportunity to practice the vocabulary orally before reading.

In order to choose the words that will constitute "key vocabulary," the teacher should think about the following (Graves et al., 1998):

a. Which words will the CLDE students encounter frequently in the text?

b. Which words are crucial to understanding the main concepts of the text?

c. Which words will the students probably not already know?

d. Which words are difficult to figure out independently or through the context of the reading?

Once the key vocabulary is chosen, the teacher can implement activities to increase retention and learning of these new words. We recommend the following activities to build vocabulary knowledge before, during, and after reading:

1. Front-load and emphasize key vocabulary of the text using the 3-way model.

2. Use repetition games, using the key vocabulary.

3. Use the vocabulary retention strategies discussed in Chapter 9

4. Structured talk around the topic with focused discussion questions.

5. Incorporate the Language Experience Approach or other oral language development program.

For a complete description of each activity listed above, see the following Web link: **www.sagepub.com/grassi.**

12.2

Strategies to Increase Comprehension of the Text Language

Overall meaning of the text—and not just specific vocabulary words—also needs to be enhanced by providing strategies to increase comprehension of the text language (Echevarria et al., 2008; Short & Echevarria, 1999). CLDE students are in the process of learning an L2. If the text is in the student's L2, teachers will need to provide strategies to increase comprehension of the language of the text as a whole. Likewise, if the student's disability affects their reading skills, making the language of the text more comprehensible can help meet the special education needs of the student as well. Chapter 9 offered foundational strategies for making any content (including a text) comprehensible. Beyond those strategies, there are specific prereading strategies that can help students access the language of the text:

1. Match texts to the reading level of the students (Eskey, 2005).

2. Front-load key concepts of the text using the 3-way model.

3. Storytell the text first, using pictures or other visual contexts.

4. Text retell in the L1.

5. Outline the text for students to examine before reading.

For a complete description of the strategies listed above, see the following Web link: **www.sagepub.com/grassi.**

12.3

Comprehension of the text also needs to be emphasized during reading. If CLDE students do not understand the text while reading, then motivation to read decreases and frustration around reading increases. Regardless of the reading level of the text, teachers can implement strategies to make the text more comprehensible to students. Ideally, the teacher would be able to match the student with a text of their language level—or a little beyond (Eskey, 2005). However, sometimes these texts are not available. In those cases, teachers must implement strategies to increase accessibility of the text during reading. We recommend the following activities:

1. Provide visual context for the main concepts.

2. Allow for L1 and L2 group discussions around the text.

3. Model the reading (read aloud).

4. Arrange partner reading, small group reading, or whole class choral reading of the text.

5. Teach jigsaw reading of the text, making individuals or pairs responsible for some part of the text that they share in groups.

6. Match the books to the reading level of the student (Eskey, 2005; Nation, 2005).

7. Provide texts in the L1.

12.4

For a complete description of the strategies listed above, see the following Web link: **www.sagepub.com/grassi.**

Strategies for Language Study

REFER TO THE CASE STUDIES

Which strategies did the teachers implement to make the text language more comprehensible to the students? How could you improve on making the text comprehensible in your classroom?

Literacy instruction for CLDE students must include specific language study. CLDE students are still acquiring grammatical and discourse competence; the teacher can use the text read in class as a basis for specific language study—focusing on key vocabulary, idioms, or grammar. In Chapter 11, we discussed using the text for grammar lessons. Those strategies are effective with any text. We also recommend the following strategies for specific language study after the text has been read and comprehended.

1. Cloze activities with gaps to fill in vocabulary or grammar.

2. Bring attention to grammar points in the text and allow students to form rules for the grammar points (see Chapter 11).

3. Reconstruct the text using grammar forms and new vocabulary.

4. Use picture and sentence matching.

> **REFER TO THE CASE STUDIES**
>
> What did each teacher do to increase grammar and language study? How could you better incorporate language study into your literacy instruction?

For a complete description of the strategies, see the following Web link: **www.sagepub.com/grassi**.

12.5

To watch a video clip of a teacher emphasizing vocabulary, oral proficiency, comprehensibility and language study, and to access a rubric with which to observe the teacher and evaluate the strategy, see the following Web link: **www.sagepub .com/grassi**.

12.6

SECTION 12.2 ACTIVITIES TO INCREASE BACKGROUND KNOWLEDGE

CASE STUDY 12.4   Cultural Relevancy and Literacy

Hawaiian language class was one of my favorites when I was in the ninth and tenth grades. It was an environment where I could learn about the place I called home. One day my Kumu (teacher) said, "I'm going to tell you about something that they do not write in history books for high school students." Instantly, she had my attention. I was excited to learn about things that I wasn't supposed to know. It would soon be the 100th anniversary of the overthrow of the kingdom of Hawaii by the United States. We were all curious because of all the news reports that we had been hearing. There were several conflicting stories and ideas. Some said that it was necessary and inevitable that Hawaii be overthrown. Others told of how the takeover devastated the Hawaiian people and led to the homelessness and joblessness that continues to plague many Hawaiians today. The mixed information confused me.

(Continued)

(Continued)

Could the tiny nation of Hawaii have survived without a takeover? As the descendant of Portuguese and Filipino immigrants to Hawaii, I wondered if I would even exist had this takeover not occurred.

Although my Kumu admittedly was biased, she did her best to present both sides for us to investigate. We read about the issues in Hawaiian and English, had discussions, took a field trip to Iolani Palace, listened to speakers, and watched videos. We were challenged to compare perspectives in the texts we read and question what we were taught. We learned that biases exist in all of us and in all texts. In our discussions, we found that the conquerors usually write the history books. The stories of those that are conquered are often lost. We wanted to learn all we could so that the stories would not disappear. These were valuable experiences that would challenge my thinking throughout my years as a student.

Another experience that shaped me as a learner was the opportunity that I had to be a part of a special cultural studies program that incorporated history and cultural study with the literature of the people of Hawaii and some of the countries from which they emigrated. My English and social studies classes that year were focused exclusively on this cultural study. My peers and I took several field trips and interviewed community and family members to gather information for an oral history investigation and project. I learned the value of seeking out different perspectives, and I began to develop a love for reading and the literature of a variety of people.

Now I am a teacher, and I cherish these lessons from my past. I look around my classroom and see 22 unique and wonderful individuals. Each day I hear different languages and ways of speaking. I am witness to a variety of interests and concerns. I want my students to know the value in each of these differences and the themes that bind them together. I want them to understand the importance of seeking out a variety of perspectives, to ask questions, and to be unsatisfied with what is simply set before them.

—Harmony Looper, Literacy teacher

Consider the case study above:

- How did the teachers tap into Harmony's background knowledge?
- How did the teachers help the students connect to the literacy?
- What elements of culturally relevant teaching were present in Harmony's class?
- Why are these strategies effective in a classroom with CLDE learners?

SOURCE: Used by permission.

Making the overarching concept of the text—and not just certain vocabulary words or key concepts—comprehensible is also important when reading with CLDE students. Making the text comprehensible involves providing *cultural* and *content schemas*. Students must be able to relate the text to their background knowledge in order to better comprehend the text and to develop the motivation to read. Many studies have indicated that rich background knowledge about the topic increases comprehension of the text (Eskey, 2005; Pressley, 2008; Van den Broek & Kremer, 2000). As Harmony puts it in Case Study 12.4, making the text relevant to the students encourages them to read. Many times, texts and textbooks are written for a specific cultural audience. If the reader is not a member of that culture, his or her comprehension of the text and motivation to read can be limited (Eskey, 2005).

Because the CLDE student has a disability, he or she may have gaps in background knowledge. Perhaps the student was pulled out of the class for special education services, or does not understand the text, has difficulty with processing the information, or lacks modifications that would help him to understand the text or content. These gaps must be filled in order for students to understand and connect with the text.

When working with CLDE students, it is important to find the gaps in background knowledge. Knowing where the gaps lie—whether in vocabulary, overarching concepts, cultural understanding, or details—can help the teacher fill in the needed information, so that students can comprehend the material and make connections between the material and their own experiences. In addition, understanding the reasons behind the gaps (language, culture, disability) is an important step before choosing an intervention in RTI.

Before reading with CLDE students, the teacher should either provide *cultural schemata* and *content schemata* or activate students' own background knowledge in order to help students better comprehend and enjoy the reading (Eskey, 2005). We suggest the following activities to help build students' background knowledge:

1. Sharing existing knowledge around the topic

2. Accessing and sharing different cultural perspectives around the topic

3. Asking "why" questions about the topic or the text

4. Sequencing activities related to the topic

5. Showing movies around the topic

6. Arranging field trips to support the topic

> **REFER TO CASE STUDY 12.4**
>
> What did Harmony's teachers do to build background knowledge before reading the text? How did her teachers value the perspective the students brought to the topic? How could you incorporate the building of background knowledge into your lessons?

7. Interviewing experts on the topic

8. Inviting the perspective of parents, student relatives, or others from diverse cultures

12.7

For a detailed description of the activities listed above, see the following Web link: **www.sagepub.com/grassi.**

12.8

To watch a video clip of a teacher increasing background knowledge before literacy instruction with CLDE students, and to access a rubric with which to observe the teacher and evaluate the strategy, see the following Web link: **www .sagepub.com/grassi.**

Section 12.3 Reading Strategy Instruction

CASE STUDY 12.5	**Reading Strategy Instruction**

I start by introducing the text, a picture book called *Where Are You Going, Manyoni?* by Catherine Stock. It has very simple text—one sentence on each page—with illustrations of Zimbabwe. There are many words that are unfamiliar because they are in an African language. To give the students some background knowledge, I tell them that the story is about a little girl who lives in Africa. I have students in my class from Africa, although not from Zimbabwe, who tell our class about their own experiences. One little boy told us about pictures his mother had that looked very much like the scenes in the book.

After we look at the book cover and discuss the setting, I talk about the reading skill we are going to work on: *inferring*. It is so important to pick a text that matches the skills I am teaching and that matches the students' abilities and interests. The text must connect with students.

I start by reading the first two pages and I stop at a word "baobab"—I say to the students, "Baobab? I really don't know what that word is and I don't know what this sentence means without knowing what this word means." I reread the sentence (I tell them what I am doing) "Hmm . . . that didn't help me. I'm going to look at the picture that goes with the baobab. Look, it is a tree—maybe baobab is a tree . . ." I have a chart and I write this idea on the chart. I want them to see me try a couple of strategies—rereading the sentence and looking at the picture. I want them to see that maybe my first try didn't work, so I try something else.

After I model a few words in the same way, we continue to read and the students take turns to infer what the new words mean as I fill out and complete the chart. We do it again the next day, continuing to decode new vocabulary in the book. After we have finished rereading the book, we check in the glossary to see if our inferences were correct. During independent reading time, they can try the new skill with sticky notes in their books.

—Jessica Bass, Elementary reading teacher

Consider the case study above:

- How does the teacher explicitly teach reading strategies?
- How does the reading lesson accommodate CLDE students?
- Which strategies could be used with both a secondary or elementary content text?

SOURCE: Used by permission.

Part of becoming a "good" reader is the ability to interact with the text, to make predictions, to ask questions, and to analyze the text for pertinent information. Cordón & Day (1996, as cited in Pressley, 2008), found that struggling readers were unable to interpret the text, evaluate its quality, review important points, and think about how ideas encountered in the text might be used in the future. Secondary students, in particular, are expected to interact with the readings on a more complex level. In standardized high school level tests, CLDE students are expected to summarize the text, analyze ideas presented in the text, and evaluate the text for accuracy and connections to prior knowledge (Fillmore & Snow, 2000). It is important that teachers explicitly teach these skills to CLDE students. Many CLDE students are below grade level in reading and have not found pleasure and enjoyment in reading. Sometimes helping students have fun with the text and interact with the text in creative manners can help motivate them to read more.

Teaching reading strategies is another way to assist students in becoming better readers (Eskey, 2005). Explicit strategy instruction at the prereading level and during reading level—such as inferring meaning from titles or pictures, asking questions about the content, making connections, summarizing, and using specific strategies to decode words—can help secondary and elementary level CLDE students become better readers. Many of these strategies are standard parts of a reading curriculum in primary elementary grades, but should also be a part of instruction with secondary level students who are learning to read in English. In order to increase reading strategy skills with CLDE students, we recommend the following activities:

Before reading

1. Predicting from words

2. Predicting from the title or first sentence

3. Predicting from key illustrations

4. Critically questioning the text using reader questions

5. Decoding words using strategy instructions

6. Completing KWL charts: what do students *know* about the topic, what do they *want* to know, what did they *learn* after reading

During reading

1. Skimming and scanning the text for meaning (Gibbons, 2002)

2. Rereading for vocabulary and grammar structures

3. Instructing students on how to read for detail

4. Pausing during reading and predicting what will happen

5. Matching voice to print

6. Critically questioning the text, and analyzing and evaluating the text

7. Pausing and reflecting: "Does that make sense?"

8. Instructing students on how to make connections with the text

9. Assigning students particular strategies to practice during mini-lessons

10. Practicing summarizing the text

> **REFER TO THE CASE STUDIES**
>
> Which reading strategies did the teachers incorporate into their lessons? What further strategy instruction could their students benefit from? Which strategies do you teach to your students? How could you improve your strategy instruction?

For a complete description of the activities listed above, see the following Web link: **www.sagepub.com/grassi.**

12.9

To watch a video clip of a teacher implementing reading strategy instruction with CLDE students, and to access a rubric with which to observe the teacher and evaluate the strategy, see the following Web link: **www.sagepub.com/grassi.**

12.10

SECTION 12.4 STRATEGIES TO HELP STUDENTS ANALYZE, ORGANIZE, AND INTERACT WITH THE CONTENT

| CASE STUDY 12.6 | Reader's Theater |

I started using Reader's Theater specifically for my more advanced readers. I wanted my students to work on their fluency skills and better interact with the text, now that they were good at decoding and comprehension skills. After the first group performed for the entire class, it was an instant hit! The whole class was begging to be next for Reader's Theater. Due to the students' enthusiasm, I discovered that this strategy is easy to differentiate for all reading levels of students.

I began to pick new scripts for all of the reading levels within my classroom. Reader's Theater was helpful for all my students to gain a deeper understanding of the text, to start sequencing of the text, and to begin understanding summarizing. In addition, it provided lots of oral practice. When the students practiced the text every day during Reader's Workshop they became more fluent and more confident; it created a whole new excitement about reading. Reader's Theater gave my students a legitimate reason to reread the text, which is a key component of successful reading. The Reader's Theater gave the students a new text to read during independent reading time and the opportunity to work with other students. Not only did my entire class start reading with more expression, fluency, and joy, but also they improved their reading levels.

—Jessica Bass, Elementary reading teacher

Consider the case study above:

- How does Reader's Theater help students interact with the text?
- How does this strategy help students organize and summarize information gathered from a text?
- How could Reader's Theater be used with primary students or with high school students?

SOURCE: Used by permission.

When working with secondary level CLDE students in particular, reading becomes even more complex and further skills should be emphasized. Fillmore (1999 as cited in Fillmore & Snow, 2000) analyzed a high school graduation exam for the type of literacy skills needed to pass the exam. Fillmore found the following reading skills were required (p. 22):

1. The ability to *summarize texts*, including the ability to interpret and infer the writer's intentions

2. The ability to *analyze texts* for various information, perspective, and mood

3. The ability to *understand and extract information from texts* and relate it to other ideas and information

4. The ability to *evaluate the evidence and arguments* presented in texts and *critique* the logic of the evidence and arguments

5. The ability to *recognize and analyze the conventions* used in various genres

6. The ability to recognize *ungrammatical written language* and the ability to make necessary corrections to grammar, punctuation, and capitalization

Many times CLDE students are overwhelmed with the information gathered from texts and are not sure how to organize, analyze, evaluate, or use the information: What are the main points? What is the true summary of the information? What information is important information and what information is insignificant? Teachers must explicitly teach the skills listed above. After a text has been read and understood, the text can be used to review the information, retain the information, and work with the information gained (both with regard to content and to grammar). The text also can be used to reinforce, review, summarize, analyze, evaluate, and retain the content learned.

Below we list after-reading strategies that can help CLDE students better work with the information gathered from the text (Copeland & Keefe, 2007; Gibbons, 2002; Gunning, 2007).

1. Organizing information from the text in graphic organizers

2. Acting out the text with Reader's Theater

3. Drawing mental images from the text

4. Using "Wanted Posters" to describe the main characters of the text

5. Using sequence charts, story boards, story maps, and time lines to delineate the text or to sequence the events of the text

6. Questioning characters in the book—"Hot Seat" or "Talk Show"

7. Using freeze frames (that is, having students construct a "frozen" scene) of main ideas in the text

8. Answering true/false statements about the text

9. Picture dictation

10. Questioning the text

11. Checking predictions about the text

12. Considering connections to the text

> For a complete description of the strategies, see the following Web link: **www.sagepub.com/grassi.**

12.11

> To watch a video clip of a teacher implementing strategies to help students analyze, organize, and interact with the content, and to access a rubric with which to observe the teacher and evaluate the strategy, see the following Web link: **www.sagepub.com/grassi.**

12.12

Summary

"Good" readers are actively involved in the text, they interrogate and interact with the text, they predict what is coming, they analyze and evaluate what they have read, they underline and take notes of important aspects of the reading, and they think about ideas presented in the text and how these relate to their current knowledge base. Becoming a "good" reader requires teachers to model reading strategies; to have a text that is interesting, comprehensible but challenging (Krashen i + 1); and to design activities that encourage exploration and interaction with the text.

Teaching reading to CLDE students is an important aspect of learning that goes beyond "reading" lessons (Table 12.1). In order for CLDE students to have access to the content-area curriculum, teachers need to make sure that reading skills and practice are incorporated explicitly in their content-area lessons. After reading this chapter, you should have a clear understanding of the importance of explicitly teaching strategies within the content areas. You also should know how to incorporate the following ideas within your lessons to support the CLDE students within your content area or general education classroom:

- Explicit reading instruction within the content areas and general education classroom for CLDE students

- Strategies to increase vocabulary, oral language proficiency, comprehensibility of the text, grammar, and language study

- Strategies to increase background knowledge

- Reading strategies

- Strategies to help students analyze, organize, and interact with the content of the text

Table 12.1 Teaching Reading to CLDE students

	Prereading Activities	During-Reading Activities	After-Reading Activities
Increase L2 vocabulary	• Front-load key vocabulary and key concepts of the text using the 3-way model • Play repetition games with key vocabulary		
Increase background knowledge on the topic	• Share existing knowledge • Ask "why" questions • Teach sequencing activities • Show movies • Teach different cultural perspectives		
Increase comprehensibility and accessibility of the text	• Match text to students • Front-load key vocabulary and key concepts of the text using the 3-way model • Use storytelling in the L1 or L2 • Text retell • Outline the text for students to examine	• Use modeled reading • Use partner reading • Use choral reading • Use jigsaw reading • Use visual context for the text • Match books to reading level • Use text in L1 • Stimulate L1–L2 group discussions	
Increase reading strategies	• Predict from words • Predict from the title or first sentence • Predict from key illustrations	• Use skimming and scanning • Use rereading for detail • Use pausing and predicting • Match voice to print	

	Prereading Activities	**During-Reading Activities**	**After-Reading Activities**
	• Use reader questions • Use strategies for decoding	• Use critical questioning • Pause and reflect • Use specific strategy instruction • Summarize the text • Analyze the text with critical questioning • Make connections with the text	
Increase grammatical knowledge of the L2			• Use cloze activities • Use noticing activities • Use text reconstruction • Use picture and sentence matching
Increase ability to analyze and organize the content of the text			• Organize information • Use Reader's Theater • Draw mental images • Make "Wanted Posters" • Use sequence charts, story boards, story maps • Use time lines • Use Hot Seat or Talk Show • Use Freeze Frame • Use True/False • Use picture dictation • Question the text • Check predictions • Use connections

12.13

To access a checklist of reading skills for any content-area classroom, see the following Web link: **www.sagepub.com/grassi.**

12.14

To access a lesson planning guide for including reading skills within content-area lessons, see the following Web link: **www.sagepub.com/grassi.**

Key Terms

Phonemic awareness

Phonics

Fluency

Vocabulary

Comprehension

Activities for Further Understanding

1. Think about your own background in reading instruction. How is what you read in this chapter similar to what you already know? What additional information did you learn?

2. If you are a secondary teacher, what strategies would you take from this chapter to help your students read the content information you assign in class?

3. If you are an elementary teacher, how will you adapt your reading instruction to better meet the needs of CLDE students?

4. Observe a secondary or elementary reading teacher. Which strategies from this chapter does the teacher employ well? How could the teacher improve on reading instruction for CLDE students?

5. Plan a lesson that includes reading. Take one strategy from this chapter and explicitly implement it in this lesson. What worked? What didn't? What would be your next steps?

Visit the Student Study Site at **www.sagepub.com/grassi** for chapter-specific study resources.

Note

1. We would like to thank Jessica Bass for her consultation on early drafts of this chapter.

Chapter 13

STRATEGIES FOR TEACHING THE WRITING PROCESS

Key Points

- ✦ Developing written expression challenges for students with special needs
- ✦ Developing expression challenges for CLDE students
- ✦ Developing expression taught explicitly to CLDE learners

CASE STUDY 13.1 | **Looking for Relevancy and Authenticity in Writing**

Like many teachers in urban settings, we are told in our school building that our students cannot afford to have one minute of their education wasted. This is especially true for our CLDE students, who are expected to perform in ways that we often feel are insurmountable. The expectation to become proficient English writers and to pass standardized tests is daunting for both teachers and students.

In preassessments, it was clear that students did not understand the reason for the writing, the audience for which they were writing, and the appropriate form to address both reason and audience. The students were writing to potential test graders as if these evaluators were their buddies, and their reasons for writing were as compelling as a playground scuffle.

It is my school's expectation that every piece of writing begins with a plan and a "TAPP" table, from which students determine the **t**opic, **a**udience, **p**urpose, and **p**roduct. Admittedly, I had spent my early teaching years not fully understanding the power of having students explicitly think through *all* these aspects of their writing. In my own early classroom demonstrations, I would quickly fill in most of the TAPP table so I could get to the *real* writing lesson. Concurrently, I would wonder why my students' writing seemed so flat. I blamed the test for forcing my students to write in inauthentic ways. This year, I realized that I wasn't teaching my students how to dissect the prompt they were given, and that I wasn't making writing authentic and relevant to them. They had no idea who they were writing to or why! My CLDE students especially needed the who and why of writing to be explicitly taught.

My students and I set off on a quest to find out what it is that readers expect of writers. We began to ask ourselves questions about our audience such as, "Who is going to read my writing?" and "What's the best way to talk to this person?" We used what we had learned from our study of different writing forms to choose a product that would best meet our purpose. For example, if we chose a persuasive essay, we wanted to know which arguments would be most compelling for our audience. We asked questions such as, "What's the difference between trying to convince our friends and trying to convince our principal that we want something?"

As a result of our investigations into all aspects of writing, students began to understand how to think about their audience, purpose, and form, and how these elements depend on each other. Their writing reflected an understanding that prompt writing can be authentic and relevant. In addition, I find prompt writing is more effective when students view its relevance. I was most pleased to find that students' overall writing improved because they were given tools to help them make their written thoughts understood more clearly.

—Harmony Looper, Literacy teacher

Consider the case study above:

- Which steps of the writing process did Harmony address with her class?
- What writing skills were her CLDE students lacking? How did Harmony address her students' needs?
- What would you change to make this lesson appropriate for your students?

SOURCE: Used by permission.

It is important for teachers to recognize that writers need to think and act explicitly to address their audience, realize their purpose, and work through a process of writing to achieve authentic written communication. Written expression is a complex process that requires explicit instruction. For CLDE students, the process can be overwhelming if teachers do not address the specific steps and skills needed to become an effective writer. In this chapter, we will address challenges CLDE students may face as they learn to write. We advocate for an explicit process approach to teaching written expression, and we outline the steps with examples of that process approach.

WRITTEN EXPRESSION CHALLENGES FOR STUDENTS WITH SPECIAL NEEDS

Students with learning and behavioral disabilities have challenges in two major areas of written expression: product problems and process problems (Isaacson, 2001; Mercer & Pullan, 2005). **Product problems** are exemplified by use of simple sentence construction (verb–object sentences or subject–verb constructions), use of few words that are usually higher-frequency words, disregard for audience, mechanical errors (spelling, punctuation, capitalization, subject–verb agreement, etc.), and poor organization and overall structure. **Process problems** are exemplified in the overall process of written communication, such as lack of systematic planning, preoccupation with mechanics, inability to monitor the writing, and lack of revision skills (Friend & Bursuck, 2009). When considering students with learning disabilities (and other students who struggle with writing), Graham and Harris (2005) describe several specific ways that a skilled writer and a struggling writer differ:

1. *Approaching.* Many students with disabilities tend to use a "knowledge-telling" approach to writing. This type of writing is done in one sitting,

without much planning, reflecting, or revising. Good writers, on the other hand, use forethought, planning, and reflection to capture the interest of the audience, logically put ideas together, and revisit their ideas to make sure the reader will understand and that the writing conveys meaning.

2. *Planning.* Generally, students with disabilities do not use good planning skills even when they are asked to plan their writing. Skilled writers think about how they are going to achieve the goals of their writing before they begin.

3. *Generating content.* Skilled writers produce much more writing. Students with disabilities tend to write much less for a variety of factors. Sometimes it is because they know little about the assigned topic. Other times, students may have difficulty accessing the knowledge they do have. In other instances, the actual physical act of writing is difficult for the student, and it becomes laborious to write all that the student actually is thinking about the topic.

4. *Persisting.* Less-skilled writers spend less time writing. A lack of persistence may be influenced by the inability to generate content as listed above.

5. *Revising.* When asked to correct or revise a text, struggling writers mostly focus on superficial errors and tend to correct handwriting, spelling, capitalization, and other more concrete errors. These writers do not consider the audience; it is difficult for them to see the perspective of the reader.

6. *Knowing what it means to write.* Most struggling writers consider the mechanics of writing, the rules of word usage, and the neatness of a paper as the definitions of "good writing." They do not consider what it means to be able to convey a thought in written words and to explain their thinking through a story. Students with disabilities often leave out major plot or genre elements in their writing.

Students with learning disabilities related to writing tend not to plan, monitor, evaluate, or revise text. They tend not to be strategic in their approach to writing tasks, and they tend to focus on the rules of writing (spelling, neatness of handwriting, what the paper should look like when finished). They want to "get through" the assignment. Because they do not always have the knowledge base to complete the writing task at hand, the product is often short, incomplete, and does not show complex thought or development of ideas (Graham & Harris, 2005). Spelling, handwriting, forming the assignment, developing content of the assignment, and putting together a written assignment are learned skills, but these skills must be taught, modeled, and practiced explicitly in lessons.

WRITTEN EXPRESSION CHALLENGES FOR CLDE STUDENTS

CLDE students face the same challenges that students with disabilities face when writing. However, the complexity of the challenges is increased due to the language acquisition process. CLDE students' writing abilities depend on many factors, including the students' special needs, the students' cultural understanding of how to write in different genres in English, the students' level of L1 literacy skills, the students' level of English oral and literacy proficiency, and the students' ability to successfully plan and revise their writing. In order for CLDE students to become "good" writers, they also need the following skills:

1. A grasp of print in the L2 and to understand the **orthographic system** of the L2 (Fillmore & Snow, 2000; Freeman & Freeman, 2004)

2. A certain level of **oral proficiency** in the L2 (August & Shanahan, 2006; Eskey, 2005, p. 566)

3. The ability to adeptly plan and organize their writing (Graham & Harris, 2005)

4. An understanding of the cultural nuances of writing in English and the ability to change their style according to the genre and the audience

5. An understanding of the process of editing and revising their writing (Graham & Harris, 2005)

Because there is an extensive list of skills CLDE students need to become proficient writers in English, explicit instruction in writing is key to their success. In this chapter, we again make an assumption that secondary and elementary teachers have been trained in the pedagogy of basic writing instruction.[1] For most elementary teachers, the skills that are taught explicitly within a general writing curriculum will be appropriate for CLDE learners—if strategies to specifically address the English language acquisition process and

REFER TO CASE STUDY 13.1

What challenges did Harmony's students face with writing? How did she address these challenges?

the special needs of the student are added. Secondary teachers have often not been given specific literacy training for working with students who are acquiring English as their L2 or for working with students who have no prior exposure to literacy; this chapter is especially pertinent to those teachers. With changing demographics and a growing number of students entering the secondary level who have not had access to schooling, secondary teachers must be well versed in how to teach writing within their content-area classrooms.

EXPLICIT INSTRUCTION OF THE WRITING PROCESS

In order to help CLDE students improve their writing skills, an explicit writing process is needed, including the following (adapted from Derewianka, 1990; with additional adaptations from Chamot & O'Malley, 1994; Gibbons, 2002; Graham & Harris, 2005; Peregoy & Boyle, 2005):

a. Activities to build background knowledge and gather the information needed to begin the piece

b. Instruction on how to organize the information gathered

c. Instruction on how to choose an appropriate genre for the purpose of the writing

d. Discernment of the audience and instruction on the type of language used with the particular audience

e. Analysis of the features of the genre chosen to determine what structures, organization, and language are needed to properly write in the specific genre

f. Models of the step-by-step planning and organization of the written piece, including co-construction of a piece with students

g. Independent writing

h. Explicit instruction in how to edit and revise the piece

Figure 13.1 provides a graphic description of the writing process.

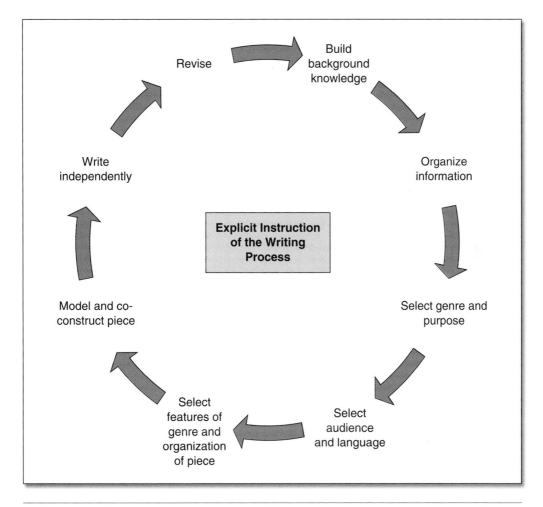

Figure 13.1   Steps of the Writing Process

Step 1. Building Background Knowledge

As mentioned in Chapter 9, much content matter requires strong background knowledge to understand. When CLDE students are asked to write about a topic, the students may or may not have background knowledge pertaining to the topic or may have culturally different content knowledge around the topic than that which the teacher expects. Therefore, students will need ample background knowledge on the topic before beginning to write. Strategies to build background knowledge of the content include the following (Chamot & O'Malley, 1994; Derewianka, 1990; Gibbons, 2002; Graham & Harris, 2005):

a. Build a **semantic web** of students' current knowledge of the topic.

b. Explicitly teach academic vocabulary that is key to understanding the topic (using the 3-way model).

c. Create a word wall of academic terms needed to write about the topic, and keep the word wall posted so students can refer to the terms when writing.

d. Introduce the topic with a KWL chart listing what students *know* about the subject, what they *want* to know about the topic. At the end of the writing project, list what students *learned* about the topic.

e. Read about the topic with students using a shared book. Note that books with plenty of visuals will help increase the comprehension of the topic for CLDE students.

f. Show visuals of the topic through PowerPoint, slide shows, or movies. (Make sure you provide students with note-taking aids when they view the visuals.)

g. Schedule a library day where you can introduce students to reference materials (in both the L1 and L2) related to the topic.

h. Use jigsaw listening where each group listens to an audiotape about a different aspect of the topic. (Make sure you provide students with note-taking aids when they listen to the audiotape.) Have students go back to their primary group and report on the tape they heard.

i. Bring in an expert on the topic and organize a class discussion or interview with the expert.

j. Where possible, organize field trips to community centers where the topic is brought to life (e.g., museums).

k. Play games around the topic.

Step 2. Organizing the Information

Many CLDE students will need assistance in organizing the information gathered and determining which information is essential and which is nonessential.

Graphic organizers and charts will assist students in putting all the information into a clear and concise format to reference when writing.

Step 3. Choosing an Appropriate Genre

CLDE students will need instruction on the various **genres** available in English and the purpose of each genre. Students need to understand why we write in specific genres, the message we try to convey by using particular genres, and the audience we attempt to reach through particular genres. Students need to understand that there are different ways that we express ourselves in writing and that they can choose the appropriate genre depending on the reason for the writing. By explaining that all writing has a purpose, teachers give students meaning for their writing. Table 13.1 shows a number of different genres we use in English and some of the different purposes for the genre.

Table 13.1 Writing Genres and Purposes

Genre	Letters/Notes	Essays/Reports	Stories/Creative Writing	Electronic Communication (email, text message)
Purpose	• To persuade • To correspond with family and friends • To argue a point with a specific person • To make a legal record of your thoughts • To thank someone • To invite someone to do something	• To state an argument • To state research or facts • To summarize or recap points • To present and explain data • To express an opinion	• To entertain • To give moral lessons • To make a point in an engaging manner • To document history or events • To creatively express ideas	• To correspond with family and friends • To correspond with businesses • To elicit a quick response • To confirm something • To invite someone • To document facts

Step 4. Discerning the Audience

Accurately discerning the audience is a key component to proficient writing. Before beginning the piece, the student should be very clear about who the audience is, the type of genre best suited for the audience, and the type of language the audience would expect. For example, if the audience is a friend and the writer needs to send a quick message, then electronic communication may be an appropriate genre. When emailing or text messaging a friend, the student may use informal language, may use slang, may use short-cut writing or specific text messaging language, may produce sentences that are grammatically incorrect, and may produce misspellings. However, when the audience is a teacher and the student uses email or text messaging to convey a message, the language must change. When emailing the teacher, the student should strive to use more formal language (no slang), should attempt grammatically correct sentences with no misspellings, and should write only about topics that are appropriate for a student–teacher relationship. Although the genre is the same—electronic communication—the audience is vastly different and requires different levels of formality. CLDE students will require explicit instruction on the different types of audiences and the writing expectations of these audiences.

Step 5. Analyzing the Genre's Features

Once the students have chosen the particular genre they will use, they need to understand the special features of the genre. Genres are constructed differently across cultures; CLDE students will need explicit instruction in how the particular genre they have chosen is constructed in English. Students will need to know the following (Gibbons, 2002):

a. Overall structure and organization of the genre

b. Special language features of the genre

Genre construction and organization will vary across cultures. Although most cultures include the same genres (i.e., narratives, reports, letters, etc.), the *way* these genres are written varies considerably. For example, some cultures are taught to write in a circular manner where the writer approaches the topic indirectly. Other cultures are taught to write in a manner where the point is alluded to but never explicitly stated. Standard academic English in the United States usually requires an organizational manner in which the topic is stated up front and in which details of the topic are explicitly stated. For example, stories are usually organized in the following manner: There is a character who lives in a particular setting. There is a problem that occurs that needs a solution. A number of events occur and the resolution is usually determined by the end of the story (Chamot & O'Malley, 1994). When students are aware of the organizational structure of the genre, it not only helps with their comprehension, but also with organizing the writing to fit that particular genre. To become effective writers in English, CLDE students need to grasp the parts of the genre (e.g., introduction, body, conclusion), and they need to analyze the information contained in each part of the genre (e.g., the introduction introduces the topic and is a lead-in to details of the topic).

Furthermore, special language features of the genre need to be detailed. Different levels of formality are used in different types of genres (e.g., stories can be told in first or third person, and persuasive papers can be written in the first or third person). Students also need to examine language features such as the use of the passive voice versus the active voice in different genres.

CLDE students will need multiple models of the genre explicitly explained to them before beginning the writing process. The teacher should consider implementing the following sequence (Derewianka, 1990; Gibbons, 2002):

1. Show an actual text of the genre and, with the whole class, break the text into parts.

2. Label each part.

3. Make note of the purpose of each part.

4. Make note of specific language features present in each part.

5. Create a wall chart of the parts of the genre for future reference.

6. Group students and let them take apart another example of the genre and label each part.

7. Ask each group to highlight special language features in the text.

For an example of different CLDE writing and an explanation of their skills with various genres, see the following Web link: **www.sagepub.com/grassi.**

13.1

Step 6. Modeling the Step-by-Step Process

Once students are familiar with the audience, the purpose of the genre, the overall structure of the genre, and any special language feature of the genre, it is time for them to attempt constructing the genre. As a first step, however, the teacher should provide scaffolding for the task by jointly constructing the genre with some students. Joint construction will aid in making the task more comprehensible and will provide added support for CLDE students who may still struggle with the construction of the written piece and the language.

The teacher should begin by asking students to recall the background knowledge on the subject matter; included in this step should be a review of the key vocabulary words needed to write the text. Next, the teacher should review the overall structure of the text and any special language features for the genre and the chosen audience. Finally, the teacher should show students how the gathered information can be put together in a structured manner in order to create a text of the specific genre.

For example, let's say the students spent a week gathering information and studying about global warming. The class has decided to write a persuasive letter to their representatives to encourage them to takes steps to stop global warming. The teacher does the following:

1. Reviews the information students have gathered concerning global warming. The teacher has already instructed the class in organizing the information in such a way that the effects of global warming have been categorized into its effects on people, weather, and endangered species.

2. Next, the teacher reviews the important vocabulary and phrases needed to adeptly discuss global warming in an academic setting.

3. The teacher then discusses the audience and the level of formality that will be needed with that audience.

4. The teacher then reintroduces the structure of a persuasive letter including the purpose, the overall structure, and any special language features of the genre.

5. Together or in small groups the class takes the information gathered and assists the teacher in co-constructing a persuasive letter. The students use the chart of information gathered and a wall chart describing the features of a persuasive letter as reference.

By co-constructing the genre step by step, CLDE students are able to watch connections being made between the information gathered, the key vocabulary and phrases used, and the manner of structuring the information to a written format that fits a specific genre.

Step 7. Independent Writing

At this step in the process, students are encouraged to write their own text individually or in pairs. Some CLDE students—especially those at a beginning level of English proficiency or with specific written expression needs—may still require scaffolding. Scaffolding for these students can be provided in the following manner:

1. Provide graphic organizers such as a "genre map" to follow step by step when writing.

2. Provide beginning students with various sentences that they can unscramble and put together in the structure of the genre.

3. Provide students with an already written text with blanks where students can fill in key vocabulary words or phrases (e.g., cloze activity).

Step 8. Editing and Revising

The final step to the writing process is instructing students on how to edit and revise their papers. CLDE students tend not to revise and edit their papers when writing in English (Graham & Harris, 2005; Leki, 1992). Therefore, teachers need to take class time to show students how to revise and edit and to explain to students the concept of multiple drafts.

Of course, one of the issues CLDE students face when revising and editing is that they may not be able to recognize their errors and therefore may not know what to edit and revise. When working with CLDE students, it is important that a teacher or another trained professional help students notice their errors in grammar, punctuation, organization, and cultural nuances and assist students in revising and editing their papers accordingly.

Many teachers use peer editing as part of the writing process. While this is a very effective strategy with native English speakers, it is not always appropriate with CLDE students. As discussed in Chapter 3, CLDE students will produce errors that would never be produced by native English speakers, and native-English-speaking students will not have the skills to explain the errors to their CLDE peers. Peer editing can be used to help CLDE students *notice* the errors, because their native-English-speaking peers will be able to point out the areas where the writing sounds "unusual." However, CLDE students will need a further step where explicit explanation of the error and instruction on how to correct it is given. Therefore, until CLDE students are at an advanced enough level at which their errors are similar to those made by native English speakers, peer editing should be used only when it is supplemented by direct instruction from the teacher or other professionals. (See Chapter 15 for strategies on written error correction with CLDE students.)

If the teacher does choose to use peer editing, a graphic organizer with step-by-step directions for the editing process is very helpful. Teachers also can have each student from the group take one editing point to focus on with the papers. For instance, each student can do one of the following:

1. Look for spelling errors and circle all misspelled words.

2. Look for punctuation errors and circle any wrong or missing punctuation.

3. Does the paper make sense? If not, circle where the student needs to make the point clearer.

4. Are there any sentences that are too long or too short or that don't make sense? Circle these sentences.

REFER TO CASE STUDY 13.1

Which steps of the writing process were missing from Harmony's initial lessons? Which steps did she eventually incorporate and how did she incorporate them? What were the results of her enhanced lessons?

---

5. Does the paper use formal, academic language? Is there slang or inappropriate language? If so, indicate where the student should use language that is more appropriate.

6. Is the paper organized according to the genre map? If not, circle areas where the student needs to reorganize.

7. Does the paper have all required parts of the genre? If not, indicate which parts are missing.

Example of Explicit Instruction of the Writing Process

On page 312 we provide examples of the writing process from typical high school and elementary school writing lessons that we have observed in classrooms across the nation. As you read through the process, keep in mind the template for bringing differentiation and cultural relevancy to the lesson in Table 13.2. Determine where you can insert choice, different perspectives, and give students the opportunity to pursue their interests.

Photo 13.2   Explicit instruction of the writing process gives students an opportunity to succeed in written expression.

Table 13.2   Bringing Differentiation and Cultural Relevancy to the Writing Process

Group Project With Choice of Topics to Pursue

This step involves expansion of the general writing assignment. The teacher starts with the general standards, then gives students choice as to multiple perspectives around the topic.

In groups, students gather information, summarize the information in a poster, and present it to the class.

Individual Writing Project on Topic of Choice

This step involves further expansion of the general writing assignment topic. Students are given the choice to fully engage with differing perspectives concerning the topic.

Students must find an underrepresented voice in the American Revolution and write a piece showing this perspective. Students have choice of one of the following: a short story, a letter, an educated opinion, a persuasive essay, a journal entry, a biography, a Venn diagram, a rap song, a poem, a song, a film script, or a newspaper article.

Look at the template for infusing differentiation and cultural relevancy into the lesson. How would you enhance the writing lesson on page 311 to include multiple perspectives and voice?

Table 13.3 walks the reader through the writing process for a Social Studies lesson on the secondary level. Following this lesson, we provide the reader with a Web link to an elementary Social Studies lesson detailing the writing process.

Table 13.3   Writing Process at the Secondary Level

<table>
<tr><td colspan="1">**Secondary Level**</td></tr>
</table>

Genre: Report on the American Revolution

Grade Level: 9th–10th

Step 1: Building background and gathering information

The teacher asks students to brainstorm and write or draw everything they can remember about the American Revolution. The teacher has numerous pictures or PowerPoint slides of the Revolution that he or she shares with the class. All visuals have labels in order for the students to match the picture with the words. As students brainstorm, if they come up with concepts that are not represented in the teacher's visuals, they draw the concept on the board and label it for all students to see. All perspectives, especially those from students of diverse cultures, are valued, affirmed, and included in the lesson. The teacher then puts the students into groups of three students each, where they are instructed to share their writings and drawings with their classmates.

The teacher then asks students to take their writings or drawings home and to review the topic with an adult, to review their textbook, their notes from class, to look at other books they may have at home, or to look up "American Revolution" on the Internet to see if they can add anything to their writing or drawings. (The teacher has books available for students to take home and the teacher has posted the school library hours and is available after school for those students who do not have computers at home or need instruction with the Internet.)

Step 2: Organizing the information gathered

The next day, the teacher asks students to share some of the information they have gathered about the Revolution. As students share, the teacher writes their answers under the categories he or she has placed across the board, for example:

Major events leading up to the Revolution

England's role in the Revolution

Significant battles of the Revolution

Role of different people in the Revolution

The categories of the graphic organizer are based solely on students' input; more categories are added if students have answers that do not fit the categories on the board. Once all the students who want to share have done so, the teacher asks students to get into their groups and further organize the information they have gathered into the categories and to organize the information in *chronological order,* adding dates where possible. The teacher models this first.

Step 3: Choosing an appropriate genre for the purpose of writing

Once the students have categorized all their information, the teacher tells them that they are going to use the information to write a report. The teacher begins by explaining why reports are written. The teacher then gives examples of the different reports they have read in class and asks students why they think the particular reports were written. The teacher writes students' answers on the board to see if they match up with his or her original "purpose" for writing a report.

Step 4: Discerning the audience and the type of language used with the audience

The teacher lets students choose who the audience will be for their report. Once students have chosen, the teacher asks students what type of language they should use with the audience: Peer language? Playground language? Formal language? The teacher leads students to think about which type of language would be most effective in a report for the audience they have chosen.

Step 5: Analyzing the features of the chosen genre

Next, the teacher instructs students on the specific features of the genre. The teacher starts by showing students the overall structure of a report. For example, the teacher could write points such as the following on the board:

Part 1 Introduction. Start with the background. Explain a little about the topic of the report. Who are the people involved? Describe the setting and characters. Introduce your topic to the reader.

Part 2 Body with details. What happened in this period? Describe, in detail, the aspects of your topic. What events led up to the Revolution? How was England involved? What were the major battles of the Revolution?

Part 3 Beginning conclusion. Was there a resolution to your topic? What was the final outcome of the Revolution?

Part 4 Ending conclusion. What are your thoughts on the topic? Do you have any opinions you would like the reader to know about?

Once these parts are on the board, the teacher shows examples of these parts by reading two or three reports with the students (the students can follow along on their hard copy). As the teacher reads with the students, the teacher stops often and asks students questions such as, What part of the report did I just read? How do you know?

The teacher then presents each student with another photocopy of a short report. He or she has students read the report in groups and circle and label each part of the report. The teacher then goes over the report with the whole class to make sure each group has correctly labeled each part of the story.

Next the teacher describes any special language features of a report. The teacher can teach this by having students *notice* specific language features in the reports they have read, or the teacher can directly tell students about the type of language used in reports. The teacher will probably want to draw students' attention to features such as the level of formality, use of the passive versus active voice, the use of first person, and the tense in which reports are written.

(Continued)

Table 13.3 (Continued)

Step 6: Modeling of the step-by-step process—co-construction of the text

The teacher constructs a report with the students. The teacher reminds students of the information they have gathered and asks them to begin by organizing the information into pieces that fit in the introduction, the body, and the conclusion.

The teacher then constructs a sample introduction with the students. When the teacher and students begin the body, the teacher points out that students have already organized the information in chronological order. To construct the body, they simply put this information into coherent sentences. The teacher models this process for the students.

The teacher walks students through the pieces of the report, and together they input the information they have gathered and sculpt the information to fit the writing expected of the audience and the genre.

Step 7: Independent Writing

The teacher instructs students to write their own reports. CLDE students are given extra support such as these:

- They are allowed to work in pairs or groups on the same report.
- They are given a genre map to follow as they write the report.
- They are given a cloze report; they fill in blanks with information, key vocabulary, or key phrases.
- They work with an adult on the writing process.

Step 8: Editing and Revising

The teacher collects all students' first drafts. The teacher carefully looks over the types of errors students are making. On the grammatical and punctuation level, the teacher chooses one error to address. The teacher also looks for errors on the organizational and discourse level—looking for flow and organization of the genre—and chooses one error on which to focus.

If most students are making the same kinds of errors, then the teacher may choose to do whole group instruction on a certain grammatical or organizational aspect. If students are producing different errors, then the teacher should help students edit individually. The teacher begins by working with one error at a time and helps students to look for that error throughout their papers and actively work to fix that error. In consequent drafts, the teacher can choose another error to work on, if this is not too overwhelming for the student. With CLDE students who are at beginning levels of English acquisition, one error at a time is sufficient.

Throughout the editing and revising process, the teacher emphasizes with students the importance of multiple drafts and provides a graphic organizer for students to follow while editing.

13.2

For an example of the writing process at the elementary level, see the following Web link: **www.sagepub.com/grassi.**

Summary

The writing process needs to be incorporated explicitly into content-area lessons throughout the general education curriculum. Many subject areas require students to be able to write for specific purposes: science reports, research projects, explanations of math strategies, narratives, summaries, stories, and so on. Teachers should address those specific writing genres within the writing process. After reading this chapter you should

- be able to describe written expression challenges of CLDE students and the skills that "good" writers use,

- have a clear understanding of the importance of explicitly teaching writing strategies within the content areas, and

- be able to implement the writing process with CLDE students.

To view a video clip of a teacher implementing the writing process with CLDE students, and a rubric with which to observe the teacher and evaluate the strategy, see the following Web link: **www.sagepub.com/grassi.**

13.3

Key Terms

Genres

Oral proficiency

Orthographic system

Process problems

Product problems

Semantic web

Activities for Further Understanding

1. Where does the writing process described in this chapter fit in the Instructional Planning Pyramid (as described in Chapter 7)? Which tier would the writing process fit in? What are your rationales for the tier you have chosen?

2. Observe a writing lesson. What steps of the writing process were explicitly taught? What would you do differently to make the lesson more appropriate for CLDE students?

3. Consider the template for differentiation and cultural relevancy. How did the teacher you observe expand the writing process to include diverse perspectives? What would you do differently?

4. Look at an example of a CLDE student's writing. What are the strengths of the student's writing? What challenges with writing does the student face? How would you approach instruction with this student?

5. Plan a writing lesson for students in your classroom. Consider the details in this chapter to be Tier 1 planning as described in Chapter 7. How can you include the writing process described in this chapter into your lesson?

Visit the Student Study Site at **www.sagepub.com/grassi** for chapter-specific study resources.

Note

1. If you need review of basic writing instruction, see the resources included on the Web site.

Chapter 14

CHALLENGES WHEN TEACHING WRITING

Key Points

✦ Addressing challenges at the grammatical level

✦ Addressing challenges at the orthographic level

✦ Addressing challenges at the cultural level

CASE STUDY 14.1 — Making Writing Concrete

No matter how much training teachers receive, we cannot ever be truly prepared for what we encounter in the classroom. I am currently teaching in a school where almost 100% of the students speak English as their L2, and many struggle with severe learning disabilities. These are my students and it is my job to teach them how to write clearly and concisely in English. Where do I begin?

My teaching experience has taught me that somehow I have to make the concept of writing less abstract. I started researching and talking to other teachers and trying to find a magical teacher text with all the "right" methods of teaching ESL students with special needs. I decided to pick and choose from all the different methods and curriculum and differentiate to meet the needs of my students the best I could.

I began to rely on observations in the classroom. I took special notice as to my students' interests, what they discussed with one another; what cultural differences between the varied cultures represented in the classroom I saw, and what nonverbal communication went on. At that point, I began to formulate a plan to teach writing.

First, I allowed my students to do activities that revolved around informal talking (most were very comfortable with talking)—interviews, student "scavenger hunts," and "culture bag" projects. We would write about these various activities, more as a reflection than as a formal report. I told them to not worry about spelling, grammar, punctuation, and so on, and just to write down their ideas. Later, we would take those ideas and work on formulating them into an actual paragraph.

At first, I allowed them to write their own paragraphs. This allowed me to assess several items, most important of them whether they knew what a "paragraph" is. Just as I had suspected, many did not. After looking at their work and getting a sense of where they were as writers, I wrote a simple seven-sentence paragraph. We dissected it on the overhead, focusing on key words like "topic sentence" and "supporting details." I then created a skeleton of a basic generic paragraph on poster paper and invited them to take my paragraph and "insert" the sentences into the skeleton. This modeling seemed to be successful.

I then took it further and used specific types of writing that I broke apart, incorporating photographs and objects (for descriptive and persuasive writing) and real-life situations that affect my students). Again, I set up a skeleton, and used one specific graphic organizer, and one model. After a few weeks, my students had become accustomed to writing and realized that writing is indeed a process.

As they began to realize that writing is a process, I introduced more terminology. We began to explore vocabulary like "word choice," "sentence fluency," and "voice." Although many of the students can rattle off these terms and their definitions, they still struggle to recognize what they look like in writing. Again, this is where modeling and examples come in: I point out examples in their writing, as well as in the writing of others. I bring in pieces of writing (often picture books), and we become critics. When we do this, however, we focus on just one trait at a time. Again, we break it into simple, manageable chunks.

Another part of the process is revising and editing. I firmly believe that this is my student's writing and not mine. Because of this, I will conference with students, but RARELY do I ever go through their writing with a red pen and mark EVERYTHING they need to fix (YUCK)! Instead, each of my students has a laminated card with specific areas to edit on one another's papers—areas such as capitalization and punctuation. Each of them also has an accompanying sheet where they tell each other what they really liked and what may need to be fixed in the other's paper. After students have edited, they discuss their "findings" with each other. The editing process not only empowers them, but also allows me to see what concepts my students have truly mastered. Students usually then do rough drafts, after which they're ready for the final draft.

Assessing my students' writing can be just as confusing and challenging as is any other aspect of teaching. One thing I had to learn was to let go of "traditional" grading and assess them as individuals. This can prove truly difficult in a time when education is driven by data and testing. To show improvements in their writing I use student-driven portfolios. Students are required to keep all their writing in a portfolio throughout the year. About once a term, they review their portfolios. Students self-evaluate based on questions such as, What is my personal best piece of writing and why? What was my favorite piece to write and why? What was the most difficult piece to write and why? This is also a great confidence booster because students can actually see their writing improving. They're not being compared against any of the other students—it's all about their own personal growth.

Finally, because of that dreaded report card, I use a lot of writing rubrics. As a class, we always go over the rubric. If it's a five-point rubric, I will give students only the requirements to earn a 5, 4, and 3—not the 2 or 1. I want them to focus on the positive. I use the same style of rubric every time, and I make the rubric trait specific. For example, if we have been discussing the trait of voice, then the trait on the rubric will focus on voice. (I always assess capitalization, punctuation, and spelling based on what I have taught.) Rubrics are easy to use. Best of all, I can design three different rubrics for one assignment to accommodate all students.

—Erin Warner, Literacy teacher

Consider the case study above:

- What steps of the writing process does Erin teach explicitly?
- What skills and challenges does she address in her writing instruction?
- How are specific needs of CLDE learners addressed?

SOURCE: Used by permission.

Photo 14.2   Cross-cultural writing can be challenging.

The writing challenges that an L2 learner presents are challenges that often are not addressed by an IEP, which considers only a special education need. The IEP usually addresses the challenges that learning and behavioral disabilities present. (These disabilities are most often in one of three areas: handwriting, spelling, or written expression [Friend & Bursuck, 2009]). Because CLDE students are not only labeled with a disability, but also are learning the English language, they tend to have additional writing difficulties beyond what is addressed in an IEP, including difficulties with grammatical, orthographic, and cultural aspects of English (see Photo 14.2). For a CLDE student, these language acquisition needs related to writing also must be addressed.

When planning for adaptations that are appropriate for a CLDE student, it is important to take into account the learning level of the student and the appropriateness of the complex writing and language instruction that we detail in this chapter. For some CLDE students, learning the reasons for the grammatical mistake will help them to write better. For other CLDE students, just being told the explicit English rule will suffice. Some students are not ready to understand fully the complexity of the rules, but will be able to apply the rule if they receive explicit instructions. We are not advocating that the teacher create simplified lessons, but that the teacher use sound professional judgment in determining how to address the explicit writing needs of the students. The strategies provided in the chapter are meant to provide information to address both the language acquisition development and the special education needs of the CLDE student.

SPECIFIC WRITING CHALLENGES FOR CLDE STUDENTS

Often, it helps to begin instruction at the challenge points that CLDE students experience when writing. The majority of CLDE students' writing challenges

that are related to English language acquisition occur at one of three levels: the
grammatical, orthographic, and cultural
levels. Below we detail the challenges in
each area and present explicit teaching
strategies for working with CLDE students
on these language acquisition challenges. It
is important to consider the complete
learning profile of your student: You must
be able to determine if your student needs
this instruction, why the student needs instruction related to this particular
issue, and to what level you will teach the language "rules." The disability that
your student has will help guide you in your teaching choices.

> **REFER TO CASE STUDY 14.1**
>
> What challenges did Erin's students have
> with writing? Which of these are related to
> the process of putting the piece together?
> Which of the challenges would require spe-
> cific instruction in grammar, orthographic,
> or cultural rules?

Challenges at the Grammatical Level

> **CASE STUDY 14.2** | **Writing Assessment**
>
> I do not need that writing class in English because since I am here, I speak only English.
> When I talking to my friends, we talk only English. When I read the book, I read only English
> book. When I writing, I use only English. I have success in English. I agree that maybe before
> I need the writing class but not now. I think you are not understand my level. I have no
> problem with writing in English. I understand how the writing is in English. I have success in
> English.
>
> Thank you
>
> —Compiled from various secondary level writing samples
>
> Consider the case study above:
>
> - What kind of writing errors does this student make? Do you notice patterns?
> - How might a learning disability affect this student's writing?
> - If you were the teacher, how would you respond? What corrections would you make?

Accurate and proficient written English is a necessary component of academic
success in elementary, secondary, and postsecondary education. Unfortunately,
many CLDE students leave U.S. secondary schools with less-than-proficient

written English—such as the example in Case Study 14.2 above. A study conducted at the University of California, Irvine, found that 60% of the first-year college students who took a competency test in English composition failed the test due to "major problems with English language skills." This was true even though many of these students had maintained a high grade point average at the secondary level (Scarcella, n.d., as cited in Fillmore & Snow, 2000, p. 23).

Many times, teachers feel that if CLDE students can speak the language, they can write the language. However, writing is a learned skill and requires skills that differ greatly from the skills needed for speaking. Written language does not have the contextual clues involved in spoken language. A writer must give many more details and more background than a speaker needs to give. As well, written English most often requires a more formal English than that required in spoken English. While ELLs may make grammatical errors during spoken conversation, they may not "get away" as easily with grammatical errors in written English.

Unfortunately, CLDE students are not always given the instruction they need to master the skills for proficient English writing. Some teachers are more apt to grade students on their effort and the content message, rather than on grammatical correctness. Grammatically incorrect papers with insightful content messages are given comments such as "Nice work!" or "Great ideas!" with little to no grammatical corrections (Fillmore & Snow, 2000). In a similar vein, some teachers give CLDE students a lower grade because of the inaccurate grammar or organization of the paper, but do not provide explicit instruction on how the student could correct the errors. In both these cases, the student knows that there are problems with the paper but may not have the skills—or the resources—to correct these errors without teacher instruction.

There are two overarching reasons for the types of (or lack of) error correction teachers give. To begin, our experience in working with teachers has indicated that the majority of teachers were not given grammar or punctuation training in English, and, therefore, do not know the rules of the English language. While these teachers "sense" that the written English is incorrect, they do not know how to explain *why* it is incorrect. As we discussed in Chapter 11, it is important that teachers procure a good grammar book or take a class in English grammar (such as grammar for TESOL teachers).

As well, we have found that teachers are sometimes given the message that error correction can impede the acquisition process and that students will "acquire" the needed grammar through exposure to the language (based on Krashen's hypotheses, 1982). This is not always true, however. From the standpoint of English language acquisition, immersion in the language does not always mean students will notice or acquire the correct form. Many students

fossilize or **stabilize** in their language acquisition—using grammatical forms that can be generally understood but that are not necessarily grammatically correct (Brown, 2007; Long, 2003). From the standpoint of the student's special needs, the student may consider writing to be a series of rules related to form and mechanics, instead of a series of rules related to substance or process (Graham & Harris, 2005). Thus, while these two needs may seem to be in contradiction, the CLDE student will need to be drawn to the errors produced in order to *notice* the error and will need explicit instruction on the rules of the English language in order to correct the error. The teacher also will need to continue to encourage the expression of the ideas in the writing so that both grammar and substance are addressed explicitly.

In Chapter 4, we provided an extensive list of the types of grammatical issues CLDE students face when learning English. When a CLDE student makes these grammar errors in a writing assignment, the teacher must not ignore the errors, assuming that they are part of the special education needs or that they will correct themselves with time. The intent of the grammar error chart is to focus on the language acquisition process and to point out explicitly that these grammatical errors need to be addressed, while taking into account the learning level of the CLDE student. In Chapter 15, we provide the reader with examples and a process for teaching the correction of grammar errors in CLDE student writing.

For a review of grammatical issues, with examples of CLDE student writing (Grades 5–12) that illustrate errors within that point, see the following Web link: **www.sagepub.com/grassi.**

14.1

CASE STUDY 14.3   **Romeo and Juliette**

The book sections we had read in the class, talking about the night costumes. The family of Juliette and the family of Romeo and the people came to that pretty festival and the people dress and have fancy costumes. Romeo love Juliette and Juliette love Romeo and the families fight together and Romeo and Juliette can not meet and they fight in the streets and they prevent Romeo to seeing to Juliette and Juliette is very sad and she don't know what to do and Romeo is very sad and he don't know what to do to see Juliette also.

—Compiled from various student
writing samples at the secondary level

(Continued)

(Continued)

Consider the case study above:

- What are the strengths of the student's writing?
- What issues with punctuation does this student have?
- What aspects of the writing process would you explicitly teach to this student?

Punctuation in English can be very hard for CLDE students to grasp. Where someone pauses in a sentence and the concept of what constitutes a "sentence" or a "paragraph" differ across cultures; these differences will show up in CLDE students' writing. CLDE students will have questions such as, "Where and when should I use a period? How many should I use? How should I connect sentences together? When and where do I use capital letters? What constitutes a paragraph?"

As noted from Case Study 14.3, the writer places random periods in the narrative because he is not sure where to stop the flow of ideas. Toward the end of the paragraph, the writer creates long sentences that represent one idea or train of thought. While such long sentences are not acceptable in written academic English, sentences of this length or longer are acceptable in many different languages. At this stage, the teacher should choose one aspect to work on—adding periods or a particular grammar point—and work with the student on one rule at a time.

Challenges at the Orthographic Level

CASE STUDY 14.4	**Teaching Phonemic Awareness at the Secondary Level**

Now, phonemic awareness may seem too elementary to teach to a group of seventh graders who have been in the States for several years, but it is what they need to become successful English writers. Many students are easily frustrated when they have to write because they are focusing more on trying to spell the words on their paper than on simply writing down the ideas they want to share. I began implementing quick 10-minute mini-lessons focused around phonemic awareness. Because my students had a difficult time differentiating between the short "e" and "i" sounds, I knew that starting with these sounds was a great starting point. I then moved them on to digraphs, root words, prefixes, suffixes, long vowels, and multisyllabic words.

I scaffolded my instruction using pictures, total physical response, and a lot of repetition so students could focus on both written and oral language. The students began understanding how the sounds fit together and transferred those sounds into words. Piece by piece, the puzzle began to illustrate a portrait. The students began building the necessary tools they would need to begin spelling words correctly on an individual basis. From days, to weeks, to months of practice, I started to see a difference in my students' confidence with writing. After a substantial amount of practicing, the students were able to write their paragraphs without having to spend more time focusing on spelling.

—Haley A. MacNeil, Middle school teacher

Consider the case study above:

- Have you observed teachers using explicit phonemic awareness strategies such as this teacher used? If so, what were the results?
- How can you incorporate specific spelling instruction into your lessons?

SOURCE: Used by permission.

It is not uncommon for CLDE student writing to be filled with spelling errors. English spelling is difficult to master because English is based on what is referred to as "deep orthography." Deep orthography is an orthographic system in which the sound of the word is not necessarily directly related to the spelling of the word (Fillmore & Snow, 2000, p. 26). Likewise, English has many different language influences (French, German, Latin, Greek, etc.) that affect the spelling and pronunciation of words (Freeman & Freeman, 2004; Moats, 2000; Nation, 2005). And, unlike many other languages of the world, English does not have a language academy to regularly review and revise the spelling of words to match the pronunciation of modern language. As a result, the sound–spelling relationship of English words can be complex.

While English spelling can cause great difficulties, the spelling of English words is often directly related to their meaning. English has many homonyms where the difference in spelling (not pronunciation) indicates the difference in their meaning: for example, ate and eight. While homonyms can be difficult to spell, they can make the text easier to read. Rather than have to read the whole sentence for contextual clues as to the meaning of the words, the meaning can be found within the spelling of the word (Freeman & Freeman, 2004).

English also has words that are related to each other. These relationships are often reflected through the spelling—for example, medicine and medical. If we were to change the spelling to match the pronunciation—medisin and medikal— the relationship between the words would be lost (Freeman & Freeman, 2004).

Finally, English spelling also reflects the origins of words. Some words are spelled in the manner they were pronounced in earlier times, and some words reflect the spelling of their origin (Freeman & Freeman, 2004).

Many languages other than English are phonetically pure. That is, there is a direct sound–letter relationship in some languages, such as Spanish, and words are pronounced as they are spelled. When CLDE students come from a phonetically pure language, they have trouble learning the spelling of English words.[1] It is not unusual for CLDE students to pass along a spelling trajectory such as depicted in Table 14.1 (Henricksen, 1999; Schmidt, 2000; Moats, 2000, p. 10).

Table 14.1 Spelling Trajectory

Step 1	Step 2	Step 3	Step 4
Can't spell the word at all; partial phoneme awareness	Knows some letters	Phonologically correct spelling; more-elaborate phoneme awareness; may know "chunks"	Fully correct spelling
Dnsrs	Dnosrs	Daynosawrs	Dinosaurs

In the narrative in the box below, the writer shows evidence of Step 2, Step 3, and Step 4 spelling:

The Fild Trip

It was the fild trip for my school. We go to the musem. My sister say it was a butiful place. My techer tell us we go to the bus stachens! To go on a bus! I am so happy! The minneit the bell rings I run outside to make the line up. My techer give us sunscream and my techer say to put on the sunscream. We make a line and we walk to the bus stachens! I was looking for my frend to walk with me. But then my frend come! I wasen't scared anymore! Me and my frend walk to the stachen and we sit on the bus. 3 minneits later we on the bus and I need water. My frend give me her water and I drincked it and I not thirsty more. This was a really funn day in the fild trip! We see many things!

—Compiled from various student writing samples at the 5th-grade level

---

Note the types of spelling errors in the narrative as listed in Table 14.2.

Table 14.2   Spelling Errors

Student spelling	Correct spelling
Butiful	Beautiful
Fild	Field
Techer	Teacher
Sunscream	Sunscreen
Stachens	Stations
Wasen't	Wasn't
Minneit	Minute

Most of the errors are good approximations of the correct spelling of the word. The narrative has phonetically correct spelling, using phonetic knowledge from both the L1 (Spanish) and the L2 (English). For example, the spelling of "fild" pulls from the phonetic knowledge of Spanish where the letter "i" makes the /ee/ sound found in English. On the other hand, the spelling of "wasen't" clearly delineates the manner in which U.S. English speakers pronounce the word "wasn't." The narrative has many correct words but the writer will need work on categorizing and word ordering. For example, to spell the word "stachens," it may help students to see the different ways in which the /sh/ sound is created in English: "sh," "tion," "cion." Once students know the various combinations to make the sound, they can better approximate words such as "stations."

It is important to note here that teachers must know how long the student has been studying the English language to know if a student is progressing at a rate that is developmentally appropriate. For example, a ninth grader who just moved to the United States and spells the word "dinosaurs" as "densrs" would be developmentally appropriate. On the other hand, a student in ninth grade who has been studying English for several years should be further along the continuum (see Table 14.1)—although a student's special needs could dictate that spelling will continue to be an issue. Many students with special needs present their disability in their spelling skills (Vaughn, Wanzek, Woodruff, & Linan-Thompson, 2007). The process of learning to spell is difficult on its own, but can become very difficult for many CLDE students, especially those who have a disability that affects the ways they associate letters with sounds or the way they perceive the letters and sounds. In order to assist students with correct spelling, teachers need to address the skills listed below:

1. Letter–sound relationship (phonics and phonemic awareness)

2. An understanding of the definition of the word and how the definition can change in different contexts

3. An understanding of the history of words (the word origin) and how the origin relates to the spelling

4. An understanding of roots, prefixes, and suffixes and how these are combined to make words

5. An understanding of any spelling rules the word contains

6. Numerous repetitions of both the spelling and the meaning

REFER TO CASE STUDY 14.4

Which of the six spelling skills did the teacher emphasize with her spelling instruction? Which skills does she still need to add to her lessons?

One of the best strategies for learning orthographic knowledge in English is to conduct investigations. A teacher can help students "discover" rules by playing games and looking for patterns in the spelling of English words. Table 14.3 is an example adapted from Freeman and Freeman (2004), who offer numerous strategies for teaching spelling:

Table 14.3   Categorizing Words

Spelled With "c"	Spelled With "k"	Spelled With "kh"	Spelled With "ch"
cat	kangaroo	khaki	chemistry
clown	kite		character
caribou	Kristin		charismatic
cartoon	king		
candy	karate		

NOTE: This table categorizes words that start with the /k/ sound to discover patterns.

When the teacher creates a chart such as Table 14.3, students begin to see the different ways in which the /k/ sound is spelled in English. Teachers can then have students brainstorm about rules that would explain the different spellings. Words for this chart can be extracted from textbooks, students' essays, story books, novels, or other written sources.

Other ideas to develop orthographic knowledge follow:

- *Create a "word wall" in the classroom.* Post index or larger cards with the words written on them on the wall, and sort them by sound, pattern, or category (e.g., science words, math terms, or topics being studied).

- *Study word origins.* When students discover the history of words and why they are spelled the way they are, it can help them to have a deeper understanding of the spelling and to retain the words longer.
  - www.wordorigins.org
  - www.wordcentral.com

- *Learn word parts.* When students are instructed on root words, prefixes, and suffixes, they can better take apart words to derive meaning and also can improve on their spelling (Nation, 2005).

- *Label the classroom or school.* Write the names of items and areas in the classroom so students can learn the spellings of commonly used words in the school.

- *Use computer programs.* There are many programs that "drill" students on word patterns and letter sounds.

- *Create personalized dictionaries or word lists.* Each student keeps a "dictionary" or word list with words that they frequently use or misspell.

- *Build a file box of words.* This is similar to the dictionary, but is a small file box of index cards with words printed on individual cards. Its value is that the cards can be used as manipulatives—taken out, alphabetized, sorted by letter patterns, and so on.

- *Create high-frequency word sheets.* Let students keep copies of high-frequency word sheets to use as references as they are writing.

REFER TO CASE STUDY 14.4

Which spelling strategies did the teacher incorporate with her students? Which strategies would be effective with your students?

- *Provide word activities.* Provide activities that give students opportunities to practice the words patterns, letter sounds, and high-frequency words used in the English language.

- *Teach spelling.* Provide explicit spelling instruction as part of language arts lessons.

14.2

> To read a case study by literacy teacher Harmony Looper, describing explicit spelling instruction and practice, see the following Web link: **www.sagepub.com/grassi.**

Challenges at the Cultural Level

Perceptions of Plagiarism

Some challenges that teachers encounter when working with CLDE learners are related to cultural and linguistic influences on students' writing. One issue that often comes up with teachers of CLDE learners is the concept of plagiarism.

We have often heard teachers state that some of their students who come from different cultures copy texts when the teacher has assigned independent work. In many cultures, students are taught that the words of published authors or masters are to be respected. One of the best ways to respect the masters is to memorize their words and use these words—rather than the students' own—in writing or on tests. In the United States, we expect originality and creativity in writing, which can appear arrogant to many CLDE students (Leki, 1992; Sowden, 2005).

As well, when CLDE students are first learning English, they struggle to accurately present their higher-level thinking in English writing. This can be a very frustrating stage, especially for CLDE students who were considered proficient speakers and writers in their L1. To compensate for a lack of vocabulary or grammar in English, CLDE students will sometimes copy words from other authors that best depict their thoughts on the topic (Leki, 1992).

Because memorization and copying of text can be prevalent among CLDE students, especially those new to English, it is important that teachers consider the following:

1. Use the opportunity to find out why the copying occurred. Did the student need more instruction on the expectations, the content, or the process of finishing the assignment? What are your next teaching steps?

2. Have patience with CLDE students, especially those who are new to the country. Consider the feat of memorizing a passage of writing in the L2 and the incredible amount of time the student must have spent in memorizing the section.

3. Explicitly teach CLDE students how to take those memorized passages and summarize them in their own words. This skill will need to be taught numerous times; it is also a valuable skill to learn for standardized tests and research and writing skills that are more advanced.

4. Explain the cultural context of summarizing in the United States, and let students know the repercussions of copying in U.S. schools.

Sharing Work

Sharing work with others also can be an issue when working with CLDE students. Many CLDE students are from cultures that emphasize the success of the group over the success of the individual. Students from cultures such as these will attempt to help their classmates during tests or other written assignments. These students do not consider their actions to be cheating; instead, they are acting in a culturally appropriate manner and their behavior should be acknowledged as such. Again, from our experience teaching CLDE students, we offer teachers the following advice:

1. Have patience with the students. Realize that they are acting in a culturally appropriate manner.

2. Explicitly explain to students how classrooms are conducted in the United States and that some activities must be done individually while others are done in groups. Explain to students the repercussions of helping out others during a test in the United States.

3. Provide for plenty of group activities where students are given the opportunity to help one another.

Cultural Perceptions of Audience

As discussed in Chapter 13, understanding the audience of the writing is key to accurate construction of English writing. Understanding the audience leads the writer to choose the most effective writing style to use with that audience, the genre to use, and the level of formality.

Understanding the audience can be difficult for any student, but the task of understanding and writing appropriately becomes much more challenging when the culture of the audience is different from that of the student. For example, if a teacher were to instruct a U.S.-born 10th-grade student to write a letter to the principal to convince her to build a skateboard park, he or she would probably understand some basic principles:

1. The tone of the letter should be formal, which the student would know how to express.

2. The letter should begin with "Dear Principal" and proceed to get to the point.

3. The point should be presented in formal language and with compelling reasons as to why a skateboard park should be built. The points should be very well organized and explicitly stated.

4. The letter should end with "Sincerely" and the student's name and signature.

A student from a culture and language outside of the United States may have a different understanding of how to construct this letter. This student may understand the same basic principles of the letter, but the *manner* in which these principles are expressed in the student's home culture and language could be vastly different from the way they are expressed in U.S. English. For example,

1. The tone of the letter should be formal.

   The manner in which formality is expressed varies widely across cultures. For example, in some languages formality is expressed through the use of pronouns and verbs—which have morphemes attached expressing levels of respect and formality. For other cultures, lengthy questions about the reader's family or flattery at the beginning of a letter are needed as a sign of respect and formality.

2. The letter should begin with "Dear Principal" and get directly to the point.

   In many cultures, getting directly to the point is considered rude and indicates a lack of respect. Many students are taught to dance around the point rather than directly state the point in order to respect the reader. Many students also are taught to write lengthy sentences and paragraphs, rather than the short, direct sentences of modern U.S. English.

3. The point should be presented in formal language and with compelling reasons as to why a skateboard park should be built.

   In many cultures, persuasion is conducted in a manner very different from how it is conducted in the United States. Some cultures assume an intelligence on the part of the reader and never directly state the point, but give hints from which the reader can decipher the point.

4. The letter should end with "Sincerely" and the student's name and signature.

   In many cultures, the endings of letters are very long and must thank the reader, wish the reader and his or her family well, and so on. Ending simply with "Sincerely" appears rude to many students.

Many CLDE students will write as if the audience were their peers—not only because they are often more fluent in BICS, but also because discerning audience can be a complex task for CLDE students. Because the cultural differences in writing can be so extreme, explicit instruction in *identifying* the audience and the writing style expectations of the audience can greatly benefit CLDE students and help them achieve English writing that is more accurate.

Summary

It is important for CLDE students to understand the writing process and know the explicit steps for writing in specific genres. Many students with disabilities struggle with written work. Their IEPs may address issues such as handwriting, spelling, and written expression. CLDE students also are learning the English language and teachers need to include explicit instruction that addresses challenges when writing in English. We advocate that these challenges be included as goals on the CLDE student's IEP as well. After reading this chapter, you should be able to

- describe and plan for challenges at the grammatical level,

- describe and plan for challenges at the orthographic level, and

- describe and plan for challenges at the cultural level.

Key Terms

Fossilize

Stabilize

Activities for Further Understanding

1. Collect writing samples from CLDE students. What specific written expression challenges do you notice? Review the activities to address the issues in this chapter. Which ones would work for your students? Which of these activities should you incorporate at the Tier 1 planning level as discussed in Chapter 7? Tier 2?

2. Teach a writing lesson using one of the strategies outlined in this chapter. What worked well? What was challenging for you? What will be your next steps in teaching writing?

3. Observe a teacher who teaches writing to CLDE students. What strategies does he or she use? What worked well? What suggestions could you offer for the lesson to better meet the needs of CLDE learners?

Visit the Student Study Site at **www.sagepub.com/grassi** for chapter-specific study resources.

Note

1. For reference that details the issues speakers of other languages will have with English spelling, grammar, and punctuation, see *Learner English: A Teacher's Guide to Interference and Other Problems, Second Edition,* by M. Swan and B. Smith (Eds.), 2006.

Chapter 15

STRATEGIES FOR
WRITTEN ERROR CORRECTION

Key Points

✦ Deciding on considerations when correcting CLDE students' writing

✦ Developing steps to error correction

✦ Studying examples of error correction strategies

CASE STUDY 15.1	Written Error Correction

It did not dawn on me that my students never had been taught English composition terms that I used every day until I said, "You have to make sure you are using the appropriate conjugation of the verb for the person you are talking about, you know, just like we do in Spanish." The general response was, "What's that?" I was stunned at the response and took a quick survey: Who knows what a verb is? Who knows what a pronoun is? Who knows what "conjugation" means? "Dialogue"? "Article"? "Tenses"? And so on.

Several hands went up for a show of understanding in basic parts of speech for English terms that they had mastered since grade school, but no hands went up for unusual terms not commonly used in English classes (articles, conjugation, etc.).

My English teacher colleagues agreed that we have the tendency to forget that we might be using technical terms with which students are not familiar, perhaps because we are so concerned with moving through the curriculum. Students' unfamiliarity with these terms does not become evident until they need to know those technicalities, at which point we have to stop, back up, and address their needs before pressing forward again.

I am happy to report that most students did better with comprehension and with writing, and that they picked up rules and terms, after I explicitly taught technical English terms and their uses in writing.

—Teresa Martinez, Literacy teacher

Consider the case study above:

- What aspects of writing were missing from the general writing curriculum?
- Why would CLDE students need instruction in specific technical aspects of writing?

SOURCE: Used by permission.

Literacy skills are essential for all students. Being able to write clearly gives a person access to full participation in society and allows that person to be less dependent on others and to make choices about what to do or learn (Copeland, 2007). Quality literacy instruction for CLDE students includes strategies that assist students in becoming proficient writers. In this chapter, we discuss strategies for error correction that support CLDE students' acquisition of written English and that support learning issues related to students' disabilities.

CONSIDERATIONS WHEN CORRECTING CLDE STUDENTS' WRITING

Historically, there have been two different philosophies in the approach of teaching literacy to students with disabilities: readiness models and functional skills. Both these philosophies are based on a deficit model and do not necessarily address all the needs of CLDE students. **Readiness models** require that students master certain skills before moving on to the next level of skills. For example, a student must know all of the letters of the alphabet before learning to write words. While this approach to teaching focuses on mastery of specific skills, this type of teaching philosophy can act as a gatekeeper, stagnating students at the lowest levels of learning.

The **functional skills approach** is another approach to teaching literacy to students with disabilities. In this teaching approach, students learn the words needed to survive in the school and in the community—words that are on signs, words needed to fill out job applications, words needed to shop in the grocery store. This approach has a narrow view of the literacy skills a student experiences, so does not give students full access to the rich opportunities in school and choices for participation in society.

Because CLDE students not only have a special education learning need, but also the need to learn English, the two philosophies listed above do not fully address their needs. Teachers need to consider how the language acquisition process plays into the students' learning and how the errors they make can be a part of the language acquisition process. Therefore, we also must consider literacy practices in the ESL field. Basically, there are two perspectives on writing correction.

One perspective advocates for model work and suggests that no student writing should be considered finished until it is at a proficient level. Advocates of this perspective feel that students learning English need good models of writing and that they should not "publish," exhibit their work, or consider their work to be a final draft until it provides a proficient model.

Another perspective sees language acquisition as a process and believes that students will pass through a developmental progression in spelling, grammar, organization, and cultural appropriateness. While error correction should occur at some level, the meaning of the written piece is the most important element. Students need time to pass through developmental stages—including producing all the errors of each particular stage (Peregoy & Boyle, 2005). This perspective advocates for celebrating what has been done well. Expecting proficient work from students at more beginning levels of English acquisition is unrealistic and could discourage further writing. Not all drafts need to become final drafts or to be published.

While any of these approaches to learning literacy and error correction may be what is needed for a particular student or a particular situation, we do not advocate for one singular approach. We advocate for an approach to error correction that perceives writing as a process, but that also is explicit in instruction (see Photo 15.2).

As discussed in Chapter 13, the **process approach** considers the context of the written piece—the audience, the purpose for writing, and the purpose of the lesson—and the type of instruction and correction suitable for each context. For example, if a student is writing a letter to the editor of the newspaper, all errors should be addressed and corrected before the letter is sent to the editor. On the other hand, if the student is learning to use more descriptive language in his or her writing, or is developing ideas around a certain topic, the teacher might overlook errors as the student concentrates on this one teaching point. In both of these examples, *readiness* skills and *functional* vocabulary will be necessary considerations. That is, the teacher may need to provide explicit examples of words that may be needed for writing a letter, or creating speech, or for using more descriptive language. The teacher also will need to make sure that the student has the needed readiness skills, such as the background knowledge for writing about a topic or an understanding of descriptive language. Using multiple approaches in the process of writing gives access to the meaningful task of communicating in written format (Peregoy & Boyle, 2005).

When using a process approach to teaching writing, the teacher also will need to decide on which aspect of the essay to grade—the teaching point, other grammatical aspects not included in the teaching point, the content message, or the essay as a whole, including all aspects. The goals of the writing process and product need to be explicitly stated to the student so that he or she understands the focus of the lessons and is clear on expected outcomes. Concurrently, the teacher can continually assess the student on all aspects of the writing, furthering learning goals, yet assign a grade on the specific objective at hand.

We believe that the teacher should not offer the student a grade until the student has had the opportunity to work with several drafts or editing phases, has received explicit feedback on errors, and has received instruction on how to correct the errors at the grammatical, punctuation, organization, orthographic, and cultural levels. It is important that students focus on meaning first, and that the meaning of their writing be the focus of the first drafts.

We also know that students and their families differ in their expectations of writing instruction, and that it is important for teachers to meet these expectations. It also is important to have realistic expectations for each student. If a child has a disability that impacts written language, it is important to take that disability into account when writing assignments are made, assessed, and graded. Adaptations, as noted on a student's IEP, must be provided and

Photo 15.2   Having students look for one error at a time as they revise is an effective strategy.

included in all lessons. That said, an open dialogue between student and teacher should provide the purpose for the writing. Teachers need to ask students the following questions: How do you want the reader to perceive you as a writer? How important is "perfection" to you? What do you want to let the reader know from your piece? The language needs of a CLDE student also should be considered on the IEP. These may need to be adapted as the student progresses through the language acquisition process. Therefore, it is doubly important when working with CLDE students to explicitly communicate the learning goals to the student and parents so there is a clear understanding as to why certain learning goals are a focus of a particular writing assignment. The teacher should explicitly explain the purpose of the lesson to the student and parents, including *why* he or she allows for errors.

When considering the writing errors of CLDE students, the teacher needs to examine why those errors have been made: Are the errors a part of the development of the language acquisition process, a result of the disability, or both? Copeland (Copeland & Keefe, 2007, p. 112) lists some possible reasons as to why errors are present in CLDE students' written work:

1. Lack of opportunities to develop writing skills due to low expectations from teachers or other adults

2. Provision of age-inappropriate literacy instruction or instruction limited to recognizing site words

3. Underlying language problems such as limited vocabulary or incomplete understanding of grammar that makes it difficult for the student to express ideas and thoughts in written form

4. Limitations in working memory that affect planning, organizing, and composing text

5. Difficulty with fine motor skills that makes handwriting laborious and time consuming and, for some with physical disabilities, impossible

6. Limited knowledge of phonics that affects the ability to spell words that the writer wishes to use in a composition

7. Lack of the technology and supports that would provide access to the writing process

For CLDE students, it is important to consider the above factors as you proceed through the steps of error correction. Teachers must be explicit and purposeful in teaching the correct ways of communicating in writing. When students have specific, appropriate, and full expectations in learning to write, opportunities for the development of language, communication, and literacy are better realized.

ERROR CORRECTION

Steps to Error Correction

When a teacher who speaks English as an L1 reads the written work of a CLDE student, the errors are easy to find because they do not "sound" right. Many teachers do not know the reasons or the grammatical rules to explain why the errors are "errors," though. When working with CLDE students, it is important that teachers be able to explicitly explain the grammatical rules to the student. This helps the student to categorize the error, to understand how to use the English written language correctly, and to have a system for remembering the rule. By using a reference point of the grammatical rule, the teacher and the student can more clearly communicate with each other about the writing. If you are a teacher who does not have a strong background in grammar—and there are many of us who do not—we encourage you to have at hand a grammar reference book to help in the correction of CLDE student work. This will help to communicate explicitly the rules of the English language.

If and when the teacher decides to address errors in student's written work, there are eight steps to guide teachers in correcting CLDE written work (Table 15.1):

Table 15.1   Steps to Error Correction of Students' Written Work

Step 1. Make note of all of the errors found in the written piece (circle them, underline them, or highlight them).

Step 2. Look at the errors for patterns. Is there one (or more) errors that are more prevalent? Is there one error that seems to disrupt the meaning of the paper more than the others? Concentrate on persistent errors or errors that disrupt the meaning first.

Step 3. Concentrate on only one error at a time.

Step 4. Begin by asking the student if he or she can self-correct. If the student is able to correct the error, then the student has acquired the rule but the rule has not yet become automatic in the student's writing. This error will not require explicit instruction. Nevertheless, it is helpful to the student if he or she is required to correct the error in the paper before he or she is given a grade.

Step 5. If the student cannot self-correct, then this error will require explicit instruction. The teacher will need to identify the type of error produced (grammatical, cultural mismatch, organizational, genre, punctuation, etc.), will need to know the rule for this error, and will need to explain this rule in a comprehensible manner.

Step 6. If the error is found in the writing of many students, then a whole class or small group instructional setting is beneficial. If the error is prevalent in only one student's writing, then the teacher should work with that student individually.

Step 7. Once the teacher has provided explicit instruction in the error, the teacher should return the paper to the student and ask him or her to correct the error in the written piece. Once the error has been corrected in the paper, then the teacher should provide a grade based on both the correctness of the error point and the content message.

Step 8. Remember that writing can backslide. As students learn new grammatical, spelling, or punctuation rules, they may slip back and produce errors in previously learned points. It will take many repetitions before proficient writing becomes automatic.

SOURCE: Adapted from Gass & Selinker, 2008; Peregoy & Boyle, 2005.

Examples of Error Correction

Below we provide examples of essays written by CLDE students at the secondary and elementary levels may look like. We walk you through the essays using the steps listed in Table 15.1 to correct the writing, and we provide examples of how to address the correction of written work. We suggest you try the steps yourself before reading our analysis of the essays.

Example 15.1 Secondary Level Essay

Me and my frend we want to play videos to each other house, and on that day i sey to my mom i going to sleep to the house of my frend, and my mom said no hide to Sandra no more, and I say OK. And wen is a 7:00 my frend call to my house and he said to me come to 3:00 P.M. to my house and on that day he going to he house and to 3:00 and i said to my mom i going to play to the house of my frend and my mom call to hes mom and hes mom sey OK and wen me go to the house of my frend and he said less go to play the videos. And we run to he house and go to hes room my frend he see sombovy coming and my frend said is sombovy coming and on that day me and my frend we run to my house get my dog.

Step 1. Make note of (underline or circle) all the errors found in the written piece.

In Example 15.1, there are numerous errors in punctuation, spelling, and grammar. Below we have highlighted some of the errors within the essay:

Me and my frend we want to play videos to each other house, and on that day i sey to my mom i going to sleep to the house of my frend, and my mom said no hide to Sandra no more and i say OK. And wen is a 7:00 my frend call to my house and he said to me come to 3:00 P.M. to my house and on that day he going to he house and to 3:00 and i said to my mom i going to play to the house of my frend and my mom call to hes mom and hes mom sey OK and wen me go to the house of my frend and he said less go to play the videos. And we run to he house and go to hes room and my frend he see sombovy coming and my frend said is sombovy coming and on that day me and my frend we run to my house get my dog

---

Step 2. Look for patterns in the errors. Is there one error that is more prevalent than the others? One error that most disrupts the meaning?

Punctuation errors. The student uses very little punctuation and will need instruction on when to use periods, capital letters, question marks, and quotation marks. This student is at the developmental stage where "and" is used in place of punctuation.

Spelling errors. The student has made spelling errors with words such as "less go," "wen," "sey," and "frend." All these errors exhibit good approximations of the correct English spelling.

Subject capitalization. The student does not capitalize the pronoun "I."

The possessive. The student has trouble forming the possessive in English.

- *house of my friend* (my friend's house)
- *he house* (his house)
- *hes mom* (his mom)

Use of auxiliary verbs. The student does not consistently add the auxiliary verb "to be" with the progressive tense.

- *he going* to he house
- i said to my mom *i going to play* to the house of my friend

Use of prepositions with verbs. The student uses the incorrect preposition with the verb or uses a preposition with a verb when none is needed.

- i going to *play to* the house of my friend
- . . . and mom *call to hes mom*

Use of the negative. The student incorrectly uses the negative form. The student uses "no" in place of do + not and uses a double negative.

- my mom said *no hide to Sandra no more*

Confusion with pronouns. The student uses "me" in the subject pronoun position instead of "I."

- and wen *me* go to the house of my friend

Prepositions for time expressions. The student uses the preposition "to" with time expressions instead of "at."

- he said to me come *to* 3:00 pm to my house
- he going to he house and *to* 3:00 and i said to my mom i going to play to the house
- and wen is a 7:00 my frend call

Use of the past tense. The student does not consistently use the past tense of verb forms and instead uses the present tense to represent the past. This is a developmental stage when acquiring the past tense (see Chapter 3 for these stages):

- On that day my frend *go* to my house
- and i *say* OK
- and wen me *go* to the house
- and when *is* a 7:00 my frend *he* see sombovy coming
- and wen me and my frend *is* in the
- and we *run* to he house
- and mom *call* to hes mom

Dummy subjects—nonreferential "it" and "there." The student skips the nonreferential subjects "it" and "there" in sentences that require them.

- and my frend said [there] is sombovy coming

Is there one (or more) errors that are more prevalent? Is there one error that seems to disrupt the meaning of the paper more than other errors?

In Example 15.1, punctuation errors are the most prevalent and appear to disrupt the meaning the most. Grammatical errors consist of

10 instances of past tense errors,

9 instances of possessive errors,

2 instances of "to" with time expressions,

3 instances of missing auxiliary verb with progressive tense,

4 instances of incorrect prepositions,

1 instance of lack of nonreferential "it" and "there,"

1 instance of improper use of the negative, and

1 instance of improper use of the subject pronoun.

Step 3. Concentrate on only one error at a time. Start with the most prevalent error in the student writing or the error that most disrupts the meaning of the paper.

In Example 15.1, punctuation errors have significant impact on meaning. We suggest teachers instruct the student on adding periods to the essay first.

After punctuation, we suggest the teacher concentrate on either formation of the possessive (three instances of possessive errors in the essay) or formation of past tense verbs (seven instances of past tense errors in the essay).

Step 4. Begin by asking the student if he or she can self-correct. If the student is able to correct the error, then the student has acquired the rule but the rule has not yet become automatic in the student's writing.

When the teacher circled the errors for the student author, the student was unable to correct the punctuation, was unable to correct all the past tense errors, but was able to correct the possessive errors.

Step 5. If the student cannot self-correct, then this error will require explicit instruction. The teacher will need to identify the type of error produced (grammatical, punctuation, cultural mismatch, organizational, genre, formality, etc.), will need to know the rule for this error, and will need to explain this rule in a comprehensible manner.

The teacher in this case was unfamiliar with the rules for punctuation so she worked with one of the English teachers in the building to help her articulate the rules for periods. Once the teacher was confident about the rules of English punctuation, she created several mini-lessons (5–10 minutes long) that were presented in an engaging and comprehensible manner (using the 3-way model).

The teacher knew the rules for formation of the past tense (add "ed" to regular verbs and memorize the form of irregular verbs) and created several mini-lessons using the class novel as a launching pad for teaching this grammar point. The class novel contained several examples of regular and irregular past tense, so the teacher listed the past tense examples from the novel on a word wall that categorized the verbs under either "Regular Verbs" or "Irregular Verbs" (Table 15.2).

Table 15.2   Verb Categories

Regular Verbs in the Past Tense		Irregular Verbs in the Past Tense	
like	liked	run	ran
gallop	galloped	sing	sang
skip	skipped	sit	sat
rain	rained	think	thought
bike	biked	drink	drank

Once the teacher had enough examples on the word wall, he worked with students to begin to categorize the words further. For example, he categorized regular past tense verbs according to the sound the "ed" ending makes:

/t/—liked

/d/—rained

/id/—fitted

The teacher categorized by spelling:

"ed" words that require a second consonant, like skip–skipped

"ed" words that change the "y" to an "i," like study–studied

The teacher categorized the irregular past into certain forms:

Verbs that take two forms in the past, like to be (was, were)

Verbs that change to the "ought" sound, like buy–bought, think–thought

Verbs that have one vowel change, like run–ran, throw–threw

A teacher also can have the students look for patterns and decide how to categorize the verbs themselves. The more the students use the verbs—through word walls, categorizing, and writing—the better they will acquire the verbs.

In the essay in Example 15.1, the student could self-correct the possessive forms, so the teacher did not create any lessons around this grammar point.

Step 6. If the error is found in the writing of many students, then a whole class or small-group instructional setting would be beneficial. If the error is prevalent in only one student's writing, then the teacher should work with that student individually.

Most of the students in the class were having trouble with punctuation, so the teacher conducted small-group lessons on punctuation during the writing block. The teacher continued with punctuation lessons once a week for the entire school year.

A small group of students were having trouble forming the past tense, especially the irregular past tense forms, so the teacher called the group aside and conducted mini-lessons with them during the novel reading period, once a week.

Because the student author was able to self-correct the possessive errors, the teacher had this student work independently in correcting the possessive errors in his essay.

Step 7. Once the teacher has provided explicit instruction in the error, the teacher should return the papers to the students and ask them to correct the error in their writing.

The student author in Essay 15.1 was a serious writer and desired perfect drafts of the majority of his stories. With this essay, the author was fine with working on punctuation, past tense forms, and forming the possessive. Once these three areas were corrected, the teacher graded the paper.

Step 8. Remember that writing can exhibit backsliding. It will take many repetitions before proficient writing becomes automatic.

The student author continued to exhibit punctuation errors for the remainder of school year. By the end of the year, however, the student was consistently adding periods, capitalizing letters, using quotation marks when appropriate, and using question marks. The student still required work with appropriate comma use.

Errors in forming the past tense and possessives continued to randomly show up in the student's work all year. However, if the teacher circled the error to draw the student's attention to the error, the student was able to self-correct in most instances. The student still had trouble correctly forming irregular past tense verb forms at the end of the school year but was observed using the word wall as a reference while writing. In order to help the student in his homework, the teacher typed up a list of all the words on the word wall and made a bookmark copy for the student to use at home.

To practice error correction with another essay on the elementary level, see the following Web link: **www.sagepub.com/grassi.**

15.1

Summary

Teachers can help the language acquisition process of CLDE students by providing quick, efficient, and accurate error correction instruction. By concentrating on only one error at a time, the teacher avoids student frustration, increases student success, and helps students acquire the rule. It is also important to consider the student's disability as it affects written communication skills and to determine if the correct adaptations have been provided as outlined in the student's IEP (fine motor skills, assistive technology, organizational tools, strategy instruction, scribes, vocabulary instruction, etc.).

After reading this chapter, you should be able to

- understand the arguments for and against explicit error instruction and other approaches to teaching literacy to CLDE students,

- understand the eight steps to error correction for student written work, and

- be able to work through the eight steps when correcting CLDE student's written work.

15.2

To read a research article concerning alternative correction and assessment of CLDE students' writing (Armon & Ortega, 2009), see the following Web link: **www.sagepub.com/grassi.**

Key Terms

Functional skills approach

Process approach

Readiness models

Activities for Further Understanding

1. Find samples of CLDE students' written work. Follow the eight steps to error correction discussed above to correct the essays. Which aspects of the eight steps were challenging for you? Where do you need to gather further information in order to work through the eight steps more effectively?

2. Observe teachers with CLDE students. Which of the eight steps discussed in this chapter do the teachers use when correcting student work? Which steps would you recommend the teacher incorporate to work more effectively with CLDE students' written work?

3. Are the eight steps to error correction appropriate with all CLDE students? Which students would benefit from the eight steps to error correction? How would you adapt the eight steps to work with other students?

4. Consider the students in your classroom. What errors are they making? How would you plan for those in Tier 1 instructional planning? How would you differentiate that instruction to meet the needs of all the students? Which aspects of the eight steps described in this chapter could fit in Tier 2?

Visit the Student Study Site at **www.sagepub.com/grassi** for chapter-specific study resources.

Glossary

3-way model   A foundational teaching strategy to make content comprehensible in the classroom. Content and directions are spoken, written down, and presented with visual context.

Accommodations   Accommodations are strategies or supports provided to help students gain full access to the content—and then to show their understanding of the content.

Acquisition vs learning hypothesis   The acquisition versus learning hypothesis claims that acquisition (the subconscious and intuitive process of "picking up" a language) is far more effective in acquiring fluency in the L2 than is just learning (the process in which students attend to the form and rules of the language).

Adequate yearly progress (AYP)   School districts must show that increasing percentages of students are reaching proficient achievement levels each year. This progress is known as AYP.

Affective filter hypothesis   The affective filter hypothesis is as follows: The lower the stress level of students, the more they are able to receive linguistic input and begin to process the language. If anxiety levels are high, concentrating and listening in class become more difficult.

Background knowledge or prior knowledge   This knowledge is the experience, knowledge, and skills that a student brings to the classroom or lesson.

Backward design model   A backward design model requires teachers to start planning the lesson from the end by determining the desired results. Teachers then build their lesson from the endpoint working backwards to plan activities and lectures that will bring students to the desired outcomes.

Backsliding   When students acquire new grammatical forms, they can sometimes return to incorrectly formed features previously acquired. This is known as backsliding—two steps forward, one step back in learning the new language.

Basic Interpersonal Communication Skills (BICS)   BICS is social language: the language students acquire when speaking informally with peers and others.

Bilingual maintenance program   This is the educational program designed to maintain the student's first language and culture while simultaneously developing English language and literacy skills. Students transition from high percentage of instruction in first language to instruction that is 50:50 home language and English.

Cognitive Academic Language Proficiency Skills (CALPS)   CALPS is the language of school and academic subjects.

Collaboration   Collaboration is an interactive process that enables teachers with diverse expertise to provide quality instructional services to students with a wide range of needs.

Comprehensible input   Comprehensible input is visual support, gestures, context, drama, stories, movies, modeling, and written instructions that makes the target language understandable.

Comprehension   Comprehension is constructing meaning from and understanding what is read.

Concurrent translation   Introducing the content first in one language then immediately translating the content to the other language.

Content   Content is the knowledge or skills taught in a lesson. Content can be differentiated, sheltered, and scaffolded to support CLDE learners.

Content and cultural schema   Content and cultural schema are the sociocultural knowledge obtained from past learning, home life, and country of origin.

Continuum of services   The continuum of services are the placement options for students with special needs, generally organized from placements most like settings for typical learners to placements least like settings for typical learners.

Co-teaching   Co-teaching occurs when two teachers work as partners to collaboratively create solutions to identify and address instructional/student problems, create units of study, plan and modify lessons, carry out classroom instruction, and supervise student work. The main goal of co-teaching is to bring intense and individualized instruction to students in a general education, content area setting, while also giving students access to the rich and full curriculum.

Cultural acquisition   This is the process of acquiring sociolinguistic competence. Includes four stages: excitement, culture shock, recovery, full recovery.

Cultural bias   Cultural bias is when a test requires students to have specific culturally based information in order to perform well on the test.

Cultural discontinuities   Cultural discontinuities are misunderstandings and confusion due to culture and language. Some mismatches that may occur when working with families of CLDE students include: perceptions of disability, perceptions of goal setting, and understandings of the special education process.

Cultural liaison   A person who can interpret the culture as well as provide access to information about cultural norms for particular situations is a cultural liaison.

Culturally and linguistically diverse exceptional students (CLDE students)   Students who are both learning English and who have a special education need are known as CLDE students.

Culturally responsive teaching   Culturally responsive teaching occurs when there is equal respect for the backgrounds and contemporary circumstances of all learners, and when there is a design of learning processes that embraces the range of needs, interests, and orientations to be found among them.

Cultural mismatches   These are unintentional clashes that occur when people of differing cultures do not understand each others' cultural norms.

Deductive lesson   This lesson involves the teacher giving an explicit explanation of the rule first, then providing examples.

Deficit system   The special education system is often defined as a deficit system because it looks at how educational and related services can "fix" what is "wrong" with a child.

Differentiating instruction (DI)   A way of approaching the planning and implementation of curriculum and instruction with an understanding that learners differ in a variety of ways including readiness levels, learning profiles, and interests. When providing differentiating instruction, teachers vary the process, product, and content associated with a particular unit or lesson of instruction.

Direct translation   Direct translating is word-for-word translation between languages. Many ideas are not directly translatable and direct translation can cause misunderstandings.

Disability categories   There are 13 specific disability categories and definitions used by the federal government to determine eligibility for special education services.

Discourse competence   The ability to connect words and sentences into stretches of comprehensible written and oral language is called discourse competence.

Discrepancy model   The discrepancy model is a model for determining eligibility for special education services for a specific learning disability. It takes into account the difference between a student's academic achievement and potential. (IQ scores are generally used to determine the potential and achievement tests are used for the current academic levels.)

Diversity pedagogy   Diversity pedagogy is an ideology that views the relationship among culture and cognition as essential to understanding the teaching-learning process.

English as a second language (ESL) program   Educational programs designed to develop English language and literacy skills as soon as possible are called ESL programs. The goal is to replace a native language with the majority language.

English language learners (ELLs)   ELLs are students who are identified as learning English.

English submersion   English submersion is when the student receives no special services and is enrolled in general education English-only classes. The goal is assimilation and replacement of the student's native language.

Equity pedagogy   Equity pedagogy is the acknowledgment that students from different backgrounds may learn in different ways.

Extrinsic motivation   Extrinsic motivation is an external factor that encourages the student to learn (the new language).

First language (L1)   The language a child first learns is L1.

Fluency   Fluency is the ability to recognize and read written words rapidly and accurately.

Fluent English Proficient (FEP)   FEP is one of the federal categories for classifying the proficiency level of an ELL student as "fluent English proficient."

Form-focused instruction   Explicit grammar teaching to enhance the communicative abilities of students is form-focused instruction.

Fossilize   Fossilizing (or stabilizing) is using grammatical forms that can be generally understood, but that are not necessarily grammatically correct.

Free and appropriate public education (FAPE)   FAPE is the requirement provided by law that guarantees all students, including students with special needs, the right to a free and appropriate public education.

Front-loading   When teachers front-load, they teach key vocabulary or information before the lesson begins.

Functional behavior assessment (FBA)   FBA is a process used to examine the function of disruptive behavior to a classroom environment or a student's learning.

Functional skills approach   Functional skills approach is a teaching approach where students learn the words needed to survive in the school and in the community.

Genre   The genre is the specific type or category of writing or reading that shares specific features such as organization, purpose, style, and voice.

Grammatical competence   The ability to communicate in the target language (both orally and written) in a grammatically correct manner is known as grammatical competence.

Graphic organizer   A graphic organizer is a visual tool that helps students organize the information read or the information presented in a lesson.

Inclusive pedagogy   Inclusive pedagogy is an emerging body of literature that advocates teaching practices that embrace the whole student in the learning process.

Individualized Education Plan (IEP)   A student's IEP is a document that is collaboratively written by school staff and parents of a student who qualifies for special education services. States the student's current levels of functioning and needs, goals and objectives for the student, evaluation measures, and special education and related services, including placement and duration. An IEP is updated annually.

Individuals with Disabilities Education Act (IDEA)   IDEA was passed first in 1990, revised in 1997, and reauthorized in 2004. This is the current special education law that continues the movement to provide access to an equal and individualized education and related services for students with disabilities.

Inductive lessons   These lessons involve presenting examples first, then giving students time to "discover" the rule on their own.

Input hypothesis   In order for students to acquire the target language, the language input they receive must be made comprehensible—through visual support, gestures, context, drama, stories, movies, modeling, and written instructions.

Instruction/assessment cycle   The instruction/assessment cycle is the instructional cycle that uses informal and formal assessment data to inform instructional decisions.

Instructional planning pyramid   This pyramid is a way to organize purposefully selected strategies, support, and placements that best meet the needs of specific students. The pyramid is organized in three tiers to represent the diverse needs of a class. Tier 1 represents core instruction and assessment, Tier 2 represents enhanced instruction and assessment, and

Tier 3 represents intensive instruction and assessment. The tiers also are used as a framework for RTI.

Instrumental orientation   Obtaining proficiency in the language for instrumental purposes (for a job, for school studies, for a promotion) is known as instrumental orientation.

Integrated content–language approach   This approach uses foundational strategies to make the content accessible to CLDE students while concurrently supporting the language acquisition process.

Integrative orientation   Obtaining proficiency in the target language in order to integrate within the culture and society is known as integrative orientation.

Interlanguage   Interlanguage is the language students use when moving from their first language to developing fluency in the second language.

Intervention team   A problem-solving committee that meets as part of a pre-referral process to support students who are not making academic progress is the intervention team. The collaborative team creates a plan of intervention strategies, data collection means, and a timeline.

Intrinsic motivation   The student wants to learn (the language) for his or her own happiness or gain. This type of motivation is more favorable for long-term retention of the language.

IRF sequence   This sequence consists of a teacher-initiated question (I), a student response (R), and teacher feedback (F) or follow-up (F).

Key academic language   The key academic language is the language needed to understand, write about, and speak about the content material. Includes both the key vocabulary, phrases, and expressions, and the grammar need to actively participate in the lesson.

Key concepts   The clearly defined learning outcomes of the lesson are the key concepts. When the teacher points these out before and during the lesson, students can focus their attention on the important points of the lesson.

Least restrictive environment (LRE)   The placement where a student with special needs will be least restricted by his or her disability and will have the most access to the full general education curriculum is the LRE.

Limited English proficiency (LEP)   LEP is a term that refers to the level of English language proficiency of students. IDEA 2004 acknowledges that acquiring a second language must be ruled out a primary reason for lower academic achievement before special education services are provided.

Making Action Plans Process (MAPs)   The MAPs process involves a gathering with family members, students, teachers, and other people who have an interest in the student. A facilitator guides the discussion, which is aimed at understanding the past, present, and future story of the child and the family.

Modeling   *See* Recasting.

Modifications   Modifications are individualized changes made to the curriculum—to assignments and to assessments—to make them more accessible to a student with special needs.

Monitor hypothesis   When students learn a language, they invoke the "monitor"—a manner of closely watching one's output for errors and mistakes (the monitor hypothesis), which, in turn, can hamper acquisition.

Monocultural   Monocultural attitudes focus on only one culture, which is generally the culture of power.

Multidisciplinary Assessment Team (MAST)   MAST is a team that conducts a full evaluation of a child and consists of specialists trained to conduct evaluations in cognitive functioning, speech and language, levels of academic achievement, social or emotional functioning, health history and current physical condition, and parent interview. The information collected is used to determine eligibility for special education services and to create an IEP.

Multiple means of expression   Multiple means of expression are ways to provide learners alternatives for demonstrating what they know.

Multiple means of representation   Multiple means of representation provide learners various ways of acquiring information and knowledge.

Multiple means of engagement   Multiple means of engagement are the variety of ways that teachers can tap into learners' interests, offer appropriate challenges, and increase motivation.

Natural order hypothesis   The natural order hypothesis suggests that second language learners acquire some features of English grammar in a predictable order.

No Child Left Behind (NCLB) Act   The NCLB law, first passed in 2001, is a reauthorization of the Elementary and Secondary Education Act of 1965. It sets high standards for student achievement, increased accountability measures, and increased criteria for "highly qualified" teachers. Students with special needs and students learning English are included in accountability reports.

Oral proficiency   A person who has oral proficiency is able to speak at a proficient level.

Orthographic system   The orthographic system is the system of written communication.

Output   Output is using the target language in speech or writing to communicate.

Output hypothesis   The output hypothesis states that student *output* is just as integral to L2 acquisition as is comprehensible *input*.

Overgeneralization   Transferring learned rules in the first language to similar grammatical situations in the second language is called overgeneralization.

Parallel teaching   Parallel teaching is a co-teaching model where the class is divided and two teachers present the same content to smaller portions of the whole group of students.

Paraprofessional (or paraeducator)   Individuals who work in schools as support to teachers, administrators, and students are paraprofessionals (or paraeducators). They are used to assist in instructional activities of all students in schools. For students with special needs, they are not primary service providers, but should be used to assist in the provisions of special education and related services.

Phonemic awareness   Phonemic awareness is the understanding that words are made up of separate units of sound that are blended.

Phonics   Phonics are the rules of how speech sounds are represented in written format. Phonics involves connecting the sounds students hear in spoken language to their alphabetic representation.

Phonology   The system of sounds within a language is phonology.

Process   The process is the way that a student accesses the content of the lesson. Differentiating the process is a way to allow CLDE students to access content in ways that support their learning needs.

Process approach   The process approach considers the context of the written piece and the type of instruction and correction suitable for each context. Looks at writing developmentally.

Process problems   Process problems are exemplified in the overall process of written communication, such as lack of systematic planning, preoccupation with mechanics, inability to monitor the writing, and lack of revision skills.

Product   The product is the manner a student demonstrates understanding of the knowledge or skills learned. Differentiating the product is a way to allow CLDE students to more accurately depict what they have learned.

Product problems   Product problems are exemplified in written communication by use of simple sentence construction, use of few words, disregard for audience, mechanical errors, and poor organization and overall structure.

Public Law 94-142 (PL 94-142)   Passed in 1975, the Education for All Handicapped Children Act (PL 94-142) granted a free and appropriate public education for all students. This law provided the groundwork for the services that all students with special needs are guaranteed today.

Readiness model   The readiness model requires that students master certain skills before moving on to the next level of skills.

Recasting   Recasting (modeling, reformulating) is where the teacher repeats what the student said, but in a grammatically correct form and in a manner that does not disrupt the conversation flow.

Reformulating   *See* Recasting.

Repetition   A key component to making the content comprehensible for ELL students is repetition.

Response to Intervention (RTI)   RTI is a process that uses levels of interventions and responses by students to the research-based interventions. A team approach is used to support classroom teachers in providing interventions, collecting data, and analyzing results. This model can be used to determine learning disability eligibility.

Second language acquisition (SLA)   SLA is the process of learning a second language.

Second language (L2)   L2 is the target language, or language the student is learning.

Section 504   Section 504 is a section of the Vocational Rehabilitation Act of 1973 that granted basic civil rights to people with disabilities in programs that receive federal funds.

Semantic web   A way of visually organizing information related to the key concept. Students brainstorm ideas and questions related to the idea they are working with. Similar to a concept map or web.

Simultaneous teaching   A co-teaching model where the content is divided and each teacher provides one part of the lesson to half of the students, after which the group switches, is known as simultaneous teaching.

Sociolinguistic competence   Pragmatics, or the ability to understand the deep cultural rules associated with language, is sociolinguistic competence.

Stabilize   *See* Fossilize.

Stages of second language acquisition   Based on the natural order hypothesis, each stage of second language acquisition is a progression, providing guidelines for the language characteristics of a student and how long the student typically exhibits behavior in the particular stage. However, there are numerous factors that contribute to second language acquisition and the amount of time a student spends in each stage is dependent on various situations.

Stage theory approach   When a child is diagnosed with a disability, the stage theory approach explains a series of emotional stages that parents progress through as they move to acceptance of the child's disability. The validity of this theory is questionable as perceptions of disability depend on a variety of complex issues.

Strategic competence   The ability to enact verbal and nonverbal communication breakdowns is strategic competence.

Target language   The target language is the language being learned.

Team teaching   Team teaching is a model of co-teaching where both teachers teach the whole class together at the same time.

Transitional bilingual educational program   Transitional bilingual educational programs are designed with the main goal of English acquisition and assimilation into the majority culture.

Two-way immersion or dual language program   These programs are educational programs that work to develop bilingualism, biliteracy, and biculturalism in both ELL and native-English-speaking students. Curriculum is generally presented in two languages.

Universal design for learning (UDL)   UDL is a concept used to ensure that all students have access to the curriculum from the point of planning by providing multiple means of representation, multiple means of expression, and multiple means of engagement.

U-shaped learning   U-shaped learning is represented by three stages: Stage 1 involves correct grammatical form. A Stage 2 learner uses incorrect form, temporarily unable to produce what had been learned. A Stage 3 learner uses correct form of target language again.

Visual context   Visual clues such as pictures, film, maps, photos, realia, artifacts, modeling, or demonstrations that help make connections to the spoken word provide the visual context.

Vocabulary   Vocabulary is the collection of words used to communicate. Students depend heavily on their oral language proficiency to develop vocabulary. Students will use the pronunciation and meaning of words in their spoken language to help them recognize words they see in print.

References

Abedi, J. (2004). The No Child Left Behind Act and English language learners: Assessment and accountability issues. *Educational Researcher, 33*, 4–14.

Abedi, J. (2005). Issues and consequences for English language learners. In J. L. Herman & E. H. Haertel (Eds.), *Uses and misuses of data in accountability testing* (pp. 175–198). Malden, MA: Blackwell.

Abu-Akhel, A. (1999). Episodic boundaries in conversational narratives. *Discourse Studies, 1*, 437–453.

Aldridge, J. (2005). The importance of oral language. *Childhood Education, 81*(3), 177–181.

Al-Hassan, S., & Gardner, R., III. (2002). Involving immigrant parents of students with disabilities in the educational process. *Teaching Exceptional Children, 34*(5), 52–58.

Andrews, J. D. (1980). The verbal structure of teacher questions, its impact on class discussion. *POD Quarterly, 2*, 129–163.

Artiles, A. J., Rueda, R., Salazar, J., & Higareda, I. (2005). Within-group diversity in minority disproportionate representation: English language learners in urban school districts. *Exceptional Children, 71*, 283–300.

August, D., & Shanahan, T. (2006). *Developing literacy in second-language learners: Report of the National Literacy Panel on Language-Minority Children and Youth.* Mahwah, NJ: Lawrence Erlbaum Associates.

Baca, L. M., & Cervantes, H. T. (2004). *The bilingual special education interface.* Columbus, OH: Pearson, Merrill Prentice Hall.

Bachman, L. (1990). *Fundamental considerations in language testing.* New York: Oxford University Press.

Baker, C. (2001). *Foundations of bilingual education and bilingualism* (3rd ed.). Buffalo, NY: Multilingual Matters.

Banks, J. A. (1997). *Educating citizens in a multicultural society.* New York: Teachers College Press.

Barbe, W. B., & Swassing, R. H. (1979). *Teaching through modality strengths: Concepts and practices.* Columbus, OH: Zaner-Bloser.

Barules, N., & Rice, S. (1993). Dialogues across difference: Continuing the conversation. In K. Geismar & G. Nicoleau (Eds.), *Teaching for change: Addressing issues of difference in the college classroom* (pp. 1–26). Cambridge, MA: Harvard Educational Review.

Beck, I., Perfetti, C., & McKeown, M. (1982). Effects of long-term vocabulary instruction on lexical access and reading comprehension. *Journal of Educational Psychology, 74*(4), 506–521.

Brett, A., Rothlein, L., & Hurley, M. (1996). Vocabulary acquisition from listening to stories and explanations of target words. *Elementary School Journal, 96*(4), 415–422.

Brown, H. D. (2007). *Principles of language learning and teaching* (5th ed.). New York: Pearson Longman.

Brown-Chidsey, R., & Steege, M. W. (2005). *Response to intervention: Principles and strategies for effective practice.* New York: Guilford.

Canale, M., & Swain, M. (1980.) Theoretical bases of communicative approaches to second language teaching and testing. *Applied Linguistics, 1,* 1–47.

Cartledge, G., Gardner, R., III, & Ford, D. Y. (2009). *Diverse learners with exceptionalities: Culturally responsive teaching in the inclusive classroom.* Upper Saddle River, NJ: Pearson Education.

Center for Applied Special Technology (CAST). (2007). Retrieved July 23, 2007, from www.cast.org.

Chamot, A. U., & O'Malley, J. M. (1994). *The CALLA handbook: Implementing the cognitive academic language learning approach.* New York: Longman.

Chaudron, C. (1988). *Second language classrooms.* Cambridge, UK: Cambridge University Press.

Chopra, R. V., Sandoval-Lucero, E., Arragon, L., Bernal, C., de Balderas, H. B., & Carrol, C. (2004). The paraprofessional role of connector. *Remedial and Special Education, 25,* 219–231.

Clark, B. (2002). *Growing up gifted* (6th ed.). Upper Saddle River, NJ: Merrill/Prentice Hall.

Collier, C. (1998, February 24–28). *Acculturation: Implications for assessment, instruction, and intervention.* Paper presented at the 27th annual meeting of the National Association of Bilingual Education, Dallas, TX. Available at http://eric.ed.gov/ERICDocs/data/ericdocs2sql/content_storage_01/0000019b/80/15/ab/46.pdf

Copeland, S. R. (2007). The power of literacy. In S. R. Copeland & E. B. Keefe, *Effective literacy instructions for students with moderate or severe disabilities* (pp. 1–6). Baltimore: Brookes.

Copeland, S. R., & Keefe, E. B. (2007). *Effective literacy instructions for students with moderate or severe disabilities.* Baltimore: Brookes.

Cordón, L. A., & Day, J. D. (1996). Strategy use on standardized reading comprehension tests. *Journal of Educational Psychology, 88,* 288–295.

Court, D., & Givon, S. (2003). Group intervention: Improving social skills of adolescents with learning disabilities. *Teaching Exceptional Children, 36*(2), 50–55.

Crawford, J. (2002). Obituary: The Bilingual Education Act, 1968–2002. *Rethinking Schools, 16*(4), retrieved from http://www.rethinkingschools.org/archive/16_04/Bi1164.shtml

Crawford, J. (2004). *Educating English learners: Language diversity in the classroom.* (5th ed.). Los Angeles: Bilingual Educational Services.

Cummins, J. (1979). Cognitive/academic language proficiency, linguistic interdependence, the optimal age question and some other matters. *Working Papers on Bilingualism, 19,* 197–205.

Cummins, J. (1981). The role of primary language development in promoting educational success for language minority students. In California State Department of Education (Ed.), *Schooling and language minority students: A theoretical framework.* Los Angeles: National Dissemination and Assessment Center.

Cummins, J. (2000). *Language, power and pedagogy: Bilingual children in the crossfire.* Clevedon, UK: Multilingual Matters.

Cummins, J. (2001). *Negotiating identities: Education for empowerment in a diverse society* (2nd ed.). Los Angeles: Association for Bilingual Education.

Cummins, J., Bismilla, V., Chow, P., Cohen, S., Giampapa, F., Leoni, L., et al. (2005). Affirming identity in multilingual classrooms. *Educational Leadership, 63*(1), 38–43.

Daniels, V. I., & McBride, A. (2001). Paraeducators as critical team members: Redefining roles and responsibilities. [Electronic version]. *NASSP Bulletin, 85*(623), 66–74.

Derewianka, B. (1990). *Exploring how texts work.* Portsmouth, NH: Heinemann.

Dillon, J. T. (1990). *The practice of questioning.* New York: Routledge, Chapman, and Hall.

Dockrell, J., Stuart, M., & King, D. (2004). Supporting early oral language skills. *Literacy Today,* 16–17.

Dörnyei, Z. (1995). On the teachability of communication strategies. *TESOL Quarterly, 29,* 55–84.

Doughty, C. (1991). Second language instruction does make a difference: Evidence from an empirical study of SL relativization. *Studies in Second Language Acquisition, 13,* 431–469.

Doughty, C. (2003). Instructed SLA: Constraints, compensation, and enhancement. In C. Doughty & M. Long (Eds.), *The handbook of second language acquisition* (pp. 256–310). Malden, MA: Blackwell.

Duff, P. (2001). Language, literacy, content, and (pop) culture: Challenges for ESL students in mainstream classes. *Canadian Modern Language Review, 58*(1), 103–132.

Dulay, H., & Burt, M. (1974). Natural sequences in child second language acquisition. *Language Learning, 24,* 37–53.

Dunn, R. (1996). *How to implement and supervise a learning styles program.* Alexandria, VA: Association for Supervision and Curriculum Development.

Dunn, R., & Dunn, K. (1975). *Educator's self-teaching guide to individualizing instructional programs.* New York: Parker.

Duplass, J. A. (2008). *Teaching elementary social studies: Strategies, standards, and Internet resources.* Boston: Houghton Mifflin.

Dutro, S., & Moran, C. (2003). Rethinking English language instruction: an architectural approach. In G. Garcia (Ed.), *English learners: Reading the highest level of English literacy.* Newark, DE: International Reading Association.

Echevarria, J., Vogt, M. E., & Short, D. (2008). *Making content comprehensible for English learners: The SIOP model* (3rd ed.). Boston: Pearson Education.

Ellis, R. (2005). Instructed language learning. In E. Hinkel (Ed.), *Handbook of research in second language teaching and learning* (pp. 713–728). Mahwah, NJ: Lawrence Erlbaum Associates.

Eskey, D. (2005). Reading in a second language. In E. Hinkel (Ed.), *Handbook of research in second language teaching and learning* (pp. 563–579). Mahwah, NJ: Lawrence Erlbaum Associates.

Farkas, S., Johnson, J., & Foleno, T. (2000). *A sense of calling: Who teaches and why. A report from Public Agenda*. ERIC ED 443 815. New York: Public Agenda Foundation.

Fillmore, L.W. (1999, February). *The class of 2002: Will everyone be there?* Paper presented at the Alaska State Department of Education, Anchorage.

Fillmore, L. W., & Snow, C. (2000). *What teachers need to know about language*. Center for Applied Linguistics, ED-99-CO-0008. Prepared with funding from the U.S. Department of Education's Office of Educational Research and Improvement. Washington, DC.

Forest, J., & Pearpoint, M. (1992). Putting all kids on the MAP. *Educational Leadership, 50*(2), 26–31.

Forest, J., Pearpoint, M., & O'Brien, J. (1996). MAPs, circles of friends, and PATH: Powerful tools to help build caring communities. In S. Stainbeck & W. Stainbeck, *Inclusion: A guide for educators* (pp. 67–86). Baltimore: Brookes.

Fotos, S. (1993). Consciousness-raising and noticing through focus on form: Grammar talk performance versus formal instruction. *Applied Linguistics, 14*, 385–407.

Freeman, D., & Freeman, Y. (2004). *Essential linguistics. What you need to know to teach reading, ESL, spelling, phonics, grammar*. Portsmouth, NH. Heinemann.

Friend, M. (2005). *Special education: Contemporary perspectives for school professionals*. Boston: Pearson.

Friend, M., & Bursuck, W. D. (2009). *Including students with special needs: A practical guide for classroom teachers* (5th ed.). Upper Saddle River, NJ: Pearson.

Friend, M., & Cook, L. (2007). *Interactions: Collaboration skills for school professionals*. Boston: Allyn & Bacon.

Fry, E. (1981). Graphical literacy. *Journal of Reading, 24*, 383–389.

Fuchs, L. S. (1996). Monitoring progress among mildly handicapped pupils: Review of current practices and research. *Remedial and Special Education, 7*(5), 5–12.

Gall, M. D. (1970). The use of questions in teaching. *Review of Educational Research, 40*(5), 707–721.

Gardner, H. (1983). *Frames of mind: The theory of multiple intelligences*. New York: Basic Books.

Gardner, R., & Lambert, W. (1972). *Attitudes and motivation in second language learning*. Rowley, MA: Newbury House.

Gass, S., & Selinker, L. (2008). *Second language acquisition: An introductory course* (3rd ed.). New York: Routledge.

Giangreco, M. F. (2003). Working with paraprofessionals. *Educational Leadership, 61*(2), 50–53.

Giangreco, M. F., Edelman, S. W., Broer, S. M., Doyle, M. B. (2001). Paraprofessional support of students with disabilities: Literature from the past decade. *Exceptional Children, 68, 45–63.*

Giangreco, M. F., Edelman, S. W., Luiselli, T. E., MacFarland, S. Z. C. (1997). Helping or hovering. Effects of instructional assistant proximity of students with disabilities. *Exceptional Children, 64, 7–18.*

Gibbons, P. (2002). *Scaffolding language, scaffolding learning.* Portsmouth, NH: Heinemann.

Government Accountability Office (GAO). (July, 2006). *Report to Congressional requesters: No Child Left Behind Act: Assistance from education could help states better measure progress of students with limited English proficiency.* GAO-06–815. Retrieved December 2006. (Updated August 2006.) Available from http://www.gao.gov/

Graham, S., & Harris, K. (2005). *Writing better: Effective strategies for teaching students with learning difficulties.* Baltimore: Brookes.

Grassi, E. (2003). *Service learning: An innovative approach to instruction for second language learners.* Unpublished dissertation, University of Colorado at Boulder.

Graves, M., Juel, C., & Graves, B. (1998). *Teaching reading in the 21st century.* Boston: Allyn & Bacon.

Gregorc, A. (1982). *An adult's guide to style.* Maynard, MA: Gabriel Systems.

Gunning, T. G. (2007). *Creating literacy instruction for all students.* Boston: Pearson.

Hall, J. K., & Walsh, M. (2002). Teacher-student interaction and learning. *Annual Review of Applied Linguistics, 22, 186–203.*

Hall, T. (2002). *Differentiated instruction.* Wakefield, MA: National Center on Accessing the General Curriculum. Retrieved July 13, 2009, from http://www.cast.org/publications/ncac/ncac_diffinstruc.html

Hall, T., Strangman, N., & Meyer, A. (2003). *Differentiated instruction and implications for UDL implementation.* Wakefield, MA: National Center on Accessing the General Curriculum.

Harry, B. (1992). Restructuring the participation of African-American parents in special education. *Exceptional Children, 59, 123–131.*

Harry, B. (2002). Trends and issues in serving culturally diverse families of children with disabilities. *Journal of Special Education, 36, 131–138, 147.*

Hatch, E. (1992). *Discourse and language education.* Cambridge, UK: Cambridge University Press.

Haynes, J. (2006). *Everything ESL.net.* Retrieved January 3, 2009, from http://www.everythingesl.net/inservices/language_stages.php

Henricksen, B. (1999). Three dimensions on vocabulary development. *Studies in Second Language Development, 21*(2), 303–317.

Hoover, J., Klinger, J., Baca, L., & Patton J. (2008). *Methods for teaching culturally and linguistically diverse exceptional learners.* Columbus, OH: Pearson/Merrill Prentice Hall.

Huang, G. (1997). *Beyond culture: Communicating with Asian-American children and families.* Teacher's College, Columbia University. Retrieved February 2, 2009, from http://www.casanet.org/library/culture/communicate-asian.htm

Idol, L., Nevin, A., & Paolucci-Whitcomb, P. (2000). *Collaborative consultation.* Austin, TX: PRO-ED.

Individuals with Disabilities Education Act (IDEA). (2004). Public Law 108-446.

Isaacson, S. (2001). Written language. In P. J. Schloss, M. A. Smith, & C. N. Schloss (Eds.), *Instructional methods for secondary students with learning and behavior problems* (3rd ed., pp. 222–245). Boston: Allyn & Bacon.

Jenkins, J. (2000). *The phonology of English as an international language.* Oxford: Oxford University Press.

Johnson, D. W., & Johnson, R. T. (1984). Building acceptance of differences between handicapped and nonhandicapped students: The effects of cooperative and individualistic instruction. *Journal of Social Psychology, 122,* 257–267.

Johnson, D. W., & Johnson, R. T. (1989). *Cooperation and competition: Theory and research.* Edina, MN: Interaction Books.

Johnson, D. W., & Johnson, R. T. (1999). Making cooperative learning work. *Theory into Practice, 38,* 67–73.

Johnson, D. W., Johnson-Holubec, E., & Johnson, R. T. (1984). *Circles of learning.* Alexandria, VA: Association for Supervision and Curriculum Development.

Kachru, Y. (2005). Teaching and learning of world Englishes. In E. Hinkel (Ed.), *Handbook of research in second language teaching and learning* (pp. 155–173). Mahwah, NJ: Lawrence Erlbaum Associates.

Kame'enui, E. J., Carnine, D. W., Dixon, R. C., Simmons, D. C., & Coyne, M. D. (2002). *Effective strategies that accommodate diverse learners.* Upper Saddle River, NJ: Merrill Prentice Hall.

Kasper, G., & Roever, C. (2005). Pragmatics in second language learning. In E. Hinkel (Ed.), *Handbook of research in second language teaching and learning* (pp. 317–334). Mahwah, NJ: Lawrence Erlbaum Associates.

Kindler, A. L. (2002). *Survey of the states limited english proficient students and available educational programs and services, 2000–2001 summary report.* Prepared for OELA by National Clearinghouse of English Language Acquisition & Language Instruction Educational Programs, Washington, DC.

Krashen, S. (1981). *Second language acquisition and second language learning.* Oxford: Pergamon.

Krashen, S. (1982). *Principles and practice in second language acquisition.* Oxford: Pergamon.

Krashen, S. (1985). *The input hypothesis.* London: Longman.

Kunnan, A. J. (2005). Language assessment from a wider context. In E. Hinkel (Ed.), *Handbook of research in second language teaching and learning* (pp. 779–794). Mahwah, NJ: Lawrence Erlbaum Associates.

Ladson-Billings, G. (1994). *The dreamkeepers: Successful teachers of African American children.* San Francisco: Jossey-Bass.

Lamb, M. (2004). Integrative motivation in a globalizing world. *System, 32,* 3–19.

Lantolf, J. (2005). Sociocultural and second language learning research: An exegesis. In E. Hinkel (Ed.), *Handbook of research in second language teaching and learning* (pp. 335–353). Mahwah, NJ: Lawrence Erlbaum Associates.

Learning Point Associates. (2004). *A closer look at the five essential components of effective reading instruction: A review of scientifically based reading research for teachers*. Report prepared with funds from the U.S. Department of Education under contract number ED-01-CO-0046/0001.

Leki, I. (1992). *Understanding ESL writers. A guide for teachers*. Portsmouth, NH: Heinemann.

Lerner, J. (2006). *Learning disabilities: Theories, diagnosis, and teaching strategies* (10th ed.). Boston: Houghton Mifflin.

Lightbown, P. (1983). Exploring relationships between developmental and instructional sequences in L2 acquisition. In H. Seliger & M. H. Long (Eds.), *Classroom oriented research in second language acquisition* (pp. 217–243). Rowley, MA: Newbury House.

Lightbown, P. (1985). Great expectations: Second language acquisition research and classroom teaching. *Applied Linguistics, 6,* 173–189.

Lightbown, P., & Spada, N. (1999). *How languages are learned* (2nd ed.). Oxford and New York: Oxford University Press.

Long, M. H. (1983). Native speaker/nonnative speaker conversation and the negotiation of comprehensible input. *Applied Linguistics, 4,* 126–141.

Long, M. H. (1996). The role of the linguistic environment in second language acquisition. In W. Ritchie & T. Bhatia (Eds.), *Handbook of second language acquisition* (pp. 413–468). San Diego: Academic Press.

Long, M. H. (2003). Stabilization and fossilization in interlanguage development. In C. Doughty & M. Long (Eds.). *The handbook of second language acquisition* (pp. 487–535). Malden, MA: Blackwell.

Macswan, J., & Rolstad, K. (2006). How language proficiency tests mislead us about ability: Implications for English language learner placement in special education. *Teachers College Record, 108*(11), 2304–2328.

Mandler, J., & Johnson, N. (1977). Remembrance of things parsed: story structure and recall. *Cognitive Psychology, 9,* 111–151.

Marston, D., Reschly, A., Lau, M., Muyskens, P., Canter, A. (2007). Historical perspectives and current trends in problem solving. In D. Haager, J. Klingner, S. Vaughn (Eds.), *Evidence-based reading practices for response to intervention*. Baltimore: Brookes.

Marzano, R. J., (2004). *Building background knowledge for academic achievement*. Alexandria, VA: Association for Supervision and Curriculum Development.

Marzano, R. J., Pickering, D. J., & Pollock, J. E. (2001). *Classroom instruction that works: Research-based strategies for increasing student achievement*. Alexandria, VA: Association for Supervision and Curriculum Development.

Massey, D. D., & Heafner, T. L. (2004). Promoting reading comprehension and social studies. *Journal of Adolescent and Adult Literacy, 48*(1), 26–40.

McCardle, P., Mele-McCarthy, J., Cutting, L., Leos, K., D'Emilio, T. (2005). Learning disabilities in English language learners: Identifying the issues. *Learning Disabilities Research & Practice, 20*(1), 1–5.

McCardle, P., Mele-McCarthy, J., & Leos, K. (2005). English language learners and learning disabilities: Research agenda and implications for practice. *Learning Disabilities Research & Practice, 20*(1), 68–78.

McGregor, G., & Vogelsberg, R. T. (1998). *Inclusive schooling practices: Pedagogical and research foundations, a synthesis of the literature that informs best practices about inclusive schooling.* Baltimore: Brookes.

McIntosh, P. (1990). White privilege: Unpacking the invisible knapsack. *Independent School, 49*(2), 31–35.

McLaughlin, B. (1990a). "Conscious" versus "unconscious" learning. *TESOL Quarterly, 24*, 617–634.

McLaughlin, B. (1990b). Restructuring. *Applied Linguistics, 11*, 113–128.

Mercer, C. D., & Pullan, P. C. (2005). *Students with learning disabilities* (6th ed.). Upper Saddle River, NJ: Pearson.

Moats, L. C. (2000). *Speech to print, language essentials for teachers.* Baltimore: Brookes.

Modern Language Association. (2006). *The MLA language map data center.* Retrieved September 15, 2006, from http://www.mla.org

Myers, C., & Bieber, B. (2007, January 19). *LD eligibility criteria and the role of RTI.* Paper presented at Courage to Risk: Nineteenth Collaborative Conference for Special Education.

Nagy, W., & Scott, J. (2000). Vocabulary processes. In M. Kamil, P. Mosenthal, P. Pearson, & R. Barr (Eds.), *Handbook of reading research* (Vol. 3, pp. 269–284). Mahwah, NJ: Lawrence Erlbaum Associates.

Nassaji, H. (2007). Elicitation and reformulation and their relationship with learner repair in dyadic interaction. *Language Learning, 57*(4), 511–548.

Nassaji, H., & Wells, G. (2000). What's the use of "traidic dialogue"? An investigation of teacher-student interaction. *Applied Linguistics, 21*, 376–406.

Nation, I. S. P. (2005). Teaching and learning vocabulary. In E. Hinkel (Ed.), *Handbook of research in second language teaching and learning* (pp. 581–596). Mahwah, NJ: Lawrence Erlbaum Associates.

National Center for Education Statistics (2002). *The condition of education, 2002.* Retrieved May 9, 2005, from http://nces.ed.gov/pubs2002/2002025.pdf

National Center for Education Statistics (2006). *The condition of education, 2006* (NCES 2006–071). Washington, DC: U.S. Department of Education.

National Clearinghouse for English Language Acquisition and Language Instruction Education Programs (NCELA). (2006). *The growing numbers of limited English proficient students, 1995/96–2005/06.* Retrieved September 1, 2006, from http://www.ncela.gwu.edu/expert/faq/25_tests.htm

National Institute of Child Health and Human Development (NICHD). (2000). *Report of the National Reading Panel. Teaching children to read: An evidence-based assessment of the scientific research literature on reading and its implications for instruction. Reports of the subgroup.* (NIH Publication No. 00-4754). Washington, DC: U.S. government Printing Office. Also available online: http://www.nichd.nih.gov/publications/nrp/report.htm

National Reading Panel. (2000). *Teaching children to read: An evidence-based assessment of the scientific research literature on reading and its implications for reading instruction.* Washington, DC: National Institute of Child Health and Human Development.

Nieto, S., & Bode, P. (2008). *Affirming diversity: The sociopolitical context of multicultural education.* Boston: Pearson.

No Child Left Behind Act of 2001 (NCLB). Public Law 107-110, 115 Stat. 1425, 20 U.S.C.

Noddings, N. (1995). A morally defensible mission for schools in the 21st century. *Phi Delta Kappan, 76*(5), 365–368.

Norris, J., & Ortega, L. (2000). Effectiveness of L2 instruction: a research synthesis and quantitative meta-analysis. *Language Learning, 50,* 417–528.

Office of Special Education and Rehabilitation Services (OSERS). (2003). *25th annual report to Congress on the implementation of the Individuals with Disabilities Education Act.* Washington, DC: U.S. Department of Education.

Office of Special Education Programs (OSEP). (2003). *25th annual report to Congress on the implementation of the Individuals with Disabilities Education Act.* Washington, DC: U.S. Department of Education.

Orkwis, R., & McLane, K. (1998). *A curriculum every teacher can use: Design principles for student access.* Topical Brief-ERIC/OSEP. ERIC Clearinghouse on Disabilities and Gifted Education.

Ortiz, A. A. (1997). Learning disabilities occurring concomitantly with linguistic differences. *Journal of Learning Disabilities, 30,* 321–332.

Ovando, C. J. (2003). Bilingual education in the United States: Historical development and current issues. *Bilingual Research Journal, 27*(1). Retrieved May 5, 2009, from http://brj.asu.edu/content/v0127_n01/documents/art1.pdf

Pearson, V. L. (1988). Words and rituals establish group membership. *Teaching Exceptional Children, 21*(1), 52–53.

Peregoy, S., & Boyle, O. (2005). *Reading, writing, and learning in ESL* (4th ed.). New York: Pearson.

Pica, T. (1994) Research on negotiation: What does it reveal about second language acquisition? *Language Learning, 44,* 493–527.

Pica, T., Holliday, L., Lewis, N., & Morgenthaler, L. (1989). Comprehensible output as an outcome of linguistic demands on the learner. *Studies in Second Language Acquisition, 11,* 63–90.

Pollard-Durodola, S., Mathes, P. G., Vaughn, S., Cardenas-Hagen, E., & Linan-Thompson, S. (2006). The role of oracy in developing comprehension in Spanish-speaking English language learners. *Topics in Language Disorders, 26*(4), 365–384.

Popham, W. J. (2007). *Classroom assessment: What teachers need to know.* Boston: Pearson.

Pressley, M. (2008). Comprehension instruction: What makes sense now, what might make sense soon. Retrieved June 11, 2008, from http://www.readingonline.org/articles/handbook/pressley/

Reed, B., & Railsback, J. (2003). Strategies and resources for mainstream teachers of English language learners. Northwest Regional Educational Laboratory. Retrieved January 2, 2009, from http://www.nwrel.org/request/2003may/textonly.html

Rolstad, K., Mahoney, K., & Glass, G. (2005). The big picture: A meta-analysis of program effectiveness research on English language learners. *Educational Policy, 19*(4), 572–594.

Rost, M. (2005). L2 listening. In E. Hinkel (Ed.), *Handbook of research in second language teaching and learning* (pp. 503–527). Mahwah, NJ: Lawrence Erlbaum Associates.

Rost, M., & Ross, S. (1991). Learner use of strategies in interaction: typology and teachability. *Language Learning, 41,* 235–73.

Sands, D., & Barker, H. (2004). Organized chaos: Modeling differentiated instruction for preservice teachers. *Teaching and Learning: The Journal of Natural Inquiry and Reflective Practice, 19*(1), 26–49.

Sands, D., Kozleski, E. B., & French, N. K. (2000). *Inclusive education for the 21st century: A new introduction to special education.* Belmont, CA: Wadsworth.

Saracho, O. N., & Spodek, B. (2007). Oracy: Social facets of language learning. *Early Childhood Development and Care, 177*(6–7), 695–705.

Scarcella, R. (n.d.). *Balancing approaches to English language instruction.* Unpublished manuscript.

Schaffner, C. B., & Buswell, B. E. (1996). Ten critical elements for creating inclusive and effective school communities. In S. Stainback & W. Stainback, *Inclusion: A guide for educators* (pp. 49–65). Baltimore: Brookes.

Schmidt, N. (2000). *Vocabulary in language teaching.* Cambridge, UK: Cambridge University Press.

Schmidt, R. W. (1990). The role of consciousness in second language learning. *Applied Linguistics, 11*(2), 129–158.

Schumann, J. (1976a). Second language acquisition: The pidginization hypothesis. *Language Learning, 26,* 391–408.

Schumann, J. (1976b). Social distance as a factor in second language acquisition. *Language Learning, 26,* 135–143.

Schumann, J. (1978). *The pidginization process: A model for second language acquisition.* Rowley, MA: Newbury House.

Schumm, J. S., Vaughn, S., Leavell, A. (1994). Planning pyramid: A framework for planning for diverse student needs during content area instruction. *The Reading Teacher, 47*(8), 608–614.

Scovel, T. (1988). *A time to speak: A psycholinguistic inquiry into the critical period for human speech.* New York: Newbury House.

Selinker, L. (1972). Interlanguage. *International Review of Applied Linguistics, 10*(2), 209–231.

Sharwood Smith, M. (1991). Speaking to many minds: On the relevance of different types of language information for the L2 learner. *Second Language Research, 72,* 118–132.

Sheets, R. H. (2005). *Diversity pedagogy: Examining the role of culture in the teaching-learning process.* Boston: Pearson Allyn & Bacon.

Short, D., & Echevarria, J. (1999). *The sheltered instruction observation protocol: A tool for teacher-research collaboration and professional development.* Report prepared for CREDE, Santa Cruz, CA.

Smith, E. C., Polloway, E. A., Patton, J. R., & Dowdy, C. A. (2007). *Teaching students with special needs in inclusive settings.* Boston: Pearson.

Sowden, C. (2005). Plagiarism and the culture of multilingual students in higher education abroad. *ELT Journal 59*(3), 226–233.

Sternberg, R. (1996). *Successful intelligence: How practical and creative intelligence determine success in life*. New York: Simon and Schuster.

Swain, M. (2005). The output hypothesis: Theory and research. In E. Hinkel (Ed.), *Handbook of research in second language teaching and learning* (pp. 471–483). Mahwah, NJ: Lawrence Erlbaum Associates.

Swain, M., & Lapkin, S. (1995). Problems in output and the cognitive process they generate: A step towards second language learning. *Applied Linguistics, 16*, 371–391.

Swan, M., & Smith, B. (Eds.). (2006). *Learner English: A teacher's guide to interference and other problems* (2nd ed.). Cambridge, UK: Cambridge University Press.

Swanborn, M. S. L., & de Glopper, K. (1999). Incidental word learning while reading: A meta-analysis. *Review of Educational Research, 69*(3), 261–285.

Tarone, E. (2005). Speaking in a second language. In E. Hinkel (ed.), *Handbook of research in second language teaching and learning* (pp. 485–502). Mahwah, NJ: Lawrence Erlbaum Associates.

Taylor, L. S., & Whittaker, C. R. (2003). *Bridging multiple worlds: Case studies of diverse educational communities*. Boston: Allyn & Bacon.

Texas Education Agency, Division of Special Education. (2000). *Coordinating for reading instruction: General education and special education working together*. Austin, TX: Special Education Reading Project.

Tharp, R. (2004). Only teachers using diversity pedagogy can be "highly qualified." *Talking Leaves, 8*(1), 1, 7.

Thomas, W. P., & Collier, V. P. (2002). *A national study of school effectiveness for language minority students' long-term academic achievement*. Center for Research in Education, Diversity, and Excellence. Santa Cruz: CA. Office of Educational Research and Improvement, Washington DC.

Thornbury, S. (2007). *How to teach grammar*. Essex, UK: Pearson-Longman.

Tomlinson, C. A. (1995). *How to differentiate in mixed-ability classrooms*. Alexandria, VA: Association for Supervision and Curriculum Development.

Tomlinson, C. A. (1999). *The differentiated classroom: Responding to the needs of all learners*. Alexandria, VA: Association for Supervision and Curriculum Development.

Tomlinson, C. A. (2000). Reconcilable differences? Standards-based teaching and differentiation. *Educational Leadership, 58*(1), 6–11.

Tomlinson, C. A., & McTighe, J. (2006). *Integrating differentiated instruction and understanding by design*. Alexandria, VA: Association for Supervision and Curriculum Development.

Trueba, H. T. (1988). English literacy acquisition: From cultural trauma to learning disabilities in minority students. *Linguistics and Education, 1*, 125–152.

Tuitt, F. (2003). Afterword: Realizing a more inclusive pedagogy. In A. Howell & F. Tuitt (Eds.), *Race and higher education: Rethinking pedagogy in diverse college classrooms* (pp. 243–268). Cambridge, MA: Harvard Graduate School of Education.

Turnbull, A., & Turnbull, R. (2001). *Families, professionals, and exceptionality: Collaborating for empowerment* (4th ed.). Upper Saddle River, NJ: Merrill/Prentice Hall.

University of Colorado at Denver. (2003). *Initial and professional teacher education program internship handbook*. Unpublished handbook.

U.S. Census Bureau. (2000). *Table 4: Difference in population by race and Hispanic or Latino origin, for the United States: 1990 and 2000* (Census 2000 PHC-T-1). Available from http://www.census.gov/population/cen2000/phc-t1/tab04.pdf

U.S. Census Bureau. (2006). *International data base*. Available from www.census.gov/ipc/www/idbnew.html

U.S. Census Bureau. (2008). *Statistical abstract of the United States: 2008*. Available at http://www.census.gov/prod/2007pubs/08abstract/educ.pdf

U.S. Department of Education (1993). *15th annual report to Congress on the implementation of IDEA*. Washington, DC: Author.

U.S. Department of Education. (2006). *Office for Civil Rights, Programs for English Language Learners*. Retrieved December 28, 2006, from http://ggsc.wnmu.edu/netc/synopsis/glossary.html#language%20proficiency. [chapter 4]

U.S. Department of Education, & National Institute of Child Health and Human Development. (2000). Washington, DC: Authors.

U.S. Department of Education, National Center for Educational Statistics (2002). *Schools and staffing survey, 1999–2000: Overview of the data for public, private, public charter, and Bureau of Indian Affairs elementary and secondary schools* (NCES 2002-313). Washington, DC: Author. Table 1.19, pp. 43–44. Available: http:nces.ed.gov/pub search/pubsinfo.asp?pubid=2002313.

U.S. Department of Education, & National Institute of Child Health and Human Development. (2003). *National symposium on learning disabilities in English language learners. Symposium summary*. Washington, DC: Author.

Valdés, G. (2003). *Expanding definitions of giftedness. The case of young interpreters from immigrant communities*. Mahwah, NJ: Lawrence Erlbaum Associates.

Valdés, G., & Figueroa, R. (1994). *Bilingualism and testing. A special case of bias*. Norwood, NJ: Ablex.

Van den Broek, P., & Kremer, K. (2000). The mind in action: What it means to comprehend. In B. Taylor, M. Graves, & P. Van den Broek (Eds.), *Reading for meaning: Fostering comprehension in the middle grades* (pp. 1–31). New York: Teachers College, Columbia University.

VanPatten, B. (1984). Processing strategies and morpheme acquisition. In F. R. Eckman, L. H. Bell, & D. Nelson (Eds.), *Universals of second language acquisition*. Rowley, MA: Newbury House.

Vaughn, S., Schumm, J., & Arguelles, M. E. (1997). The ABCDEs of co-teaching. *Teaching Exceptional Children, 30*(2), 4–10.

Vaughn, S., Wanzek, J., Woodruff, A. L., & Linan-Thompson, S. (2007). Prevention and early identification of students with reading disabilities. In D. Haager, J. Klingner, & S. Vaughn, *Evidence-based reading practices for response to intervention*. Baltimore: Brookes.

Verplaetse, L. S. (1998). How content teachers interact with English language learners. *TESOL, 7*(5), 24–28.

Villa, R., & Thousand, J. (1992). Student collaboration: An essential for curriculum delivery in the 21st century. In S. Stainbeck & W. Stainbeck (Eds.), *Curriculum considerations in inclusive classrooms: Facilitating learning for all students* (pp. 117–142). Baltimore: Brookes.

Wagner, R. K., Francis, D. J., Morris, R. D. (2005). Identifying English language learners with learning disabilities: Key challenges and possible approaches. *Learning Disabilities Research & Practice, 20*(1), 6–15.

Walther-Thomas, C., Bryant, M., & Land, S. (1996). Planning for effective co-teaching: The key to successful inclusion. *Remedial and Special Education, 17*(4), 255–264.

Wehby, J. H., Symons, F. J., & Canale, J. A. (1998). Teaching practices in classrooms for students with emotional and behavioral disorders: Discrepancies between recommendations and observations. *Behavioral Disorders, 24*(1), 51–56.

Wei, L. (2000). Unequal election of morphemes in adult second language acquisition. *Applied Linguistics, 21*(1), 106–140.

Wells, G. (1993). Reevaluating the IRF sequence: A proposal for the articulation of theories of activity and discourse for the analysis of teaching and learning in the classroom. *Linguistics and Education, 5,* 1–17.

Wiese, A. M., & Garcia, E. (1998, Winter). The Bilingual Education Act: Language minority students and equal educational opportunity. *The Bilingual Research Journal.* Retrieved May 5, 2009, from http://findarticles.com/p/articles/mi_qa3722/is_199801/ai_n8762946/?tag=content;c011

Wiggins, G., & McTighe, J. (1998). *Understanding by design.* Alexandria, VA: Association for Supervision and Curriculum Development.

Williams, J. (2005). Form-focused instruction. In E. Hinkel (Ed.), *Handbook of research in second language teaching and learning* (pp. 671–691). Mahwah, NJ: Lawrence Erlbaum Associates.

Wlodkowski, R. J., & Ginsberg, M. B. (1995). *Diversity and motivation: Culturally responsive teaching.* San Francisco: Jossey-Bass.

Woolfolk, A. (2007). *Educational psychology.* Boston: Allyn & Bacon.

Wright, W. D. P., & Wright, P. D. (2007). *Special education law* (2nd ed.). Harbor House Law Press: Hartfield, VA.

Yell, M. L. (1998). *The law and special education.* Upper Saddle River, NJ: Merrill.

Zehler, A. M., Fleischman, H. L., Hopstock, P. J., Pendzick, M. L., & Stephenson, T. G. (2003). *Descriptive study of services to LEP students and LEP students with disabilities* (No. 4 Special topic report: Findings on special education LEP students). Arlington, VA: Development Associates, Inc.

Zehler, A. M., Fleischman, H. L., Hopstock, P. J., Stephenson, T. G., Pendzick, M. L., & Sapru, S. (2003). *Descriptive study of services to LEP students and LEP students with disabilities* (Contract No. ED-00-CO-0089). Policy Report: Summary of Findings Related to LEP and SPED-LEP students. Report prepared for U.S. Department of Education, Office of English Language Acquisition (OELA), Language Enhancement, and Academic Achievement of Limited English Proficient Students.

Index

Note: In page references, p indicates photos, f indicates figures and t indicates tables.

Abedi, J., 5, 117
Abu-Akhel, A., 218
Academic achievements:
  classroom environments and, 197
  eligibility for special education
    and, 128
  IEP meetings and, 127
  input hypothesis and, 65p
  language acquisitions and, 211
  laws and, 8, 18
  program options and, 15
  testing and, 77, 117, 128–129
Academically gifted students, 133–135,
  147–148, 181
Academic skills:
  CALPS and, 79
  CLDE student eligibility process
    and, 122
  labels and, 114
  L1/L2 and, 67–68
  See also Skills
Academic success:
  differentiation and, 167, 171,
    172–173
  discourse competence and, 90
  family involvement and, 33–34
  group work and, 239
  organizing/accessing information and,
    223, 224, 225–226
  RTI and, 131
  See also Success

Accommodations, 19t, 20t, 142, 237, 349
Accountability, xxii–xxiii
Acculturation, 69–70
  cultural acquisition and, 98
  multidisciplinary evaluations and, 124
Acquisition. See Cultural acquisition;
  Language acquisition; Second
  Language Acquisition (SLA)
Acquisition vs. learning hypothesis,
  66, 349
Adequate Yearly Progress (AYP),
  115, 158, 349
Administrators, 145, 148
Affective filter hypothesis, 59, 63–64,
  234, 349
African Americans, 7, 40
Age issues:
  bias and, 124–125
  grammatical competence and, 85
Alaska Native students, 6–7
Aldridge, J., 280
Al-Hassan, S., 34, 123, 124, 126
Ambiguity, 216, 259
American Indian students, 6–7
Andrews, J. D., 206
Anger, 40, 96
Anxiety:
  cultural acquisition and, 97
  feedback and, 260
  language errors and, 258
  participation and, 234

Appreciation, 160, 237

Arguelles, M. E., 154

Arizona, 10

Arragon, L., 158

Artiles, A. J., 5, 16

Asian Americans, 40

Assessment/instruction cycle, 165

Assessments:
 BICS/CALPS and, 80t
 CLDE student eligibility process
  and, 119
 English language and, 115
 goals of, 111
 GT students and, 134–135
 intervention teams and, 122
 language proficiency and, 77
 NCLB and, 115–116
 planning and, 166
 reclassification of ELLs and, 118
 study skills and, 225
 See also Testing

Assimilation:
 cultural acquisition and, 97
 programs and, 14f, 15–16
 social distance and, 70t

Attention issues, 227, 251

August, D., 68, 275, 276, 277, 280, 301

Autism, xviii, 16, 19t, 113t

Baca, L., 117, 181

Bachman, L., 105n 1

Background knowledge, 285–288,
  293, 349
 error correction and, 338
 reading strategies and, 289
 special education and, 219–220
 writing skills and,
  302, 303–304, 308
 See also Prior knowledge

Backsliding, 57, 247, 349

Backward design model, 178–179, 179t,
  186, 213–214, 349

Baker, C., 13, 16

Banks, J. A., 189, 190, 196, 234

Barbe, W. B., 209

Barker, H., 165

Barules, N., 195

Basic Interpersonal Communication Skills
  (BICS), 78–80, 104, 274, 333, 350
 assessing, 80t
 characteristics of, 78t
 language proficiency and, 77
 tools for assessing, 80t
 See also Communication

Bass, J., 296n

Beck, I., 280

Behavioral issues:
 classroom environments and, 192
 FBA and, 132–133
 GT students and, 135
 IEP and, 320
 paraprofessionals and, 159, 160
 team teaching and, 154–155
 vocabulary development and, 276
 writing skills and, 299

Beliefs, 197

Bernal, C., 158

Bevan-Brown, J., xviii

Bias:
 classroom environments and, 193, 197
 cultural, 117, 350
 eligibility for special education and,
  129
 GT students and, 134–135
 multidisciplinary evaluations and,
  124–125

Bicultural issues:
 cultural acquisition and, 97
 GT students and, 135
 laws and, 9
 placement options and, 23
 program options and, 14–15

Bieber, B., 181, 183

Bilingual Education Act (BEA), 8, 9, 10

Bilingual issues, 152, 153
 CALPS and, 80
 cultural acquisition and, 98
 differentiation and, 169–170
 discourse competence and, 91
 GT students and, 135
 intervention teams and, 122
 laws and, 8–13, 9
 NCLB and, 10
 paraprofessionals and, 160

placement options and, 23, 23t
program options and, 14–15
RTI and, 130
specialist and, 121, 141, 148
Bilingual maintenance program, 11t, 12t, 14–15, 350
Biliteracy:
laws and, 9
program options and, 14–15
Bismilla, V., 87
Black students, 7, 40
Bode, P., 234
Boyle,O., 280, 302, 337, 341, 388
Brett, A., 280
Broer, S. M., 159
Brown, H. D.:
backsliding and, 57
feedback and, 261
grammar and, 323
grammatical competence and, 86
grammatical forms and, 323
interlanguage and, 52, 58
language errors and, 257, 258, 259
sociolinguistic competence and, 95
U-shaped learning and, 57
Brown-Chidsey, R., 128
Bryant, M., 154
Bureaucracies, 111
Bursuck, W. D., 20, 249, 299, 320
Burt, M., 53, 56, 59, 73n
Buswell, B. E., 236, 237

California, 9–10, 12t
Canale, J. A., 235
Canale, M., 77, 80, 81, 245, 261
Canter, A., 180
Cardenas-Hagen, E., 280
Caregivers:
CLDE student eligibility process and, 122–123
GT students and, 135
IEP meetings and, 126
intervention teams and, 122
Carnine, D. W., 204
Carrol, C., 158
Cartledge, G., 34, 40, 41, 42, 43, 126, 134, 135, 192

Casteneda v. Pickard, 9
Center for Applied Special Technology (CAST), 176
Cervantes, H. T., 117
Chamot, A. U., 302, 304, 307
Chaudron, C., 206
Choice:
classroom environments and, 190
classroom management and, 184
differentiation and, 167
participation and, 237
teaching, 321
Chopra, R. V., 158
Chow, P., 87
Churches, 38, 70t, 100
Civil rights, xvi–xvii, 16, 114
Civil Rights Act of 1964, 8
Clark, B., 134
Classroom environments.
See Environments
Coaching, 131
Cognitive Academic Language Proficiency Skills (CALPS), 78–80, 104, 350
assessing, 80t
characteristics of, 78t
discourse competence and, 89–90
GT students and, 135
language proficiency and, 77
Cohen, S., 87
Collaboration, 141, 142–143, 145p, 145t, 350
CLDE student eligibility process and, 119
IEP meetings and, 126
paraprofessionals and, 159
teachers and, xxii
tips for, 145–146, 145–146t
See also Co-teaching
Collier, C., 104
Collier, V. P., 15
Communication, 104
behavioral issues and, 132
classroom environments and, 195

collaboration and, 143, 144
cultural acquisition and, 98
differentiation and, 176–177
error correction and, 340–341
family involvement and, 41, 42
feedback and, 260
grammar instruction and, 267
grammatical competence and, 81.
    See also Grammatical competence
group work and, 244
language errors and, 259
language proficiency and, 77
MAPs and, 43, 44
paraprofessionals and, 160
participation and, 249, 250, 251
strategic competence and, 100–103
teachers and, xxii
team teaching and, 154, 155
trusting relationships and, 38
vocabulary development and, 276
writing skills and, 299, 306
See also Basic Interpersonal
    Communication Skills (BICS)
Communicative competence, 77, 80–81,
    81t, 104, 105n 1
Community centers, 38, 100, 304
Compensatory strategies, 100–101, 135
Comprehensible input, 64–66, 209,
    245, 350
Comprehension, 283–284, 293, 350
    background knowledge and, 220,
        286–287
    collaboration and, 143
    differentiation and, 171
    ELL students and, 206–207
    fluency and, 276
    genre and, 307
    group work and, 239, 243–244
    IEP meetings and, 126
    input hypothesis and, 64, 65–66
    key concepts and, 211, 214
    language acquisition and, 211
    language study and, 284
    literacy instruction and, 278
    note taking and, 223
    oral language proficiency and,
        277, 280–281

participation and, 250
repetition and, 211–212
special education issues and, 216
success and, 209
team teaching and, 152–153
3-way model and, 205, 229, 265,
    283, 345
time for L1 grouping and, 221
visual context and, 208
vocabulary development and,
    276, 280, 282
Concepts:
    background knowledge and, 287
    CALPS and, 79–80
    comprehension and, 284
    differentiation and, 176
    input hypothesis and, 66
    key, 213–214
    participation and, 237
    planning and, 165
    visual context and, 208
Concept webbing, 218
Concurrent translation, 160–161,
    221, 350
    See also Translations
Conferences, 35
Confidence, 193, 260
Conflict resolution, 144
Content, 350
    background knowledge and, 219
    classroom environments and, 196–197
    differentiation and, 172–175, 176
    instructional planning pyramid
        and, 183
    participation and, 249
    time for L1 grouping and, 221
    vocabulary development and, 282
Content schemas, 217–218, 287, 350
Continuum of services, 21, 21f, 350
Conversations:
    BICS/CALPS and, 79
    discourse competence and, 89–90
    feedback and, 261, 262
    group work and, 239
    language errors and, 258
    planning and, 166
    strategic competence and, 100

Cook, L., 142, 147, 148, 154, 159
Copeland, S. R., 292, 336, 339
Co-planning, 144–145, 155
   See also Planning
Cordón, L. A., 289
Co-teaching, 147, 350
   collaboration and, 144–145, 146–148
   models of, 148–157, 155–157t
   paraprofessionals and, 160
Counseling, 18t, 98
Court, D., 236
Coyne, M. D., 204
Crawford, J., 10, 13
Cultural acquisition, 26, 94, 350
   CLDE student eligibility process
      and, 121
   RTI and, 131
   stages of, 95–97, 95f
   team teaching and, 152–153
Cultural bias, 117, 350
   See also Bias
Cultural brokers:
   CLDE student eligibility process
      and, 121
   collaboration and, 142
   cultural acquisition and, 98
   GT students and, 135
   IEP meetings and, 126
Cultural discontinuities, 39–42, 351
Cultural displays, 192–193
Cultural liaisons, 99t, 151
   CLDE student eligibility process
      and, 123
   collaboration and, 143, 144
   cultural acquisition and, 98, 100
   family involvement and, 40–41
   GT students and, 135
   home visits and, 35
   IEP meetings and, 126
   intervention teams and, 122
   MAPs and, 43
   multidisciplinary evaluations and, 124
   RTI and, 131–132
Culturally and Linguistically Diverse
     (CLD) families, 33–34
Culturally relevant teaching, 19, 161,
   189, 196, 237

Culturally responsive teaching, 151, 189,
   196, 197
Cultural mismatches, 35, 97, 351
Cultural relevancy, 285–286, 310,
   311t, 316
Cultural schema, 217–218, 225,
   287, 350
Culture:
   background knowledge and, 287
   behavioral issues and, 132
   classroom environments and, 190, 197
   home visits and, 34–35
   literacy instruction and, 277
   making the content relevant to,
      172–173
   multidisciplinary evaluations and, 124
   participation and, 235, 250
   planning and, 165
   public education and, 188
   school, 144–146
   school meetings and, 38–39
   sociolinguistic competence and, 93
   translations and, 38
   United States and, 43, 218
   writing skills and, 330–333
Culture shock:
   behavioral issues and, 132
   CLDE student eligibility process
      and, 121
   multidisciplinary evaluations and, 124
Cummins, J., 67, 77, 78, 87
Curriculum:
   background knowledge and,
      218, 219–220
   CLDE students and, 23–24, 120
   collaboration and, 141
   co-teaching and, 147
   differentiation and, 167, 169, 171, 176
   group work and, 243
   instructional planning pyramid
      and, 183
   laws and, 8
   participation and, 235, 237, 250
   planning and, 165
   reading and, 289, 293
   RTI and, 129
   scaffolding and, 168

school meetings and, 39
teacher training and, 26
writing skills and, 301–302
Cutting, L., 5

Daniels, V. I., 158
Data:
  behavioral issues and, 132
  CLDE student eligibility process and, 119, 122
  co-teaching and, 148, 149, 150
  cultural acquisition and, 99t
  discourse competence and, 92t
  error analysis and, 263
  family stories and, 42
  grammatical competence and, 87–88t
  IEP meetings and, 127
  instruction/assessment cycle and, 111
  MAPs and, 46
  multidisciplinary evaluations and, 123
  paraprofessionals and, 159
  reclassification of ELLs and, 118
  RTI and, 129, 131
Day, J. D., 289
De Balderas, H. B., 158
Decision making:
  collaboration and, 143
  family involvement and, 41, 42
  IEP meetings and, 126
  paraprofessionals and, 158
  participation and, 237
Deductive lessons, 151, 267–268
Deep orthography, 325
Deficit system, 40, 151
De Glopper, K., 215
D'Emilio, T., 5
Democracy, 188, 190
Depression, 96, 98
Derewianka, B., 302, 304, 307
Developmental issues, 276
Dialogue, 193–194, 194t, 195–196
Differentiating Instruction (DI), 165, 351
  accessing academic information and, 226
  application of, 175t, 178t
  backward design model and, 178

planning/classroom management and, 184–185
  product and, 170–172, 172p
  UDL and, 175–177, 177t
  writing skills and, 311t
Dillon, J. T., 247
Direct translations, 38, 89t, 113t, 126, 151
  See also Translations
Disabilities:
  background knowledge and, 287
  comprehension and, 283
  emotional response to, 40
  error correction and, 339, 347
  feedback and, 260
  laws and, 16, 114 .*See also* Laws
  perceptions of, 40–41
  phonics and, 276
  reading and, 276, 277
  spelling and, 327–328
  testing and, 123
  vocabulary development and, 276
  writing skills and, 300, 333
Disability categories, 6–7, 24, 113, 113t, 151
Discipline:
  classroom management and, 184–185
  paraprofessionals and, 159
  special education law and, 18t
Discourse competence, 62t, 88–92, 90p, 351
  communicative competence and, 81t
  errors/examples and, 89t
  strategies for language study and, 284
  tools for assessing, 92t
Discrepancy model, 18–19, 352
  eligibility and, 128–129
Discrimination, 8, 10t, 16, 20t
Disorders, 249, 251
Diversity:
  classroom environments and, 195, 197
  groupings and, 238–239, 239p
  participation and, 236, 237
Diversity pedagogy, 189, 352
Dixon, R. C., 204
Dockrell, J., 280
Dörnyei, Z., 100, 101

Doughty, C., 66, 86, 258
Dowdy, C. A., 236
Doyle, M. B., 159
Dropouts, 15, 96
Dual language, 358
    funding and, 9, 12t
    program options and, 14–15
Duff, P., 246
Dulay, H., 53, 56, 59, 73n
Dunn, K., 209
Dunn, R., 209
Duplass, J. A., 227
Dutro, S., 203, 204, 210, 211, 212, 213, 223, 239, 262

Echevarria, J., 203, 204, 206, 210, 211, 283
Edelman, S. W., 159
Education:
    justice and, xvi–xvii
    political will and, xviii–xix
    schools and, 111, 321–322
Educational history, 142, 276
Education and Rehabilitation Services (OSERS), 5, 6, 7, 128
Elementary and Secondary Education Act (ESEA), 8, 10t, 16
Ellis, R., 258, 267
E-mail/Internet, 223, 225, 226, 305t, 306
Embarrassment, 190, 250
Emotional issues:
    black students and, 7
    disabilities and, 6t
    evaluations and, 123
    fluency and, 276
    group work and, 240–241
    interlanguage and, 56–57
    laws and, 113t
    multidisciplinary teams and, 123
    parents and, 40
    separate schools and, 22
    teacher training and, 119
English as a Second Language (ESL), 15–16, 352
    behaviors of, 7
    bilingual teachers and, 112

CLDE student eligibility process and, 121
identification of, 3
intervention teams and, 122
laws and, 8–13
paraprofessionals and, 160
placement options and, 23t
RTI and, 130
specialists and, 141, 148, 170
strategies and, 152, 153
teacher training and, 26
team teaching and, 152–153
English language:
    front-loading and, 210
    programs and, 15–16
    as prominent world language, 85
    pronunciation and, 325
    punctuation and, 324
    rules and, 320, 321, 322, 323, 324
    spelling and, 325–330, 326t, 327t, 328t
    testing and, 117
    See also Language
English language acquisition.
    See Language acquisition
English Language Learners (ELLs), xxiv, 9–10, 10t, 85, 90, 352
    affective filter hypothesis and, 63
    assessment/classification of, 115–119, 116f, 118t
    behavioral issues and, 132
    bureaucracies and, 111
    CALPS and, 78
    CLDE student eligibility process and, 119, 121
    comprehension and, 206–207
    cultural knowledge and, 218
    demographics of, 3–5, 4f
    eligibility for special education services and, 114–119, 128
    grammatical errors and, 82–84t
    GT students and, 135
    input hypothesis and, 66
    key points and, 206–207
    laws and, 10–13t
    learning disabilities and, 7
    L1/L2 and, 68

motivation and, 69
multidisciplinary evaluations and, 124
NCLB and, 115, 117
participation and, 247t
placement and, 13–14, 14f, 24–25
reclassification of, 118t
social/psychological distance and,
    69–71
strategies for, 203–205
visual context and, 208
English language proficiency tests, 115
English submersion, 16, 352
Environments:
    comfortable, 64, 235–236, 237, 238,
        249, 257
    discourse competence and, 89
    learning risks and, 257
    participation and, 234, 251
    relationships and, 190–193
Equality, xv–xvi
Equity pedagogy, 189, 192, 352
Error correction, 257
    verbs and, 343–346, 345t, 347
    Web sites and, 347
    writing skills and, 336–347, 341t
Errors:
    discourse competence and, 89t
    input hypothesis and, 64
    interlanguage and, 52–53
    interlingual, 257, 258
    oral language and, 257
    participation and, 234
    phonological, 85t
    sociolinguistic competence and, 94–95t
    spelling and, 327t
    strategic competence and, 102t
    writing skills and, 336
Eskey, D., 275, 277, 280, 283, 284, 287,
    289, 301
ESL pull-out, 14f, 16, 23t
Ethnicity, 6t, 193
    bias and, 124–125
European Americans, 40
Evaluations:
    CLDE student eligibility process and,
        123–125
    laws and, 17t, 114

Exams. *See* Assessments; Testing
Expectations:
    group work and, 239–240
    participation and, 237, 241
    teachers and, 204
Extrinsic motivation, 69, 352
    See also Motivation

Family involvement:
    academic success and, 33–34
    classroom environments and, 197
    CLDE student eligibility process and,
        119, 122–123
    CLDE students and, 34–39
    collaboration and, 33–34,
        41, 142
    communication and, 41, 42
    cultural acquisition and, 96, 98,
        99–100
    cultural discontinuities and, 39–42
    cultural liaisons and, 40–41
    cultural perceptions of disabilities
        and, 40
    empowering, 42–46
    home visits and, 34–35
    IEP meetings and, 125–127
    intervention teams and, 122
    involvement of, 33–34, 42
    meetings and, 38, 41–42
    special education/bilingual education
        and, xxii
    team teaching and, 154
    trusting relationships and, 34–39
    See also Parent involvement
Farkas, S., 26
Federal laws, 114, 122
    See also Laws
Feedback, 268, 269
    error correction and, 338
    IRF sequence and, 246
    language errors and,
        258, 259–262, 263
    output and, 245
Field trips:
    background knowledge and, 287
    visual context and, 208
    writing skills and, 304

Figueroa, R., 77
Fillmore, L. W., 86, 204, 289, 291, 301, 322, 325
First language (L1), 116f, 352
  CALPS and, 79
  CLDE student eligibility process and, 121
  cultural acquisition and, 100
  family involvement and, 33–34
  interlanguage and, 51f, 52, 53
  justice education and, xvi–xvii
  L2 and, 67
  language acquisition and, 51
  natural order hypothesis and, 59
  school meetings and, 38
  time and, 220–222
  writing skills and, 301
Fleischman, H. L., 4, 5, 7, 24, 26
Flow charts, 224
Fluency issues, 103, 276, 352
  acquisition vs. learning hypothesis and, 66
  BICS and, 78
  CALPS and, 78
  differentiation and, 171
  grammatical competence and, 85, 86
  group work and, 242
  language acquisition and, 51
  language errors and, 258, 259
  participation and, 249
Fluent English Proficient (FEP), 60t, 116, 352
  reclassification of ELLs and, 117–119, 118t
Foleno, T., 26
Ford, D. Y., 34
Forest, J., 42
Form-focused instruction, 66, 263–264, 352
Fossilize, 274, 323, 352, 357
Fotos, S., 267
Francis, D. J., 3
Free and Appropriate Public Education (FAPE), 16, 17t, 19t, 114, 352
Freeman, D., 301, 325, 326, 328
Freeman, Y., 301, 325, 326, 328
French, N. K., 24

Friend, M., 142, 147, 148, 154, 159, 203, 235, 249, 299, 320
Front-loading, 210, 214–216, 282, 352
  comprehension and, 283
  oral language proficiency and, 282
  special education issues and, 216
  vocabulary development and, 283
  Web site and, 212
Frustration:
  classroom management and, 184–185
  comprehension and, 284
  cultural acquisition and, 96
  error correction and, 347
  organization strategies and, 224
  reading and, 215
  strategic competence and, 102, 103
  vocabulary instruction and, 280
  writing skills and, 330
Fry, E., 280
Fuchs, L. S., 149
Functional Behavior Assessment (FBA), 132–133, 133f, 133t, 352
  collaboration and, 141, 149
  Web site for, 133
Functional skills approach, 337, 353
Functional vocabulary, 338
Funding, xviii–xix
  co-teaching and, 145
  disability categories and, 113
  grants and, 8–9
  justice education and, xvii–xviii
  laws and, 8–9
  2004 reauthorization of IDEA and, 18
  translators and, 38

Gall, M. D., 247
Games:
  orthographic knowledge and, 328
  vocabulary development and, 283
  writing skills and, 304
Garcia, E., 8, 9
Gardner, H., 209
Gardner, R., III, 34, 68, 123, 124, 126
Gass, S., 52, 53, 57, 60, 93, 257, 263, 341
Gender issues, 124–125

Genre, 312t, 353
  error correction and, 345
  Web sites and, 307
  writing skills and, 301, 305, 305t,
    306–308, 309, 315, 333
Gestures:
  discourse competence and, 89–90
  input hypothesis and, 64
  strategic competence and, 101
Giampapa, F., 87
Giangreco, M. F., 159, 160
Gibbons, P., 241, 290, 292, 302, 304,
    306, 307
Gifted and Talented (GT), 133–135,
    147–148, 181
Gifted and Talented Students Education
    Act, 134
Ginsberg, M. B., 189, 195, 196
Givon, S., 236
Glass, G., 15
Global error, 260
Goals:
  children with special needs and, 40, 41
  classroom management and, 184
  collaboration and, 143
  co-teaching and, 147
  data and, 111
  feedback and, 260
  group work and, 243, 244
  IEP and, 127, 204
  instructional planning pyramid and,
    181, 183
  language acquisition and, 51
  MAPs and, 44
  participation and, 236
  perceptions of, 41
  writing skills and, 300, 338–339
Government Accountability Office
    (GAO), 117
Grading, 338
Graham, S., 299, 301, 302, 304,
    309, 323
Grammar, 212–213, 213t, 263–268
  differentiation and, 170
  errors and, 323
  front-loading and, 216
  grammatical competence and, 86

language errors and, 258–259
language study and, 285
literacy instruction and, 277
punctuation and, 324
spelling and, 325–330, 326t, 328t, 337t
Web sites and, 268, 269
Grammar points, 324
  error correction and, 345
  input hypothesis and, 64
  interlanguage and, 52, 58
  language study and, 285
Grammar rules:
  error correction and, 340–341
  interlanguage and, 53
  language acquisition and, 263–264, 264p
  language errors and, 258
  See also Rules
Grammar structures, 260, 290
Grammatical code, 68
Grammatical competence, 81–85, 81t,
    270n1, 353
  errors/examples and, 82–84t
  tools for assessing, 87–88t
Grammatical correctness, 56–57
Grammatical morphemes, 56t
Grammatical patterns, 52
Grammatical structures, 216–217, 257
Grants, 8–9
  See also Funding
Graphic organizers, 228, 353
  backward design model and, 178, 179t
  key concepts and, 214
  key points and, 207
  organizing/accessing information and,
    223, 227
  reading skills and, 292
  visual context and, 208
  writing skills and, 304–305, 309
Graphing, 224
Grassi, E., 248
Graves, B., 211, 282
Graves, M., 211, 282
Gregorc, A., 209
Grouping strategies:
  co-teaching and, 149, 151
  participation and, 238–244, 239p
  team teaching and, 152, 153

Group work:
  checklist for, 242t
  language acquisition and, 241
  Web sites and, 243
Group work checklist, 242t
Gunning, T. G., 292

Hall, J. K., 246
Hall, T., 168, 176
Harris, K., 299, 301, 302, 304, 309, 323
Harry, B., 34, 40
Hatch, E., 88
Haynes, J., 61
Heafner, T. L., 226
Health issues, 123, 124
Henricksen, B., 326
Higareda, I., 5
Hispanics, 3–5
  cultural perceptions of disabilities and, 40
  overrepresentation/underrepresentation
    of, 6–7
Holliday, L., 245
Home care, 22
Home language, 9
  intervention teams and, 122
  LRE and, 22
  programs and, 15
  survey, 115
  translation and, 38
Home visits, 36–37
  family involvement and, 34–35
  RTI and, 131–132
Homework:
  cultural acquisition and, 96
  error correction and, 347
  school meetings and, 39
Hoover, J., 181, 183
Hopstock, P. J., 4, 5, 7, 24, 26
Hospital care, 22
Huang, G., 40
Human rights, xvi–xvii, xvii
Hurley, M., 280

Identity:
  classroom environments and, 191,
    192–193, 195–197
  cultural acquisition and, 97

  culturally relevant teaching and, 189
  justice education and, xvi
Idol, L., 142
Inclusive pedagogy, 188, 189, 195,
    196, 353
Individualized Education Plan (IEP),
    17t, 20, 353
  challenges and, 320
  collaboration and, 143
  co-teaching and, 148
  cultural discontinuities and, 39–42
  feedback and, 260
  goals and, 204
  grammar instruction and, 265
  instructional planning pyramid and,
    180, 181, 183
  instruction/assessment cycle and,
    111–113
  language acquisition and, 51
  laws and, 18
  literacy instruction and, 277
  meetings and, 125–127, 125t
  paraprofessionals and, 159
  required elements in, 125t
  reviewing/monitoring and, 127
  special education laws and, 114
  team teaching and, 154
  trusting relationships and, 35
Individuals with Disabilities Education
    Act (IDEA), 6n, 16, 353
  accountability and, xxii–xxiii
  categories of, 17t
  defining disabilities and, 113
  eligibility and, 119, 128
  family involvement and, 33–34, 42
  GT students and, 133
  IEP meetings and, 125
  paraprofessionals and, 159
  placement options and, 22–23
  reauthorization of, 18, 19t, 20t, 24
  RTI and, 19, 137n 2
  special education services and, 114
Inductive lessons, 267, 353
Information:
  accessing, 226, 227
  differentiation and, 175
  organizing/accessing, 223–228

Input hypothesis, 59, 64–66, 65p, 205, 353
Institute of Child Health and Human Development (NICHD), 4
Instructional design methods, 196
Instructional planning pyramid, 179–181, 180t, 185, 353–354
Instruction/assessment cycle, 111–113, 112f, 353
    CLDE student eligibility process and, 119
    multidisciplinary team and, 125
    special education law and, 114
    team teaching and, 155
Instrumental orientation, 68, 354
Integrated content–language approach, 204, 228, 233, 244, 354
Integrative orientation, 68, 354
Intelligence, 18, 128–129
Intelligence tests, 128, 135
Interactions:
    classroom environments and, 190–191, 193–194
    participation and, 239
Interdependence, xvii
Interlanguage, 51f, 71, 234, 251, 354
    developmental sequence of, 53–56, 54–55t, 56t
    emotion and, 56–57
    errors and, 51–53, 52–53t, 58
    multidisciplinary evaluations and, 124
Interlingual errors, 257
Internet/e-mail, 223, 225, 226, 305t, 306
Interpreters:
    behavioral issues and, 132
    children and, 126
    collaboration and, 142
    IEP meetings and, 126
    multidisciplinary evaluations and, 124
    school meetings and, 38
Interventions:
    CLDE student eligibility process and, 121–122
    collaboration and, 143
    co-teaching and, 149
    IEP and, 127

instructional planning pyramid and, 180t, 181, 183
instruction/assessment cycle and, 112
response to, 128, 129–132, 130f.
    See also Response to Intervention (RTI)
special education laws and, 114
Intervention teams, 110, 354
    behavioral issues and, 132
    CLDE student eligibility process and, 121–122
    collaboration and, 141, 142
    GT students and, 135
    MAPs and, 46
Interviews, 118, 123
Intralingual errors, 258
Intrinsic motivation, 69, 354
    See also Motivation
IQ tests, 128, 135
IRF sequence, 246, 253, 354
Isaacson, S., 299

Javits, J. K., 134
Jenkins, J., 85
Jigsaw reading, 284, 304
Johnson, D. W., 236, 240
Johnson, J., 26
Johnson, N., 218
Johnson, R. T., 236, 240
Johnson-Holubec, E., 236
Juel, C., 211
Justice, xv–xvi
    leadership and, xviii
    political will and, xviii–xix

Kachru, Y., 85
Kame'enui, E. J., 204, 215, 216
Kasper, G., 97
Keefe, E. B., 292, 339
Key academic language, 210–211, 213t, 354
    front-loading and, 214–215, 217
    participation and, 247t
    special education issues and, 216
    Web site and, 212
Key concepts, 210p, 213–214, 354
    front-loading and, 210, 216
    paraprofessionals and, 161

special education issues and, 216
Web sites and, 214, 217
See also Concepts
Key vocabulary, 213t
  language acquisition and, 210–211
  language study and, 284
  oral language proficiency and, 282
  repetition and, 211–212
  special education issues and, 216–217
  vocabulary development and, 283
  writing skills and, 308, 309
Kindler, A. L., 4, 115
King, D., 280
King, M. L., xvii
Klinger, J., 181
Kozleski, E. B., 24
Krashen, S., 59, 63, 64, 65, 66, 204,
  205, 234, 243, 322
Krashen's hypotheses, 63, 322
Kremer, K., 287
Kunnan, A. J., 125
KWL charts:
  background knowledge and,
    218, 219
  reading strategies and, 290
  time for L1 grouping and, 221
  writing skills and, 304

Labeling:
  CLDE students and, 3
  ELLs and, xxii
  GT students and, 134
  IDEA and, 128
  identification of CLDE students and,
    5, 6–8, 6t
  instructional planning pyramid
    and, 183
  laws and, 18
  reclassification of ELLs and, 119
  special education/bilingual education
    and, xxi
  testing and, 117
  treatments and, 114
Ladson-Billings, G., 190, 191, 196
Lamb, M., 68
Lambert, W., 68
Land, S., 154

Language:
  background knowledge and, 287
  key academic, 213t
  literacy instruction and, 277–278
  writing skills and, 302, 306
  See also English language
Language acquisition, 51, 277
  challenges and, 320–321
  CLDE student eligibility process
    and, 121
  collaboration and, 141, 142
  co-teaching and, 150, 151
  differentiation and, 171
  error correction and, 337, 339
  grammar and, 322–323
  grammar rules and, 263–264, 264p
    .See also Rules
  group work and, 241
  IEP meetings and, 126
  interlanguage and, 58
  key concepts and, 210–211
  multidisciplinary evaluations and, 124
  NCLB and, 10
  participation and, 234
  planning and, 165, 166
  scaffolding and, 204
  special education services and, 114
  stages of, 60t
  See also Second Language
    Acquisition (SLA)
Language disorders, 249
Language Experience Approach, 283
  Web sites and, 281
Language proficiency, 77, 104
Language proficiency tests, 115–117
Language skills, 77, 79
  See also Skills
Language study, 284–285
Lantolf, J., 65, 88
Lapkin, S., 234, 245
Lau, M., 180
Lau v. Nichols, 9
Laws:
  CLDE students and, 3, 8–13
  ELLs and, 10–13t
  federal, 114, 122
  intervention teams and, 122

PL 94–142, 16, 20–21, 357
special education and, xxii, 16–20,
    17–18t, 112, 113t, 114
Leadership:
    justice and, xviii
    school meetings and, 39
Learning disabilities:
    eligibility for special education and,
        128–129
    ELLs and, 7
    IEP and, 320
    laws and, 18
    participation and, 249
    RTI and, 131
    writing skills and, 299, 300–301
Learning Point Associates, 276
Learning profiles, 166
Learning styles:
    classroom environments and, 192, 197
    differentiation and, 168
    grammar instruction and, 265
    participation and, 239
    planning and, 165, 166
Least Restrictive Environment (LRE),
    20, 354
    CLDE students and, 22–24, 23t
    co-teaching and, 149
    curriculum and, 23
    IEP meetings and, 126
    laws and, 17t, 21
    legislation/litigation and, 19t
    placement options and, 22–24, 23t
Leavell, A., 180
Leki, I., 309, 330
Leoni, L., 87
Leos, K., 5, 124
Lerner, J., 249
Lesson planning, 166–167
    background knowledge and, 218
    differentiation and, 176
    grammar instruction and, 265
    key concepts and, 214
    See also Planning
Lewis, N., 245
Liaisons. See Cultural liaisons
Lightbown, P., 52, 53, 54, 55, 56, 57,
    66, 257

Limited English Proficiency (LEP),
    18, 117, 354
Linan-Thompson, S., 280, 327
Linguistic skills, 131, 168, 177
Listening skills, 249, 251
Literacy skills, 277
    CLDE student eligibility process
        and, 121
    cultural relevancy and, 285–286
    error correction and, 337–338, 340
    L1/L2 and, 67–68
    planning and, 166
    programs and, 14–16
    secondary level and, 274–275
    teaching, 337
    writing skills and, 301, 302
    See also Skills
Long, M. H., 65, 88, 204, 323
Low-income, 8
Luiselli, T. E., 159

MacFarland, S. Z. C., 159
MacSwan, J., 7
Mahoney, K., 15
Making Action Plans Process (MAPs),
    42–46, 355
Mandler, J., 218
Marston, D., 180
Marzano, R. J., 203, 204, 214, 215, 219
Massachusetts, 10
Massey, D. D., 226
Mathes, P. G., 280
Matrix Analogies Tests, 135
McBride, A., 159
McCardle, P., 5, 7, 124
McGregor, G., 204, 209
McIntosh, P., 198n
McKeown, M., 280
McLane, K., 176
McLaughlin, B., 57, 58, 204
McTighe, J., 178, 203, 204, 214, 236
Meaning:
    classroom environments and, 196
    comprehension and, 277, 283
    error correction and, 337, 338, 343,
        344–345
    feedback and, 260

participation and, 250
reading strategies and, 289, 290
spelling and, 325, 328
vocabulary development and, 282
writing skills and, 300, 305
Mele-McCarthy, J., 5, 7, 124
Memory issues:
    background knowledge and, 219
    error correction and, 340
    participation and, 251
    vocabulary development and, 215, 276
    writing skills and, 330–331
Mercer, C. D., 299
Meyer, A., 176
Minority students, 8–9
Misidentification, 133
Moats, L. C., 325, 326
Modeling, 355
    differentiation and, 170
    feedback and, 261–262
    input hypothesis and, 64
    instructional planning pyramid
        and, 183
    note taking and, 223
    paraprofessionals and, 159
    participation and, 249, 250
    reading and, 293
    visual context and, 207, 208
    writing skills and, 307–308
Modern Language Association (MLA), 3
Modifications, 124, 355
Monitor hypothesis, 59, 66, 355
Monitoring, 131, 183
    See also Observations
Monocultural issues, 235, 355
Moran, C., 203, 204, 210, 211, 212,
    213, 223, 239, 262
Morgenthaler, L., 245
Morphemes, 73n
Morris, R. D., 3
Motivation:
    background knowledge and, 287
    classroom environments and, 190,
        196, 197
    comprehension and, 284
    differentiation and, 171, 174
    extrinsic, 69, 352

grammar instruction and, 267
interlanguage and, 53
intrinsic, 69, 354
learning language and, 69t
SLA and, 68–69, 69t, 72
vocabulary instruction and, 280
Motor skills, 340
Movies, 64
Multidisciplinary Assessment Team
    (MAST), 110, 114, 123–125, 355
Multiple means of engagement, 176,
    177t, 355
Multiple means of expression,
    176, 177t, 355
Multiple means of representation, 176
Muyskens, P., 180
Myers, C., 181, 183

Naglieri Non-Verbal Abilities Test, 135
Nagy, W., 282
Nassaji, H., 246, 258, 261
Nation, I. S. P., 211, 284, 325, 329
National Center for Educational
    Statistics (NCES), 4, 26
National Center for Education Statistics
    (NCES), 4
National Clearinghouse for English
    Language Acquisition, 4
National Institute of Child Health and
    Human Development (NICHD),
    4, 5, 25, 26, 246, 276
National Literacy Panel on Language-
    Minority Children and Youth,
    68, 277, 280
National Reading Panel, 276
Native language proficiency test, 115
Natural order hypothesis, 59, 355
Negation, 54t
Nevin, A., 142
Nieto, S., 234
No Child Left Behind (NCLB), 10, 355
    accountability and, xxii–xxiii
    CLDE student eligibility process
        and, 119
    ELLs assessments and, 115, 117
    English proficiency and, 203
    grammar instruction and, 265

GT students and, 134
legislation/litigation and,
    12t, 20t
paraprofessionals and, 159
placement options and, 14, 22–23
RTI and, 19
Noddings, N., 237
Norris, J., 258, 263
Note taking, 228
    comprehension and, 206–207
    organizing/accessing information and,
        223, 225, 226, 227
    writing skills and, 304

O'Brien, J., 42
Observations:
    behavioral issues and, 133
    CLDE student eligibility process
        and, 121
    co-teaching and, 148, 149–150
    differentiation and, 168
    multidisciplinary evaluations and,
        123, 124
    participation and, 246
    planning and, 166
    reclassification of ELLs and, 118
    RTI and, 131
Office of Civil Rights, 9
Office of Special Education and
    Rehabilitation Services (OSERS),
    5, 6, 7, 128
Office of Special Education Programs
    (OSEP)., 6, 24, 159, 160
O'Malley, J. M., 302, 304, 307
Open houses, 35
Oral language issues, 278–279,
    280p, 356
    assessments and, 131–132
    comprehension and, 280–281
    discourse competence and, 88
    ELLs assessment/classification and,
        116–117
    errors and, 257, 322
    L1/L2 and, 68, 277
    NCLB and, 115
    proficiency and, 279–282
    reading and, 277, 280, 293

vocabulary development and,
    276, 279–282
Web site and, 285
writing skills and, 301
Organization skills, 223–228
    genre and, 306–307
    Web sites and, 228
    writing skills and, 304–305
Orkwis, R., 176
Ortega, L., 258, 263, 348
Orthographic knowledge, 328, 329, 338
Orthographic system, 301, 325, 356
Ortiz, A. A., 119
Output, 356
    acquisition vs. learning hypothesis
        and, 66
    comprehensible input and, 245
    input hypothesis and, 65
    instructional planning pyramid
        and, 181
    participation and, 234
Ovando, C. J., 9
Overgeneralization, 52, 52t, 61t, 83t,
    89t, 258, 356

Pacific Islanders, 6–7
Paolucci-Whitcomb, P., 142
Parallel teaching, 150, 151, 156t, 356
Paraprofessionals, 158–161, 356
    differentiation and, 169–170
    group work and, 239
    instructional planning pyramid
        and, 181
    time for L1 grouping and, 221
Parent involvement:
    CLDE student eligibility process and,
        119, 122–123
    cultural acquisition and, 96, 99–100
    goals and, 339
    grammatical competence and, 86–87
    GT students and, 134, 135
    IEP meetings and, 125–127
    instructional planning pyramid
        and, 181
    intervention teams and, 122
    interviews and, 123, 124, 131–132
    multidisciplinary evaluations and, 124

permissions and, 122–123
planning and, 166
special education and, 112
team teaching and, 155
See also Family involvement
Participation, 232–233, 247t
    classroom environments and, 195p
    CLDE student eligibility process
      and, 120
    ELL students and, 206
Patton, J. R., 236
Patton J., 181
Pearpoint, M., 42
Pearson, V. L., 236
Pendzick, M. L., 4, 5
Peregoy, S., 280, 302, 337, 341, 388
Perfetti, C., 280
Permissions:
    CLDE student eligibility process and,
      122–123
    parents and, 122–123
    special education laws and, 114
Phonemes, 85, 276
Phonemic awareness, 274, 276, 356
    grammatical competence and, 87
    secondary level and, 324–325
    spelling and, 328
Phonics, 276, 356
    error correction and, 340
    grammatical competence and, 87
    spelling and, 327, 328
Phonological transfer, 87, 88t
Phonology, 81t, 356
    grammatical competence and, 84–85, 85t
    interlanguage and, 52
    language proficiency and, 77
Phrasing, 250
Physical condition evaluation, 123
Pica, T., 88, 245
Pickering, D. J., 203
Pidginization hypothesis, 69–70
Placement decisions, 20p, 24, 28, 111, 112
    ELL students and, 13–14, 14t
Planning:
    backward design model and,
      178–179, 179t
    challenges and, 320

classroom management and, 184–185
CLDE students and, 184
collaboration and, 143, 144, 145
co-teaching and, 148
curriculum and, 176
differentiation and, 167–175
group work and, 239–240, 241
instruction and, 165
key concepts and, 214
participation and, 236, 237–238
team teaching and, 151–152, 153, 154
writing skills and, 299–300, 301, 302
See also Individualized Education Plan
    (IEP); Lesson planning
Policies:
    discipline and, 159 .*See also* Discipline
    meetings and, 39
    school districts and, 114
    social justice and, xviii
    special/bilingual education and,
      xxii, 135
Political issues:
    English only instruction and, 9
    justice and, xviii–xix
    program placement and, 14
Pollard-Durodola, S., 280
Pollock, J. E., 203
Polloway, E. A., 236
Popham, W. J., 111
Portfolios, 118, 319
Poverty, 8
PowerPoint, 171, 172p
    differentiation and, 174
    visual context and, 207
    writing skills and, 304
Pragmatics, 35, 77, 92, 357
Prereading strategies, 283, 289–290
Preservice teacher seminar, 235
Pressley, M., 280, 287, 289
Prior knowledge, 219, 349
    content/cultural schemas and, 217–218
    reading strategies and, 289
    See also Background knowledge
Problem-solving:
    CLDE student eligibility process and,
      120f, 122
    collaboration and, 141, 143

co-teaching and, 148–149
RTI and, 130f
Procedural knowledge, 226, 228
Process, 165, 356
    differentiation and, 169–170
    laws and, 18
Process approach, 299, 338, 356
Process problems, 299, 356
Product, 356
    differentiation and, 170–172, 172p
    instructional planning pyramid and, 181
Product problems, 291–301, 299, 357
Proficiency:
    ELLs assessment/classification and,
        115–117
    L2 reading and, 277
    participation and, 251
Pronunciation:
    English language and, 325
    grammatical competence and, 86
    language errors and, 257, 258, 325
    spelling and, 325–326, 326t, 327t
Proposition 227, 9–10
Psychological distance, 69–70, 71t
Puberty, 85
Public Agenda study, 26
Public Law 94–142 (PL 94–142), 16,
        20–21, 357
    See also Laws
Pullan, P. C., 299
Pull-out program, 14f, 16, 23t
Punishment. See Discipline

Railsback, J., 61
Read aloud, 65p
    comprehension and, 284
    grammatical competence and, 87
Reader's theater, 291, 292, 295t
Readiness models, 337, 357
Readiness skills:
    differentiation and, 173
    error correction and, 338
    planning and, 165, 166–167
Reading disabilities, 276
Reading skills, 275, 291–292, 293
    CALPS and, 79
    comprehension and, 284

ELLs assessment/classification and,
        116–117
    NCLB and, 115
    oral language proficiency and, 280
    teaching, 294–295t
    vocabulary knowledge and, 215
    Web sites and, 296
    See also Skills
Reading strategies, 288–290, 294
Recasting, 261–262, 355, 357
    See also Modeling
Reciprocity, 143
Reed, B., 61
Reformulating, 261–262, 355, 357
    See also Modeling
Rehabilitation Act, 16, 19t
Repetition, 211–212, 261, 311, 357
    grammar rules and, 268
    reading and, 283, 294t
    spelling and, 328
    vocabulary and, 206
    Web site and, 212
    writing and, 341t, 347
Reschly, A., 180
Residential facility, 21f, 22
Resources:
    classroom environments and, 190
    cultural acquisition and, 99–100
    organizing/accessing, 223–228
    Web sites and, 28, 105
Respect:
    classroom environments and, 194, 195
    collaboration and, 143
    culture and, 332
    feedback and, 260
    home visits and, 35
    paraprofessionals and, 159
    participation and, 237
    school meetings and, 38–39
    sociolinguistic competence and, 92, 93
Response to Intervention (RTI), 18–19,
        137n 2, 357
    background knowledge and, 287
    CLDE students and, 129–132, 130f
    co-teaching and, 148–149
    eligibility and, 128
    funding and, 18

instructional planning pyramid and, 179–181, 180t
problem-solving cycle and, 130f
Web site and, 129
Restructuring, 57–58
Retention issues:
  background knowledge and, 220
  participation and, 251
  vocabulary development and, 215, 282–283
Revision skills, 299
Rice, S., 195
Risk taking:
  classroom environments and, 257
  language errors and, 259
  participation and, 234, 235, 236, 249
Rituals, 236–237
Roever, C., 97
Rolstad, K., 7, 15
Ross, S., 211
Rost, M., 85, 206, 207, 211, 218, 223, 234
Rothlein, L., 280
Round Robin, 214
Rueda, R., 5
Rules:
  cultural acquisition and, 97
  English language and, 320, 321, 322, 323, 324
  error correction and, 345, 347
  grammar and, 86, 263–264, 264p
  L1/L2 and, 68
  school meetings and, 39
  sociolinguistic competence and, 93
  spelling and, 328
  See also Grammar rules

Salazar, J., 5
Sandoval-Lucero, E., 158
Sands, D., 24, 40, 114, 147, 148, 165, 180, 226
Sapru, S., 4
Saracho, O. N., 280
Scaffolding:
  differentiation and, 168
  ELLs and, 203–204
  group work and, 243
  instructional planning pyramid and, 181–182, 183
  language acquisition and, 204
  organizing/accessing information and, 226, 227
  special education/bilingual education and, xxi
  writing skills and, 308, 309
Scarcella, R., 322
Schaffner, C. B., 236, 237
Schmidt, N., 326
Schmidt, R. W., 259
Schools:
  bureaucracies and, 111
  U.S. secondary, 321–322
Schumann, J., 54, 69, 70, 71, 96
Schumm, J. S., 154, 180
Scott, J., 282
Scovel, T., 85
Second Language Acquisition (SLA), 58, 60–61t, 73n, 357, 358
  acquisition vs. learning hypothesis and, 66
  affective filter hypothesis and, 63–64
  input hypothesis and, 64–66
  motivation and, 68–69, 69t, 72
  natural order hypothesis and, 59
  paraprofessionals and, 160
  psychological factors and, 71t
  social/psychological distance and, 69–71, 70t, 71t
  sociolinguistic competence and, 93
  teacher training and, 26
  See also Language acquisition
Second language (L2), 357
  CALPS and, 79
  CLDE student eligibility process and, 121
  grammatical competence and, 81, 85.
    See also Grammatical competence
  input hypothesis and, 64, 65
  interlanguage and, 51, 52, 53, 57–58
  language acquisition and, 51
  language proficiency and, 77
  L1/L2 and, 67, 68
  motivation and, 69
  school meetings and, 38
  social distance and, 69–70, 70t

Section 504, 16, 19t, 357
Self-esteem, 235, 240
Self-image, 236
    See also Identity
Selinker, L., 51, 52, 53, 57, 60, 93, 257, 263, 341
Semantics, 77, 81t
Semantic web, 207, 220, 223, 304, 357
Seminars, 192
Sentence structure, 52, 79, 126, 249
Shanahan, T., 68, 275, 276, 277, 280, 301
Sharwood Smith, M., 64
Sheets, R. H., 189, 190, 192, 234
Sheltered English, 16
Short, D., 203, 204, 283
Short-term objectives, 111, 125t
Simmons, D. C., 204
Simultaneous teaching, 150–151, 156t, 357
Skills:
    cognitive, 135
    collaboration, 142–143, 145, 350
    communication, 244, 251
    differentiation and, 171
    functional, 337, 353
    group work and, 242
    language, 77, 79, 117, 210
    linguistic, 131, 168, 177
    listening, 249, 251
    motor, 340
    participation and, 237
    planning and, 166
    revision, 299
    study, 226–227, 228
    team teaching and, 153–154
    tracking, 68
    See also Academic skills; Literacy skills; Organization skills; Readiness skills; Reading skills; Writing skills
Smith, B., 334n
Smith, E. C., 236
Smith, S., 64
Snow, C., 86, 204, 289, 291, 301, 322, 325
Social distance, 69–70, 70t, 71t

Social interaction skills:
    co-teaching and, 147
    discourse competence and, 89
    group work and, 239–240, 244
    input hypothesis and, 65
    labels and, 114
    participation and, 236, 250, 251
    school meetings and, 39
    strategic competence and, 103
Social justice, xviii
Sociolinguistic competence, 81t, 92–100
    cultural acquisition and, 95–97, 95f
    errors/examples and, 94–95t
    tools for assessing, 99t
Sowden, C., 330
Spada, N., 52, 53, 54, 55, 56, 57, 66, 257
Special education:
    background knowledge and, 219–220
    bureaucracies and, 111
    CALPS and, 79
    CLDE student eligibility process and, 122
    comprehension and, 283
    co-teaching and, 148
    cultural acquisition and, 98
    discourse competence and, 90–91
    eligibility and, 113–114, 128–129
    IEP meetings and, 125–127
    instructional planning pyramid and, 183
    instruction/assessment cycle and, 111–113
    laws and, xxii, 16–20, 17–18t, 112, 113t, 114
    legislation/litigation and, 19–20t
    LRE/ESL and, 23t
    MAPs and, 46
    professionals and, 142
    RTI and, 129–132
    strategic competence and, 102–103
    strategies for, 203–205
    teacher training and, 26
Special needs students. *See* Students with special needs
Specially Designed Academic Instruction in English (SDAIE), 16

Speech issues:
   disabilities and, 249, 260
   grammatical errors and, 82–84t
Speech/language specialist, 148
Spelling:
   categorizing words and, 328t
   errors and, 327, 327t, 342, 343, 346
   grammar and, 325–330, 326t, 328t, 337t
   phonics and, 327, 328
   pronunciation and, 325–326, 326t, 327t
   Web sites and, 329, 330
Spelling trajectory, 326t
Spodek, B., 280
Stabilize, 323, 357
Stage theory approach, 40, 358
Standardized testing, 117, 119, 124
   differentiation and, 171
   grammar instruction and, 265
   paraprofessionals and, 158
   writing skills and, 330–331
   See also Testing
Standards:
   bilingual education and, 9
   participation and, 237
Steege, M. W., 128
Stephenson, T., 4, 5, 7, 24, 26
Stereotypes, 191–192, 193
   See also Bias
Sternberg, R., 209
Strangman, N., 176
Strategic competence, 81t, 100–103, 358
   errors/examples and, 102t
   tools for assessing, 103t
Strategies:
   bilingual, 152, 153
   compensatory, 100–101
   differentiation, 184–185
   ESL, 152, 153
   grouping, 244
   organization, 224
   prereading, 283
   reading, 288–290, 294
   special education and, 203–205
Stress:
   cultural acquisition and, 96
   feedback and, 260
   participation and, 234

Stuart, M., 280
Students:
   intervention teams and, 122
   special education and, 112
   teachers and, 190–193
Students with special needs:
   CLDE student eligibility process
      and, 119
   continuum of services for, 21f
   grammar and, 323
   human rights and, xvii
   independence and, 41
   literacy instruction and, 277
   multidisciplinary evaluations and, 124
   placement options and, 20–22, 20p,
      21f, 24–25
   spelling and, 327
   writing skills and, 301, 302
Study skills, 225, 226–227, 228, 230
Success:
   comprehension and, 209
   error correction and, 347
   feedback and, 261
   L2 reading and, 277
   teachers and, 204
   writing skills and, 301, 311p, 321–322
   See also Academic success
Support:
   bureaucracies and, 111
   classroom environments and, 190
   CLDE student eligibility process
      and, 122
   co-teaching and, 148, 150
   cultural acquisition and, 96, 98,
      99–100
   differentiation and, 169, 170
   FAPE and, 114
   IEP meetings and, 126
   input hypothesis and, 64
   instructional planning pyramid and,
      181, 183
   instruction/assessment cycle and, 112
   intervention teams and, 122
   MAPs and, 43
   natural order hypothesis and, 59
   paraprofessionals and, 159
   participation and, 236–237, 250

planning and, 166
reclassification of ELLs and, 118, 119
RTI and, 129
teachers and, 164
Surveys:
   home language and, 115
   participation and, 248–249
Swain, M., 50, 65, 77, 80, 81, 105n 1,
   204, 234, 245, 261
Swan, M., 334n
Swanborn, M. S. L., 215
Swassing, R. H., 209
Symons, F. J., 235

Target language, 358
   discourse competence and, 90
   input hypothesis and, 64, 65
   integrative orientation and, 68
   motivation and, 69
   natural order hypothesis and, 59
Tarone, E., 84, 85
Taylor, L. S., 43
Teachers:
   accountability and, xxii–xxiii
   collaboration and, 142, 144p
   cultural acquisition and, 99
   error correction and, 340–341
   goals and, 339
   GT students and, 134, 135
   IEP meetings and, 125–127
   instructional planning pyramid
      and, 181
   labels and, 114
   literacy and, 275
   organization strategies and, 224
   paraprofessionals and, 159
   RTI and, 129–130
   special education and, 112
   students and, 190–193
   success and, 204
   support and, 164
   trusting relationships and, 34–35
Teacher training:
   CLDE student eligibility process
      and, 119
   co-teaching/co-planning and, 145

ELL/special education strategies
   and, 203
funding and, 18
grammar/punctuation and,
   263–264, 322
GT students and, 134
laws and, 8–9 .*See also* Laws
new directions in, 25–26
placement options and, 23
RTI and, 131
Web site and, xxiv
writing skills and, 301–302
See also Training
Team teaching, 150, 351–352, 356t, 358
   co-teaching and, 151–152
Testing:
   academic achievement and, 77, 117,
      128–129
   bias and, 124–125
   CLDE student eligibility process
      and, 123
   culture and, 331
   eligibility for special education and,
      128–129
   ELLs assessment/classification and,
      115–118
   GT students and, 134–135
   IEP meetings and, 126
   intelligence and, 128, 135
   language proficiency and, 77
   matrix analogies and, 135
   organizing/accessing information
      and, 223
   paraprofessionals and, 158
   RTI and, 130
   writing skills and, 322
   See also Assessments; Standardized
      testing
Texas Education Agency, 142, 151, 154
Tharp, R., 26
Theoharis, G., xviii
Think-pair-share, 170, 214
Thomas, W. P., 15
Thornbury, S., 53, 86, 257, 258, 259,
   261, 264, 265, 266, 270n 2
Thousand, J., 237

3-way model, 349
    background knowledge and, 304
    comprehension and, 205, 229, 265,
        283, 345
    co-teaching and, 157t
    cultural schemata and, 218
    error correction and, 345
    grammar instruction and, 265
    group work and, 241
    teaching reading to CLDE students
        and, 294t
    UDL and, 176, 177t
    vocabulary development and, 283
    Web sites and, 210
    writing skills and, 304
Time:
    classroom environments and, 194, 197
    collaboration and, 143
    comprehension and, 206
    co-teaching/co-planning and, 145
    cultural acquisition and, 98
    differentiation and, 169, 170, 176
    grammar instruction and, 265, 267
    group work and, 243–244
    L1 and, 220–222
    participation and, 249, 250–251
    RTI and, 129
    team teaching and, 154, 155
    vocabulary knowledge and, 215
    writing skills and, 300, 309
Title VII, 8, 11t, 12t
Tomlinson, C. A., 165, 203, 204,
    226, 235
Tracking skills, 67–68
Training, 203
    cultural awareness and, 144
    mislabeling/overrepresentation/
        underrepresentation and, 8
    paraprofessionals and, 160
    See also Teacher training
Transitional bilingual educational
    program, 15, 358
Translations:
    concurrent, 160–161, 221, 350
    direct, 38, 126, 151
    GT students and, 135

IEP meetings and, 126
    paraprofessionals and, 160–161
    school meetings and, 38
    strategic competence and, 101
Trauma:
    brain injury and, 16
    cultural acquisition and, 96
    MAPs and, 43
Trueba, H. T., 3
Trust issues:
    collaboration and, 143
    communication and, 38
    family involvement and, 34–35
    home visits and, 34–35
    team teaching and, 151, 154
Tuitt, F., 189, 193, 196, 234
Turnbull, A., 41
Turnbull, R., 41
Two-way immersion or dual language
    program, 14, 358

Universal Design for Learning (UDL),
    175–177, 358
    applications of, 177t
    classroom management and, 184–185
University of Colorado at Denver,
    152, 154
U.S. Census Bureau, 3, 4, 5, 6
U.S. Department of Education,
    4, 77, 134
U.S. Department of Education (USDOE),
    4, 5, 77
    GT students and, 134
    teacher training and, 25, 26.
        See also Teacher training
U-shaped learning, 57–58, 72, 358
    error analysis and, 263
    restructuring and, 57

Valdés, G., 77, 135
Values:
    classroom environments and,
        192, 196, 197
    participation and, 237
Van den Broek, P., 287
VanPatten, B., 73n

Vaughn, S., 154, 180, 280, 327
Verplaetse, L. S., 246
Villa, R., 237
Violence, 96, 98
Visual context, 66, 207–208, 358
Visual learners, 206–207
Vocabulary knowledge, 276, 358
  background knowledge and, 219, 287
  CALPS and, 79
  comprehension and, 280
  differentiation and, 170
  interlanguage and, 52
  language acquisition and, 211
  language errors and, 258
  language proficiency and, 77
  language study and, 285
  literacy instruction and, 277
  participation and, 237, 249, 251
  reading and, 214–215
  reading strategies and, 290, 293
  Web sites and, 215
Vogelsberg, R. T., 204, 209
Volunteers, 88t, 100

Wagner, R. K., 3
Walsh, M., 246
Walther-Thomas, C., 154
Wanzek, J., 327
Web sites, xxv
  background knowledge and, 219, 288
  backward design and, 214
  classroom management and, 185
  CLDE student eligibility process
      and, 120
  comfortable environments and, 238
  comprehension and, 283, 284
  content/cultural schemas and, 218, 220
  cultural acquisition and, 98
  disability categories and, 7, 113
  English language assessments and, 115
  error correction and, 347
  extended output and, 251
  FBA and, 133
  front-loading and, 212
  genre and, 307
  grammar and, 268, 269, 323
  grouping strategies and, 244

group work and, 243
high/low-context cultures and, 43
home language survey and, 115
home visits and, 35, 37
IEP and, 127
inventories for various student levels
    and, 167
key academic language and, 212
key concepts and, 214, 217
language acquisition/learning
    disabilities and, 103
language experience approach
    and, 281
language study and, 285
language surveys and, 115
laws and, 13
learning disability eligibility and, 128
L1 grouping and, 222
organization skills and, 228
reading skills and, 296
reading strategies and, 290, 292
repetition and, 212
resources and, 28, 105
RTI/discrepancy models and, 129
sociolinguistic competence and, 95
special education referral process
    and, 127
special needs case study and, 33
spelling and, 329, 330
testing bias and, 125
3-way model and, 210
vocabulary development and, 215, 283
writing skills and, 314, 315, 348
Wehby, J. H., 235
Wei, L., 73n
Wells, G., 246
White board work, 214
Whittaker, C. R., 43
Wiese, A. M., 8, 9
Wiggins, G., 178, 213, 236
Williams, J., 261
Wlodkowski, R. J., 189, 195, 196
Woodcock–Johnson math subtest, 128
Woodruff, A. L., 327
Woolfolk, A., 209
Workshops, 182, 192
Wright, P. D., 20

Wright, W. D. P., 20
Writing skills, 299, 302–303, 303f
  assessments and, 321
  BICS/CALPS and, 79
  challenges and, 320
  cultural/linguistic influences on,
    330–333
  discourse competence and, 89–91
  ELLs assessment/classification and,
    116–117
  error correction and, 336–347, 341t
  genres and, 301, 305, 305t, 306–308,
    309, 315, 333

goals and, 338–339
grammatical errors and, 82–84t, 322
NCLB and, 115
relevancy/authenticity and, 298
secondary level and, 312–314t
success and, 301, 311p
U.S. secondary schools and,
    321–322
Web sites and, 314, 315, 348

Yell, M. L., 17

Zehler, A. M., 4, 5, 7, 24, 26

About the Authors

Elizabeth A. Grassi is associate professor of linguistically and culturally diverse education at Regis University. Prior to joining the Regis faculty, Elizabeth was a K–12 teacher and coordinator of ESL/language acquisition programs both in the United States and abroad.

Heidi Bulmahn Barker is associate professor of elementary and special education at Regis University. Prior to joining the Regis faculty, Heidi worked in both special and general education teaching positions.

Supporting researchers for more than 40 years

Research methods have always been at the core of SAGE's publishing program. Founder Sara Miller McCune published SAGE's first methods book, *Public Policy Evaluation*, in 1970. Soon after, she launched the *Quantitative Applications in the Social Sciences* series—affectionately known as the "little green books."

Always at the forefront of developing and supporting new approaches in methods, SAGE published early groundbreaking texts and journals in the fields of qualitative methods and evaluation.

Today, more than 40 years and two million little green books later, SAGE continues to push the boundaries with a growing list of more than 1,200 research methods books, journals, and reference works across the social, behavioral, and health sciences. Its imprints—Pine Forge Press, home of innovative textbooks in sociology, and Corwin, publisher of PreK–12 resources for teachers and administrators—broaden SAGE's range of offerings in methods. SAGE further extended its impact in 2008 when it acquired CQ Press and its best-selling and highly respected political science research methods list.

From qualitative, quantitative, and mixed methods to evaluation, SAGE is the essential resource for academics and practitioners looking for the latest methods by leading scholars.

For more information, visit **www.sagepub.com**.